What Viewers Are Saying About
America's Test Kitchen

"I have watched a lot of cooking shows, and many of them were a waste of time. America's Test Kitchen *is by far the best I have ever seen. You understand the everyday cook. Most of us don't grocery shop at places that sell the most exotic and expensive products. I enjoy your recipes because I know they will be good. I also appreciate your product testing. By following your suggestions, I have saved a lot of money."*

Frances Williamson
via e-mail

"It just doesn't get any better than your flourless chocolate cake! In fact, if you can only bake one chocolate cake, this should be it."

Mindy Keys
Pittsburg, California

"I watched your show for the first time today on NJ Public Television. Bravo!!!! A cooking show that had a brain! I am so tired of the glitz that is featured nowadays on many cooking shows. I enjoyed your show because it reflected science rather than cute quips."

Bruce
via e-mail

"You have the best cooking show on TV. Not only the recipes, but all of the other interesting cooking and equipment information."

Tom and Annie
West Bend, Wisconsin

"Thank you for your show . . . it is the best cooking show on television! Every recipe of yours that I have made has been fabulous. My favorites are the raspberry-oat squares and the country-style Greek salad. I tell my friends that you are the Consumer Reports of the kitchen. I appreciate all the testing you do to make your viewers' lives easier. Please don't ever quit!"

Victoria Siegel
St. Louis, Missouri

"I just LOOOOOOVE the show. Finally, a cooking show that uses 'regular' ingredients we can find at the grocery store. I access your Web site all the time to find recipes and also tips about equipment if I want to make a purchase. I have to say that all the tips and recipes I have tried from your show have been 'phenomenal.'"

Patti Butz
Chicago, Illinois

"I am 61 years young, with a passion for cooking and baking, and have been doing it 'with love' for the past 50 years, or so. Just when I think that I have perfected something, I see a new tip or suggestion on your show to make it even better. It never ceases to amaze me that I always learn something new, every time I see your show. How great is that?"

Nancy Awve
Milwaukee, Wisconsin

"I just wanted to send a note to let you know that this show is the very best cooking show EVER!!! I have learned so very, very much and have improved my cooking substantially purely due to tips and things I learned from the show. DON'T CHANGE A THING!! I have watched cooking shows for as long as I can remember, but this is the only show that has provided truly useful and practical information. PLEASE, PLEASE continue to produce the show exactly the way you have been doing . . . it is OUTSTANDING."

Becky
Ritzville, Washington

"I love America's Test Kitchen. I watch it regularly on WTTW from Chicago. It is the most informative and truly applicable show of its type. I think of it as The Joy of Cooking televised. Love the information, recipes, hosts . . . it's all great, don't change a thing."

Amy Tollas
Sawyer, Michigan

"So far, every single thing we've tried from watching your show on PBS has been a complete success. While we love the show, I have to admit that we are sorry to see that everything you show works as well as or better than you say it will. We really didn't need MORE great things to eat."

Robert and Lori Fore
Surprise, Arizona

"Just a quick note of thanks for your WONDERFUL show on PBS! My daughter and I stumbled across your show one afternoon, and now we are hooked. Finally, a cooking show for regular people that features food we would actually eat! I did not grow up in a house where people cooked, and I am totally enjoying the process of learning to cook."

Alisa Rawlins
Vancouver, Washington

AMERICA'S TEST KITCHEN LIVE!

AMERICA'S TEST KITCHEN LIVE!

BY THE EDITORS OF
COOK'S ILLUSTRATED

ILLUSTRATIONS
John Burgoyne

PHOTOGRAPHY
Daniel J. van Ackere
Carl Tremblay

AMERICA'S TEST KITCHEN
BROOKLINE, MASSACHUSETTS

America's Test Kitchen
17 Station Street
Brookline, MA 02445

ISBN 0-936184-82-5
Library of Congress Cataloging-in-Publication Data
The Editors of *Cook's Illustrated*

America's Test Kitchen Live!: The All-New Companion to America's Favorite Public Television Cooking Series
1st Edition

ISBN 0-936184-82-5 (hardback): $29.95
1. Cooking. 1. Title
2004

Manufactured in the United States of America

Distributed by America's Test Kitchen
17 Station Street, Brookline, MA 02445

Editor: Jack Bishop
Series Designer: Amy Klee
Jacket Designer: Beth Tondreau
Book Production Specialist: Ron Bilodeau
Photographers: Carl Tremblay (color and selected black-and-white food photography);
Daniel J. van Ackere (documentary and silhouette photography and color photograph on page 86);
Keller + Keller (color photograph on page 200)
Illustrator: John Burgoyne
Production Manager: Jessica Lindheimer Quirk
Copyeditor: Cheryl Redmond
Proofreader: Jean Rogers
Indexer: Cathy Dorsey

CONTENTS

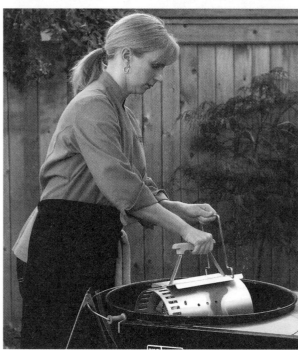

PREFACE

AS I WRITE THIS, MY WIFE, ADRIENNE, AND I ARE organizing an end-of-summer pig roast for our small Vermont town. Much like putting on a TV show, it involves a lot of planning: We have to order the pig and have it butterflied, get more than 50 pounds of charcoal for the cooker, draw up a guest list, hire an old-time band (fiddler, frail banjo, and guitar), put together a list of desserts (we do the pig and desserts; neighbors bring the other covered dishes), make sure there is wood for the late-night sauna after the roast, and then go over the guest list one more time to make sure that nobody has been left out.

All of this reminds me a great deal of the filming of *America's Test Kitchen*. Sure, it involves a lot of hard work and planning, but it is also a party of sorts, and you, the audience, are invited. If you are new to *America's Test Kitchen*, you should know that everyone on the show actually works there. It is a real place just outside of Boston and is also the home of *Cook's Illustrated* magazine. I am happy to say that much of the original cast from the first season (2001) is still together: test cooks Julia Collin Davison and Bridget Lancaster, tasting expert Jack Bishop, equipment guru Adam Ried, and me, Christopher Kimball, the host. This season (2005), we will also be introducing you to a few new faces from our kitchen, including test cooks Erika Bruce, Rebecca Hays, and Jeremy Sauer.

Of course, this is just the tip of the iceberg. Our kitchen has almost two dozen test cooks, 40 burners, 20 ovens, and more cookware than we can keep track of. We test a recipe 10, 20, 30, even up to 100 times to get it right. After a recipe is done, we make it with the wrong cookware and bad ingredients to see what will happen. We send it out to *Cook's Illustrated* readers who have volunteered to make the recipes at home and then give us their no-nonsense feedback. But on the show, what we want to do above all is to take you behind the scenes to show you why recipes so often fail and how to make them a success. And, please, this is real home cooking. We will never tell you that you can cook a gala dinner for 12 in just 20 minutes; we all know about promises made and promises not kept, especially in the kitchen.

Like our pig roast, *America's Test Kitchen* is mostly about the people we invite to join us. Cooking is not about perfect food; it is about the process of bringing folks together around the table and sharing a meal. As I often say, "Happy Meals Are Made at Home," and that is the higher purpose of our show.. We want to give you the recipes and the confidence to get back into the kitchen and do good work. There is nothing wrong with meatloaf and mashed potatoes when made well. (Most "gourmet" cooking, at least in my opinion, is best left to restaurant chefs.) Home cooking ought to be straightforward, dependable, and satisfying. That is what we are all about.

One last thing you might notice about our show: We look like we're having fun. There are no scripts and no speechwriters. Everything is filmed "live" in that we never really know what is going to happen—and neither do you. Julia and I may disagree about technique. I may not choose the same winner that our panel chose in an earlier blind tasting. (In the bottled water tasting, I chose Boston tap water!) Or Adam may have me demonstrate a particularly useless kitchen gadget in an effort to show you what not to buy. The show is very much like our everyday test kitchen: unpredictable, surprising, practical, and, on occasion, inspiring.

My family just attended our local Fireman's Parade last weekend. My daughter Caroline and I baked a chocolate cake for the "Win a Cake" booth and dropped it off just before the parade started. (To win a cake, you bet 25 cents on a number, the wheel of fortune is spun, and you hope for the best.) I noticed that there were more than 50 cakes in that booth, all donated by local bakers. Some were works of art, but most were simple enough: Bundt cakes, sheet cakes, cupcakes, and layer cakes covered with everything from sprinkles to a whipped chocolate fudge frosting. In a moment, I understood why we do the show. We want to bring folks back into the kitchen, where they belong. For our part, we are happy to share our recipes, our food, and our time. For your part, we hope to see you each week in our kitchen, *America's Test Kitchen*.

Christopher Kimball
Founder and editor, *Cook's Illustrated* magazine
Host, *America's Test Kitchen*
Brookline, Massachusetts, 2004

WELCOME TO AMERICA'S TEST KITCHEN

AMERICA'S TEST KITCHEN IS A VERY REAL 2,500-SQUARE-foot kitchen located just outside of Boston. It is the home of *Cook's Illustrated* magazine and is the Monday through Friday destination of more than two dozen test cooks, editors, food scientists, tasters, photographers, and cookware specialists. Our mission is to test recipes over and over again until we understand how and why they work and until we arrive at the "best" version.

Our television show highlights the best recipes developed in the test kitchen during the past year—those recipes that our test kitchen staff makes at home time and time again. These recipes are accompanied by our most exhaustive equipment tests and our most interesting food tastings.

Christopher Kimball, the founder and editor of *Cook's Illustrated* magazine, is host of the show and asks the questions you might ask. It's the job of our two chefs, Julia Collin Davison and Bridget Lancaster, to demonstrate our recipes. They show Chris what works, what doesn't, and explain why. In the process, they discuss (and show us) the best and worst examples from our development process—the bread that burned, the cake that collapsed, and the pork chops that were tough.

Adam Ried, our equipment guru, shares the highlights from our detailed testing process in Equipment Corner segments. He brings with him our favorite (and least favorite) gadgets and tools. He tells you which knives performed best in a dozen kitchen tests and shows why most stain removers are nearly worthless.

Jack Bishop is our ingredient expert. He has Chris taste our favorite (and least favorite) brands of common food products—everything from bacon and chocolate ice cream to bottled water and chicken. Chris may not always enjoy these exercises (fish sauce is not much fun to taste), but he usually learns something as Jack explains what makes one brand superior to another.

Although there are just five cooks and editors who appear on the television show, another 50 people worked to make the show a reality. Executive chefs Erin McMurrer and Dawn Yanagihara ran the "back kitchen," where all the food that appeared on camera originated. Along with the on-air crew, Erin and Dawn also planned and organized the 26 television episodes shot in May 2004. Melissa Baldino researched the Q & A segments, and Garth Clingingsmith organized the tasting and equipment segments.

During the actual filming, chefs Stephanie Alleyne, Erika Bruce, Keith Dresser, Sean Lawler, Jeremy Sauer, and Diane Unger-Mahoney were in the kitchen from early in the morning to late at night helping Erin and Dawn cook all the food needed on set. Nadia Domeq and Nina West were charged with the herculean task of making sure all the ingredients we needed were on hand. Kitchen assistants

Katie Archimbault, Barbara Akins, Maria Elena Delgado, Ena Guidel, Rebecca King, and Cali Todd also worked long hours. Garth Clingingsmith, Becky Hays, Charles Kelsey, and Nina West helped coordinate the efforts of the kitchen with the television set by readying props, equipment, and food.

The staff of A La Carte Communications turned our recipes, tastings, testing, and science experiments into a lively television show. Special thanks to executive producers Geoffrey Drummond and Nat Katzman; director Herb Sevush; coordinating producer Richard Dooley; production manager Anne-Sophie Brieger; director of photography Dean Gaskill; and editor Hugh Elliot. We also appreciate the hard work of the video production team, including Stephen Hussar, Michael McEachern, Peter Dingle, Eliat B. Goldman, Gilles Morin, Brenda Coffey, Tommy Hamilton, Patrick Ruth, Jack McPhee, Aaron Frutman, Kaliel Roberts, Mark Romanelli, and Paul Swensen.

We also would like to thank Hope Reed, who handles station relations, and the team at American Public Television that presents the show: Cynthia Fenniman, Chris Funkhauser, Judy Barlow, and Tom Davison. Thanks also for production support from DGA Productions, Boston; Paul Swensen Productions, Santa Rosa, California; and Zebra Productions, New York.

Sub-Zero, Wolf, Vendange Wines, and Viva Towels helped underwrite the show, and we thank them for their support. Equipment for the show was supplied by Olgo Russo at A. Russo & Sons, Mahoney's Garden Center of Cambridge, Massachusetts, and DuPont Corian.

We hope this book gives you an inside look at America's Test Kitchen. We are passionate about our work, and we hope you enjoy our recipes as well as reading about the process by which they were created. Our mission is pretty simple. We want to help make you a better cook. We hope that our television show and this book will do just that. If you have comments or questions about the show or the book, contact us at www.americastestkitchen.com. Visit www.cooksillustrated.com for information about *Cook's Illustrated* magazine.

AMERICA'S TEST KITCHEN LIVE!

Bridget and Chris taste an array of easy appetizers—beef satay, spinach dip with pita chips, and spiced nuts.

APPETIZERS

CHAPTER I

When preparing and serving appetizers, you're also answering the front door, pouring drinks, and catching up with old friends who know their way to the kitchen. Appetizers are, after all, party food. If you're the host, you can bet that having lots of time alone in the kitchen is an unlikely proposition.

The challenge, then, when choosing appetizers is to find recipes that won't keep you away from guests for very long. But a quick appetizer that doesn't taste very good isn't worth the bother. If the only choice is some bland dip and tired crudités, we'd rather go hungry and wait for dinner.

We've chosen recipes for this chapter that deliver big flavor without much work. This means spiced nuts that are not overly sweet (the most common flaw in other recipes), spinach dip that is bold and creamy (not watery and insipid), and beef satay that is tender and vibrant (rather than the usual cold shoe leather with sticky, sweet sauce). These recipes will start any meal on the right note.

SPICED NUTS

WHAT WE WANTED: Party nuts that are packed with flavor but not overly sticky or sweet.

At parties, spiced nuts usually disappear faster than the host can replenish the bowl. But most spiced nuts are made with a heavy sugar syrup, which can leave your hands sticky and cause the nuts to clump together in unappealing, indelicate clusters.

Finding the right coating method required a good deal of testing. The most common technique, boiling the nuts in a thick, sweet syrup, was not even an option because it made the nuts sticky. Another popular method, toasting or sautéing the nuts in butter or oil before tossing them with spices, dulled the finish of the nuts and made them taste bland or oily. A third possibility, coating the nuts with a spiced egg white mixture, created such a chunky, candy-like coating that the nuts themselves were barely visible.

Our answer came when we made a light glaze for the nuts from very small amounts of liquid, sugar, and butter. It worked like a charm. This treatment left the nuts shiny and just tacky enough for a dry spice coating to stick perfectly, giving the nuts both a consistent, beautiful appearance and plenty of flavor.

Kosher salt is important here because it adds crunch and has a clean flavor. If you can, make the nuts ahead of time; as they sit, they will better absorb the flavorings.

Toasting the nuts (before they are coated) is also key to developing their flavor. We like the even heat of the oven for this task. Make sure the oven isn't too hot (350 degrees is ideal) and shake the pan once or twice to turn the nuts so they toast evenly. Finally, stick close by the oven. Nuts can go from perfectly toasted to burnt in a few minutes.

WHAT WE LEARNED: Glaze toasted nuts with butter, sugar, and a little liquid (we like either rum or water) and then toss them with the spices for an even, light coating.

SPICED PECANS WITH RUM GLAZE

Makes about 2 cups

The spiced nuts can be stored in an airtight container for up to 5 days.

2 cups (8 ounces) raw pecan halves

spice mix
2 tablespoons sugar
¾ teaspoon kosher salt
½ teaspoon ground cinnamon
⅛ teaspoon ground cloves
⅛ teaspoon ground allspice

rum glaze
1 tablespoon rum, preferably dark
2 teaspoons vanilla extract
1 teaspoon light or dark brown sugar
1 tablespoon unsalted butter

1. Adjust an oven rack to the middle position and heat the oven to 350 degrees. Line a rimmed baking sheet with parchment paper and spread the pecans on it in an even layer; toast for 4 minutes, rotate the pan, and continue to toast until fragrant and the color deepens slightly, about 4 minutes longer. Transfer the baking sheet with the nuts to a wire rack.

2. FOR THE SPICE MIX: While the nuts are toasting, stir the sugar, salt, cinnamon, cloves, and allspice together in a medium bowl; set aside.

3. FOR THE GLAZE: Bring the rum, vanilla, brown sugar, and butter to a boil in a medium saucepan over medium-high heat, whisking constantly. Stir in the toasted pecans and cook, stirring constantly with a wooden spoon, until almost all the liquid has evaporated, about 1½ minutes.

4. Transfer the glazed pecans to the bowl with the spice mix; toss well to coat. Return the glazed spiced pecans to the parchment-lined baking sheet to cool.

MEXICAN-SPICED ALMONDS, PEANUTS, AND PUMPKIN SEEDS

Makes about 2 cups

The spiced nuts can be stored in an airtight container for up to 5 days.

- 1¼ cups (4½ ounces) sliced almonds
- ⅔ cup (3 ounces) roasted unsalted shelled peanuts
- ¼ cup (1 ounce) raw pumpkin seeds

mexican spice mix
- 1 tablespoon sugar
- 1 teaspoon kosher salt
- ¼ teaspoon ground cinnamon
- ¼ teaspoon ground cumin
- ¼ teaspoon ground coriander
- ⅛ teaspoon cayenne
- ⅛ teaspoon garlic powder

simple glaze
- 2 tablespoons water
- 1 teaspoon light or dark brown sugar
- 1 tablespoon unsalted butter

1. Adjust an oven rack to the middle position and heat the oven to 350 degrees. Line a rimmed baking sheet with parchment paper and spread the almonds on it in an even layer. Toast for 4 minutes and rotate the pan; add the peanuts and pumpkin seeds, spreading them in an even layer. Continue to toast until fragrant and the color deepens slightly, about 4 minutes longer. Transfer the baking sheet with the nuts and seeds to a wire rack.

2. FOR THE SPICE MIX: While the nuts and seeds are toasting, stir the sugar, salt, cinnamon, cumin, coriander, cayenne, and garlic powder together in a medium bowl; set aside.

3. FOR THE GLAZE: Bring the water, brown sugar, and butter to a boil in a medium saucepan over medium-high heat, whisking constantly. Stir in the toasted nuts and seeds and cook, stirring constantly with a wooden spoon, until the nuts are shiny and almost all the liquid has evaporated, about 1½ minutes.

4. Transfer the glazed nuts and seeds to the bowl with the spice mix; toss well to coat. Return the glazed and spiced nuts and seeds to the parchment-lined baking sheet to cool.

INDIAN-SPICED CASHEWS AND PISTACHIOS WITH CURRANTS

Makes about 2 cups

The spiced nuts can be stored in an airtight container for up to 5 days.

- 1¼ cups (6 ounces) raw cashews
- ½   cup (2 ounces) raw unsalted shelled pistachios
- 2   tablespoons currants

indian spice mix
- 1   tablespoon sugar
- 1   teaspoon kosher salt
- 1   teaspoon curry powder
- ¼   teaspoon ground cumin
- ¼   teaspoon ground coriander

simple glaze
- 2   tablespoons water
- 1   teaspoon light or dark brown sugar
- 1   tablespoon unsalted butter

1. Adjust an oven rack to the middle position and heat the oven to 350 degrees. Line a rimmed baking sheet with parchment paper and spread the cashews on it in an even layer; toast for 4 minutes, rotate the pan, and toast for 4 minutes more. Add the pistachios, spreading them in an even layer; continue to toast until fragrant and the color deepens slightly, about 2 minutes. Transfer the baking sheet with the nuts to a wire rack; add the currants.

2. FOR THE SPICE MIX: While the nuts are toasting, stir the sugar, salt, curry powder, cumin, and coriander together in a medium bowl; set aside.

3. FOR THE GLAZE: Bring the water, brown sugar, and butter to a boil in a medium saucepan over medium-high heat, whisking constantly. Stir in the nut mix and cook, stirring constantly with a wooden spoon, until the nuts are shiny and almost all the liquid has evaporated, about 1½ minutes.

4. Transfer the glazed nuts and currants to the bowl with the spice mix; toss well to coat. Return the glazed and spiced nuts and currants to the parchment-lined baking sheet to cool.

Q&A

What's the best way to store nuts?

Improper storage and a harsh kitchen environment (think hot, bright, or humid) are enough to make a good nut go bad. Nuts are filled with oils that can spoil rather quickly, even when stored in a cool, dark, dry cabinet. When this happens, the nuts taste rancid and must be discarded. To avoid such a costly mistake, the test kitchen stores all shelled nuts in the freezer. Sealed in a freezer-safe, zipper-lock storage bag, nuts will stay fresh tasting for months, if not a year. And there's no need to defrost them. Frozen nuts chop up just as easily as (if not more so than) fresh. You can toast nuts straight from the freezer, but you might need to add a minute or two to the oven time.

SPINACH DIP

WHAT WE WANTED: Spinach dip—a quick, simple concoction made with vegetable soup mix, sour cream, and frozen spinach—often tastes simply awful. We wanted a rich, thick, and creamy spinach dip brimming with big, bold flavors. Could we bring this old-fashioned recipe into the twenty-first century?

In 1954, America was introduced to what would become our most popular party fare: Lipton's onion soup mix combined with sour cream. Spinach dip—made with vegetable soup mix, sour cream, and frozen spinach—was hot on its heels.

Fifty years later, most spinach dips are still based on soup mixes, and the flavors are still flat, exorbitantly salty, and nowhere near fresh. Yet a good spinach dip can be made easily enough with just a few fresh ingredients, a couple of kitchen tools, and no more than 30 minutes of preparation. (A good onion dip takes much longer because the onions must be caramelized in a skillet for at least 45 minutes.) We set out to rejuvenate spinach dip, without compromising its quick and easy appeal.

To begin, we gathered five varieties of spinach: curly (or crinkly), flat (or smooth), semi-savoy (a hybrid of the two), baby, and, for the sake of comparison, frozen spinach. We then trimmed, washed, chopped, and wilted the fresh spinaches in hot pots (we simply thawed the frozen spinach), made the dips, chilled them until thickened, and let tasters dig in. The results were so surprising we had to tally them twice. Frozen spinach was the victor. Tasters liked its "familiar," "intense" flavor and even used the word "fresh" to describe it. The fresh varieties were too "meek," their flavor lost among the other ingredients. After a few more tests to determine the best consistency, we found that 20 to 30 seconds in the food processor chopped the thawed frozen spinach into small, manageable bits and made the dip smooth and creamy.

The '50s were creeping their way back into our recipe—frozen spinach, no cooking (so far), and speedy preparation—but we weren't about to backtrack on flavor. Armed with a host of fresh herbs and other pungent ingredients, we began developing the flavor components for the dip sans soup mix. Among the herbs, parsley and dill were by and large the standards, and they worked appealingly well when combined. Onions and shallots were problematic, however, as they required cooking to mellow their astringency and soften their crunch. We weren't cooking the spinach and thought it would be a waste of time and effort to start pulling out pots and pans now. In the end, a combination of raw scallion whites and a single small clove of garlic added the perfect amount of bite and pungency. With a dash of hot pepper sauce for a kick and some salt and pepper, the dip came out of the processor light, fresh, and full of bold flavors—far better than the soup mix recipe and not much more work.

The only problem remaining was that the dip, which took only about 15 minutes to make, took almost two hours to chill. Wanting to skip this polar timeout, we found the solution was simple enough. Instead of thawing the spinach completely, we simply thawed it only partially. Before processing, we microwaved the frozen block for three minutes on low, broke it into icy chunks, and squeezed each to extract a surprising amount of liquid. The chunks were still ice cold and thoroughly cooled the dip as they broke down in the processor. Although our hands were slightly numb, the dip was quick to make, thick, creamy, and cool enough for immediate service.

WHAT WE LEARNED: Frozen spinach actually makes a better-tasting dip than fresh spinach. Use the food processor to chop partially thawed spinach and then enrich it with sour cream, mayonnaise, and a mixture of fresh herbs and seasonings.

CREAMY HERBED SPINACH DIP

Makes about 1½ cups, serving 8 to 10

Partial thawing of the spinach produces a cold dip that can be served without further chilling. If you don't own a microwave, the frozen spinach can be thawed at room temperature for 1½ hours, then squeezed of excess liquid. The garlic must be minced or pressed before going into the food processor; otherwise, the dip will contain large chunks of garlic.

1	(10-ounce) box frozen chopped spinach
½	cup sour cream
½	cup mayonnaise
3	medium scallions, white parts only, sliced thin (about 2 tablespoons)
1	tablespoon chopped fresh dill leaves
½	cup packed fresh parsley leaves
1	small garlic clove, minced or pressed through a garlic press (about 1 teaspoon)
¼	teaspoon hot pepper sauce, such as Tabasco
½	teaspoon salt
¼	teaspoon ground black pepper
½	medium red bell pepper, diced fine

1. Thaw the spinach in a microwave for 3 minutes at 40 percent power. (The edges should be thawed but not warm; the center should be soft enough to be broken into icy chunks.) Squeeze the partially frozen spinach to remove excess water.

2. In a food processor, process the spinach, sour cream, mayonnaise, scallions, dill, parsley, garlic, hot pepper sauce, salt, and pepper until smooth and creamy, about 30 seconds. Transfer the mixture to a serving bowl and stir in the bell pepper; serve. (The dip can be covered with plastic wrap and refrigerated for up to 2 days.)

VARIATIONS

SPINACH DIP WITH BLUE CHEESE AND BACON

If making this dip in advance, hold off sprinkling the bacon over the top until just before serving.

Cut 3 ounces (about 3 slices) bacon into ¼-inch pieces and fry them in a small skillet over medium-high heat until crisp and browned, about 5 minutes; using a slotted spoon, transfer the bacon to a paper towel–lined plate and set aside. Follow the recipe for Creamy Herbed Spinach Dip, omitting the dill, hot pepper sauce, salt, and red bell pepper, and processing 1½ ounces crumbled blue cheese (about ⅓ cup) along with the spinach. Season with salt; before serving, sprinkle the bacon over the dip.

SPINACH DIP WITH FETA, LEMON, AND OREGANO

Do not substitute dried oregano for the fresh oregano in this recipe.

Follow the recipe for Creamy Herbed Spinach Dip, omitting the hot pepper sauce, salt, and red bell pepper, and processing 2 tablespoons fresh oregano leaves, 2 ounces crumbled feta cheese (about ½ cup), and 1 tablespoon lemon juice plus 1 teaspoon grated lemon zest along with the spinach. Season with salt.

CILANTRO-LIME SPINACH DIP WITH CHIPOTLE CHILES

This dip is particularly good served with tortilla chips.

Follow the recipe for Creamy Herbed Spinach Dip, omitting the hot pepper sauce and red bell pepper, and processing ¼ cup packed fresh cilantro leaves, 1 tablespoon seeded and minced chipotle chiles in adobo (about 2 medium chiles), 1 tablespoon lime juice plus ½ teaspoon grated lime zest, ½ teaspoon light brown sugar, and ⅛ teaspoon ground cumin along with the spinach.

PITA CHIPS

WHAT WE WANTED: An accompaniment to dips that would taste better than the store-bought alternatives.

Because pita chips are essentially pieces of toast made from pita bread, we figured that developing this recipe was going to be a breeze. Surprisingly, it took more than a few tests to get the results we were after.

We took advantage of the pocket in the middle of each pita by first cutting the pitas into two thin, round layers. Thin one-layer chips not only baked more evenly than double-layered chips but also were easier to dip and eat. Next, we tried baking two batches—one plain, the other brushed with a little olive oil. Hands down, we preferred the crisp, flavorful chips made with a little oil. The oil made all the difference between authentic pita chips and boring pita toast. Not only did the oil matter but, surprisingly, which side of the pita was oiled made a difference as well. After the pita is cut into layers, each chip has two distinct sides—one smooth (the exterior of the original pita bread), the other rough (the inside of the original bread). When the oil was brushed onto the smooth side, tasters claimed the chips felt greasy. Not so when the oil was brushed onto the rough side, which seemed to absorb it.

We also noted that it made a difference which side was facing up or down during baking. When baked rough-side down, the chips stuck to the cookie sheet, requiring a fair amount of prying to remove. But when they were baked smooth-side down, no such problem developed. Finding it necessary to flip the chips during baking for an even toasting, we decided to begin with the smooth side down, giving the rough side a chance to toast so it wouldn't stick.

WHAT WE LEARNED: Cut each pita into two thin rounds and then into chips so they will bake more evenly. Brush the chips with oil and then make sure to start the chips smooth-side down on the baking sheet so they won't stick.

PITA CHIPS
Makes 48 chips, enough to accompany 2 cups dip

4	(8-inch) pita breads, split and cut into 6 wedges
¼	cup olive oil
1	teaspoon salt

1. Adjust the oven racks to the upper- and lower-middle positions and heat the oven to 350 degrees. Spread the pita wedges, smooth-side down, over 2 rimmed baking sheets. Brush each chip lightly with oil and sprinkle with salt.

2. Bake the chips until lightly browned, about 6 minutes. Flip the chips so their smooth side is up. Continue to bake until the chips are fully toasted, about 6 minutes longer. Cool the chips before serving.

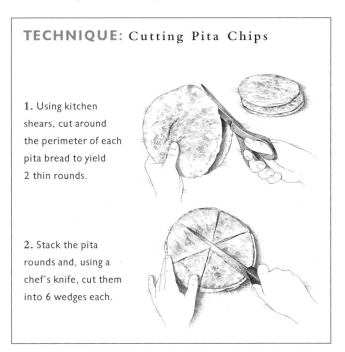

TECHNIQUE: Cutting Pita Chips

1. Using kitchen shears, cut around the perimeter of each pita bread to yield 2 thin rounds.

2. Stack the pita rounds and, using a chef's knife, cut them into 6 wedges each.

BEEF SATAY

WHAT WE WANTED: Tender meat that is easily pulled apart into small bites right off the skewer. The accompanying peanut sauce should be potent and spicy, with just a hint of sweetness.

Slender slices of marinated beef weaved onto bamboo skewers and thrown briefly on the grill are a traditional Indonesian favorite, known as satay (or saté). The meat has a sweet yet salty flavor, and the skewers are served as an appetizer, snack, or light main course alongside a spicy peanut sauce. All too often, however, the beef is tough and sliced so thick it doesn't pull apart, leaving you with an ungainly mouthful of meat. The peanut sauce can be graceless, with a glue-like consistency and muddy peanut flavor. Not only would finding the right cut of beef and slicing it correctly be key for a tender satay, but we wondered how to make the exotic-tasting marinade and accompanying peanut sauce.

Starting with the beef, we surveyed the local meat counter for possibilities. Skipping over the expensive cuts such as top loin, rib eye, and tenderloin, we focused on the cheaper cuts more appropriate for marinating and skewering—sirloin, sirloin flap, round, skirt, flank, and blade steaks. Bringing these cheaper cuts back to the test kitchen, we immediately noted that slicing the raw beef into thin strips is a difficult task. To make it easier, we found it best to firm the meat in the freezer for about 30 minutes. Sliced, skewered, and cooked, these various cheaper cuts of meat produced substantially different textures. Steaks from the round were the worst, with a tough, dry texture, followed closely by chewy sirloin, and stringy sirloin flap (a cut from the bottom sirloin). The blade steaks tasted great and were fairly tender, but their small size made it difficult to slice them into long, elegant strips. Both the skirt and flank steaks were easy to slice and tasted best. Since skirt steak can be difficult to find and is a bit more expensive, flank steak is the best option.

We found the key to tenderness hinges on slicing the meat perpendicular to its large, obvious grain. Using a small, 1½-pound flank steak, we could make about 24 skewers, enough for 12 people as an appetizer. Although satay is classically grilled, we found the broiler to be a simpler and more party-friendly cooking method. Thin wooden skewers worked better than metal skewers, which tend to be thicker and tore up the small pieces of meat. Protecting the bamboo skewers with foil, however, is necessary to prevent them from burning or catching on fire. Cooked roughly six inches from the broiler element, these thinly sliced pieces of meat are done in only six to seven minutes.

Having found a tender cut of meat, we focused next on adding flavor with the marinade. Researching a variety of traditional Indonesian recipes, we noted that most were

based on a combination of fish sauce and oil. Using vegetable oil, we tested various amounts of fish sauce, but tasters simply did not like its fermented fish flavor in combination with the beef. Replacing it with soy sauce, although not traditional, worked well; the soy sauce lent its salty, fermented flavor without any "fishiness."

We then tried adding other flavors such as coconut milk, lime juice, Tabasco, Asian chili sauce, sugar, and an array of fresh herbs. Coconut milk dulled the beef's natural flavor, while the tart, acidic flavor of lime juice tasted out of place. Asian chili sauce added a pleasant, spicy heat without the sour, vinegary flavor that Tabasco contributed. The sweet, molasses flavor of the brown sugar added a welcome balance to the hot chili sauce and salty soy, while enhancing the beef's ability to brown under the broiler. Garlic and cilantro rounded out all of these flavors nicely. Marinating the beef for more than one hour turned the texture of the thin sliced beef mushy, while less time didn't give the meat long enough to pick up the marinade flavors. One hour of marinating was perfect.

Lastly, we focused on the peanut sauce. Using creamy peanut butter, we tried spicing it up using a variety of flavorings. In the end, the same ingredients used in the marinade also tasted good in the peanut sauce—soy sauce, Asian chili sauce, dark brown sugar, garlic, cilantro, and scallion. This time, however, lime juice added a welcome burst of tart acidity. We then stumbled on the obvious way to keep the sauce from being too thick or pasty: Thin it with hot water. Pairing perfectly with the flavor of the marinated beef, the peanut sauce turns these exotic-tasting skewers into an authentic satay.

WHAT WE LEARNED: Choose flank steak and use thin wooden skewers so the meat won't tear. Marinating the beef for an hour in a potent mixture of soy sauce, chili sauce, brown sugar, cilantro, garlic, and scallions adds flavor. The same ingredients work well in the peanut sauce, which should be thinned with hot water and sparked with fresh lime juice.

BEEF SATAY

Serves 12

Meat that is partially frozen is easier to slice into thin strips. Asian chili sauce is available in most supermarkets under the name Sriracha. A chili-garlic sauce, known as sambal, could also be used; however, it is much spicier. Use 6-inch-long skewers for this recipe; you'll need about 24.

1½	pounds flank steak
¼	cup soy sauce
¼	cup vegetable oil
2	tablespoons Asian chili sauce, or more to taste
¼	cup packed dark brown sugar
¼	cup minced fresh cilantro leaves
2	medium garlic cloves, minced or pressed through a garlic press (about 2 teaspoons)
4	scallions, white and green parts, sliced thin
1	recipe Spicy Peanut Dipping Sauce (recipe follows)

1. Cut the flank steak in half lengthwise and freeze it for 30 minutes.

2. Combine the soy sauce, oil, chili sauce, brown sugar, cilantro, garlic, and scallions in a measuring cup; set aside. Remove the flank steak from the freezer and slice each piece across the grain into ¼-inch-thick strips. Weave the meat onto individual bamboo skewers. Dunk the meat end of each skewer in the marinade to coat; lay the skewers in a shallow dish, propping up the exposed ends of the skewers to keep them clean. Pour the remaining marinade over the meat. Refrigerate for exactly 1 hour.

3. Adjust an oven rack to the top position and heat the broiler. Following the illustration on page 12, lay the skewers on a wire rack set over a rimmed baking sheet and cover the skewer ends with foil. Broil for 6 to 7 minutes, flipping the skewers over halfway through, until the meat is browned. Serve immediately with the peanut sauce.

SPICY PEANUT DIPPING SAUCE

Makes about 1½ cups

This sauce can be made a day in advance and refrigerated. Bring the sauce to room temperature before serving.

- ½ cup creamy peanut butter
- ¼ cup hot water
- 1 tablespoon soy sauce
- 2 tablespoons juice from 1 lime
- 2 tablespoons Asian chili sauce
- 1 tablespoon dark brown sugar
- 1 medium garlic clove, minced or pressed through a garlic press (about 1 teaspoon)
- 1 tablespoon chopped fresh cilantro leaves
- 2 scallions, white and green parts, sliced thin

Whisk the peanut butter and hot water together in a medium bowl. Stir in the remaining ingredients. Transfer to a small serving bowl.

TECHNIQUE: Arranging the Skewers

Using a narrow strip of aluminum foil, cover the exposed portion of each skewer to prevent burning. Secure the foil by crimping it tightly at the edges.

TASTING LAB: Salsa

THE MEXICAN WORD FOR "SAUCE," SALSA GENERICALLY refers to a chilled tomato relish that is seasoned with garlic, onions, cilantro, and/or chiles. It sounds simple enough, but if you've ever tried supermarket salsas, you know that simple doesn't always translate into good. In fact, after tasting nine brands of jarred and refrigerated salsas, we can tell you that simple can taste downright awful.

There are two types of supermarket salsa: refrigerated, which only last a month or two, thanks to added preservatives; and bottled salsas, which will stay "fresh" for over a year (thanks to vacuum sealing and, yes, preservatives). The two types vary texturally: refrigerated salsas are raw and have a texture that most resembles homemade, while bottled salsas are cooked, with a more saucy consistency. Refrigerated salsas are often store or regional brands; we found one that was widely distributed. We tasted this brand alongside eight popular bottled brands, all in the basic version (no roasted garlic or chipotle) at a medium level of spiciness.

While none of the salsas measured up to homemade (few supermarket products do), we did find three that we can recommend. The refrigerated salsa topped the ratings, with a flavor and texture that compared most favorably with homemade. Two jarred salsas, Old El Paso and Tostitos, were also recommended for their clean, bright flavors and chunky textures. Conversely, our lowest rated salsas, Herdez and Embasa, were downgraded for muddy flavors and soupy textures.

So if you don't have time to make salsa to go with those chips, head for the refrigerator case for the best store-bought salsa. Jars of Old El Paso and Tostitos are decent options, too.

Rating Salsas

FIFTEEN MEMBERS OF THE *COOK'S ILLUSTRATED* STAFF TASTED ALL OF THE SALSAS PLAIN, WITH CHIPS offered for dipping. The salsas are listed in order of preference based on their scores in this tasting. Look for these salsas in supermarkets nationwide.

RECOMMENDED
Santa Barbara Medium Salsa (refrigerated) **$3.49 for 16 ounces**
Tasters liked this "fresh-tasting" refrigerated salsa, praising its "good herbal flavors."

RECOMMENDED
Old El Paso Thick 'n Chunky Medium Salsa **$2.79 for 16 ounces**
Our favorite bottled salsa was called "spicy" and "bright."

RECOMMENDED
Tostitos Restaurant Style Medium Salsa **$3.29 for 16 ounces**
Although this salsa received decent scores, tasters were not overly enthusiastic about this sample, calling it "not bad" and "very mild."

NOT RECOMMENDED
Muir Glen Organic Medium Salsa **$3.99 for 16 ounces**
Tasters complained about the "mushy" texture and "ketchup-y" flavor.

NOT RECOMMENDED
Taco Bell Home Thick 'n Chunky Medium Salsa **$2.69 for 16 ounces**
One taster quipped, "Is this salsa or tomato sauce?"

NOT RECOMMENDED
Newman's Own Medium Salsa **$2.69 for 16 ounces**
This salsa was deemed "bland" and "sweet."

NOT RECOMMENDED
Green Mountain Gringo Medium Salsa **$3.99 for 16 ounces**
There were several complaints about the "cooked flavor" in this "too sweet" salsa.

NOT RECOMMENDED
Herdez Medium Salsa Casera **$2.99 for 16 ounces**
"Tastes like unseasoned canned tomatoes" was the general consensus about this bland offering imported from Mexico.

NOT RECOMMENDED
Embasa Medium Salsa Mexicana **$2.95 for 16 ounces**
A "gluey" texture and "bitter" aftertaste sank this salsa to the bottom of the ratings.

Canned beans can be the basis of a great soup if you follow our simple method for infusing them with flavor.

SIMPLE soups

Not surprisingly, the differences in flavor between soup from a can and homemade soup are immeasurable. The former is usually too salty, mushy, and altogether unappealing. But most cooks are under the impression that good soup takes all day to prepare. Maybe that's what our mothers wanted us to think, but the truth is that homemade soup need not be a complicated affair.

Rich chicken stock is the basis for many soups, including our favorite, chicken noodle soup. Simply put, there's no way to make this kind of brothy soup without homemade stock. We found an unusual technique and a remarkably simple recipe (just four ingredients, plus salt and water) that yields great stock in less than an hour.

Pasta e fagioli (pasta and beans) is well known to Italian-Americans. This hearty peasant soup deserves a wider audience. It's a meal in a bowl and can be made from pantry ingredients most cooks will have on hand.

CHICKEN STOCK

WHAT WE WANTED: A stock potent enough to use in a simple chicken noodle soup that doesn't take all day to cook. Was there a way to make great stock quickly?

Most standard chicken stocks are not flavorful enough for a robust chicken soup. They are fine if ladled into risotto, but we wanted a stock that really tastes like chicken. We knew that the conventional method—simmering chicken parts and aromatics, such as onions, carrots, and celery, in water for hours—was part of the problem. This method takes too long (at least three hours) to extract flavor from the chicken. We wanted to see if we could do better, and in less time.

We tried blanching a whole chicken on the theory that blanching keeps the chicken from releasing foam during cooking. The blanched chicken was then partially covered with water and placed in a heatproof bowl over a pan of simmering water. Cooked this way, the chicken never simmered, and the resulting stock was remarkably clear, refined, and full-flavored. The only problem: It took four hours for the stock to take on sufficient flavor. We also noted that our 4-pound chicken was good for nothing but the garbage bin after being cooked for so long.

A number of recipes promote roasting chicken bones or parts and then using them to make stock. The theory, at least, is that roasted parts will flavor stock in minutes, not hours. We gave it a try several times, roasting chicken backs, necks, and bones—with and without vegetables. We preferred the stock made with roasted chicken parts and vegetables, but the actual chicken flavor was too tame.

Finally, we tried a method described by Edna Lewis in her book *In Pursuit of Flavor* (Knopf, 1988). She chops a chicken into small pieces and then sautés it with an onion until the chicken loses its raw color. The pot is then covered, and the chicken and onion cook over low heat until they release their rich, flavorful juices, which takes about 20 minutes. Only at that point is the water added, and the stock is simmered for just 20 minutes longer.

We knew we were onto something as we smelled the chicken and onion sautéing, and the finished stock confirmed what our noses had detected. The stock tasted pleasantly sautéed, not boiled. We had some refining to do, though. For once, we had made too strong a brew.

First, we tried using more water. The stock was less intense, but just the right strength to make a base for some of the best chicken soup we've ever tasted. We made the stock twice more, once without the onion and once with onion, celery, and carrot. The onion added a flavor dimension we liked; the extra vegetables neither added nor detracted from the final soup, so we left them out.

After much trial and error, we had a recipe that delivered liquid gold in just 40 minutes. While this recipe requires more hands-on work (hacking up a chicken, browning an onion, then the chicken parts), it is ready in a fraction of the time required to make stock by traditional methods.

If you are making a soup that needs some chicken

meat, use a whole chicken. The breast is removed in two pieces and reserved. The rest of the bird—the legs, back, and wings—is hacked into small pieces, browned, and then sweated with the onions. The water is added to the pot along with the reserved breast pieces. After 20 minutes of simmering time, the breast meat is perfectly cooked, ready to be skinned and shredded when cool. The hacked-up chicken pieces are strained and discarded. We particularly liked the tidiness of this method: One chicken yields one pot of soup.

If you are making a soup that doesn't require chicken meat, use four whole legs that have been cut into 2-inch pieces. Don't try to salvage the meat from the legs. After five minutes of sautéing, 20 minutes of sweating, and another 20 minutes of simmering, the meat is void of flavor.

One note about this method. We found it necessary to cut the chicken into pieces small enough to release their flavorful juices in a short period of time. A meat cleaver, a heavy-duty chef's knife, or a pair of heavy-duty kitchen shears makes the task fairly simple. Cutting up the chicken for stock doesn't require precision.

To cut up a whole chicken, start by removing the whole legs and wings from the body; set them aside. Separate the back from the breast, then split the breast and set the halves aside. Hack the back crosswise into three or four pieces, then halve each of these pieces. Cut the wing at each joint to yield three pieces. Leave the wing tip whole, then halve each of the remaining joints. Because of their larger bones, the legs and thighs are the most difficult to cut. Start by splitting the leg and thigh at the joint, then hack each to yield three to four pieces.

WHAT WE LEARNED: An unusual method—one that calls for browning small pieces of chicken, sweating them in a covered pot with an onion, and then simmering them for just 20 minutes—yields rich stock that's perfect for soup.

TECHNIQUE:
Using a Cleaver to Cut Up Chicken

Chicken hacked into small pieces with a meat cleaver will give up its flavor in record time. To cut through bone, place your hand near the far end of the cleaver handle, curling your fingers securely around it in a fist. Handle the cleaver the way you would a hammer, holding your wrist stiff and straight and letting the weight of the blade's front tip lead the force of the chop.

QUICK CHICKEN STOCK FOR SOUP

Makes about 2 quarts

This soup yields plenty of perfectly cooked white meat that can be used in soups. Make sure to reserve the breast pieces in the refrigerator until step 2—they should not be browned. To make stock without meat for soup, use 4 pounds of cut-up legs, wings, or back. If you use a cleaver, you will be able to cut up the chicken parts quickly. A chef's knife or kitchen shears will also work, albeit more slowly. See the illustration above for tips on using a cleaver.

1   tablespoon vegetable oil
1   whole chicken (about 4 pounds), breast removed, split, and reserved; remaining chicken cut into 2-inch pieces
1   medium onion, cut into medium dice
2   quarts boiling water
2   teaspoons salt
2   bay leaves

1. Heat the oil in a large stockpot or Dutch oven over medium-high heat. Add half of the chopped chicken pieces and cook until no longer pink and the skin is lightly browned, 4 to 5 minutes. Transfer the cooked chicken to a bowl. Brown the remaining chicken pieces and transfer them to the bowl with the first batch. Add the onion and cook until colored and softened slightly, 2 to 3 minutes. Return the chicken pieces to the pot. Reduce the heat to low, cover, and cook until the chicken releases its juices, about 20 minutes.

2. Increase the heat to high; add the boiling water, reserved chicken breast pieces, salt, and bay leaves. Return to a simmer, then cover and barely simmer until the stock is rich and flavorful, about 20 minutes.

3. Remove the breast pieces from the pot and set aside. When cool, discard the skin and bones from the breast pieces and shred the meat into bite-size pieces. Strain the stock into a container and discard the solids. Skim the fat from the stock and reserve for later use in the soup. (The shredded chicken, strained stock, and fat can be covered and refrigerated separately up to 2 days.)

TECHNIQUE:
Freezing Small Portions of Stock
In the test kitchen, we ladle the cooled stock into nonstick muffin tins and freeze. When the stock is frozen, twist the muffin tin just as you would twist an ice tray. Place the frozen blocks in a zipper-lock plastic bag and seal it tightly.

1. An alternative is to pour stock into a coffee mug lined with a quart-size plastic zipper-lock bag.

2. Place the filled bags in a large, shallow roasting pan and freeze. Once the stock is frozen solid, the bags can be removed from the pan and stored in the freezer.

EQUIPMENT CORNER: Fat Separators

IS THERE ANYTHING AS FRUSTRATING AS SKIMMING THE fat from the top of a homemade soup, sauce, or stock? Endlessly blotting with messy paper towels, flaccid lettuce leaves, or, worst of all, ladling ounces of delicious liquid down the drain just to remove a few droplets of oil, defatting is probably the most thankless task in the kitchen. Luckily, separating liquid fat is easy to do with a specially designed fat separator, aka gravy strainer or soup strainer. Anticipation was high as we recently lined up eight widely available fat separators and put them to the test. In addition to their individual performance, the separators would also be judged on their price, material, capacity, handle comfort, and ease of use. Faced with a wide range of designs and price tags, we were out to find the fat separator that would finally liberate us from our skimming woes.

Fat separators typically come in three formats: pitcher-type measuring cups with sharply angled spouts opening out from the base of the cup; ladles with slots around the perimeter; and "fat mops," brushes with long, soft bristles made from plastic fibers. Such extreme design differences raise the obvious question—which kind works best? Fat-separating ladles offer a series of slot-shaped holes along one side of the ladle that allow fat to drain into the bowl of the ladle so it can be discarded. Our testers found this to be a tedious process requiring fine control of the ladle, which, when dipped too low, let in the broth along with the fat. Although we tested only one, fat mops are designed to wick away fat from stews, gravies, soups, chilis, and fried foods—items for which it would be impossible to use another kind of fat separator. This clever design proved successful in smaller capacities but was unable to effectively defat large amounts of liquid. The pitcher-type separators offered convenience, reliable performance, and, owing to the large capacity, a level of efficiency that the other styles could not provide.

Because of its oblong shape, the Trudeau Gravy Separator ($9.99) had the widest mouth of all, a point in its favor. The Trudeau also had an integrated strainer, which is helpful when you're defatting pan drippings that are still mixed with chunks of aromatic vegetables, herb sprigs, or other flavorings. The "As Seen on TV" OMI Original Fat Mop ($4.99) turned out to be pretty interesting. In our tests, it did in fact prove effective with chunky tomato sauce and pot-au-feu. Strictly speaking, however, the Fat Mop is not intended for use with large amounts of liquid. If we could have just one fat separator in the kitchen, Trudeau's version of the common pitcher type would be our choice. For another five bucks, though, the Fat Mop makes a useful supplement, especially if you have to remove fat from chunky stews and chilis. Between the two, neither the fat nor the process of removing it should be cause for anxiety.

Rating Fat Separators

WE TESTED EIGHT FAT SEPARATORS BY SIMMERING 1 GALLON OF CANNED LOW-SODIUM CHICKEN BROTH WITH 10 ounces of rendered chicken fat for 30 minutes. The stock was allowed to cool for 15 minutes prior to testing. Each of the fat separators was evaluated on its price, material, capacity, performance, handle comfort, and ease of use. The fat separators are listed in order of preference. See www.americastestkitchen.com for up-to-date prices and mail-order sources for top-rated products.

HIGHLY RECOMMENDED
Trudeau Gravy Separator with Integrated Strainer, Model 099-1105 $9.99

The clear-cut winner. Its wide, oblong shape makes it easy to pour into, the integrated strainer is a great feature, and an angled shield near the spout prevents spillovers. Reasonably priced, too.

RECOMMENDED
Pedrini Gravy Separator $14.95

This model has the largest capacity of all the contestants at 5 cups. Its very ergonomic handle was also praised by the testers.

RECOMMENDED
East Hampton Industries Souper Strain, No. 824 $5.69

The basic design of this separator is certainly function over form, but its performance was strong. Because the handle is not attached to the bottom of the cup, this separator was slightly unstable at full capacity.

RECOMMENDED
OMI (Oil Mop, Inc.) The Original Fat Mop $4.99

This tool was inefficient when defatting large quantities of liquid, but it worked like a champ on stews, sauces, and other chunky dishes. Does not clean easily, but at $4.99 a pop, it is inexpensive enough to replace periodically.

RECOMMENDED
East Hampton Industries Gravy Strain, No. 823 $2.49

Works as well as its big brother but lost some points because of its small capacity.

RECOMMENDED
Catamount Glass 2-Cup Fat Separator/Strainer $16.95

This model won points for its measurement lines that are printed in dark ink and are therefore very easy to read. Unfortunately, difficulty pouring and a lofty price tag hurt this separator in our rankings.

NOT RECOMMENDED
WMF Profi Plus 11-inch Stainless Steel Fat Skimming Ladle $19.99

Although it performed decently as a ladle-style skimmer, it required considerable steadiness and patience to defat the stock.

NOT RECOMMENDED
East Hampton Industries Skim It Fat Separator, No. 826B $4.99

Even considering its reasonable price, this separator performed poorly in most of the tests. It was difficult to dip into the liquid with enough precision to control the flow of fat, and the design only works with large volumes of liquid.

CHICKEN NOODLE SOUP

WHAT WE WANTED: A great chicken noodle soup with tender, flavorful vegetables and perfectly cooked noodles.

With homemade chicken stock on hand, making chicken noodle soup is a relatively easy proposition. Add some vegetables, herbs, and noodles and you've got a great bowl of soup. We did have several questions, though. Which vegetables are best added to this soup? Should the vegetables be sautéed first, or can diced vegetables simply be simmered in chicken stock? As for the pasta, which kind of noodles work best, and should they be cooked in the soup or in a separate pot of boiling water?

We tackled the vegetable issue first. We tested a wide range of vegetables, including onions, carrots, celery, leeks, potatoes, zucchini, tomatoes, and mushrooms. We concluded that the classic mirepoix ingredients (onions, carrots, and celery) should be part of a basic chicken noodle soup. Other vegetables are fine choices, but we concluded that they are more appropriate for variations. For instance, tomatoes and zucchini give chicken noodle soup an Italian character, and spring vegetables are a natural choice with delicate orzo.

To settle the issue of how to cook the vegetables, we prepared two batches of soup. For the first batch, we sautéed the onions, carrots, and celery in a little vegetable oil until softened and then added the chicken stock. For the second batch, we simply simmered the sliced vegetables in stock. We found that sautéing brought out flavors in the vegetables and made a big difference in the finished soup.

We saw a few recipes that suggested saving chicken fat skimmed from homemade stock and using this fat as a cooking medium for the vegetables. We tested this method and found that chicken fat does in fact add another level of chicken flavor to the soup. Although not essential, it makes sense to use chicken fat if you have planned ahead and saved the congealed fat skimmed from the surface of your stock.

In addition to the vegetables, we found the use of thyme and parsley brightened flavors. We added dried thyme along with the chicken stock so it would have time to soften and permeate the stock. To preserve its freshness, the parsley is best added just before serving.

The noodles were the last (and the most important) element that we needed to investigate. Although dried egg noodles are the most common choice, we ran across several recipes that suggest fresh or dried pasta. Before testing various noodles, we decided to clarify the issue of how to cook them. We simmered egg noodles in the soup as well as in a separate pot of salted water. The noodles cooked in the soup pot shed some starch that clouded the soup slightly but not horribly so. In contrast, noodles cooked in a separate pot and added to the finished soup left it completely clear.

The effect on the soup, however, paled in comparison to the effect on the noodles. Noodles cooked separately tasted bland and did not meld with the soup. The noodles cooked in the soup absorbed some of the chicken stock, giving them a rich, well-rounded flavor. We concluded that you must cook the noodles in the soup.

We identified five possible noodle choices—Pennsylvania Dutch dried egg noodles, dried linguine, dried spaghetti, fresh fettuccine, and fresh linguine. We cooked 2 ounces of each in a pot of chicken soup. Tasters preferred the egg noodles to either the fresh or dried pasta. These noodles cooked up very soft and yielding. They were tender to the bite and nearly melted in the mouth. In addition to their texture, tasters liked the ridged edges on these noodles, which provide nooks and crannies that can trap pieces of vegetable. (See the Tasting Lab on page 22 for brand recommendations.)

WHAT WE LEARNED: Sauté the onion, carrot, and celery in chicken fat (reserved from the stock) for maximum flavor. Cook the egg noodles right in the soup pot so they can absorb some chicken flavor.

CHICKEN NOODLE SOUP

Serves 6 to 8

Three components from the stock—chicken fat, strained stock, and shredded breast meat—are all used to make this soup, but each goes into the pot at a different point in the process.

2 tablespoons chicken fat (reserved from making stock) or vegetable oil
1 medium onion, cut into medium dice
1 large carrot, peeled and sliced ¼ inch thick
1 celery rib, sliced ¼ inch thick
½ teaspoon dried thyme
1 recipe Quick Chicken Stock for Soup (page 17), stock and meat separated
2 cups (3 ounces) wide egg noodles
¼ cup minced fresh parsley leaves
Ground black pepper

1. Heat the chicken fat in a large stockpot or Dutch oven over medium-high heat. Add the onion, carrot, and celery and cook until softened, about 5 minutes. Add the thyme and stock and simmer until the vegetables are tender and the flavors meld, 10 to 15 minutes.

2. Add the noodles and shredded chicken and cook until just tender, 5 to 8 minutes. Stir in the parsley and pepper to taste, adjust the seasonings, and serve.

VARIATIONS

CHICKEN SOUP WITH ORZO AND SPRING VEGETABLES

Follow the recipe for Chicken Noodle Soup, replacing the onion with 1 medium leek, rinsed thoroughly, quartered lengthwise, then sliced thin crosswise. Substitute ½ cup orzo for the egg noodles. Along with the orzo, add ¼ pound asparagus, trimmed and cut into 1-inch lengths, and ¼ cup fresh or frozen peas. Substitute 2 tablespoons minced fresh tarragon leaves for the parsley.

CHICKEN SOUP WITH SHELLS, TOMATOES, AND ZUCCHINI

Follow the recipe for Chicken Noodle Soup, adding 1 medium zucchini, cut into medium dice, with the onion, carrot, and celery and increase the sautéing time to 7 minutes. Add ½ cup chopped tomatoes (fresh or canned) with the stock. Substitute 1 cup small shells or elbow macaroni for the egg noodles and simmer until the noodles are cooked, about 10 minutes. Substitute an equal portion of fresh basil for the parsley. Serve with grated Parmesan, if desired.

TASTING LAB: Egg Noodles

EGG NOODLES ARE NOT THE STARS OF THE PASTA WORLD. They lack the panache of penne, the sultriness of spaghetti, the rotundity of rotini. Yet they are essential in chicken noodle soup. Noodles that are mealy or pasty have no place in your cupboard.

Classic egg noodles are thick, wide ribbons of pasta that have a slightly higher fat content than other kinds of pasta because of their high percentage (up to 20 percent) of eggs. Their firm, sturdy texture is what makes them so appealing.

We chose eight widely available brands and tasted them plain (tossed in a small amount of canola oil to prevent clumping). We were looking for a clean, slightly buttery flavor and a firm yet yielding texture. The top two finishers were clearly superior to the rest of the pack. Problems with the rest of the field included excessive thickness, gumminess, off flavors, or no flavors (the only no-yolk brand in the testing fell victim to the last problem). In two cases, the flaws were serious enough to sink the noodles to the "not recommended" category.

The top choice, Light 'n Fluffy, was praised for its "clean, neutral" flavor and superior texture. Close behind was Black Forest Girl, a German brand found in the international aisle of some supermarkets (or by mail order from www.germandeli.com), and described by fans as "yummy" with a "wheaty" flavor and "firm" texture.

Rating Egg Noodles

FIFTEEN MEMBERS OF THE *COOK'S ILLUSTRATED* STAFF TASTED ALL OF THE EGG NOODLES, WHICH WERE BOILED, drained, and tossed with a tiny amount of canola oil to prevent clumping. The noodles are listed in order of preference based on their scores in this tasting. Brands are available in supermarkets.

HIGHLY RECOMMENDED
Light 'n Fluffy Wide Egg Noodles **$1.95 for 12 ounces**
This brand won fans with its "buttery" flavor and "firm, delicate" texture.

HIGHLY RECOMMENDED
Black Forest Girl Extra Broad Noodles **$3.29 for 8.8 ounces**
"Has bite, but is tender," wrote one fan of these expensive German noodles. Tasters were split on flavor; some praised its "clean, neutral" flavor, while others found it "bland."

RECOMMENDED
Streit's Wide Egg Noodles **$1.59 for 12 ounces**
This brand was praised for "good pasta flavor," though many found the texture "too thick and gummy."

RECOMMENDED
Manischewitz Wide Egg Noodles **$1.49 for 12 ounces**
"Your everyday noodle," wrote one taster. Both fans and detractors noted the "substantial egg flavor."

RECOMMENDED
Pennsylvania Dutch Homestyle Egg Noodles **$1.39 for 16 ounces**
Fans praised the "wheaty" flavor, though many found these noodles "slightly gummy."

RECOMMENDED
Mueller's Hearty Wide Egg Noodles **$1.79 for 16 ounces**
"Very neutral," wrote one taster of this popular supermarket brand, which many tasters found "familiar."

NOT RECOMMENDED
No Yolks Cholesterol Free Egg Noodle Substitute **$2.05 for 12 ounces**
Not surprisingly, there were few fans of this "substitute," which was deemed "too firm" by most tasters, who also lamented that there was "no egg flavor."

NOT RECOMMENDED
Goodman's Wide Egg Noodles **$2.79 for 16 ounces**
Tasters were put off by the texture of these "thick, gummy" noodles and their "stale" flavor.

PASTA E FAGIOLI

WHAT WE WANTED: A rich broth with perfectly cooked pasta and beans.

Pasta fazool, the Italian-American version of Italy's pasta e fagioli (pasta and bean soup) is hearty, thick, almost stew-like, and always orange-red in color from the presence of tomatoes. Each spoonful is laden with pasta and beans, and the soup is full of harmonious flavors, with no one taste standing out. The vegetables are cut small and used as accents to the pasta. Typically, in mediocre pasta fazool, the beans have no flavor, the pasta is mushy, the broth is too tomatoey, and the soup is bland. We wanted to make a pasta fazool that would make any Italian-American family proud.

We began by preparing a half dozen recipes, most of which followed a similar procedure. First the aromatics (vegetables and often some pork product) were sautéed in olive oil. Then the tomatoes and broth went into the pot, followed by the beans and, finally, the pasta. Almost all of these recipes produced bland soups with mushy pasta. The soup with the best flavor took more than four hours to prepare and used dried beans. Although the long hours at the stove paid off, the speed with which some other recipes came together was certainly appealing. So the challenge became clear. Could we make a really good soup using canned beans, a shortcut that would save hours of cooking time?

Many recipes for pasta e fagioli contain pancetta (unsmoked Italian bacon), while completely Americanized recipes call for regular bacon. The simplest recipes avoid the pork and use only olive oil. Our first test showed that even a small amount of a pork product added much flavor to the soup, so we sautéed 3 ounces of finely diced pancetta in 1 tablespoon olive oil. We served this batch to tasters alongside a version made with the same amount of bacon and oil. The pancetta gave the soup a subtler pork flavor, but tasters did not mind the stronger, smokier flavor of regular bacon. (Pancetta is preferred, but you can use either.)

Most Italian recipes use the same quartet of aromatic vegetables: onions, celery, carrots, and garlic. Tasters liked the onions, celery, and garlic but were divided over the sweetness of the carrots. We decided to omit carrots from the recipe.

In most recipes, the aromatics are sautéed, and then the pan is deglazed with either tomatoes or broth. For the tomatoes, we tried crushed, diced, and sauce. The crushed tomatoes and tomato sauce were overpowering, but the diced tomatoes worked well, helping to intensify the flavors of the aromatics. We also tested chicken broth, a close second to the tomatoes (we would add the broth later), and white wine, the latter simply turning the soup sour.

Cranberry beans, a beautiful pink-and-white-mottled variety, are popular in Italy but hard to find in this country. We tested two common substitutes, pinto beans and red kidney beans. Neither had the sweet, delicate flavor of a cranberry bean, so we tried cannellini beans, also known as white kidney beans. Tasters found these oval-shaped beans to be sweet and creamy and most like cranberry beans. Smaller white beans (navies and great Northerns) did not have quite enough heft for this soup but are certainly fine if that's what you have on hand.

Although a taste test (see page 27) revealed some good choices among canned beans, we wanted to find a way to boost their flavor. Our first thought was to add the beans to the tomato mixture, a step that might infuse them with the flavors of the pancetta, oil, and vegetables. We prepared two batches of soup—one with beans and broth added simultaneously and one with beans added to the tomatoes and cooked for 10 minutes prior to adding the broth. The results were black and white. The beans added to the tomato mixture adopted its flavors readily, easily beating out the bland beans added later in the recipe.

The makeup of the broth was also critical. Although chicken broth is standard in many recipes, tasters felt that the resulting pasta fazool tasted like chicken soup. We tried water instead of chicken stock, adding some Parmesan rind to boost flavor. This test was a success, but we went on to try a 60/40 combination of broth and water, retaining the cheese rind. This soup was the winner: good body, good flavor, and not too "chickeny."

For additional flavorings, we added oregano and red pepper flakes to the pot with the aromatic vegetables; tasters approved. Parsley is typically added at the end of cooking, and it took just one test to show that it brightened the flavor and color of the soup. The last flavor-enhancing idea—a long shot, perhaps—was a teaspoon of minced anchovy fillet. Tasters could not identify what was different about the batch with anchovy, but everyone agreed that it was more complex and fuller in flavor.

Our tests showed that pasta with relatively small shapes is best in this soup. Larger shapes, like elbows and shells, crowded out the other ingredients and soaked up too much broth. Tiny pasta, such as stars and pastina, was lost next to the more sizable beans and tomatoes.

WHAT WE LEARNED: Construct a flavorful base with pancetta, sautéed aromatic vegetables, oregano, pepper flakes, anchovies, and tomatoes. Cook canned beans directly in this mixture before adding chicken broth and water. Finish by cooking a small pasta shape right in the soup pot.

ITALIAN PASTA AND BEAN SOUP (PASTA E FAGIOLI)

Serves 8 to 10

This soup does not hold well because the pasta absorbs the liquid, becomes mushy, and leaves the soup dry. You can, however, make the soup in two stages. Once the beans are simmered with the tomatoes, before the broth and water are added, the mixture can be cooled and refrigerated for up to 3 days. When ready to complete the soup, discard the Parmesan rind (otherwise it will become stringy), add the liquid, bring the soup to a boil, and proceed with the recipe.

1	tablespoon extra-virgin olive oil, plus more for drizzling
3	ounces pancetta or bacon, chopped fine
1	medium onion, chopped fine
1	celery rib, chopped fine
4	medium garlic cloves, minced or pressed through a garlic press (about 1 heaping tablespoon)
1	teaspoon dried oregano
¼	teaspoon red pepper flakes
3	anchovy fillets, minced to a paste
1	(28-ounce) can diced tomatoes
1	piece Parmesan cheese rind, about 5 inches by 2 inches
2	(15.5-ounce) cans cannellini beans, drained and rinsed
3½	cups low-sodium chicken broth
2½	cups water
	Salt
8	ounces small pasta shape (see page 26)
¼	cup chopped fresh parsley leaves
	Ground black pepper
	Grated Parmesan cheese for the table

1. Heat the oil in a large heavy-bottomed stockpot or Dutch oven over medium-high heat until shimmering. Add the pancetta and cook, stirring occasionally, until it begins to brown, 3 to 5 minutes. Add the onion and celery and cook, stirring occasionally, until the vegetables are softened, 5 to 7 minutes. Add the garlic, oregano, red pepper flakes, and anchovies and cook, stirring constantly, until fragrant, about 1 minute. Add the tomatoes with their liquid, scraping up any browned bits from the pan bottom. Add the cheese rind and beans; bring to a boil, then reduce the heat to low and simmer to blend the flavors, 10 minutes. Add the chicken broth, water, and 1 teaspoon salt; increase the heat to high and bring to a boil. Add the pasta and cook until tender, about 10 minutes (refer to the package instructions to better estimate pasta cooking time).

2. Discard the cheese rind. Off the heat, stir in 3 tablespoons of the parsley; adjust the seasonings with salt and pepper to taste. Ladle the soup into individual bowls; drizzle each serving with olive oil and sprinkle with a portion of the remaining parsley. Serve immediately, passing the grated Parmesan separately.

VARIATION

ITALIAN PASTA AND BEAN SOUP WITH ORANGE AND FENNEL

Ditalini and orzo are especially good pasta shapes for this variation.

Trim 1 medium fennel bulb of its stalks and fronds; trim the bottom ½ inch. Halve the bulb lengthwise and, using a paring knife, remove the core. Slice the bulb lengthwise into ¼-inch-thick strips, then chop fine. Follow the recipe for Italian Pasta and Bean Soup, cooking the fennel along with the onion and celery and adding 2 teaspoons grated orange zest and ½ teaspoon fennel seeds along with the garlic, oregano, pepper flakes, and anchovies. Proceed as directed.

GETTING IT RIGHT: The Four Best Shapes for Pasta e Fagioli

Ditalini
These "little thimbles" are ½ inch square when cooked, about the same size as the beans and tomatoes. They create the chunkiest soup.

Tubetini
These "tiny tubes" are similar in shape to ditalini but not even half the size when cooked. The soup will have a more brothy appearance.

Conchigliette
These "small shells," the largest of the recommended pasta shapes, are close to ¾ inch square when cooked.

Orzo
This rice-shaped pasta cooks up thinner than the beans but has a similar shape and length, making the soup look a bit more refined.

TECHNIQUE: Freezing Small Portions of Soup

1. Set out a number of 10- to 12-ounce paper cups for hot beverages and fill each with a portion of cooled soup (but not all the way to the top). Label, wrap, and freeze each cup.

2. Whenever you want a quick cup of soup, remove as many servings as necessary from the freezer and microwave them until they're hot and ready to serve.

TASTING LAB: Canned White Beans

WE SAMPLED FOUR CANNED WHITE BEANS IN OUR SEARCH for the best beans for this soup. Because so few brands of canned cannellini beans (our favorite for this soup) are distributed nationwide, we broadened our taste test to include other white beans with widespread distribution. We tasted each contender twice: straight from the can (after being drained and rinsed) and prepared in our recipe for pasta e fagioli made without the pasta.

The tasting had two clear winners, one clear loser, and one brand with mixed comments from tasters. Westbrae great Northern beans had the best flavor and texture—described as "earthy" and "creamy" by our tasters—but they were a bit small for our soup recipe. Progresso cannellini beans were "plump" and "sweet" and were the perfect size for soup. Eden navy beans were small and broken and rejected by our

tasters. Goya cannellini beans received mixed scores. Their flavor received high marks, but tasters were put off by their "weird" gray color and "tough" skins.

BEST CANNED WHITE BEANS
Westbrae organic great Northern beans (left) had great flavor but are a bit small for soup. Progresso cannellini beans (right) are excellent in soup (although their flavor is a bit less complex).

Chris watches Julia demonstrate the secrets to a quick cheese bread—the perfect accompaniment to our hearty lentil soup.

A SOUP supper

Soup for supper is an appealing concept, especially on a cold, snowy night. But for soup to work as a main course, it better be hearty. A light, clear broth simply won't do.

Lentil soup fits the bill, but more often than not this soup is starchy, thick, and stodgy. It may be hearty, but who wants to eat more than a few spoonfuls let alone a big bowl? Our goal when developing this recipe was clear: create a vibrant lentil soup around which we could build a meal. It would be substantial and satisfying but not leaden.

We cannot live by soup alone. A salad might round out the meal, but we usually want some bread, and preferably something homemade. Since our lentil soup is a relatively straightforward affair, a complex yeast bread that takes all day to prepare doesn't feel like the right choice. Instead, we turned to a quick cheese bread, ready for the oven after just 15 minutes of work. This full-flavored bread is so good, you might want to skip the soup and have bread for dinner. Certainly not a balanced meal, but delicious nonetheless.

LENTIL SOUP

WHAT WE WANTED: Lentil soup is cheap to make, quick to make, and when properly prepared, tastes great—maybe even better—the next day. We wanted a hearty lentil soup worthy of a second bowl, not the tasteless variety we have so often encountered.

We started our testing process for lentil soup by preparing five representative recipes, and two discoveries came quickly to light. First, garlic, herbs, onions, and tomatoes are common denominators. Second, texture is a big issue. None of our tasters liked the soup that was brothy or, at the other extreme, the one that was as thick as porridge. They also gave a big thumbs down to those that looked like brown split pea soup. Consequently, recipes that included carrots, tomatoes, and herbs were lauded for their brighter colors (and flavors). There was also a clear preference for the subtle, smoky depth that meat provides. The next step was to determine which lentils to buy and how to cook them.

Brown, green, and red lentils are the most common choices on supermarket shelves. At specialty markets and natural food stores, you can also find black lentils and French green lentils (lentils du Puy), the latter being the darling of chefs everywhere. In addition to color differences, lentils can be divided according to their size—large or small—and to whether they are split, like peas, or not. Ordinary brown and green lentils are large, while red, black, and lentils du Puy are small. Red lentils are often sold split and are used most frequently in Indian dishes such as dal.

To make some sense of all of this, we made five pots of lentil soup, each one using a different color lentil. Red lentils were out; they disintegrated when simmered. All four of the remaining choices produced an acceptable texture, but tasters preferred, as expected, the earthy flavor and firm texture of the lentils du Puy. To our surprise, however, the larger green and brown lentils fared reasonably well,

exceeding the low expectations of the test kitchen.

Next, we set out to test cooking methods. Some lentils, especially the large brown and green varieties, have a greater tendency to fall apart if overcooked, even for just a few minutes. Searching for a way to avoid this problem, we employed a common Indian culinary trick: sweating the lentils in a covered pan with aromatic vegetables prior to adding the liquid. Using brown lentils, we cooked up two batches and, bingo, we had solved the problem! The sweated lentils remained intact, while the unsweated lentils had broken down.

To better understand this phenomenon, we set up a series of tests. We sweated one batch of lentils with just onions and carrots. In the second batch we added salt, and in the third batch we added vinegar to test the role of acids. The results were clear. The first batch—without any salt or acid—was the worst, with a very mushy texture. The lentils sweated with salt were the most intact, while the vinegar helped keep the lentils firm but it was not as effective as the salt (at least in amounts that would taste good). So why did we get these results? When legumes are cooked, their pectin breaks down into a gelatinous goo, similar to jam. Salt and acids (such as those found in canned tomatoes or vinegar) reinforce the original insoluble pectin and retard its conversion to gel. Sweating the lentils with bacon, canned tomatoes, and salt (as well as aromatic vegetables and herbs) not only ensured an ideal texture but boosted the flavor of the legumes as well.

One issue concerning texture remained. Tasters wanted a chunkier soup and did not like the brothy base. We tried pureeing a few cups of the soup and then adding it back to the pot. Tasters praised the contrast of the now creamy base with the whole lentils and found the entire soup more interesting.

Pork was the meat of choice in all of the recipes we examined. We found that the lentils cooked too quickly to absorb the smoky flavor that a ham bone or hock can impart. Prosciutto and pancetta were too mild. Tasters preferred the smoky flavor of bacon and liked the textural addition of the bacon bits. Another advantage bacon offered was rendered fat. We used it to sauté the vegetables and aromatics, which further infused the soup with smoky flavor. Bay leaves, thyme, and parsley rounded out the other flavors and added a touch of bright green to the pot.

Last, but not least, was the question of liquids. We prepared two batches, one with water and one with chicken broth. Neither was ideal. Water produced a soup that was not as rich in flavor as desired, while the broth-only version tasted too much like chicken soup. After several more tests, we concluded that a mix of 3 parts broth to 1 part water produced a hearty depth of flavor without being overpowering.

Many recipes call for the addition of vinegar or lemon juice just before the soup is served. We stirred a touch of balsamic vinegar into the pot at completion, and tasters gave this soup a perfect 10.

With our recipe complete, we developed a few variations. Stirring a hefty amount of spinach into the pot at the end of cooking created a popular version: lentil soup with greens. For a spicier and more exotic rendition, we added some of the aromatic spices used in North African cooking—cumin, coriander, cinnamon, and cayenne—and substituted cilantro for the parsley and lemon juice for the vinegar.

WHAT WE LEARNED: Almost any lentil (other than red lentils) can be used to make soup. To keep the lentils from losing their shape as they cook, sweat them with the sautéed aromatic vegetables, bacon, and tomatoes before adding the liquid to the soup pot. Lentil soup needs plenty of acidity, so use white wine as part of the broth and finish the soup with balsamic vinegar.

HEARTY LENTIL SOUP

Serves 4 to 6

Lentils du Puy, sometimes called French green lentils, are our first choice for this recipe, but brown, black, or regular green lentils are fine, too. Note that cooking times will vary depending on the type of lentils used. Lentils lose flavor with age, and because most packaged lentils do not have expiration dates, try to buy them from a store that specializes in natural foods and grains. Before use, rinse and then carefully sort through the lentils to remove any small stones.

3   ounces (3 slices) bacon, cut into ¼-inch pieces
1   large onion, chopped fine
2   medium carrots, peeled and chopped medium
3   medium garlic cloves, minced or pressed through a garlic press (about 1 tablespoon)
1   (14.5-ounce) can diced tomatoes, drained
1   bay leaf
1   teaspoon minced fresh thyme leaves
1   cup (7 ounces) lentils, rinsed and picked over
1   teaspoon salt
    Ground black pepper
½   cup dry white wine
4½ cups low-sodium chicken broth
1½ cups water
1½ teaspoons balsamic vinegar
3   tablespoons minced fresh parsley leaves

1. Fry the bacon in a large stockpot or Dutch oven over medium-high heat, stirring occasionally, until the fat is rendered and the bacon is crisp, 3 to 4 minutes. Add the onion and carrots; cook, stirring occasionally, until the vegetables begin to soften, about 2 minutes. Add the garlic and cook until fragrant, about 30 seconds. Stir in the tomatoes, bay leaf, and thyme; cook until fragrant, about 30 seconds. Stir in the lentils, salt, and pepper to taste; cover, reduce the heat to medium-low, and cook until the vegetables are softened and the lentils have darkened, 8 to 10 minutes.

2. Uncover, increase the heat to high, add the wine, and bring to a simmer. Add the chicken broth and water; bring to a boil, cover partially, and reduce the heat to low. Simmer until the lentils are tender but still hold their shape, 30 to 35 minutes; discard the bay leaf.

3. Puree 3 cups of the soup in a blender until smooth, then return to the pot. Stir in the vinegar and heat the soup over medium-low until hot, about 5 minutes. Stir in 2 tablespoons of the parsley and serve, garnishing each bowl with some of the remaining parsley. (The soup can be made up to 2 days in advance. After adding the vinegar in step 3, cool the soup to room temperature and refrigerate it in an airtight container. To serve, heat it over medium-low until hot, then stir in the parsley.)

VARIATIONS

HEARTY LENTIL SOUP WITH SPINACH
Follow the recipe for Hearty Lentil Soup, replacing the parsley with 5 ounces baby spinach. Continue to heat the soup, stirring frequently, until the spinach is wilted, about 3 minutes; serve.

GETTING IT RIGHT:
A Good Sweat Makes a Difference

| **Firm Lentils** | **Mushy Lentils** |

Sweating the lentils with salt and an acidic component (from the canned tomatoes) retards the conversion of pectin-like compounds to a gel. Once sweated, these lentils easily remain intact during a long simmer in broth (left) while becoming tender on the inside. Lentils simmered without first being sweated fall apart (right) if overcooked.

HEARTY LENTIL SOUP WITH FRAGRANT SPICES
Follow the recipe for Hearty Lentil Soup, adding 1 teaspoon ground cumin, 1 teaspoon ground coriander, 1 teaspoon ground cinnamon, and ¼ teaspoon cayenne along with the garlic; substitute lemon juice for the balsamic vinegar and minced fresh cilantro leaves for the parsley.

TASTING LAB: Lentils

LENTILS COME IN VARIOUS SIZES AND COLORS, AND the differences in flavor and texture are surprisingly distinct. Tasters evaluated five kinds of lentils in our soup, rating them in terms of taste, texture, and appearance. Here's what we found, with the lentils listed in order of preference.

Lentils du Puy
These green lentils are smaller in size than the more common brown and green varieties. While they take their name from the city of Puy in central France, they are also grown in North 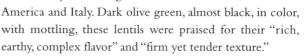 America and Italy. Dark olive green, almost black, in color, with mottling, these lentils were praised for their "rich, earthy, complex flavor" and "firm yet tender texture."

Black Lentils
Like lentils du Puy, black lentils are slightly smaller than the standard brown lentils. They have a deep black hue that tasters likened to the color of caviar. In fact, some markets refer to them as beluga lentils. Tasters liked their "robust, earthy flavor" and "ability to hold their shape while remaining tender." A few tasters found the color of the soup made with them "too dark and muddy."

Brown Lentils

These larger lentils are the most common choice in the marketplace and are a uniform drab brown. Tasters commented on their "mild yet light and earthy flavor." Some found their texture was "creamy," while others complained that they were "chalky." But everyone agreed that they held their shape and were tender inside.

Green Lentils

Another larger lentil, this variety is the same size as the brown lentil and is greenish-brown in color. Although tasters accepted the "mild flavor" of these lentils and liked the way they "retain their shape while being tender," most complained that the soup made from them looked unappealing.

Red Lentils

These small orange-red lentils "completely disintegrate when cooked." They made a soup that looked "anemic."

EQUIPMENT CORNER:
Vegetable Peelers

THE OXO GOOD GRIPS PEELER HAS BEEN A STANDARD IN our test kitchen since our 1998 rating of vegetable peelers. But two new peelers—the Oxo I-Series and Messermeister serrated—recently led us back into the kitchen for another look. We tested these peelers on thin-skinned fruits and vegetables, tough-skinned squash, and craggy root vegetables. They were evaluated on sharpness, maneuverability, comfort, and the downward pressure required to peel.

Oxo's new I-Series line offers a completely redesigned vegetable peeler that we found to be exceptionally sharp. In addition to its new feature—replaceable blades—the I-Series peeler (which costs about $10) also dons a sleek, more slender handle—something the Good Grips model lacks. And tipping the scale at nearly a quarter pound (3.75 ounces), we liked the heft of the I-series, compared with the lighter Good Grips (which weighs only 2.25 ounces). It may sound like a picky difference, but testers felt that the balance of extra weight on the I-Series falls to the blade end, making it seem like the peeler does some of the work for you. After extensive use, we recognized the likelihood that the I-Series might cause some hand strain; however, you would have to peel a lot of potatoes to notice.

The Messermeister serrated blade peeler ($5.50) looks a bit like the Oxo Good Grip peeler, except for the zigzag blades. We were surprised that this peeler—which we took for a novelty—could rival and even replace a Good Grips at the usual peeling tasks. And what makes this peeler exceptional is its ability to peel ripe peaches and tomatoes—a difficult task, even for the noticeably sharper I-Series peeler. The only problem with the Messermeister is its narrow 2¾-inch diameter black rubber handle. Testers complained of difficulties getting a good grip. For most peeling chores, including potatoes and apples, we prefer the Oxo I-Series, but we recommend keeping the Messermeister on hand just to deal with peaches and tomatoes.

In addition to these basic peelers, we've noticed that several companies are now making julienne peelers. A skilled chef with a sharp knife can turn a carrot into a pile of perfect julienne (pieces that measure ⅛-inch square by 2 to 3 inches in length) in minutes. The rest of us, however, might need a little assistance. Julienne peelers promise to help you "julienne your way to restaurant-style presentations" and "add authenticity to Asian dishes."

Shaped like a Y-peeler, julienne peelers have one flat blade and one blade set with a row of tiny metal teeth. When you run the blades over the surface of the food, the flat blade removes a strip of food and the teeth cut it into perfectly squared strips—in theory.

Unfortunately, most of the peelers we tested shredded rather than julienned, and the resulting shreds were nowhere near the elongated square shape of a proper julienne. Also, the jagged blades were often bent out of alignment, making the tool little more than a crude, hand-held juicer. The one exception was the Oxo Good Grips Julienne Peeler ($6.99). This peeler could produce perfectly squared slices of carrot and zucchini with no trouble and could even julienne blocks of firm cheddar. This model also offers a cover for the nasty little protruding blades. Should the small blades come out of alignment, they can be bent back into shape rather easily. If your knife skills are not up to julienning vegetables, this peeler is a good addition to your kitchen.

BEST PEELERS

The sleek-handled Oxo I-Series peeler (left) is our favorite all-purpose peeler. The Messermeister peeler (center) works great on delicate fruit, but the handle is less than ideal. Save this model for tomatoes and peaches. And for julienning vegetables, we recommend the Oxo Good Grips Julienne Peeler (right). See www.americastestkitchen.com for up-to-date prices and mail-order sources for these top-rated products.

TASTING LAB: Mail-Order Bacon

TO FIND OUT IF PREMIUM BACON REALLY TASTES BETTER than our supermarket favorite, Farmland, we cooked up six popular smokehouse brands and summoned our tasters.

First a little on how bacon is made. All bacon starts with a pork belly. The spare ribs are removed from the belly's interior, the skin is taken off the exterior, and the remaining slab is trimmed.

The next step is curing, which is generally done in one of two ways. Many small producers of artisan (aka smokehouse or premium) bacon choose to dry-cure by rubbing the slab with a dry mixture of seasonings (which always includes salt and sugar). Large producers usually inject the slabs with a liquid brine containing salt, sugar, and sometimes liquid smoke for flavor; sodium phosphate for moisture retention during processing and cooking; ascorbate or sodium erythorbate to accelerate the curing process and promote color retention; and a curing salt that includes sodium nitrite to stave off bacteria and set flavor and color characteristics. (Are you still hungry for supermarket bacon?) Once the cure has been applied or injected, the slabs are hung. If a dry cure has been applied, this process could stretch up to one week. Curing with an injected brine can be completed in a mere one to three hours and so is quite cost-efficient.

The final step is thermal processing—which can take as few as four to five hours or as many as 24, depending on the processor. During thermal processing, the cured pork bellies are smoked and partially cooked to an internal temperature of roughly 130 degrees, after which they finally merit the term bacon. The bacon is chilled to approximately 24 degrees, pressed to square it off for uniform slicing, sliced to the processor's specifications, and packaged. A package of regular-cut bacon usually contains between 18 and 22 slices, $\frac{1}{16}$ inch thick, per pound, whereas a package of thick-cut bacon, sometimes called country style, contains 12 to 16 slices, $\frac{1}{8}$ inch thick, per pound.

So how did our six expensive mail-order brands do against Farmland, our favorite supermarket bacon? Although every one of these premium bacons outscored Farmland, in some cases the differences in scores were minimal. Several premium bacons had strong flavor characteristics, erring on the side of salty or smoky or sweet, which overwhelmed tasters who were looking for meaty flavor and balance, just as they had with the supermarket brands. That said, the top finisher, Niman Ranch, was a hands-down winner over Farmland. So premium bacons are better than the best supermarket bacon. But they're also much more expensive. Be prepared to pay up to 250 percent more for the experience and shop carefully to make sure that extra money is well spent.

Rating Mail-Order Bacons

TWENTY-FOUR MEMBERS OF THE *COOK'S ILLUSTRATED* STAFF TASTED ALL OF THE BACONS, WHICH WERE COOKED TO the same degree of doneness. The bacons are listed in order of preference based on their scores in this tasting. For up-to-date prices and mail-order information on these products, see www.americastestkitchen.com.

HIGHLY RECOMMENDED

Niman Ranch Dry Cured Center Cut Bacon
Oakland, California

$8 for 12 ounces

Tasters found this bacon hearty, rich, balanced, and smoky. One taster said, "Yum . . . what bacon should be."

RECOMMENDED

New Braunfels Smokehouse Comal County Smoked Sliced Bacon
New Braunfels, Texas

$8.25 for 1 pound

This was deemed overly smoky by many tasters, though one said, "Has all the right elements. I could eat a lot of this one."

RECOMMENDED

Burgers' Smokehouse Sliced Country Bacon, Sugar Cured and Hickory Smoked
California, Missouri

$18.95 for 2 pounds

This bacon was characterized by many as too salty and lacking in deep meaty flavor.

RECOMMENDED

Nodine's Smokehouse Apple Bacon
Torrington, Connecticut

$5.50 for 1 pound

Over and over, tasters commented on the sweetness of this bacon, using adjectives such as "caramelized," "candy-sweet," and "mapley."

RECOMMENDED

Nueske's Smoked Bacon
Wittenberg, Wisconsin

$19.95 for 2 pounds

Nearly every taster zeroed in on this bacon's strong smoky character, with comments such as "whoa, smoky!," "crazy-smoky," "carbon-like," and "tastes like a campfire."

RECOMMENDED

Edwards Virginia Bacon, Hickory-Smoked, Country Style, Dry Cured
Surry, Virginia

$4 for 12 ounces

"Too salty," "way salty," "very salty," "overpowering salt," "salty like Ruffles potato chips." Get the picture?

QUICK CHEESE BREAD

WHAT WE WANTED: A moist, hearty quick bread with bits of cheese tossed throughout, plus a cheesy crust.

Cheese bread sounds like a great idea, a pairing of two of America's favorite foods. Unlike pizza, wherein bread dough is merely topped with cheese, a true cheese bread involves a more intimate relationship, going well beyond the quick blind date in which the two ingredients are merely thrown together and then heated. Good cheese bread displays a subtle balance of flavor and texture, neither party getting the upper hand. But most of the recipes we tested offered the worst of both worlds: dry bread and no cheese flavor.

Our first step was to create a working recipe that consisted of 3 cups flour, 1 tablespoon baking powder, 6 tablespoons melted butter, 2 cups milk, and 1 egg. For the cheese, we chose shredded cheddar, the most frequently used type in our stack of research recipes. Our working recipe had lots of problems, but we could now test every variable.

First, we tinkered with the amount of butter. Starting with 6 tablespoons, we worked our way down to a mere 3, putting an end to the slick hands and lips we'd been

experiencing after eating a piece of the bread. Less fat also pushed the bread away from the texture of a delicate cake and toward that of a hearty muffin. The single egg we'd been using turned out to be just right.

Because we wanted a rich loaf, similar to a good banana bread, we replaced a portion of the milk in each of two breads with scoops of yogurt and sour cream, respectively. Given that this was cheese bread, it also seemed logical to try cottage cheese, cream cheese, goat cheese, and ricotta. In the end, most tasters chose the sour cream–based bread. It was rich and moist without being greasy. The sour cream also added a nip of tartness to the bread, offsetting the richness of the cheese without overpowering it.

Test results showed that small chunks of cheese, not shreds, were best, as they melted into luscious, cheesy pockets. In terms of the cheese itself, we tested five readily available types: extra-sharp cheddar, Muenster, Asiago, Gruyère, and Monterey Jack. Cheddar and Asiago were the leaders of the pack, with Muenster and Monterey Jack being too mild and Gruyère too pungent (although we liked this last cheese in a variation that also included bacon). We quickly determined that excess cheese weighed down the bread, causing it to collapse into itself. With a modest 4 ounces of cheese, the bread had plenty of flavor but still rose to its full potential.

We had arrived at the top crust. We wanted rich flavor and color. The solution was a topping of shredded Parmesan. We then decided to coat the bottom of the pan with cheese as well, thus doubling the cheesy exterior. Nutty and salty, every bite was packed with flavor. The Parmesan also turned the crust a deep bronze color.

WHAT WE LEARNED: Sour cream adds richness and flavor to this bread, and whole milk is the best choice for the liquid ingredient. Small chunks of cheese melt into luscious cheesy pockets. For a crust with great flavor and crunch, sprinkle the loaf pan as well as the batter with Parmesan.

QUICK CHEESE BREAD

Makes one 9 by 5-inch loaf

If using Asiago, choose a mild supermarket cheese that yields to pressure when pressed. Aged Asiago that is as firm as Parmesan is too sharp and piquant for this bread. If, when testing the bread for doneness, the toothpick comes out with what looks like uncooked batter clinging to it, try again in a different—but still central—spot; if the toothpick hits a pocket of cheese, it may give a false indication.

>   3   ounces Parmesan cheese, shredded on the large
>   holes of box grater (about 1 cup)
>   3   cups (15 ounces) unbleached all-purpose flour
>   1   tablespoon baking powder
>   ¼   teaspoon cayenne
>   1   teaspoon salt
>   ⅛   teaspoon ground black pepper
>   4   ounces extra-sharp cheddar cheese, cut into
>   ½-inch cubes, or mild Asiago, crumbled into
>   ¼- to ½-inch pieces (about 1 cup)
>   1¼ cups whole milk
>   3   tablespoons unsalted butter, melted
>   1   large egg, beaten lightly
>   ¾   cup sour cream

1. Adjust an oven rack to the middle position and heat the oven to 350 degrees. Spray a 9 by 5-inch loaf pan with non-stick cooking spray, then sprinkle ½ cup of the Parmesan evenly over the bottom of the pan.

2. In a large bowl, whisk the flour, baking powder, cayenne, salt, and pepper to combine. Using a rubber spatula, mix in the cheddar, breaking up clumps. In a medium bowl, whisk together the milk, melted butter, egg, and sour cream. Using a rubber spatula, gently fold the wet ingredients into the dry ingredients until just combined (the batter will be heavy and thick). Do not overmix. Scrape the batter into the prepared loaf pan; level the surface with a rubber spatula. Sprinkle the remaining ½ cup Parmesan evenly over the surface.

3. Bake until deep golden brown and a toothpick inserted into the center of the loaf comes out clean, 45 to 50 minutes. Cool in the pan on a wire rack 5 minutes; invert the loaf onto the rack, turn right-side up, and continue to cool until warm, about 45 minutes. Cut into slices and serve.

VARIATION

QUICK CHEESE BREAD WITH BACON, ONION, AND GRUYÈRE

1. Cut 5 ounces (5 slices) bacon into ½-inch pieces and fry in a medium nonstick skillet over medium heat, stirring occasionally, until crisp, about 8 minutes. Using a slotted spoon, transfer the bacon to a paper towel–lined plate and pour off all but 3 tablespoons fat from the skillet. Add ½ cup minced onion to the skillet and cook, stirring frequently, until softened, about 3 minutes; set skillet with onion aside.

2. Follow recipe for Quick Cheese Bread, substituting Gruyère for cheddar, adding the bacon and onion to the flour mixture along with the cheese, and omitting the butter.

Q & A

What's the best way to wrap quick breads before freezing them?

Wrap the cooled loaf tightly with a double layer of aluminum foil and then place it in a large, plastic zipper-lock bag. When protected this way, the loaf will keep for several months in the freezer. When you're ready to serve the bread, remove it from the freezer, slip the foil-wrapped bread out of the bag, place it on the center rack of a 375-degree oven, and bake until the loaf yields under gentle pressure, 10 to 15 minutes. Remove the foil (watch out for steam) and return the loaf to the oven for a few minutes to crisp the crust. Cool the bread on a rack for 15 minutes to make slicing easier.

Bridget serves up a taste of Louisiana in a big bowl.

REGIONAL classics

On occasion local dishes become so popular that they transcend their region. Gumbo is a taste of Louisiana in a big old bowl. Its distinct aroma and flavor are like a quick trip to the bayous outside of New Orleans. Gumbo is Louisiana and Louisiana is gumbo.

The history of Cincinnati chili dates back almost a century to an Ohio diner. This dish combines Middle Eastern spices with homespun Midwestern cooking to create an American original, served with buttered spaghetti, kidney beans, cheddar cheese, and chopped onions.

Our goal when developing our versions of these dishes was to remain faithful to originals while making the recipes approachable for cooks who may not have grown up with them. Regional classics must remain authentic, or they lose their distinct personality. But if the dishes require hard-to-find ingredients or difficult techniques, no one will make them. We've balanced authenticity with practicality in our renditions of these regional classics.

GUMBO

WHAT WE WANTED: A true Louisiana gumbo with a rich, thick sauce studded with shrimp and sausage.

Gumbo usually includes some combination of seafood, poultry, or small game along with sausage or some other highly seasoned, cured smoked pork. Also present is the Creole and Cajun "holy trinity" of onion, bell pepper, and celery. Quite often, gumbos are thickened with okra or ground dried sassafras leaves, known as filé (pronounced fee-LAY) powder. Last, but very important, most gumbos are flavored with a dark brown roux. For us, this roux is the heart of a good gumbo.

In classic French cooking, a roux is nothing more than flour cooked gently in some type of fat to form a paste that is used to thicken sauces. If the flour is just barely cooked, you have a white roux; if cooked to a light beige, you have a blond roux. When it reaches the color of light brown sugar, you have brown roux. Creole and Cajun cooks push this process to the outer limit. When they make roux, they keep cooking until the flour reaches a shade of very dark brown, sometimes just short of black. This breaks down the starches in the flour to the point where the roux offers relatively little thickening power. Instead, it imbues gumbo with a complex, toasty, smoky flavor and a deep, rich brown color that define the dish. The problem is that the flour can burn very easily, and the only safeguards against that are relatively low heat and constant stirring.

Most of the recipes we saw called for cooking the roux over low heat while stirring constantly for anywhere from 40 to 60 minutes. Since the roux truly does need to be stirred constantly as it cooks to avoid burning the flour, which will give the mixture a noticeable bitter taste, time was the first issue we had to tackle. We decided on 20 minutes as our limit for stirring. Any longer than that, we reasoned, and most cooks would probably skip over this dish.

To hit that 20-minute mark, we knew we'd have to increase the heat and probably preheat the oil before adding the flour. We also thought we'd try a microwave roux, instructions for which we'd seen along the way. For our testing, we began with the widely used 1:1 ratio of all-purpose flour to vegetable oil, using ½ cup of each.

Some cooks recommend heating the oil until it smokes and then cooking the roux over high heat. Though this method produced a very dark roux, about the color of bittersweet chocolate, in less than 10 minutes there was too much sizzle and smoke. The process felt out of control, and the specter of burnt roux loomed large.

We slowed things down a bit, preheating the oil over medium-high heat for two minutes (to well below the smoke point) before adding the flour, then lowering the heat to medium to cook the roux. At the 20-minute stopping point, the roux had cooked to a deep reddish brown, about the color of a shelled pecan or a dirty penny. It had started to smoke once or twice, but it cooled fairly quickly when we removed it from the heat, stirred it for a minute, then returned it to the burner. In all, the process was much less nerve-wracking than the high-heat methods we had tried, and it yielded absolutely acceptable results. Unfortunately, though, another problem popped up. We began to have trouble incorporating the simmering stock into the roux. The roux and stock generally would mix smoothly, but sometimes they wouldn't, and the result was little globs of brown flour floating in a layer of oil at the surface. Nonetheless, we pressed on with our testing of the roux.

We tried different ratios of fat to flour, varying them by as much as 6 tablespoons up and down from the ½-cup starting point, but none improved on the original 1:1 ratio in terms of either taste or performance. Switching the all-purpose flour from a high-protein, unbleached Northern brand to a slightly lower-protein, bleached national brand improved the texture of the gumbo slightly, making it a little smoother and more satiny. The gumbo's consistency also benefited from a thorough skimming of the foam from the surface of the liquid, both just after it had come to a boil and throughout the simmering time.

The microwave roux had seemed vaguely promising until the day we turned the test kitchen into a scene from a *Lethal Weapon* movie by putting a superheated, microwave-safe bowl with its smoking hot contents down on a damp counter. The bowl did not merely shatter; it exploded, literally raining glass shards and globs of fiery hot roux into every corner of the room. We were very lucky that no one was hurt and, sure enough, a quick call to the test kitchens at Corning Consumer Products confirmed that they do not recommend heating oil in any Pyrex product for 10 minutes on high in the microwave.

Throughout the roux testing, the occasional separation of the flour and oil upon the addition of simmering liquid continued to perplex us. All along, we had followed the instructions in most of the recipes we'd studied to add simmering stock, which is about 200 degrees, to a hot roux-vegetable mixture, also about 200 degrees.

But there is another, if less popular, school of thought. Legendary New Orleans restaurateur Leah Chase advises cooling either the roux or the stock before combining them. Sure enough, cooling the stock (which took less time than cooling the roux) did the trick. Room-temperature stock, at about 75 degrees, mixed into the hot roux beautifully; stock at about 150 degrees also mixed in very well and was only slightly less smooth than its cooler counterpart. In terms of the timing in the recipe, then, we decided to make a concentrated shrimp stock and cool it rapidly by adding ice water rather than making the full amount and allowing it to cool at its own slow pace. This quick-cooling technique brought the stock to about 110 degrees within minutes, and the gumbo made with this concentrated, then diluted, stock easily passed muster with tasters.

The rest of the recipe development process focused on testing the wide range of ingredients and flavorings we encountered on our trip and in our research. First, we experimented with the liquid. Our testing thus far had been done with a simple shrimp stock made by simmering the shells in water. We tried boiling the shells in chicken stock instead of water, combining equal parts shrimp and chicken stock, adding bottled clam juice to the shrimp stock, and adding small amounts of white wine and beer to the gumbo. The clam juice did the trick, adding a depth of flavor that supplemented the 20-minute roux.

Two big flavoring questions concerned tomatoes—some say that gumbo just isn't gumbo without them—and garlic. Well, our tasters said that gumbo was just fine without tomatoes, but they gave the thumbs up to garlic, six cloves of it, in fact. We tried what seemed like a hundred seasoning variations and finally settled on a simple combination of dried thyme and bay leaves. Our experiments with different proportions of onion, bell pepper, and celery in the holy trinity notwithstanding, the classic ratio of 1 part celery to 2 parts pepper to 4 parts onion tasted best. We did, however, switch from the traditional green bell pepper to red peppers, preferring their sweeter, fuller flavor.

The gumbos we tasted in Louisiana were only subtly spicy, with the pepper heat very much in the background. You want to feel a slight heat in the back of your throat after you've swallowed a couple of spoonfuls. A mere ½ teaspoon of cayenne did the trick for our tasters, all of whom favored the powder over the vinegary taste of bottled hot sauce.

Last, we considered whether to thicken the gumbo with okra or filé powder. We think both are probably acquired tastes. Thus far, everyone had been satisfied without either, and because both added distinct—and to some, unwelcome—flavors, we decided to reserve them for the variations on our master recipe.

WHAT WE LEARNED: Make the roux over medium-high heat with an equal mixture of vegetable oil and flour. Cook the roux, stirring constantly, for about 20 minutes or until the color is dark reddish brown. To keep the gumbo silky smooth, add lukewarm stock (made with bottled clam juice and shrimp shells) to the hot roux. Finally, okra and filé powder are traditional but optional ingredients.

CREOLE-STYLE SHRIMP AND SAUSAGE GUMBO

Serves 6 to 8

Making a dark roux can be dangerous. The mixture reaches temperatures in excess of 400 degrees. Therefore, use a deep pot for cooking the roux and long-handled utensils for stirring it and be careful not to splash it on yourself. One secret to smooth gumbo is adding shrimp stock that is neither too hot nor too cold to the roux. For a stock that is at the right temperature when the roux is done, start preparing it before you tend to the vegetables and other ingredients, strain it, and then give it a head start on cooling by immediately adding ice water and clam juice. So that your constant stirring of the roux will not be interrupted, start the roux only after you've made the stock. Alternatively, you can make the stock well ahead of time and bring it back to room temperature before using it. Spicy andouille sausage is a Louisiana specialty that may not be available everywhere; kielbasa or any fully cooked smoked sausage makes a fine substitute. Gumbo is traditionally served over white rice.

1½	pounds small shrimp (51 to 60 per pound), shells removed and reserved
1	cup clam juice
3½	cups ice water
½	cup vegetable oil
½	cup all-purpose flour, preferably bleached
2	medium onions, chopped fine
1	medium red bell pepper, stemmed, seeded, and chopped fine
1	medium celery rib, chopped fine
6	medium garlic cloves, minced or pressed through a garlic press (about 2 tablespoons)
1	teaspoon dried thyme
	Salt
¼	teaspoon cayenne
2	bay leaves
1	pound smoked sausage, such as andouille or kielbasa, sliced ¼ inch thick
½	cup minced fresh parsley leaves
4	medium scallions, white and green parts, sliced thin
	Ground black pepper

1. Bring the reserved shrimp shells and 4½ cups water to a boil in a stockpot or large saucepan over medium-high heat. Reduce the heat to medium-low and simmer for 20 minutes. Strain the stock and add the clam juice and ice water (you should have about 2 quarts of tepid stock, 100 to 110 degrees); discard the shells. Set the stock aside.

2. Heat the oil in a Dutch oven or large, heavy-bottomed saucepan over medium-high heat until it registers 200 degrees on an instant-read thermometer, 1½ to 2 minutes. Reduce the heat to medium and gradually stir in the flour with a wooden spatula or spoon, making sure to work out any lumps that may form. Continue stirring constantly, reaching into the corners of the pan, until the mixture has a toasty aroma and is deep reddish brown, about the color of an old copper penny or between the colors of milk chocolate and dark chocolate, about 20 minutes. (The roux will thin as it cooks; if it begins to smoke, remove the pan from the heat and stir the roux constantly to cool slightly.)

3. Add the onions, bell pepper, celery, garlic, thyme, 1 teaspoon salt, and cayenne to the roux and cook, stirring frequently, until the vegetables soften, 8 to 10 minutes. Add 1 quart of the reserved stock in a slow, steady stream while stirring vigorously. Stir in the remaining quart of stock. Increase the heat to high and bring to a boil. Reduce the heat to medium-low, skim the foam from the surface, add the bay leaves, and simmer, uncovered, skimming the foam as it rises to the surface, about 30 minutes. (The mixture can be covered and set aside for several hours. Reheat when ready to proceed.)

4. Stir in the sausage and continue simmering to blend the flavors, about 30 minutes. Stir in the shrimp and simmer until cooked through, about 5 minutes. Off the heat, stir in the parsley and scallions and season with salt, ground black pepper, and cayenne to taste. Serve immediately.

VARIATIONS

SHRIMP AND SAUSAGE GUMBO WITH OKRA

Fresh okra may be used in place of frozen, though it tends to be more slippery, a quality that diminishes with increased cooking. Substitute an equal amount of fresh okra for frozen; trim the caps, slice the pods ¼ inch thick, and increase the sautéing time with the onion, bell pepper, and celery to 10 to 15 minutes.

Follow the recipe for Creole-Style Shrimp and Sausage Gumbo, adding 10 ounces thawed frozen cut okra to the roux along with the onions, bell pepper, and celery. Proceed as directed.

SHRIMP AND SAUSAGE GUMBO WITH FILÉ

Follow the recipe for Creole-Style Shrimp and Sausage Gumbo, adding 1½ teaspoons filé powder along with the parsley and scallions after the gumbo has been removed from the heat. Let rest until slightly thickened, about 5 minutes. Adjust the seasonings and serve.

Q & A

What's the best way to buy shrimp?

Even the most basic market now sells several kinds of shrimp. We cooked more than 100 pounds to find out just what to look for (and avoid) at the supermarket.

Should you buy fresh or frozen? Because nearly all shrimp are frozen at sea, you have no way of knowing when those "fresh" shrimp in the fish case were thawed (unless you are on very personal terms with your fishmonger). We found that the flavor and texture of thawed shrimp deteriorate after a few days, so you're better off buying frozen.

Should you buy peeled or unpeeled? If you think you can dodge some work by buying frozen shrimp that have been peeled, think again. Someone had to thaw those shrimp in order to remove their peel, and the shrimp can get pretty banged up (compare the left and center photos).

Should you buy treated shrimp? Make sure to check the ingredient list. Frozen shrimp are often treated or enhanced with additives such as sodium bisulfate, STP (sodium tripolyphosphate), or salt to prevent darkening (which occurs as the shrimp age) or to counter "drip loss," the industry term referring to the amount of water in the shrimp that is lost as they thaw. We have found that treated shrimp have a strange translucency and an unpleasant texture and suggest that you avoid them (see right photo). Look for the bags of frozen shrimp that list "shrimp" as the only ingredient.

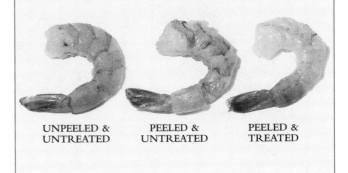

UNPEELED &   PEELED &   PEELED &
UNTREATED   UNTREATED   TREATED

SCIENCE DESK:
How to Thicken Gumbo

IN A CREOLE OR CAJUN DARK ROUX, MOST OF THE STARCH in the flour breaks down in the cooking, so the roux does more to flavor the stew than thicken it. That leaves the task to one of two other traditional Southern ingredients, okra and filé powder. (It's also possible, as we do in our master recipe, to go without either one for a slightly thinner stew.)

Okra pods, said to have been brought to the southern United States from Africa by the slave trade, are slender, green, usually about 3 inches in length, ridged in texture, tapered in shape, and often slightly fuzzy. The interior of the pods is sticky and mucilaginous, so once they are cut open, they thicken any liquid in which they are cooked. Okra's flavor is subtle, with hints of eggplant, green bean, and chestnut. In our gumbo testing, we could detect no taste difference between fresh and frozen okra.

The other possible thickener, filé powder, is made of ground dried sassafras leaves. It is said to have been introduced to the settlers of southern Louisiana by the native Choctaw Indians. Filé, also referred to in Louisiana as gumbo filé, adds both a gelatinous thickness and a subtle, singular flavor to gumbo. Though difficult to describe precisely, the flavor is distinctly earthy, with notes of straw, bay, marjoram, and oregano. Filé is as much a hallmark of authentic Louisiana cooking as dark roux and the holy trinity of onion, bell pepper, and celery. Filé is used in one of two ways. Diners can sprinkle a little bit onto their portion of gumbo right at the table, or the cook can stir some into the pot at the very last moment of cooking or even once the pot has come off the heat. In our recipe variation, we prefer to add it to the pot, which mellows the flavor somewhat. In stores that carry it, pale green filé powder is generally sold in tall, slender, 1-ounce jars.

One thing on which most Creole and Cajun cooks agree is that you should never use okra and filé together because the gumbo will get too thick, even gummy.

GETTING IT RIGHT:
The Temperature Matters

Lukewarm stock and constant stirring are the keys to gumbo with the right consistency. The roux in the spoonful of gumbo on top is dispersed smoothly in the liquid. The roux in the second spoonful of gumbo (below) has broken, with globs of browned flour floating in oil.

GETTING IT RIGHT: Making a Roux

With flour just added to the oil, the roux at left is very light in color. After about 10 minutes of cooking, the mixture browns to about the color of peanut butter (center). The completed dark roux (right) is a deep reddish brown, almost the color of dark chocolate. A long-handled, straight-edged wooden spatula is best for stirring the roux. Be sure to scrape the pan bottom and reach into the corners to prevent burning. The cooking roux will have a distinctive toasty, nutty aroma. If it smells scorched or acrid, or if there are black flecks in the roux, it has burned.

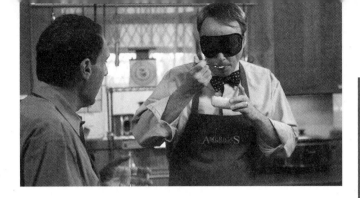

TASTING LAB: Long-Grain White Rice

THE BEAUTY OF WHITE RICE RESIDES IN ITS NEUTRAL flavor, which makes it good at carrying other flavors. But is all long-grain white rice created equal? We set up a few taste tests to find out.

We rounded up a converted rice, three standard supermarket options, and an organic white rice available in bulk from a natural foods market. These samples were tasted plain and in our Mexican Rice recipe (page 168). All five brands rated well in the Mexican Rice. Flavor differences were minuscule. With so many potent ingredients in this recipe (tomatoes, chiles, lime juice), these results are not terribly surprising. The most noticeable difference was an unpredictable variance in cooking time. According to the U.S. Rice Producers Association, the age of the rice, its moisture content, and the variety used can affect the rate of water uptake. Inconsistent cooking times are barely noticeable in plain rice, but they can become more apparent when other ingredients—such as the tomatoes and aromatics in our Mexican rice—are added to the pot. When making Mexican Rice, we suggest checking for doneness after 30 minutes and be prepared to keep the rice in the oven a bit longer.

When tasted plain, all of the rices were noted for being "clean" and "like rice should be," with the exception of Uncle Ben's. This converted rice failed to meet our standards on all fronts. Converted rice is processed in a way that ensures separate grains, a firm texture, and more pronounced flavor. Those "round," "rubbery" grains and the telltale yellowish tint immediately brought back not-so-fond memories of "dining hall rice." Tasters agreed that some "stickiness" and minor "clumping" make for more natural-looking and better-tasting rice. So when choosing long-grain rice, you really can't go wrong, as long as you avoid converted rice.

Rating Long-Grain White Rices

TWENTY-TWO MEMBERS OF THE *COOK'S ILLUSTRATED* staff participated in the tasting. We tasted the rices plain and in our Mexican Rice recipe (page 168). With the exception of the Uncle Ben's rice, tasters liked all the rices in both applications. Since scores were so close within the recommended category, these rices are listed in alphabetical order. All brands are available in supermarkets.

RECOMMENDED

Canilla Extra Long Grain Enriched Rice

$2.19 for 48 ounces

The "distinct flavor" was likened to Jasmine rice.

RECOMMENDED

Carolina Extra Long-Grain Enriched Rice

$1.79 for 32 ounces

"Not many nuances" made this rice a good, clean slate on which to add flavor.

RECOMMENDED

Sem-Chi Organically Grown Florida Long Grain Rice

$1.99 for 48 ounces

This rice was rated the "chewiest," with "roasted" and "nutty" flavors.

RECOMMENDED

Stop & Shop Long Grain Enriched Rice

$1.19 for 32 ounces

This rice was liked for its neutrality and "chewy" texture.

NOT RECOMMENDED

Uncle Ben's Converted Enriched Long Grain Rice

$3.89 for 32 ounces

The "assertive rice flavor" was "too much" and bordered on being "stale." Even worse was the "bouncy" texture, reminiscent of the "cafeteria" rice.

CINCINNATI CHILI

WHAT WE WANTED: An authentic version of this Midwestern classic flavored with Middle Eastern spices and served over spaghetti.

Redolent of cinnamon and warm spices, Cincinnati chili is unlike any chili served in Texas or the rest of the country, for that matter. On sight alone, its sauciness makes it look more like a Sloppy Joe filling or some strange sauce for pasta. One taste reveals layers of spices you expect from Middle Eastern or North African cuisine, not food from the American heartland.

Legend has it that Cincinnati chili was created in the 1920s by a Macedonian immigrant named Athanas Kiradjieff. He ran a hot dog stand called the Empress, where he served his chili over hot dogs. This deluxe hot dog eventually morphed into the "five-way" concoction beloved by locals.

Cincinnati chili is as much about the garnishes, or "ways," as the chili itself. On its own, it is merely one-way Cincinnati chili. Served over buttered spaghetti, it is two-way. Add shredded cheddar cheese and it becomes three-way. Chopped onions make it four-way, and the final garnish, for five-way chili, is with warmed kidney beans.

To get a handle on this unusual chili, we tested a number of recipes. We noticed two problems. First, most of the versions tested were much too greasy. Second, the myriad spices used in many recipes were overwhelming. Our goals were clear—cut the fat and figure out which spices were essential and which were not.

In most chili recipes, the meat is browned to build flavor and render some fat, which can be spooned off. Cincinnati chili is unique because it calls for boiling ground beef instead of browning it. The boiled meat had a texture described as "wormy" by most tasters, which, as odd as it sounds, pairs well with the pasta and the other accompaniments. But boiling the meat can make it difficult to rid the meat of excess fat, particularly since traditional recipes use the blanching liquid as the base for the chili.

We decided to try replacing the ground chuck (80 to 85 percent lean), which is the usual choice for chili, with ground round (90 percent lean). This idea sounded great, but tasters felt that the flavor of the chili made with ground round suffered. Ground chuck has a beefier flavor, so we would have to figure out some way to eliminate the excess grease from the final dish.

For our next batch of chili, we added the beef to salted, boiling water and blanched it for three minutes, or until an unappetizing raft of oily meat foam had risen to the surface. We then drained the beef and discarded the water—along with the fat. The resulting chili was grease-free but lacked the body and flavor that fat provides. We had gone too far. Next, we cut the blanching time back to only 30 seconds, and the results were much better. The chili was rich and fully flavored, without being slick or greasy.

Like curries in India, the spice mixture in Cincinnati chili varies from recipe to recipe (and house to house). Some mixes contain just two or three spices, while others embrace the entire spice cabinet and are more evocative of a Moroccan souk than an Ohio hot dog stand. We hoped to isolate the key flavors and create a streamlined spice mixture.

We had uncovered all kinds of incongruous combinations in our research, including one recipe that called for coriander, cardamom, turmeric, and nutmeg—a simply dreadful mixture. Tasters also objected to cloves and mace, both of which were deemed too overpowering. Chili powder, cinnamon, and cayenne pepper were essential, although the latter had to be used sparingly.

Cumin, in addition to the small amount of cumin already blended into the chili powder, proved too much, so it was pulled. The cinnamon was not strong enough in early batches and was almost doubled in the final recipe. We were almost content with the basic spice mixture, but it needed a little more depth. After trying several ideas, a combination of black pepper and allspice proved winning.

Many recipes call for unsweetened chocolate, but we figured that cocoa powder would achieve much the same thing and would be easier to add along with the spices. (Further testing bore out the hypothesis.) Dried oregano rounded out our list of "spices." To further boost the flavors of our spice mixture, we toasted it in the oil before adding the liquid ingredients.

While the spices vary from recipe to recipe, the aromatics are consistently onion and garlic. Most recipes add them to the water with the meat. We decided to draw out a little more flavor and sweetness by sautéing them.

As far as the liquids go, most recipes call for tomato sauce and water. We tried to replace the generic canned tomato sauce suggested in most recipes with canned whole peeled tomatoes that we pureed in the blender. While the canned tomatoes made the chili taste a bit brighter, the chili made with canned tomato sauce was favored by most tasters.

Tasters felt that the water did little to improve the chili and wondered if it should be replaced. To add body, we tried using red wine as part of the liquid. We decided it was superfluous due to the strength of the rest of the flavors. In the end, we went with canned chicken broth for the sake of convenience. To keep the chicken flavor from dominating, we used half chicken broth and half water. A small amount of cider vinegar (very traditional) brightened the broth. Some brown sugar added the necessary sweetness to balance the vinegar and spices.

We turned our attention to the garnishes. After several tests, we realized it was best to leave tradition alone. Sure you could do without the beans or onions, but why compromise? Five-way Cincinnati chili is almost sacrosanct.

WHAT WE LEARNED: Use ground chuck for the best flavor and blanch it for 30 seconds to give the meat its characteristic texture. Add a mix of spices and cocoa powder to create depth of flavor. A combination of chicken broth, water, and tomato sauce becomes a rich base for the chili, while some vinegar and brown sugar enliven all the other flavors.

CINCINNATI CHILI

Serves 6 to 8

Choose a relatively plain tomato sauce—nothing too spicy or herbaceous. To warm the kidney beans, simmer them in water to cover for several minutes and then drain.

chili

2	teaspoons salt, plus more to taste
1½	pounds ground chuck
2	tablespoons vegetable oil
2	medium onions, chopped fine (about 2 cups)
2	medium garlic cloves, minced or pressed through a garlic press (about 2 teaspoons)
2	tablespoons chili powder
2	teaspoons dried oregano
2	teaspoons cocoa
1½	teaspoons ground cinnamon
½	teaspoon cayenne
½	teaspoon ground allspice
¼	teaspoon ground black pepper
2	cups low-sodium chicken broth
2	cups water
2	tablespoons cider vinegar
2	teaspoons dark brown sugar
2	cups tomato sauce
	Tabasco sauce

accompaniments

1	pound spaghetti, cooked, drained, and tossed with 2 tablespoons unsalted butter
12	ounces sharp cheddar cheese, shredded
1	(15-ounce) can red kidney beans, drained, rinsed, and warmed
1	medium onion, chopped fine (about 1 cup)

1. FOR THE CHILI: Bring 2 quarts of water and 1 teaspoon of the salt to a boil in a large saucepan. Add the ground chuck, stirring vigorously to separate the meat into individual strands. As soon as the foam from the meat rises to the top

(this takes about 30 seconds) and before the water returns to a boil, drain the meat into a strainer and set it aside.

2. Rinse and dry the empty saucepan. Set the pan over medium heat and add the oil. When the oil is warm, add the onions and cook, stirring frequently, until the onions are soft and browned around the edges, about 8 minutes. Add the garlic and cook until fragrant, about 1 minute. Stir in the chili powder, oregano, cocoa, cinnamon, cayenne, allspice, black pepper, and the remaining 1 teaspoon salt. Cook, stirring constantly, until the spices are fragrant, about 30 seconds. Stir in the broth, water, vinegar, sugar, and tomato sauce, scraping the pan bottom to remove any browned bits.

3. Add the blanched ground beef and increase the heat to high. As soon as the liquid boils, reduce the heat to medium-low and simmer, stirring occasionally, until the chili is deep red and has thickened slightly, about 1 hour. Adjust the seasonings, adding salt and Tabasco sauce to taste. (The chili can be refrigerated in an airtight container for up to 3 days. Bring to a simmer over medium-low heat before serving.)

4. TO SERVE: Divide the buttered spaghetti among individual bowls. Spoon the chili over the spaghetti and top with the cheese, beans, and onion. Serve immediately.

EQUIPMENT CORNER:
Useful Kitchen Gadgets

THERE ARE HUNDREDS OF KITCHEN GADGETS ON THE market today. Over the years, we've pretty much tested them all. Sure, we've come across some real duds, but we've also uncovered some true gems. The following is a list of gadgets that we couldn't live without in the test kitchen, or at home. See www.americastestkitchen.com for up-to-date prices and mail-order sources.

Taylor Classic Oven Guide Thermometer
$14.95
Temperature readings are spot on with our favorite thermometer—it even passed our knock-over test with flying colors! Not only is it the most accurate thermometer we've tested, it's also the most stable, in part because of its 4-inch length—and it hangs.

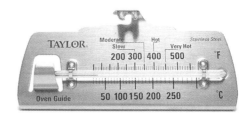

Polder Electronic Clock/Stopwatch/Timer
$12.99

A well-deserved honorable mention in our useful gadget lineup, the Polder times up to 10 hours and can be worn around your neck (so it goes where you go).

Polder Cooking Thermometer/Timer
$24.99

With its easy, intuitive design, this gadget is the secret weapon for properly cooked meat. It has a 4-foot-long thermometer probe cord and a loud alarm (great for outside grilling), and it's magnetized (sticks right to the side of the oven).

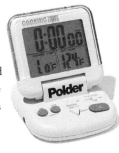

Oxo Oven Thermometer
$11.99

We like the Oxo, a superb new-comer to the market, for its large, bold-print numbers, glass back panel (that allows light from the oven to illuminate the numbers), and adjustable clip (that attaches the thermometer to the oven rack).

Microplane Zester/Grater
$12.95

The combination of very sharp teeth and a solid handle makes grating cheese a breeze. It also makes quick work of ginger and citrus zest.

Oxo Good Grips Locking 12-Inch Tongs
$9.99

These stainless steel tongs with rubber handles earned high marks in our battery of tests. We use them for everything, from retrieving corn on the cob from boiling water to turning large roasts in the oven.

Oxo Good Grips Stainless Steel Multi-Purpose Scraper & Chopper
$7.99

It's perfect for scraping sticky dough off the counter or cutting board. The wide metal blade makes it easy—and safer than a sharp chef's knife blade—to transfer chopped ingredients from the cutting board to a sauté pan.

KitchenArt Adjust-A-Cup
$9.95

It effortlessly measures and releases hard-to-measure ingredients such as molasses, shortening, and peanut butter. Every bit of the ingredient is removed from the cup with ease.

Egg Slicer
$5–$8

In addition to slicing hard-boiled eggs, we use the model with smooth wire blades to cut mushrooms and strawberries.

Keith checks the progress of his simple gravy recipe that uses basic pantry items—and no meat.

PORK CHOPS and gravy

CHAPTER 5

It sometimes seems like the simplest recipes suffer the worst fate in modern cookbooks. Maybe it's because no one really cares enough about these dishes to get them right. Most of these recipes are not terribly sexy. But when done right, this kind of food can be incredibly satisfying and comforting.

Stuffed pork chops, gravy, and glazed carrots almost always fall into this disappointing category. The pork chops are dry and bland. In theory, the gravy should help mitigate these problems, but all too often the gravy has odd chemical flavors (caused by the use of "gravy enhancers"), and the texture is either lumpy or too thick. And the carrots are so sweet they might as well be dessert.

The test kitchen was committed to breathing new life into these old-fashioned American recipes. Taste the results of our labor—we hope you'll think we succeeded.

STUFFED PORK CHOPS

WHAT WE WANTED: Most stuffed pork chops are extremely dry and bland. We wanted the stuffing to be especially flavorful to offset the mildness of the pork, and we wanted the chops to be moist and juicy.

A simple garlic and herb bread stuffing seems an easy way to load flavor and richness into today's leaner pork chops. Whenever stuffing occurs, however, a host of challenges enters the kitchen. Chief among them is bringing the stuffing (often bound with raw eggs) up to a safe internal temperature without overcooking the surrounding meat. Many of the recipes we consulted employ a crude strategy to tackle this problem—surround the chops in liquid and cook them for an hour or more. This old-fashioned technique (essentially a braise) may have worked with fattier chops, but modern-day pork is lean and tender—much better suited to searing in a hot skillet, which can then be used to make a quick pan sauce.

Determining which type of chop to stuff was fairly simple. Rib chops were the obvious choice for their higher fat content (making them less likely to dry out) and wide, unbroken eye of meat. Center-cut or loin chops, on the other hand, are divided down the middle like a T-bone steak, making them tough to stuff. Thick-cut rib chops (about 1½ inches) are widely available and big enough to handle a hearty amount of filling.

Our favorite recipe for sautéing thick-cut pork chops pointed the way. We knew from our testing that the best results came from brining the chops beforehand and then finishing them in a hot oven instead of in the pan. As stuffed chops require more time in the oven than unstuffed ones, the brining step was crucial for retaining moisture. By first cutting a pocket in each chop, we allowed the brine to penetrate to the center of the meat.

No amount of brining could save a pork chop from 30 minutes in a 450-degree oven, however. That's about how long it took for the stuffing inside of the seared chops to reach a temperature of 160 degrees, the minimum temperature for the safe consumption of raw eggs. By that time, temperature of the meat near the edges of the chop had topped 180 degrees, and the meat was dry and tough. Using eggs to bind the stuffing was evidently out—but did we, in fact, need them?

It seemed so at first. Without the eggs, the stuffing had been loose and crumbly, spilling out all over the plate when the chops were served. Our working method for stuffing the chops had been part of the problem. We slit the pork chops open from the side and spooned loose stuffing into the middle, then tried using toothpicks to keep the chops closed. But the toothpicks interfered with the searing of the meat and did a poor job of keeping the chop closed in the heat of the oven as the pork contracted and curled open.

When it came time to plate the chops, we had to dig the toothpicks out of the meat (we missed one once), which only encouraged the stuffing to come tumbling out.

Some careful knife work solved the problem. Instead of butterflying the meat, we made an inch-long cut in the side of the chop with a thin boning knife, then used the blade to clear a cavity in the center of the meat without any further cuts at the edge. We stuffed the meat through this smaller opening, and the natural shape of the chop held the stuffing in place. No eggs, no toothpicks. Furthermore, the natural juice from the brined pork moistened the stuffing while the chop cooked.

Next we experimented with adding bacon and sausage to our basic bread stuffing. The flavors were overbearing, tasters said, and the extra meat made the stuffing too salty. (Thanks to the brine, the juice from the pork was enough to season the stuffing without adding extra salt.) Tasters preferred the simpler version made with garlic and fresh herbs. A few tablespoons of cream added richness and enough moisture to bring the stuffing together.

The meat near the edges of the chops still tended to dry out when left in the oven until the stuffing reached 145 degrees, the temperature that recipes with non-egg stuffings recommend. Our standard operating procedure is to tent resting meat loosely with aluminum foil to allow the juices to redistribute while the residual heat gently brings the internal temperature to the desired doneness. In this case, we were able to pull the meat from the oven when the temperature at the center of the stuffing was just 130 degrees. After 5 to 10 minutes of resting, the temperature of the pork and the stuffing had evened out around 145 degrees.

WHAT WE LEARNED: Use cream rather than eggs to bind a stuffing made with fresh bread, garlic, herbs, and aromatic vegetables. Because the stuffing doesn't contain eggs, the chops can be cooked to a lower (and more palatable) internal temperature. Start the chops in a skillet to develop a nice brown crust but finish cooking them through on a sheet pan in a hot oven.

TECHNIQUE: Stuffing Pork Chops

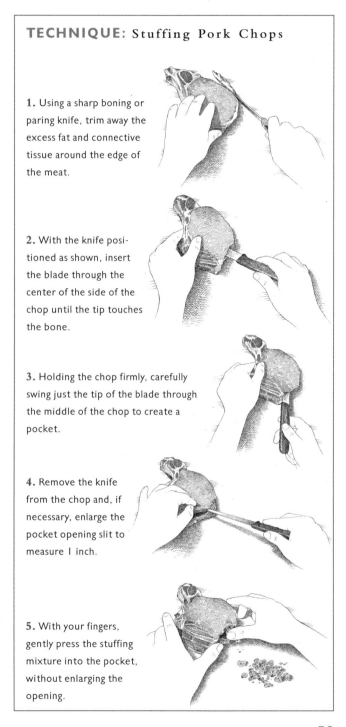

1. Using a sharp boning or paring knife, trim away the excess fat and connective tissue around the edge of the meat.

2. With the knife positioned as shown, insert the blade through the center of the side of the chop until the tip touches the bone.

3. Holding the chop firmly, carefully swing just the tip of the blade through the middle of the chop to create a pocket.

4. Remove the knife from the chop and, if necessary, enlarge the pocket opening slit to measure 1 inch.

5. With your fingers, gently press the stuffing mixture into the pocket, without enlarging the opening.

STUFFED PORK CHOPS

Serves 4

These stuffed pork chops may be served with All-Purpose Gravy (page 57), applesauce, or Quick Ginger-Apple Chutney (recipe follows). The gravy is best made before you start the chops and then reheated as needed. If you choose to serve the chops with the chutney instead, prepare it in the skillet used to cook the chops while the chops are in the oven.

chops

4	bone-in rib loin pork chops, 1½ inches thick (about 12 ounces each)
¾	cup packed light brown sugar
½	cup Diamond Crystal Kosher Salt, 6 tablespoons Morton Kosher Salt, or ¼ cup table salt
	Ground black pepper
1	tablespoon vegetable oil

GETTING IT RIGHT:
Buying the Right Chop

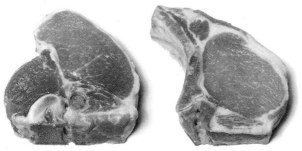

CENTER-CUT CHOP   RIB CHOP

When shopping, make sure to buy the right kind of pork chops. A center-cut chop (left) has a bone running through the middle and will be very hard to stuff. The bone runs along the outside of rib chop (right), making it much easier to cut a large pocket in the side of the chop. We find that rib chops are also juicier and more flavorful than center-cut chops, and they are our top choice for cooking, even when stuffing is not part of the equation.

stuffing

3	tablespoons unsalted butter
1	small onion, diced small
1	medium celery rib, diced small
½	teaspoon salt
2	medium garlic cloves, minced or pressed through a garlic press (about 2 teaspoons)
2	teaspoons minced fresh thyme leaves
1	tablespoon minced fresh parsley leaves
2	cups ¼-inch bread cubes from 1 baguette
2	tablespoons heavy cream
⅛	teaspoon ground black pepper

1. FOR THE CHOPS: Following the illustrations on page 53, cut a small pocket through the side of each chop. Dissolve the sugar and salt in 6 cups of cold water in a gallon-size, zipper-lock plastic bag. Add the pork chops and seal the bag, pressing out as much air as possible. Refrigerate until fully seasoned, about 1 hour.

2. FOR THE STUFFING: Melt the butter in a 12-inch skillet over medium heat until the foaming subsides. Add the onion, celery, and salt and cook until the vegetables are softened and beginning to brown, about 10 minutes. Add the garlic and herbs and cook until fragrant, about 1 minute. Transfer to a medium bowl, add the bread cubes, cream, and pepper, and toss well to combine. Using a rubber spatula, press the stuffing lightly against the sides of the bowl until it comes together.

3. TO STUFF, SEASON, AND COOK THE CHOPS: Adjust an oven rack to the lower-middle position, place a shallow roasting pan or rimmed baking sheet on the rack, and heat the oven to 450 degrees. Remove the chops from the brine, rinse, and pat dry with paper towels. Place one quarter of the stuffing (about ⅓ cup) in the pocket of each pork chop. Season the chops with pepper.

4. Heat the oil in a heavy-bottomed 12-inch skillet over high heat until shimmering. Lay the chops in the skillet and cook until well browned and a nice crust has formed, about 3 minutes. Turn the chops over with tongs and cook until well browned and a nice crust has formed on the second side, 2 to 3 minutes longer.

5. Using the tongs, transfer the chops to the preheated pan in the oven. Roast until an instant-read thermometer inserted into the center of the stuffing registers 130 degrees, about 15 minutes, turning the chops over once halfway through the cooking time. Transfer the chops to a platter, tent loosely with foil, and let rest at least 5 minutes. Check the internal temperature; it should register 145 degrees.

QUICK GINGER-APPLE CHUTNEY

Makes enough for 4 pork chops
This chutney works well with pork chops or roast pork.

1	tablespoon vegetable oil
1	small onion, cut into ½-inch dice
2	Granny Smith apples, peeled, cored, and cut into ½-inch dice
1	tablespoon minced ginger
¼	teaspoon ground allspice
⅛	teaspoon cayenne
¼	cup packed light brown sugar
1	cup apple cider
	Salt and ground black pepper

While the chops are in the oven, pour off any fat in the skillet used to sear the chops. Add the oil and heat over medium-high heat until shimmering. Add the onion and apples and cook, stirring occasionally, until softened and browned, about 10 minutes. Stir in the ginger, allspice, and cayenne and cook until fragrant, about 1 minute. Add the sugar and cider and bring to a boil, scraping the browned bits off the pan bottom, until the cider is slightly thickened, about 4 minutes. Season with salt and pepper to taste.

Q & A

Should pork be cooked until well done, and why do recipes often mention different temperatures?

The reason you will see different recommended finished temperatures for pork is simple: Some sources are concerned with safety first, while other sources put a premium on palatability. Guidelines for cooking pork to temperatures as high as 190 degrees originated decades ago when pork quality was inconsistent and fears of trichinosis ran high. Today the risk of trichinosis is nearly nonexistent in the United States. What's more, even when the trichina parasite is present, it is killed when the temperature of the meat rises to 137 degrees.

Both the U.S. Department of Agriculture and the National Pork Board recommend cooking pork to a final internal temperature of 160 degrees. If you are concerned about contamination from salmonella (which is possible in any type of meat, including beef), you must cook the pork to 160 degrees to be certain that all potential pathogens are eliminated. Unfortunately, given the leanness of today's pork, these recommendations result in dry, tough meat.

In the test kitchen, we have found cooking modern pork beyond 150 degrees to be a waste of time and money. We cook pork chops to a final internal temperature of 145 degrees—the meat will still be slightly rosy in the center and juicy. Depending on the size of the chops and the cooking method, the chops will probably need to be removed from the heat source before they reach this temperature. As the chops rest and the juices are redistributed throughout the meat, the internal temperature will continue to climb. Follow recipes as to when to take the chops off the heat and then check the temperature again just before serving to make sure it has reached 145 degrees. Of course, if safety is your top concern, cook all meat (including pork) until it is well done; that is, when the internal temperature reaches 160 degrees.

ALL-PURPOSE GRAVY

WHAT WE WANTED: We wanted to make really good gravy without a roast, using only canned broth and a few vegetables. Was this even possible?

Gravy, by definition, is a thickened sauce made of meat juices and pan drippings, usually left over from a roast. But what if you don't have a roast on hand and want gravy for some mashed potatoes or pork chops? What if you are limited to just some canned broth and a few vegetables? The problem is that a roast provides concentrated flavor through the fond, the browned bits at the bottom of the roasting pan. Without these small flavor jewels, a professional chef would say that any gravy is a lost cause. However, being fond (no pun intended) of lost causes, we set out to create a top-notch all-purpose gravy that could be made quickly, without one special ingredient, including a roast.

Our first thought was to turn to the supermarket shortcuts for making gravy, including products such as Kitchen Bouquet and Gravy Master. The results were unacceptable (see page 58 for details). Next, we researched gravy recipes that can be made without a roast and without homemade stock. They ran the gamut from a six-minute gravy prepared in the microwave to one that had more than 20 ingredients and took 1½ hours to make. The flavors were, to say the least, disappointing. Most were thick and bland with no meat flavor; others were just downright frightening with odd, out-of-place Asian overtones.

What we did learn from all this testing was that some combination of supermarket broth and sautéed vegetables thickened with flour was the likely solution, given the fact that this approach seemed to deliver the most authentic, richest flavor. We began our recipe development with the liquid base. We quickly ruled out both water and vegetable broth because they made flavorless gravies. This left us with three options: chicken broth, beef broth, or a combination of both. Using a base recipe (some sautéed vegetables and

flour), we prepared two batches of gravy, one using beef broth, the other using chicken. Tasters agreed that the beef broth gravy was acidic and contained a metallic aftertaste. On the other hand, the chicken broth was well liked, although the strong poultry flavor was inappropriate for all-purpose gravy. Finally, we tried equal amounts of chicken and beef broth and found that combination to be a winner.

We had started with a standard mirepoix (a mixture of onions, carrots, and celery) that was lightly sautéed in oil. While this combination of vegetables lent the gravy a balanced sweetness and body, it failed to accent the gravy's meatiness or impart any roasted flavor. We replaced the mirepoix in our basic recipe with 1 cup of mushrooms in one test and 2 cups of onions, lightly caramelized, in a second test. The gravy made with the mushrooms was a complete miss. Both the color and the appearance became muddy, and the overall flavor was bland and vegetal. The caramelized onions didn't perform much better. One taster thought that the gravy tasted like French onion soup.

However, we did learn an important lesson from these tests. The process of caramelizing onions creates a fond on the bottom of the pan—not unlike the fond created after roasting meat—which gave the gravy an appealing nutty-brown color; we could also detect the hint of a pleasant roasted essence. It occurred to us that the development of a vegetable fond might be the key to increasing the gravy's flavor. We went back to the original mirepoix and merely extended the cooking time until the vegetables were well browned. This meant cooking the vegetables in butter (for more flavor) over medium-high heat for about seven minutes. As we had hoped, the gravy had a more pronounced roasted, meaty flavor. Much to our delight, we also found that if we chopped the vegetables in the food processor, we not only saved time but also created a better-tasting fond in less time due to the smaller pieces.

The last step in gravy making involves thickening. Our

basic recipe called for browning the vegetables in butter and then sprinkling flour over them to create a roux, the classic combination of fat and flour that thickens liquids. We then whisked in the broth and simmered the gravy until thickened, after which time the raw flour taste had dissipated. We also tested other thickeners (cornstarch and arrowroot) and thickening techniques (making a paste of butter and flour that is added to the gravy at the end of the cooking time). Believe it or not, we also tried gingersnaps, as suggested in one of the initial test recipes. Each of these options (even the gingersnaps) thickened the gravy to a similar consistency, but they created other problems. The cornstarch and arrowroot variations tasted fine but had an unappealing, translucent quality; the gingersnaps, meanwhile, produced a gravy that tasted like cake batter. All in all, the butter-based roux produced a superior gravy.

Still short in terms of depth of flavor, we thought to employ a technique used by Creole cooks in making gumbo and cooked the roux until it was the color of milk chocolate, far beyond the pale blond color of previous tests. Much to our amazement, this simple technique substantially boosted the flavor of the gravy, helping to develop complex flavor elements in our simple recipe. In conjunction with the caramelized vegetable fond, the toasted flour provided an unexpectedly rich roasted flavor as well as a bold meaty flavor—exactly what we had been looking for. And the gravy's color was now a rich, deep brown as well.

We were close, but we still wanted to test some of the more unusual flavor-building ingredients, including miso (which made the gravy taste like a stir-fry sauce), coffee (which colored the gravy but added no flavor), and molasses (which thickened the gravy but made it sweet and bitter). In the end, we opted for a more classic combination of dried thyme, bay leaf, and peppercorns.

WHAT WE LEARNED: To make good gravy without a roast, you must eke out as much flavor as possible from every ingredient. Brown the vegetables and the flour thoroughly, and add both beef and chicken broth.

ALL-PURPOSE GRAVY

Makes 2 cups

This gravy can be served with almost any type of meat and with mashed potatoes as well. The recipe can be doubled. If doubling it, use a Dutch oven so that the vegetables brown properly and increase the cooking times by roughly 50 percent. The finished gravy can be frozen. To thaw it, place the gravy and a tablespoon of water in a saucepan over low heat and slowly bring it to a simmer. It may appear broken or curdled as it thaws, but a vigorous whisking will recombine it.

1   small carrot, peeled and chopped into rough
    ½-inch pieces (about ½ cup)
1   small celery rib, chopped into rough ½-inch
    pieces (about ½ cup)
1   small onion, chopped into rough ½-inch pieces
    (about ¾ cup)
3   tablespoons unsalted butter
¼   cup unbleached all-purpose flour
2   cups low-sodium chicken broth
2   cups low-sodium beef broth
1   bay leaf
¼   teaspoon dried thyme
5   whole black peppercorns
    Salt and ground black pepper

GETTING IT RIGHT:
Process the Vegetables

In addition to saving time, chopping the carrot, celery, and onion in a food processor breaks down the vegetables' cell walls and speeds the release of their flavors when cooked. Because the vegetables are strained out of the finished gravy, the fact that the food processor makes them mushy is not a big deal.

1. Process the carrot in a food processor until broken into rough ¼-inch pieces, about five 1-second pulses. Add the celery and onion; pulse until all the vegetables are broken into ⅛-inch pieces, about five 1-second pulses.

2. Heat the butter in a large heavy-bottomed saucepan over medium-high heat. When the foaming subsides, add the vegetables and cook, stirring frequently, until softened and well browned, about 7 minutes. Reduce the heat to medium; stir in the flour and cook, stirring constantly, until thoroughly browned and fragrant, about 5 minutes. Whisking constantly, gradually add the broths; bring to a boil, skimming off any foam that forms on the surface. Reduce the heat to medium-low and add the bay leaf, thyme, and peppercorns. Simmer, stirring occasionally, until thickened and reduced to 3 cups, 20 to 25 minutes.

3. Strain the gravy through a fine-mesh strainer into a clean saucepan, pressing on the solids to extract as much liquid as possible; discard the solids. Adjust the seasonings with salt and pepper to taste. Serve hot.

TASTING LAB: Gravy Additives

IN OUR RESEARCH, WE FOUND SEVERAL RECIPES THAT called for Kitchen Bouquet or Gravy Master. Although we had heard of these ingredients, we had never before cooked with them. A trip to the supermarket revealed that these were not the only gravy "additives" that are available.

These products, which primarily consist of caramel or caramel coloring, vegetable extracts, salt, and preservatives, are made to impersonate fond, the little flavor-packed bits left in the pan after roasting meat. Since fond was exactly what we were trying to replicate in our all-purpose pantry gravy, we thought these items might be the key to the best recipe.

We choose four gravy additives, two powders and two liquids, and prepared four gravies following the instructions on each of the packages. Overall results were dismal and tasters all complained that the gravies tasted artificial. While the theory behind the supermarket additives—a store-bought replacement for the time-consuming fond—was right on, the results were off base. Our suggestion: Build your own fond with fresh vegetables and leave these items on the shelf.

GETTING IT RIGHT: Building Great Flavor from Ordinary Ingredients

BROWNING VEGETABLES

ADDING BROTH AND HERBS

PRESSING VEGETABLES

In the absence of pan drippings, making a good-tasting gravy requires several crucial flavor-building steps. To start, the vegetables must be well browned (left). Caramelizing the sugars in the vegetables gives the gravy a complex roasted flavor. Browning the flour also heightens the roasted flavor of the gravy and gives it a distinctive chestnut color. A combination of beef and chicken broth contributes a rich, well-rounded, meaty flavor. Whisking the broths in slowly (center) releases the vegetable fond from the bottom of the pan and ensures a lump-free gravy. When straining the finished gravy, it is important to press on the vegetables (right) to extract as much flavor as possible. Straining also guarantees a velvety smooth gravy.

GLAZED CARROTS

WHAT WE WANTED: Fully tender, well-seasoned carrots with a glossy, clingy, yet modest glaze.

Glazing is probably the most popular way to prepare carrots. However, glazed carrots are often saccharine and ill-suited as a side dish on a dinner plate. These defamed vegetables, adrift in a sea of syrup, often lie limp and soggy from overcooking or retain a raw, fibrous resistance from undercooking.

To rescue glazed carrots from such poor treatment, we began with how to prepare the carrots for cooking. Matchsticks were out from the get-go—we were looking for simplicity, not to improve our knife skills. A bag of "baby" carrots unceremoniously emptied into a pan for cooking revealed pieces of wildly different girth, with some more than twice as big around as others. Surely these would cook unevenly, so we halved the large pieces lengthwise. Gone was the convenience of this product. Once these baby carrots were cooked, tasters remarked that they were shy on both carrot flavor and good looks. We peeled regular bagged carrots and cut them on the bias into handsome oblong shapes. Once cooked, these comely carrots earned much praise for their good flavor. Slender bunch carrots (sold with their tops on and at a higher price), also cut on the bias, were no more flavorful, and their diminutive size lacked presence. Regular bagged carrots it was.

Most recipes suggest that the carrots need to be steamed, parboiled, or blanched prior to glazing, resulting in a battery of dirtied utensils. Instead, we put the carrots with a bit of liquid in a skillet (nonstick, for the sake of easy cleanup), along with some salt and sugar for flavor, covered the skillet, and simmered. Mission accomplished: The carrots were cooked through without much ado. Chicken broth as a cooking liquid lent the carrots savory backbone and a full, round flavor, whereas water left them hollow and wine turned them sour and astringent. We tried swapping the sugar for more compelling sweeteners but found brown sugar too muddy flavored, maple syrup too assertive, and honey too floral (but good for a variation, we noted). We stood by clean, pure, easy-to-measure granulated sugar.

We moved on to finessing the glaze. After the carrots simmered for a few minutes, when just on the verge of tender (they would see more heat during glazing, so we simmered them shy of done), we lifted the lid from the skillet, stepped up the heat, and let the liquid reduce to 2 tablespoons. (If the liquid is not reduced, it is thin and watery.) Finally, we added butter, cut into small pieces for quick melting, and a bit more sugar to encourage glaze formation and to favorably increase sweetness. All of this resulted in a light, clingy glaze that with a few more minutes of high-heat cooking took on a pale amber hue and a light caramel flavor. A sprinkle of fresh lemon juice gave the dish sparkle, and a twist or two of freshly ground black pepper provided depth. We were surprised, as were our tasters, that glazed carrots could be this good and this easy.

WHAT WE LEARNED: Avoid bags of "baby" carrots (often filled with carrots of varying sizes) and choose more flavorful bagged, full-size carrots that can be sliced to yield ovals that will cook more evenly. Cooking and glazing the carrots is one single operation. Start by cooking the sliced carrots in a covered skillet with chicken broth, salt, and sugar. Remove the lid and glaze with a little butter and a bit more sugar.

GLAZED CARROTS

Serves 4

A nonstick skillet is easier to clean, but this recipe can be prepared in any 12-inch skillet with a cover.

1	pound carrots (about 6 medium), peeled and sliced ¼ inch thick on the bias (see the illustration below)
½	teaspoon salt
3	tablespoons sugar
½	cup low-sodium chicken broth
1	tablespoon unsalted butter, cut into 4 pieces
2	teaspoons juice from 1 lemon
	Ground black pepper

1. Bring the carrots, salt, 1 tablespoon of the sugar, and the chicken broth to a boil in a 12-inch nonstick skillet, covered, over medium-high heat. Reduce the heat to medium and simmer, stirring occasionally, until the carrots are almost tender when poked with the tip of a paring knife, about 5 minutes. Uncover, increase the heat to high, and simmer rapidly, stirring occasionally, until the liquid is reduced to about 2 tablespoons, 1 to 2 minutes.

2. Add the butter and remaining 2 tablespoons sugar to the skillet. Toss the carrots to coat and cook, stirring frequently, until the carrots are completely tender and the glaze is light gold, about 3 minutes. Off the heat, add the lemon juice and toss to coat. Transfer the carrots to a serving dish, scraping the glaze from the pan into the dish. Season to taste with pepper and serve immediately.

VARIATIONS

GLAZED CARROTS WITH GINGER AND ROSEMARY

Cut a 1-inch piece of fresh ginger crosswise into ¼-inch coins. Follow the recipe for Glazed Carrots, adding the ginger to the skillet along with the carrots and adding 1 teaspoon minced fresh rosemary along with the butter. Discard the ginger pieces before serving.

HONEY-GLAZED CARROTS WITH LEMON AND THYME

Follow the recipe for Glazed Carrots, substituting an equal amount of honey for the sugar and adding ½ teaspoon minced fresh thyme leaves and ½ teaspoon grated lemon zest along with the butter.

GLAZED CURRIED CARROTS WITH CURRANTS AND ALMONDS

Lightly toasting the curry powder in the warm, dry skillet brings forth its full flavor.

Toast ¼ cup sliced almonds in a 12-inch nonstick skillet over medium heat until fragrant and lightly browned, about 5 minutes; transfer to a small bowl and set aside. Off the heat, sprinkle 1½ teaspoons curry powder in the skillet; stir until fragrant, about 2 seconds. Follow the recipe for Glazed Carrots, adding the carrots, salt, sugar, and chicken broth to the skillet with the curry powder. Add ¼ cup currants along with the butter; add the toasted almonds along with the lemon juice.

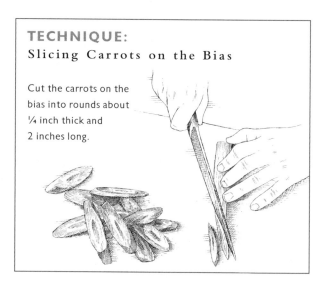

TECHNIQUE:
Slicing Carrots on the Bias

Cut the carrots on the bias into rounds about ¼ inch thick and 2 inches long.

GLAZED CARROTS WITH ORANGE AND CRANBERRIES

Dried cherries can be used in place of the cranberries if you prefer.

Follow the recipe for Glazed Carrots, adding ¼ cup dried cranberries with the carrots in step 1 and replacing ¼ cup of the chicken broth with ¼ cup orange juice and ½ teaspoon grated orange zest. Reduce the amount of sugar in step 2 to 1 tablespoon and omit the lemon juice.

GLAZED CARROTS WITH BACON AND PECANS

The rich caramel flavor of brown sugar goes well with the bacon and pecans.

    3   ounces (about 3 slices) bacon, cut into
        ½-inch pieces
    ⅓   cup chopped pecans
    1   pound carrots (about 6 medium), peeled
        and sliced ¼ inch thick on the bias (see the
        illustration on page 60)
    ½   teaspoon salt
    3   tablespoons light brown sugar
    ½   cup low-sodium chicken broth
    ½   teaspoon minced fresh thyme leaves
    1   tablespoon unsalted butter, cut into 4 pieces
    2   teaspoons juice from 1 lemon
        Ground black pepper

1. Cook the bacon in a 12-inch nonstick skillet over medium-high heat until crisp. Transfer the cooked bacon to a paper towel–lined plate to drain. Remove all but 1 tablespoon of the bacon drippings from the pan. Add the pecans and cook until fragrant and slightly browned, about 3 minutes. Transfer the pecans to the plate with the bacon.

2. Add the carrots, salt, 1 tablespoon of the brown sugar, the chicken broth, and thyme to the skillet. Bring to a boil, covered, over medium-high heat. Reduce the heat to medium and simmer, stirring occasionally, until the carrots are almost tender when poked with the tip of a paring knife, about 5 minutes. Uncover, increase the heat to high, and simmer rapidly, stirring occasionally, until the liquid is reduced to about 2 tablespoons, 1 to 2 minutes.

3. Add the butter and remaining 2 tablespoons brown sugar to the skillet. Toss the carrots to coat and cook, stirring frequently, until the carrots are completely tender, about 3 minutes. Off heat, add the lemon juice and toss to coat. Transfer the carrots to a serving dish, scraping the glaze from the pan into the dish. Season to taste with pepper and serve immediately.

TECHNIQUE: Impromptu Salt Cellars

Measuring from the pouring spout on a cardboard container of salt can be frustrating when the salt flows out in an uncontrollable rush. Here are two ways around this problem.

A. Use a lidded sugar shaker or covered sugar bowl as a salt cellar. The lid keeps out any grease or dust but can be easily removed to grab a quick pinch.

B. Turn the salt container itself into a salt cellar by cutting off the top of the partially empty salt container with a serrated knife. Cover the container with a sheet of plastic wrap and secure it with a rubber band. When you want to measure salt, remove the plastic cover and stick the measuring spoon right into the box.

Julia is willing to try almost any idea—
even cooking a whole chicken in a skillet.

TWO ROAST chickens

Despite its apparent simplicity, roast chicken is a hard recipe to get right. First, you've got to deal with the skin, which never seems to crisp up properly. Then there's the odd structure of the bird, with legs and wings tucked close against the body (and thus slow to cook through), while the delicate breast is exposed directly to the oven heat. The fact that dark meat tastes better when cooked to a higher temperature makes it nearly impossible to get the entire bird properly cooked. And even if you do everything right, roast chicken can be a bit plain.

This chapter looks at two inspired takes on roast chicken. Our roast lemon chicken starts by following a conventional path but ends with a twist. And there's nothing conventional about cooking a butterflied chicken under a brick. But these two recipes do have some things in common. Both deliver crisp skin and lots of flavor. Best of all, these two roast chicken recipes are fairly easy to execute.

ROAST LEMON CHICKEN

WHAT WE WANTED: Moist, evenly roasted chicken, with crisp skin, and a bright, pure lemon flavor without a trace of bitterness.

From the simplest incarnation (throw a whole lemon into the cavity of a chicken) to the most ridiculous (smother a chicken with homemade candied lemon peel), there are as many ways to make roast lemon chicken as there are cooks ready to try it. But while this familiar dish suffers from an identity crisis, one thing is sure: Roast lemon chicken can be disappointing. The chicken itself can be dry and uninteresting, tasting nothing like lemon or, even worse, bursting with bitter citric acidity. The accompanying pan sauce (if any) usually suffers a similar fate—bland, with no lemon flavor, or pucker-up harsh.

Our goal was simple: Find a way to bring out the full potential of the two main ingredients. Although such a quest seemed simple and straightforward, we soon discovered that the path to success would be a long and winding one.

We used our favorite basic roast chicken as a starting point, including no lemons in the initial testing. We brushed a chicken with melted butter, placed it wing-side up in an oiled V-rack, and roasted it in a moderate oven set to 375 degrees. After 20 minutes, we flipped the chicken, other wing-side up, and roasted it for 20 more minutes. Finally, we rotated the chicken breast-side up and roasted it for a final 25 minutes. This chicken was exceptionally good. Rotating the bird while it roasted kept the breast meat from drying out before the thigh meat was done, yielding an evenly roasted bird. The only downside was the lack of a crackling crisp skin. To solve this problem, we raised the oven temperature to 450 degrees while the chicken was breast-side up. Now the chicken skin was nicely browned and reasonably crisp. Satisfied with our results, we decided to introduce a little lemon into the game.

We threw a whole lemon, cut in half, into the cavity of the chicken and roasted it according to our method. While this did not produce lemon-flavored chicken, the meat was perfumed with a light lemon essence. Cutting the lemon into smaller pieces helped to develop the lemon flavor, although it was still a bit muted. We also tossed in several cloves of garlic and a handful of fresh thyme, but while the garlic flavor was pleasantly evident, the thyme lent little of its flavor to the meat. At this point, lemon testing was interrupted by one annoying occurrence. Invariably, the small pieces of lemon and garlic would tumble out of the chicken each time it was turned. This problem was readily solved by stitching the skin of the cavity closed using a long wooden skewer. We also wondered if we could simplify the recipe by turning the bird only once instead of three times, so we started the chicken breast-side down (rather than wing-side down) at 375 degrees and then flipped it breast-side up just before raising the temperature to 450. We had the perfect roasting method—or at least we thought so.

Our next step was to heighten the lemon flavor. Our first test involved making a compound butter to which we added finely grated lemon zest. We spread the butter under the skin of the chicken and proceeded to roast it. While the lemon flavor was notable, it came with an unpleasant bitter flavor. Next we marinated the chicken in a mixture of lemon juice, lemon zest, and herbs. But no matter how long we let the chicken soak in the marinade (even overnight), the lemon flavor failed to travel much beyond the skin. Next we tried soaking the chicken in a brine (a saltwater solution) flavored with lemon juice and lemon peel, but this gave the chicken a weird, lemonade-like flavor that tasted artificial. Still, the test wasn't a complete wash because the brining without the lemon flavorings turned out a superior chicken—moist, juicy, and well seasoned.

But at what cost? Now, owing to the moisture added by the brine, the chicken skin had lost its crispy texture. We

thought that a blast from the broiler might do the trick, but because the chicken was still in whole form, it browned unevenly. A colleague then suggested a method that she had picked up working in a restaurant. After cutting the roast chicken into parts, we put them back, skin-side up, in the roasting pan and broiled them, producing a deep brown skin that was crackling crisp. An added benefit of the brine/roast/broil method is that the meat, which is face-down in the pan drippings, becomes extremely moist and succulent.

Now we had a perfectly good, evenly roasted, well-seasoned chicken with very crisp skin and ultra-moist meat. But we couldn't yet sell this dish as roast lemon chicken—we needed a lemon-infused pan sauce to really make this chicken shine. Working with the pan drippings as the basis for a lemony sauce, we added a squirt of lemon juice to the pan drippings. This was exactly what we were looking for—a sauce with bright, pure lemon flavor. Now all that was necessary was a little butter to thicken the sauce and some fresh parsley and thyme to lend an herbal note. Served with the sauce on the side, this roast lemon chicken—perfectly cooked, crisp-skinned, and lemon-scented—was one we could be proud of.

WHAT WE LEARNED: Place a quartered lemon in the cavity to perfume the chicken as it roasts. For crisp skin, quarter the roast chicken and then run the pieces under the broiler. And for a final hit of lemon flavor, make a quick lemon pan sauce to accompany the chicken.

CRISPY ROAST LEMON CHICKEN

Serves 3 to 4

If using a kosher chicken, skip the brining and begin with step 2. Broiling the fully roasted and quartered chicken skin-side up as it sits in a shallow pool of sauce crisps and browns the skin while keeping the meat succulent. If you decide to skip the broiling step, go directly from quartering the chicken to finishing the sauce with lemon juice, butter, and herbs.

1   cup Diamond Crystal Kosher Salt, ¾ cup Morton Kosher Salt, or ½ cup table salt
1   whole chicken (3½ to 4 pounds), trimmed of excess fat, giblets removed and discarded, chicken rinsed and patted dry
       Vegetable cooking spray
2   medium lemons
6   medium garlic cloves, crushed and peeled
4   tablespoons (½ stick) unsalted butter, 2 tablespoons melted and the remaining 2 tablespoons chilled and cut into 2 pieces
       Ground black pepper
1¾ cups low-sodium chicken broth
1   tablespoon minced fresh parsley leaves
1   teaspoon minced fresh thyme leaves

1. Dissolve the salt in 2 quarts cold water in a large bowl, stockpot, or Dutch oven. Immerse the chicken in the brine and refrigerate 1 hour. Remove the chicken from the brine and pat dry with paper towels.

2. Adjust an oven rack to the lower-middle position; heat the oven to 375 degrees. Spray a V-rack with cooking spray and set in a flameproof roasting pan.

3. Cut 1 of the lemons lengthwise into quarters. Place the lemon quarters and garlic in the cavity of the chicken. Following the illustration on page 66, thread a long wooden skewer through the flaps of skin on either side of the cavity. Turn the skewer and rethread back through the skin flaps.

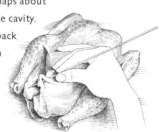
Repeat stitching as necessary to shut the cavity. Brush the breast side of the chicken with 1 tablespoon of the melted butter and season generously with pepper. Place the chicken breast-side down in the V-rack, then brush the back with the remaining 1 tablespoon melted butter and season generously with pepper.

4. Roast the chicken 40 minutes. Remove the roasting pan from the oven; increase the oven temperature to 450 degrees. Using 2 large wads of paper towels, rotate the chicken breast-side up; add 1 cup of the chicken broth to the roasting pan. Return the roasting pan to the oven and continue roasting until the thickest part of a thigh registers 165 to 170 degrees on an instant-read thermometer, about 35 to 40 minutes longer. Remove the roasting pan from the oven; tip the V-rack to let the juices from the chicken cavity run into the roasting pan. Transfer the chicken to a cutting board and let rest, uncovered, while making the sauce. Remove the V-rack from the roasting pan.

5. Adjust the oven rack to the upper-middle position; heat the broiler. Skim the fat from the drippings in the roasting pan, add the remaining ¾ cup chicken broth, and set the roasting pan over high heat on a burner. Simmer the liquid, scraping the pan bottom with a wooden spoon to loosen the browned bits, until reduced to ½ cup, about 4 minutes; set aside off heat.

6. Discard the lemons and garlic from the chicken cavity. Following the illustrations on page 68, cut the chicken into quarters. Pour the accumulated chicken juices into the roasting pan, then place the chicken quarters, skin-side up, into the sauce in the roasting pan; broil the chicken until the skin is crisp and deep golden brown, 3 to 5 minutes. Transfer the chicken to a serving platter.

7. Halve the remaining lemon lengthwise; squeeze the juice of one half into the roasting pan; cut the remaining half into 4 wedges and set aside. Whisk the remaining 2 tablespoons butter into the sauce until combined; stir in the parsley and thyme. Adjust the seasoning with salt and pepper to taste. Serve the chicken with the pan sauce and lemon wedges.

EQUIPMENT CORNER:
Countertop Rotisserie Ovens

IS THERE ANYTHING AS HUNGER-INDUCING AS A ROTIS-serie oven? Just thinking about a deliciously greasy lamb souvlaki, a Chinatown window jam-packed with Peking ducks, or the mesmerizing merry-go-round of chicken at the local Boston Market can send us on a half-hour trek toward the nearest rotisserie joint. Well, according to a recent infomercial and a slew of imitators, any cook with a wealth of counter space can now have that authentic rotisserie flavor at home. Too good to be true, you say? We picked up five of the most popular and easily accessible countertop rotisserie ovens to see if our dream could become a reality.

To evaluate the ovens, we decided to roast a whole chicken, a 4-pound beef rib roast, and a pork tenderloin in

each one. We also selected one recipe from each machine's instruction manual and cooked it in its respective oven.

Countertop rotisserie ovens come in two distinct styles—horizontal roasters and vertical roasters. The two horizontal roasters were the George Jr. Rotisserie ($100) and the Ronco Showtime Jr. ($74.98). The chickens cooked in these ovens were decent, but the lurid, ashen pork tenderloins were entirely unappetizing and utterly bland. The beef rib roasts browned beautifully but, when sliced, revealed egregiously uneven cooking—the perimeter of the roasts was well done, while the very core was medium. The George Jr. oven also had its share of flaws. The instruction manual suggested securing our 4-pound beef roast in an 8-inch-square by 2¼-inch-deep basket—an utterly impossible feat. (The roast had to go directly on the spit.) In addition, this rotisserie oven was difficult to clean, and the recipe we tested for Dijon Mustard Steaks was lousy. Since the Ronco Showtime Jr. did a slightly better job at roasting the chicken and was easier to load, unload, and clean, we thought it the best of its kind.

The others, all vertical roasters, were the Betty Crocker Vertisserie Plus ($100), the Farberware Vertical Rotisserie ($75), and the Sunbeam Carousel Rotisserie ($80). The first two looked surprisingly similar and were, hands down, the most simple to use. The Sunbeam was the most awkward to use, and it managed to perform just as poorly as its vertical roasting cousins. On a positive note, this model was entertaining to watch. Several spectators were captivated by the pirouetting "spit-roasted cobra"—baby back ribs threaded on the center skewer in a serpentine "S" shape.

As our tests indicated, rotisserie nirvana will continue to be accessible only by automobile. Although we had high hopes that our rotisserie cravings would be satiated by these countertop counterfeits, it seems as if we will have to keep an eye out for the next generation of infomercials.

Rating Countertop Rotisserie Ovens

IN EACH OVEN, WE ROASTED A WHOLE BRINED CHICKEN, a 4-pound beef rib roast, and a pork tenderloin. Then, we selected one recipe from each recipe booklet/instruction manual and cooked it in its respective oven. In general, we found that the two horizontal ovens produced a more moist and flavorful chicken than the vertical roasters, but overall we could find little to recommend a countertop rotisserie oven of any type. The ovens are listed below in order of preference.

RECOMMENDED WITH RESERVATIONS
Ronco Showtime Jr. $74.98
The top performer won points for ease of use and for including a surprisingly tasty recipe, Ron's Spicy Lemon Pepper Chicken Wings.

RECOMMENDED WITH RESERVATIONS
George Jr. Rotisserie $100
This model performed nearly as well as the Ronco oven but was more difficult to operate. It lost points because of difficulty fitting the rib roast in the suggested roasting basket.

NOT RECOMMENDED
Betty Crocker BCF6000 Vertisserie Plus $100
Although we found this model to be the easiest to operate, the vertical spit cooked the meats poorly in most of our tests.

NOT RECOMMENDED
Farberware Vertical Rotisserie $75
Similar to the Betty Crocker model but with a smaller capacity, this oven was comparatively lightweight and fragile.

NOT RECOMMENDED
Sunbeam Carousel Rotisserie $80
This oven performed poorly in almost all the tests and seemed very flimsy. It did win style points with those who enjoyed watching meats pirouette just beyond the clear oven door.

TECHNIQUE:
Quartering the Chicken after Roasting

1. Cut into the chicken where the leg skin meets the breast.

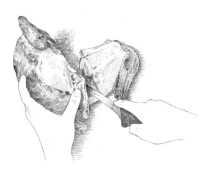

2. Pull the leg quarter away from the carcass. Cut through the thigh joint to remove the leg quarter.

3. Cut down along one side of the breastbone, pulling the breast meat away as you cut.

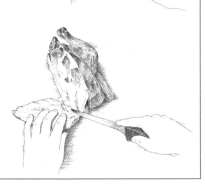

4. Use a knife to cut through the wing joint. Repeat on the second side to remove the other leg and breast quarters.

Q&A

Is there a way to get the benefits of brining (that is, moister meat) without so much salt?

We often hear from readers who like the moisture that brining gives to chicken and turkey but find that the meat sometimes tastes too salty. To see if salt-sensitive cooks could brine with less salt, we tested reducing the salt in our standard brine. Unfortunately, we found there was no marked difference between birds brined in a half-strength solution and non-brined samples. The brined birds were a bit saltier than the unbrined birds, but they were not substantially moister, which, after all, is the most important reason to brine a chicken or turkey.

Although brining offers great benefits in terms of flavor and texture, it may not be right for all cooks. But before eliminating this technique from your repertoire, make sure that you are using the right salt at the right strength for brining. Remember that 1 cup table salt equals 1½ cups Morton Kosher Salt but 2 cups Diamond Crystal Kosher Salt.

CHICKEN UNDER A BRICK

WHAT WE WANTED: A perfectly cooked butterflied chicken with super-skin crisp that could be on the table—with some roasted potatoes—in less than one hour.

Cooking a butterflied chicken under a brick in a skillet not only looks cool but also shaves half an hour off the cooking time of a regular roast chicken and produces an amazingly crisp skin. The brick helps keep the chicken flat as it cooks, forcing all of the skin to make contact with the pan. Yet, after trying a few recipes, we noted two big problems. First, the beautiful, crisp skin often turns soggy or greasy as the chicken finishes cooking. Second, the chicken is often marinated, but we found the marinade scorches in the hot pan.

We also noted a few problems that could be immediately rectified. Not only did we find that a single brick on top of the chicken didn't offer an even distribution of weight but that very few people actually have bricks hanging about in the kitchen. Also, we found that chickens much larger than three pounds were difficult to fit into a 12-inch skillet.

To start, we set the idea of a marinade aside for the moment and focused on the cooking method. Using two unmarinated, butterflied chickens, we tested the difference between pounding the chicken to an even thickness with a mallet and simply pressing it flat by hand. When pounded with a mallet, the super-flat chicken cooked very evenly, and more of the skin made contact with the pan, thus turning crisp. By comparison, only portions of skin on the thicker sections of the chicken flattened by hand were nicely browned.

We cooked these chickens according to the method cited in most of the recipes we researched—skin-side down first with bricks on top, then flipped to cook the underside, replacing the bricks to help keep the chicken flat. This, however, didn't work. After the chickens were flipped and the weight placed back on top, the skin (which was now crisp and delicate) was torn to pieces and steamed itself flaccid.

We then tried not replacing the bricks after the chicken was flipped, but the skin still turned rubbery from the steam and splattering oil. Next, we tried cooking the underside of the chicken first, finishing breast-side down, but this didn't work either. By flipping time, the pan was so loaded with grease and burned bits that the skin had no chance of looking pretty. It was greasy, spotty, and slightly bitter.

We then decided to try a different approach altogether. We cooked the chicken skin-side down underneath the bricks until it had a beautiful color. We then removed the bricks, flipped the bird over, and finished it, still in the skillet, in a 450-degree oven. The hot, dry air of the oven ensured that the skin remained crisp and intact as the meat finished cooking through. As for the bricks, we found that heavy cans and a cast-iron pot worked just as well (see the recipe headnote for further ideas).

Why is dark meat dark?

Leg muscles are exercised much more than breast muscles. As a result, leg muscles contain more myoglobin, a compound that helps store oxygen in muscle cells. Muscles with a high concentration of myoglobin are darker than muscles with little myoglobin. Increased exercise also makes muscle tissue tougher, which is why most recipes suggest cooking dark meat to a higher internal temperature than white meat. While breast meat is done at 160 degrees, we find that dark meat should be cooked to an internal temperature of 165 to 170 degrees for maximum palatability.

Based on our oven-finish method, we quickly figured out an easy way to include a flavorful marinade as well as some accompanying potatoes. Brushing the marinade onto the crisp chicken before finishing it in the oven was the obvious answer to our initial scorching problem. The heat of the oven fused the marinade to the skin without ruining its crisp texture, and the brief cooking time made it easy to retain the fresh, potent flavors in the marinade. Tasters preferred a simple oil-based marinade made with garlic, lemon, thyme, and a kick of red pepper flakes.

We found an easy method for roasting potatoes, too. We simply threw them into the pan underneath the chicken before it went into the oven. Emerging from the oven fragrant and gorgeous, the chicken must rest for 10 minutes, during which time the potatoes are returned to the oven to finish cooking and pick up some color.

WHAT WE LEARNED: With the help of both the stovetop and the oven, a complete meal can be made in a skillet. Start by browning the weighted chicken skin-side down in the skillet, remove the chicken from the pan, add some potatoes, and place the chicken back in the pan on top of the potatoes. Finish cooking the chicken and potatoes in the oven.

CHICKEN UNDER A BRICK WITH HERB-ROASTED POTATOES

Serves 4

Instead of two bricks and a rimmed baking sheet, you may use a heavy cast-iron skillet loaded with several cans or a large stockpot partially filled with water. Be careful when removing the pan from the oven, as the handle will be hot.

- 1   small whole chicken (about 3 pounds), trimmed of excess fat, giblets removed and discarded, chicken rinsed and patted dry
      Salt and ground black pepper
- 2   tablespoons plus 1 teaspoon vegetable oil
- 3   medium garlic cloves, minced or pressed through a garlic press (about 1 tablespoon)
- 1   tablespoon minced fresh thyme
- ⅛   teaspoon red pepper flakes
- 2   tablespoons juice from 1 lemon, plus 1 lemon, cut into wedges
- 1½   pounds small Red Bliss potatoes, scrubbed, dried, and cut into ¾-inch wedges
- 1   tablespoon minced fresh parsley leaves

1. Following the illustrations on page 71, remove the backbone from the chicken and pound flat with a rubber mallet. Season the chicken with salt and pepper to taste.

2. Adjust an oven rack to the lowest position and heat the oven to 450 degrees. Heat 1 teaspoon of the oil in a heavy-bottomed 12-inch ovenproof nonstick skillet over medium-high heat until it begins to smoke. Swirl the skillet to coat evenly with oil. Place the chicken, skin-side down, in the hot pan and reduce the heat to medium. Place the weight (see the note above) on the chicken and cook, checking every 5 minutes or so, until evenly browned, about 25 minutes. (After 20 minutes, the chicken should be fairly crisp and golden; if not, turn the heat up to medium-high and continue to cook until well browned.)

3. Meanwhile, mix the remaining 2 tablespoons oil, garlic, 1½ teaspoons of the thyme, the pepper flakes, lemon juice, ½ teaspoon salt, and ¼ teaspoon black pepper in a small bowl and set aside.

4. Using tongs, carefully transfer the chicken, skin-side up, to a clean plate. Pour off any accumulated fat in the pan and add the potatoes, sprinkling them with ¼ teaspoon salt, ⅛ teaspoon black pepper, and the remaining 1½ teaspoons thyme. Place the chicken, skin-side up, on the potatoes and brush the skin with the reserved thyme–lemon juice mixture.

5. Transfer the pan to the oven and roast until the thickest part of the breast registers 160 degrees on an instant-read thermometer, 10 to 15 minutes longer. Transfer the chicken to a cutting board and let rest 10 to 15 minutes.

6. Return the skillet with the potatoes to the oven and roast until browned and cooked through, about 10 minutes. Using a slotted spoon, transfer the potatoes to a large bowl, leaving the fat behind. Toss the potatoes with the parsley. Cut the chicken into pieces. Serve the chicken and potatoes immediately with the lemon wedges.

TECHNIQUE: Butterflying a Chicken

1. With the breast side down and the tail of the chicken facing you, use poultry shears to cut along the length of one side of the backbone.

2. With the breast side still down, turn the neck end to face you, cut along the other side of the backbone and remove it.

3. Turn the chicken breast-side up. Open the chicken on the work surface. Use the palm of your hand to flatten the chicken, then pound it with the flat side of a mallet to a fairly even thickness.

A four-ingredient compound butter flavored with garlic and lemon gives a big flavor boost to pan-seared shrimp.

FLASH in a pan

CHAPTER 7

Dinner in less than 20 minutes is the holy grail of weeknight cooking. Many recipes make good on this promise, but most ultimately reflect the minimal effort exerted on the part of the cook. They are fine in a pinch but rarely worth making again. But it doesn't have to be this way.

For this chapter, we started with two quick-cooking classics—sautéed chicken cutlets and pan-seared shrimp—and worked to elevate them from the everyday. We refused to employ lengthy ingredient lists or difficult techniques, and the total preparation and cooking time had to remain under the 20-minute mark. We've figured out the secrets to these dishes and what separates the merely serviceable from the truly memorable. So heat up your skillets and get ready to cook.

SAUTÉED CHICKEN CUTLETS

WHAT WE WANTED: Sautéed super-thin cutlets are satisfying midweek fare, except when they are tough and dry. We set out to improve chicken paillards.

The ultra-thin sautéed chicken cutlets known as paillards owe their invention to Monsieur Paillard, a Parisian restaurateur of the late nineteenth century. Although his namesake juicy cutlets are now legendary, the test kitchen quickly came to the conclusion that he took the secret of chicken paillards to his grave, given the bland, dry, shoe-leather-tough chicken cutlets we prepared from a wide variety of recipes.

Classically defined, a paillard is a cutlet trimmed or pounded to a wafer-thin thickness of ¼ inch. Technically speaking, a paillard can be any variety of meat, although it is most often associated with poultry. Any thicker than ¼ inch and it's a workaday cutlet; any thinner and it overcooks at the mere sight of a skillet. The recipes we found offered little or conflicting advice about preparation and loaded the cutlets with sauces ranging from basic to baroque (demi-glace, truffles, and cockscombs). We decided to tackle the cutlets first and deal with a sauce in due time.

The first step, of course, was to flatten the chicken into cutlets. We sandwiched whole boneless, skinless breasts between plastic wrap and went at them with a heavy meat pounder. By the time the meat was ¼ inch thick, our hands were throbbing—it took a long time to get a cutlet that was more than an inch thick this thin. Even worse, the cutlet looked as if it had gone a few hard-fought rounds with a heavyweight (the edges were frayed and the interior was mottled with peek-a-boo holes). More important, the cutlets were not even in thickness, so there was no way they could cook properly. Following the lead of another paillard recipe, we halved the breasts horizontally before pounding. Roughly ½ to ¾ inch thick, these cut breasts required less pounding, were consistently even, and also ended up being

a reasonable size for skillet cooking. (The first round of cutlets ended up the size of dinner plates.) A sharp chef's knife proved essential for this task, something not everyone has at home. We solved this problem by chilling the chicken breasts in the freezer for about 15 minutes, which firmed the chicken sufficiently to slice with just about any knife.

We also learned a bit about using a meat pounder. Brute force is out. The chicken breaks apart when hit too hard. We had better luck with a firm yet gentle stroke—methodical, not murderous. Moistening the plastic wrap with a little water—a common technique when pounding cutlets—appeared to help by allowing the cutlet to slide under the mallet's assault. Seasoned generously with salt and pepper, the cutlets were ready for cooking.

A 12-inch skillet was the obvious choice for a pan as it could fit a recipe's worth of cutlets into just two batches. But the eternal question loomed: nonstick or traditional? Nonstick made for goof-proof cooking and easy cleanup, but the coating prevented the buildup of fond—the bits of meat that stick to the pan during cooking and lend depth and body to pan sauces. Not willing to sacrifice flavor for the sake of convenience, we chose a traditional skillet.

For our first attempt at cooking the cutlets, we heated a scant 2 teaspoons vegetable oil in the skillet until shimmering and then cooked each side of the cutlets until golden brown. The attractive coloring masked a leathery, desiccated texture. Increasing the heat to medium-high yielded slightly moister cutlets, but the texture was still too dry.

Thinking that a hotter initial temperature (which would get the cutlets in and out of the pan as quickly as possible) might be the key, we heated the skillet over medium-high until the oil was smoking. The resulting cutlets were promising, though the edges were very tough and the meat just shy of appealing. On a whim, we tried partially freezing the cutlets before cooking, but the cutlets browned less and the meat was just as dry. Weighting the cutlets with a heavy lid and pressing forcefully with a spatula also accomplished little.

Confident that high heat was the right direction, we revisited our method. Did both sides of the cutlet have to be browned for the best flavor? Or was it necessary to brown just one side, as is the case with fish fillets? We thoroughly browned the first side, about two minutes, and cooked the second side until just opaque—mere seconds. While the cutlet was just shy of fully cooked, it heated through within a few minutes' repose in a warm oven (long enough to make a pan sauce), and the results were the best yet: juicy, tender, and flavorful. Those pesky tough edges, however, persisted.

We thought more oil in the skillet might protect the edges, which it did, but the excess oil also splattered wildly and coated both the stovetop and the cook in a shower of grease. Rubbing the cutlet with oil before seasoning was a better approach, as it kept splattering to a minimum. But then it occurred to us: Why not replace the water used to lubricate the cutlets during pounding with oil? A scant ½ teaspoon per cutlet was all that was necessary to thinly coat each cutlet. Once cooked, the cutlets were—in their entirety—ideal. Shielded by a veneer of oil, both the edges and the interior were moist, tender, and juicy.

Now ready to prepare a couple of pan sauces, we searched through classic French cookbooks for inspiration, first settling on an apple and mustard sauce. We sautéed shallots in the "dirty" skillet and reduced some apple cider to concentrate it (and deglaze the fond), then finished with whole-grain French-style mustard, parsley, and butter. A shot of apple cider vinegar cut the sweetness and sharpened the apple flavor. We made a second sauce with chicken broth, white wine vinegar, tomato paste, and a large pinch of brown sugar that was finished with butter. Shallots, thyme, and white wine were the basis for a third sauce.

WHAT WE LEARNED: The cutlets must be halved horizontally before they are pounded. Coating the cutlets with oil as they are pounded keeps their edges from drying out when cooked. To keep the cutlets juicy, they should be browned on only one side.

SAUTÉED CHICKEN CUTLETS WITH MUSTARD-CIDER SAUCE
Serves 4

To make slicing the cutlets in half even easier, pop the chicken into the freezer until firm, about 15 minutes.

chicken cutlets
4   boneless, skinless chicken breasts (6 to 8 ounces each), prepared according to the illustrations on page 76
     Salt and ground black pepper
     Vegetable oil

mustard-cider sauce
2   teaspoons vegetable oil
1   medium shallot, minced (about 3 tablespoons)
1¼ cups apple cider
2   tablespoons cider vinegar
2   teaspoons whole-grain mustard
2   teaspoons minced fresh parsley leaves
2   tablespoons unsalted butter
     Salt and ground black pepper

1. FOR THE CHICKEN: Adjust an oven rack to the middle position and heat the oven to 200 degrees. Season both sides of each cutlet with salt and pepper. Heat 2 teaspoons of oil in a 12-inch skillet over medium-high heat until smoking. Place 4 cutlets in the skillet and cook without moving them until browned, about 2 minutes. Using a spatula, flip the cutlets and continue to cook until the second sides are opaque, 15 to 20 seconds. Transfer to a large heatproof plate. Add 2 teaspoons of oil to the now-empty skillet and repeat to cook the remaining cutlets. Cover the plate loosely with foil and transfer it to the oven to keep warm while making the sauce.

2. FOR THE SAUCE: Off the heat, add the oil and shallots to the hot skillet. Using residual heat, cook, stirring constantly, until softened, about 30 seconds. Set the skillet over medium-high heat and add the cider and vinegar. Bring to a simmer, scraping the pan bottom with a wooden spoon to loosen any browned bits. Simmer until reduced to ½ cup, 6 to 7 minutes. Off the heat, stir in the mustard and parsley; whisk in the butter 1 tablespoon at a time. Season with salt and pepper and serve immediately with the cutlets.

VARIATIONS

SAUTÉED CHICKEN CUTLETS WITH TOMATO, THYME, AND WHITE WINE VINEGAR SAUCE

Follow the recipe for Sautéed Chicken Cutlets with Mustard-Cider Sauce, adding 2 teaspoons tomato paste along with the shallot, substituting 1 cup low-sodium chicken broth for the cider and 3 tablespoons white wine vinegar for the cider vinegar, and adding 1½ teaspoons light brown sugar and 6 sprigs fresh thyme along with the liquids. Omit the mustard and parsley.

SAUTÉED CHICKEN CUTLETS WITH SHALLOT AND WHITE WINE SAUCE

Follow the recipe for Sautéed Chicken Cutlets with Mustard-Cider Sauce, substituting ½ cup dry white wine and ¾ cup low-sodium chicken broth for the cider, omitting the vinegar and mustard, replacing the parsley with 1 teaspoon minced fresh thyme, and increasing the butter to 3 tablespoons.

GETTING IT RIGHT:
How Pounding Can Fail

If you try to pound a whole breast (most are more than an inch thick) without first splitting it in half, the end result is ragged. We found that halving the breast horizontally and then pounding it yielded neat, even paillards.

TECHNIQUE:
Preparing Chicken Paillards

1. Lay each cutlet tenderloin-side down (the floppy, thin piece of meat attached to the breast) and smooth the top with your fingers. Any yellow fat will slide to the periphery, where it can be trimmed with a knife.

2. Tenderloins tend to fall off or disintegrate during pounding, so they are best removed and reserved for another use, such as a stir-fry.

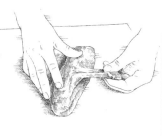

3. Holding the knife parallel to the cutting board, halve each breast horizontally to form two cutlets of even thickness.

4. Pour ½ teaspoon vegetable oil in the center of a sheet of plastic wrap. Turn one cutlet in the oil to coat. Top with a second sheet of plastic wrap and pound gently to an even ¼-inch thickness. Repeat with the remaining cutlets, adding additional oil as needed.

Q & A

Is there a non-alcoholic substitute for white wine in pan sauces?

Our first impulse was to replace wine or vermouth with an equal amount of broth, but upon testing we found that sauces prepared this way lacked acidity and balance. After several rounds of tests, we found four ingredients—dealcoholized white wine (Sutter Home Fre, for example), verjus (the unfermented juice of unripe wine grapes), lemon juice, and white wine vinegar—that could make up for the lack of acidity. Formulas are summarized below. For ingredients added when the sauce is ready to serve, use the lower amount, taste, and add more if greater acidity is desired.

ALCOHOL-FREE PAN SAUCES
To replace ½ cup wine or vermouth, try:

Ingredient	When to Add
¼ cup each DEALCOHOLIZED WINE and CHICKEN BROTH	Use to deglaze the pan
2–4 tablespoons VERJUS	Just before serving
½–1 teaspoon LEMON JUICE	Just before serving
½–1 teaspoon WHITE WINE VINEGAR	Just before serving

TASTING LAB: Chicken Cutlets

IN A WORLD OF LOW-FAT FANATICISM AND A SOCIETY obsessed with weight, it is not surprising that boneless, skinless chicken breasts are a standard in many home kitchens. No fat, no fuss, and unfortunately, no flavor. We've come up with countless recipes to add zip to these otherwise boring birds, but we never stopped to look at the chicken itself. Was there a difference in flavor among the popular brands? Do terms like "organic," "free range," "natural," or "kosher" have any real bearing on the quality of the meat?

To find out, we gathered six brands of boneless, skinless chicken breasts, broiled them without seasoning, and had 20 tasters sample the chickens side by side. Among the contenders were one kosher bird, two "natural," and one "free-range." The remaining two were just "chicken."

The U.S. Department of Agriculture defines "natural" as "a product containing no artificial ingredients or added color and is only minimally processed (a process which does not fundamentally alter the raw product)…" In the case of the chicken, it means there are no antibiotics or hormones, and the birds are fed a vegetarian diet. "Free-range" means exactly what it says: The birds are not confined to small cages but allowed to roam freely. Some people find that this excess motion yields tougher meat, but our tasters did not find this to be the case.

As in our last tasting of whole chickens, Empire Kosher topped the charts, this time tying for first place with all-natural Bell & Evans. The only kosher bird, Empire won points with tasters for its superior flavor: namely, salt. The koshering process involves coating the chicken with salt to draw out any impurities; this process, similar to brining, results in moist, salty meat (for this reason, we do not recommend brining kosher birds). Springer Farms All-Natural and Eberly's Free Range chickens also scored well.

Last place finishers (and lowest priced) Perdue and White Gem (our local store brand) were downgraded for poor texture and unnatural flavor. Tasters were also put off by the brash yellow color of the birds.

In the end, it seems that more money can buy you a better bird and, many would argue, a better-for-you bird. (Kosher birds are also all-natural and contain no hormones or antibiotics.) As for lower-priced supermarket staples and store brands, a cheaper price does indicate a cheaper product.

Rating Chicken Cutlets

TWENTY MEMBERS OF THE *COOK'S ILLUSTRATED* STAFF TASTED ALL OF THE CHICKEN CUTLETS, WHICH WERE cooked to the same degree of doneness under a broiler and without seasoning. The chicken cutlets are listed in order of preference based on their scores in this tasting. All brands are available in supermarkets, although distribution for poultry products is generally not nationwide.

RECOMMENDED

Empire Kosher Chicken Breast Boneless and Skinless

$6.69 per pound

This top finisher was deemed "nicely seasoned" and "buttery." Others praised its "great texture—no dryness." Almost all tasters noted the "salty" flavor.

RECOMMENDED

Bell & Evans Naturally Raised Boneless Skinless Breast

$5.99 per pound

Tied for first place, this all-natural chicken was praised for its "good texture" and "clean flavor." Though a minority of tasters found it "bland," most favored its "clean," "rich" flavor.

RECOMMENDED

Springer Mountain Farms Boneless Skinless Breasts

$5.99 per pound

"Tastes like chicken," wrote one taster of this boutique brand from Georgia. Many found this chicken to have a "natural flavor," though others found it "bland."

RECOMMENDED

Eberly's Free Range Young Organic Chicken Boneless Skinless Breast

$7.99 per pound

"Nondescript," wrote one taster of the only free-range chicken in the tasting, "though very tender." Others found the taste "slightly sour."

NOT RECOMMENDED

Perdue Fit 'N Easy Skinless and Boneless Fresh Chicken Breasts

$4.99 per pound

This supermarket staple lost points for its "unnatural" flavor, "mustard color," and "chalky" texture. Some tasters complained of an unpleasant aftertaste.

NOT RECOMMENDED

White Gem Boneless Skinless Chicken Breast

$4.29 per pound

There were no fans of this store brand from Stop & Shop supermarkets, which tasters found "chewy," "mushy," "stringy," and "bland." One taster wrote simply, "awful."

PAN-SEARED SHRIMP

WHAT WE WANTED: Nicely browned shrimp that were still juicy, moist, and tender.

Having prepared literally tons of shrimp in the test kitchen and in our own home kitchens, we have found that pan-searing produces the ultimate combination of a well-caramelized exterior and a moist, tender interior. If executed properly, this cooking method also preserves the shrimp's plumpness and trademark briny sweetness.

That being said, a good recipe for pan-seared shrimp is hard to find. Of the handful of recipes we uncovered, the majority resulted in shrimp that were variously dry, flavorless, pale, tough, or gummy—hardly appetizing. It was time to start some serious testing.

We quickly uncovered a few basic rules. First, tasters unanimously favored shrimp that were peeled before being cooked. Peeled shrimp are easier to eat, and unpeeled shrimp fail to pick up the delicious caramelized flavor that pan-searing provides. Second, the shrimp were best cooked in a 12-inch skillet; its large surface area kept the shrimp from overcrowding the pan and steaming—a surefire way to prevent caramelization. Third, oil was the ideal cooking medium, favored over both a dry pan (which made the shrimp leathery and metallic tasting) and butter (which tended to burn).

Next, in pan-searing the shrimp, we found that in the time it took to get the shrimp to brown, they turned out tough and overcooked. Looking for another way to promote browning in a shorter time frame, we thought to add a pinch of sugar to the shrimp. Not only did the sugar caramelize into a nice brown crust, it also accentuated the natural sweetness of the shrimp, nicely setting off their inherent sea-saltiness.

Even in a 12-inch skillet, 1½ pounds of shrimp must be cooked in two batches or they will steam instead of sear. The trick was to develop a technique that neither overcooked the shrimp nor let half of them turn cold while the other half finished cooking. To prevent overcooking, we tried searing the shrimp on one side, removing the pan from the flame, and then allowing the residual heat to finish cooking the other side of the shrimp. This worked like a charm. Better yet, the residual heat from the pan also solved the cold shrimp problem. As soon as the second batch finished cooking (the first batch was now near room temperature), we tossed the first batch back into the pan, covered it, and let residual heat work its magic once again. After about a minute, all of the shrimp were perfectly cooked and piping hot. Now all we needed were a few ideas for some quick sauces.

We tested sauces made from assertive ingredients such as garlic, ginger, and chipotle chile mixed with plenty of acidity as a foil for the shrimp's richness. The most successful of these sauces were those that clung to the shrimp like a glaze. All of them could easily be made ahead of time and quickly tossed with the shrimp during the last stage of cooking, once the pan was removed from the heat.

WHAT WE LEARNED: Season peeled shrimp with salt, pepper, and sugar (to promote browning) before cooking them in a very hot pan. Cook just ¾ pound of shrimp at a time, searing on just one side, and then use residual heat to cook the second side. Finish the shrimp with a potent flavored butter or glaze.

PAN-SEARED SHRIMP

Serves 4

The cooking times below are for extra-large shrimp (there are 21 to 25 in 1 pound). If this size is not available in your market, buy large shrimp—the next size down—and adjust the cooking time slightly. Either a nonstick or a traditional skillet will work for this recipe, but a nonstick simplifies cleanup. See page 43 for tips on buying shrimp.

    2   tablespoons vegetable oil
    1½   pounds extra-large shrimp (21 to 25 per
         pound), peeled and deveined
    ¼   teaspoon salt
    ¼   teaspoon ground black pepper
    ⅛   teaspoon sugar

Heat 1 tablespoon of the oil in a 12-inch skillet over high heat until smoking. Meanwhile, toss the shrimp, salt, pepper, and sugar in a medium bowl. Add half of the shrimp to the pan in a single layer and cook until spotty brown and the edges turn pink, about 1 minute. Remove the pan from the heat. Using tongs, flip each shrimp and let stand until all but the very center is opaque, about 30 seconds. Transfer the shrimp to a large plate. Repeat with the remaining tablespoon of oil and the remaining shrimp. After the second batch has stood off the heat, return the first batch to the skillet and toss to combine. Cover the skillet and let stand until the shrimp are cooked through, 1 to 2 minutes. Serve immediately.

VARIATIONS
PAN-SEARED SHRIMP WITH GARLIC-LEMON BUTTER

Beat 3 tablespoons softened unsalted butter with a fork in a small bowl until light and fluffy. Stir in 1 medium garlic clove, minced, 1 tablespoon lemon juice, 2 tablespoons chopped parsley, and ⅛ teaspoon salt until combined. Follow the recipe for Pan-Seared Shrimp, adding the flavored butter when returning the first batch of shrimp to the skillet. Serve with lemon wedges, if desired.

PAN-SEARED SHRIMP WITH GINGER-HOISIN GLAZE

Stir 2 tablespoons hoisin sauce, 1 tablespoon rice vinegar, 1½ teaspoons soy sauce, 2 teaspoons grated fresh ginger, 2 teaspoons water, and 2 scallions, sliced thin, together in a small bowl. Follow the recipe for Pan-Seared Shrimp, substituting an equal amount of red pepper flakes for the black pepper and adding the hoisin mixture when returning the first batch of shrimp to the skillet.

PAN-SEARED SHRIMP WITH CHIPOTLE-LIME GLAZE

Stir 1 chipotle chile in adobo, minced, 2 teaspoons adobo sauce, 4 teaspoons brown sugar, 2 tablespoons lime juice, and 2 tablespoons chopped fresh cilantro leaves together in a small bowl. Follow the recipe for Pan-Seared Shrimp, adding the chipotle mixture when returning the first batch of shrimp to the skillet.

EQUIPMENT CORNER:
Cookware Cleaning Products

IF YOU COOK A LOT (LIKE WE DO), YOU CLEAN A LOT. In the test kitchen, we've long debated the merits of various cleaning methods and cleansers. We decided to end the debate and apply the same exhaustive methods we use to develop recipes to figure out the best, most efficient ways to clean cookware. We dirtied pots and pans by burning food onto surfaces. We also rounded up the worst-looking cookware in the test kitchen (and in our kitchens at home) to test methods for bringing a new shine to old pans.

Along the way, we tested a dozen cleansers on pots and pans made from a variety of materials. After weeks of work, our testers' hands were rough and chapped, but we did find some winners and losers among these cleansers. And by the end of this marathon cleaning session, the cookware in the test kitchen was looking much brighter.

Cast iron

Old, well-seasoned cast-iron pans have become heirlooms, making it hard to find even dirty, rusty, perfectly cruddy pans for a bargain at yard sales and flea markets. If you are lucky enough to find one, it deserves a place on the stovetop. After scraping up a couple of dirty pans with several grades of sandpaper and emery cloth—both being too harsh for even these badly rusted pans—we settled on the following method to restore pans that have been subject to such neglect.

First, rub the pan with fine steel wool and wipe out loose dirt and rust with a cloth (repeat until the pan is largely cleared of rust). Then place the pan on the burner over medium-low heat and add enough vegetable oil to coat the pan bottom heavily. Heat it for five minutes, or until the handle is too hot to touch; turn off the burner. Add enough salt to form a liquid-like paste and, wearing a work or gardening glove, scrub with a thick wad of paper towels, steadying the pan with a potholder. Repeat the heating and scrubbing steps until the pan is slick and black.

And to maintain a clean pan, we recommend the following after each use of the pan: Rinse the pan thoroughly in hot water, wipe it dry, and then coat it with a thin film of vegetable oil, wiping off any excess oil with paper towels. If hot water does not work to rid the pan of stuck-on food, try a washcloth to scrub the pan with salt.

Copper

We came across a number of ways for removing tarnish: a salted lemon half, Worcestershire sauce, tomato sauce, ketchup, vinegar, cream of tartar and water, yogurt, even boiling milk. Enterprising and interesting as they all are, these home remedies were not as effective as the traditional commercial polishes we tried, which not only removed tarnish but added shine. Among the home remedies, ketchup was the only one that effectively removed tarnish. Unfortunately, it did not add shine.

But if you're desperate to clean up a tarnished copper pan and have no commercial polish on hand, we recommend spreading an even layer of ketchup over the surface of a pan with a paper towel or dishcloth. After five minutes, wipe off the ketchup with a damp towel or sponge. Wash the pan with warm water and dishwashing liquid, and dry.

Stainless steel, nonstick, and hard-anodized aluminum

We found that these pans, which see the most action in the kitchen, present similar cleaning challenges. We identified three types of cleaning tasks: everyday messes on just-used cookware, stubborn messes that have built up over time, and burnt, blackened messes that make the cookware almost unusable.

When testing ways to handle these three types of jobs, we continually ran into stern warnings about mixing cleaning chemicals—bleach and ammonia in particular, as well as commercially prepared cleansers (which may contain bleach, ammonia, or any other harmful chemicals). When combined, bleach and ammonia create chloramine gases that are highly irritating to the lungs and can cause coughing and choking. With these warnings in mind, we forged ahead with testing.

For cleaning everyday messes, you can soak the pan overnight in sudsy water, but is there an alternative if you don't want to be greeted with greasy dishwater in the morning? Yes. Boil water in it. And you don't need to add either vinegar or baking soda to the water, as some sources recommend. We tried these formulas and they were no more effective than plain water. (The boiling water method is especially kind to nonstick cookware, as it allows you to clean the sensitive surface without any rough scrubbing.)

Fill the pan halfway with tap water and put it on the stovetop, uncovered. Bring the water to a boil and continue to boil briskly for about three minutes, and then turn off the burner. Next, using a wooden spatula, scrape the pan and then pour off the water. Let the pan sit for a few minutes and the residue will flake off as the pan dries. Wash the pan with hot water and dishwashing liquid, and dry.

Unfortunately, we found that our neat trick of boiling water in a pan doesn't clean up the stubborn, brown, sometimes tacky residue seared into a pan from many past meals. Neither does boiling water work on two forms of discoloration a pan may suffer: rainbows and brown tints likely caused by prolonged exposure to heat in excess of 500 degrees.

After tests with dishwashing liquid, SOS pads, and various home remedies, such as baking soda, we found two powdered cleansers—Bar Keepers Friend and Cameo—to be superior for these tasks. Stainless steel responded especially well to this technique, but it is also safe for nonstick surfaces. For anodized aluminum surfaces, do not use Bar Keepers Friend; Cameo can be used, although some manufacturers recommend Soft Scrub, which we found to be less effective.

Start by moistening the pan with water, then shake a film of cleanser over it to cover. Using a copper scrubber for stainless steel or a nylon scrubber for nonstick or anodized aluminum, scrub the pan; we found that circular motions work best. Finish cleaning the pan by washing it out with hot water and dishwashing liquid, and dry.

For pans with a stainless steel exterior that has been deeply, darkly blackened and seems immune to any amount of scrubbing with powdered cleanser, we did find a cleanser of last resort: oven cleaner. We recommend its use only on the exterior of pans (so this method is fine on pans with steel exteriors and nonstick interior finishes) and in extreme cases; ideally, you'll treat a pan with oven cleaner only once, to get it back up to snuff. Oven cleaner should not be used on hard-anodized aluminum pans. If possible, bring the pan to a shady spot outdoors; otherwise, clean the pan in a well-ventilated room, with the windows wide open.

Place the pan upside down on newspapers and, wearing rubber gloves, apply an even layer of cleaner. Let it sit for 20 minutes (or the time recommended on the can). With the gloves still on and using an old damp cloth or sponge, wipe off the oven cleaner. Discard the newspapers and thoroughly rinse or discard the cloth or sponge. Thoroughly rinse the pan in the sink under warm running water, then wash it with dishwashing liquid; thoroughly rinse again and dry.

BEST CLEANSERS FOR CAST IRON

We found that a thick paste of warm vegetable oil and salt does the best job of bringing rusty cast-iron pots and pans back to life.

BEST CLEANSERS FOR COPPER

Among widely available polishes, Weiman Metal Polish did the best job of removing tarnish and adding shine to copper pots and pans. Ketchup does a great job of removing tarnish but won't add a brilliant luster to copper cookware.

BEST CLEANSERS FOR STAINLESS STEEL, NONSTICK, AND ANODIZED ALUMINUM

We found Bar Keepers Friend and Cameo to be the most effective in removing stubborn messes from most of the cookware in the test kitchen. Cameo can be used on stainless steel, anodized aluminum, or nonstick surfaces; Bar Keepers Friend is too harsh for anodized aluminum but works well on stainless steel or nonstick surfaces.

Pan-Seared Shrimp **page 80**

Salad with Apples, Walnuts, Dried Cherries, and Herb Baked Goat Cheese **page 259**

French Onion Soup **page 263**

Sweet and Tangy Oven-Barbecued Chicken **page 102**

Campanelli with Asparagus, Basil, and Balsamic Glaze **page 175**

Hearty Lentil Soup **page 31**

Quick Cheese Bread **page 37**

Mexican Rice **page 168**

Chicken Enchiladas with Red Chili Sauce **page 162**

Mushroom Risotto **page 235**

Polenta with Gorgonzola **page 255**

93

Salsa Verde **page 141**

94

Crispy Roast Lemon Chicken **page 69**

Creole-Style Shrimp and Sausage Gumbo **page 42**

Pasta all'Amatriciana **page 239**

Classic Macaroni and Cheese **page 107**

FAMILY favorites

CHAPTER 8

Cooking for a family isn't as easy as it was once. In Norman Rockwell pictures, the entire clan (with aunts, uncles, cousins, and grandparents) is gathered around the table with a dozen different dishes in front of them. No one has soccer practice or is working late. No one is on a weird diet, and the kids seem to eat the same thing as the adults.

Times have certainly changed, and meals are much more rushed. But we think it's important for families to spend an hour every evening gathered around the table. The challenge for the modern cook is figuring out what to make. Dishes that require all-day attention won't work, and kids today are much more likely to express their own opinions about what they want to eat. (As for dieters, well, you can't please everyone.)

The recipes in this chapter represent the best of modern home cooking. They are delicious, relatively straightforward fare that will appeal to young and old. What kid—or adult—won't look forward to macaroni and cheese or barbecued chicken?

OVEN-BARBECUED CHICKEN

WHAT WE WANTED: The idea—barbecued chicken straight from your oven—is a great one. Unfortunately, the real thing is often dry and tough, with a tasteless, baked-on sauce. Could we save this recipe and create an oven-barbecued chicken with a rich and tangy sauce?

When you hear the phrase "hospital food," what do you see in your mind's eye? That's right—plain baked chicken, the very portrait of bland institutional fare, a culinary yawn. The need to dress up this dull, workaday recipe probably inspired the idea of oven-barbecued chicken, which should, in theory at least, add sweet, tangy, spicy flavors to tender chicken by way of a rich, tomatoey sauce in the classic Kansas City style. In our experience, though, the idea remains just that—a theory. As expected, the five initial recipes we tried in the test kitchen delivered tough, rubbery, or unevenly cooked chicken in sauces ranging from pasty and candy-sweet to greasy, stale, thin, or commercial tasting.

Monumental as these problems seemed, we were inspired by the challenge. Surely this dish would be worthwhile if the chicken was juicy, tender, and evenly cooked and the sauce tasted fresh and multidimensional, clinging to the chicken in a thick, lightly caramelized coat.

The recipes we scoured indicated that our chicken options were wide open, as they called for, variously, half chickens, quarter chickens, whole chickens cut into serving pieces, bone-in breasts, thighs, drumsticks, and wings, and even meat that was cooked, boned, shredded, and mixed with barbecue sauce, à la pulled pork. To methodically test each option, we cobbled together a basic baking procedure: Bake the chicken at 350 degrees until partially done, coat with barbecue sauce—a bottled brand from the supermarket for now—and continue baking until the chicken is cooked through, basting with the sauce several times along the way.

Success was elusive. The halved and quartered chickens cooked unevenly and were awkward to eat. Butchering a whole chicken was more work than we saw fit to do for an easy Tuesday-night supper. Of course, purchasing cut-up serving pieces eliminated the work, but time and time again we found them to be sloppily butchered or even mismatched. Using a single cut of chicken, such as all breasts or thighs, helped with the evenness of cooking, at least, and we confirmed that tasters preferred the mild white meat of the breasts as a backdrop for the sauce. Shredding the cooked chicken to mix with the sauce was a messy, tedious process, so we settled on breasts as our best option.

One of the first problems to solve was the skin, which was consistently flabby, rubbery, and fatty. Any fat that rendered from the skin during cooking left the sauce not thick and clingy but greasy and loose, so it slid right off the chicken. To cover our bases, we tried cooking the chicken skin-side down in a preheated pan, slashing the skin lightly to expose extra surface area and expedite rendering, and air-drying the chicken prior to cooking. In the end, we rejected all of these methods as either not successful enough or too fussy for a quick weeknight dinner.

The solution, we hoped, would be to jettison the skin entirely. We gave skinless, boneless breasts a whirl and were delighted to find that they made for a dramatic improvement. The chewy skin became a nonissue, and we discovered an extra benefit in that both sides of the chicken breasts were now coated with sauce.

We were next determined to achieve our goal of a fresh, lively sauce with a properly thick and sticky texture. Could we find it in a bottled sauce? Hoping for an easy out, we tried several types, from supermarket standards to fancy mail-order products. We had the best luck with Bull's-Eye, a sauce that won a blind tasting here in the test kitchen, but we still felt that a homemade sauce could lift this recipe from pretty good to great.

That certainly didn't mean that the sauce had to be complicated. We began with our own Simple Sweet and Tangy Barbecue Sauce, a quick-cooked number developed several years ago. Although this sauce took about half an hour to prepare and required the use of a food processor and strainer, it did offer both fresh, balanced flavors and a thick, clingy texture.

Rather than building a new recipe from the ground up, we tried stripping this one down to make it even faster and simpler. After dozens of tests, we learned that ketchup, Worcestershire, mustard, molasses, chili powder, and cayenne were absolutely necessary, as were maple syrup and the tang of cider vinegar. We substituted grated onion for the onion juice in the original recipe and eliminated the hot pepper sauce, garlic, and liquid smoke. Only four minutes over medium heat were needed to blend the flavors, which became further concentrated when the sauce cooked again on the chicken.

We tried a few other flavoring tricks, including rubbing the chicken with a dry spice rub and marinating it overnight in the sauce before cooking it, but none was worth the effort. Brining was also a bust. The extra seasoning was superfluous in the face of the assertively flavored barbecue sauce, and the extra moisture in the meat from the brine tended to thin the sauce.

In terms of cooking temperature and method, we tried dousing the chicken with sauce and then baking it as well as dredging the chicken in seasoned flour and pan-frying it before undertaking an intricate dance of baking and basting. Both approaches failed.

From there, we focused on oven mechanics, testing various oven rack positions, various combinations of low and high temperatures (from 325 to 500 degrees), and additions of sauce at various points during cooking. Alas, despite the moniker "oven-barbecued," none of these oven-based methods worked, although we did learn that lower oven temperatures cooked the irregularly shaped chicken breasts evenly and that higher temperatures helped to concentrate the sauce.

Standing in the kitchen, scratching our heads after the umpteenth test, we looked at the skillet of waiting barbecue sauce and an idea flashed. We remembered a method we had used to make maple-glazed pork roast. It involved searing the roast in a skillet, reducing the glaze in the same skillet, and then finishing the roast in that already hot skillet in the oven. Would a similar technique help us to master our current challenge?

The first attempt showed promise, but it wasn't perfect because the exteriors of the breasts were dry from aggressive pan-searing. The solution was to sear the chicken breasts very lightly, just until they began to color and develop a slightly rough surface to which the sauce could adhere. The chicken was then removed from the pan, the sauce made, the chicken added back and coated with sauce, and the pan slipped under the broiler. The results were good, but the heat of the broiler had dried out the chicken a bit. The solution was to start the skillet in a 325-degree oven and then finish it under the broiler. The chicken was now juicy and thickly coated with a perfectly concentrated sauce.

WHAT WE LEARNED: Boneless, skinless breasts are the best choice for this recipe. Lightly brown the breasts in a hot skillet, build a quick sauce in the empty pan, return the chicken to the pan, and bake until the chicken is nearly cooked. Finish the recipe by turning the oven to broil to caramelize the sauce.

SWEET AND TANGY OVEN-BARBECUED CHICKEN

Serves 4

Real maple syrup is preferable to imitation syrup, and "mild" or "original" molasses is preferable to darker, more bitter types. If you are content to use bottled sauce, we had the best luck with Bull's-Eye Original, winner of a blind tasting held last year. Use 1¾ cups of sauce and, in step 3, reduce the sauce cooking time from 4 minutes to 2 minutes.

Some notes on equipment: First, to grate the onion, use a Microplane grater or the fine holes of a box grater. Second, resist the temptation to use a nonstick skillet; most nonstick skillets are not broiler-safe. Third, and most important, you should make this recipe only in an in-oven broiler; do not use a drawer-type broiler. Finally, be aware that broiling times may differ from one oven to another. For instance, in one editor's powerful professional-style oven, the chicken took just 4 minutes to reach 160 degrees, so we urge you to check the chicken for doneness after only 3 minutes of broiling. You may also have to lower the oven rack if your broiler runs very hot.

1 cup ketchup
2 tablespoons finely grated onion
2 tablespoons Worcestershire sauce
2 tablespoons Dijon mustard
3 tablespoons molasses
2 tablespoons maple syrup
3 tablespoons cider vinegar
1 teaspoon chili powder
¼ teaspoon cayenne
4 boneless, skinless chicken breasts, 6–7 ounces each (with tenderloins), patted dry with paper towels
Salt and ground black pepper
1 tablespoon vegetable oil

1. Adjust an oven rack to the upper-middle position, about 5 inches from the upper heating element; heat the oven to 325 degrees. Whisk the ketchup, onion, Worcestershire, mustard, molasses, maple syrup, vinegar, chili powder, and cayenne together in a small bowl; set aside. Season the chicken with salt and pepper.

2. Heat the oil in a heavy-bottomed, nonreactive 12-inch ovenproof skillet over high heat until beginning to smoke. Brown the chicken skinned-side down until very light golden, 1 to 2 minutes; using tongs, turn the chicken and brown until very light golden on the second side, 1 to 2 minutes longer. Transfer the chicken to a plate and set aside.

GETTING IT RIGHT: Oven-Barbecued Chicken, Reinvented in a Skillet

1. Lightly brown the chicken, transfer the pieces to a plate, and pour off the fat from the skillet.

2. Add the sauce ingredients to the empty pan and cook until a heatproof spatula leaves a clear trail.

3. Return the chicken to the skillet, turn to coat with sauce, then spoon more sauce over each piece.

4. Bake the chicken and sauce in the skillet, broil to caramelize the sauce, and then serve.

3. Discard the fat in the skillet; off the heat, add the sauce mixture and, using a wooden spoon, scrape up the browned bits on the bottom of the skillet. Simmer the sauce over medium heat, stirring frequently with a heatproof spatula, until the sauce is thick and glossy and a spatula leaves a clear trail in the sauce, about 4 minutes. Off the heat, return the chicken to the skillet and turn to coat thickly with the sauce; set the chicken pieces skinned-side up and spoon extra sauce over each piece to create a thick coating.

4. Place the skillet in the oven and cook until the thickest parts of the chicken breasts register 130 degrees on an instant-read thermometer, 10 to 14 minutes. Set the oven to broil and continue to cook until the thickest parts of the chicken breasts register 160 degrees, 5 to 10 minutes longer. Transfer the chicken to a platter and let rest 5 minutes. Meanwhile, whisk to combine the sauce in the skillet and transfer to a small bowl. Serve the chicken, passing the extra sauce separately.

GETTING IT RIGHT: The Problem with Packaged Chicken Breasts

Uniformly sized chicken breasts will cook more evenly than breasts of varying sizes. Unfortunately, it's difficult to discern the size of individual breasts when they're squished into a supermarket package (left). Once we removed the breasts from this package (right) and weighed them, we discovered that one breast weighed 9 ounces, two weighed 6 ounces, and one weighed just 4½ ounces. To prepare oven-barbecued chicken, we recommend buying a family pack with at least six breasts and then freezing the largest and smallest breasts for future use in a stir-fry, where size won't matter.

THESE BREASTS LOOK THE SAME . . . BUT OUT OF THE PACKAGE, THEY ARE QUITE DIFFERENT.

EQUIPMENT CORNER:
Stain Removal Products

FOOD-STAINED CLOTHING IS A SAD REALITY IN OUR test kitchen. Tired of throwing out otherwise perfectly good shirts, we decided to get serious about laundry and put 16 supermarket stain removers to the test. These products fell into four categories: pretreaters, laundry additives, spot removers, and oxygen-based powders.

Pretreaters
These products are applied to the stained garment, which is then thrown into the wash. This group included Spray 'n Wash, Shout, Zout, Shout Ultra Gel, Shout Action Gel, Extra-Strength Spray 'n Wash, and Spray 'n Wash Stain Stick.

Laundry additives
These products go right into the machine with the wash to boost the stain-removing power of the detergent used. Both products in this group were made by Spray 'n Wash, one a liquid additive and one a concentrated tablet referred to as Actionball.

Spot removers
These products are applied to clothes, rubbed to remove the stains, and finally washed. Those tested included Gonzo Stain Remover, Amodex Premium Spot Remover, and Didi Seven Ultra Super Concentrated Cleaner.

Oxygen-based powders
These products are diluted with water to make a soaking solution for garments. Once the stains are gone, the clothes can be washed. This group included All Oxi-Active, Shout Oxy Power, Clorox Oxygen Action, and Oxi-Clean.

For our tests, we took plain 100 percent cotton T-shirts and dirtied them with the foods most infamous for leaving

unrelenting stains: pureed blueberries, pureed beets, black coffee, red wine, ketchup and yellow mustard (to simulate a hot dog mishap), melted bittersweet chocolate, and chili (which also covered grease stains). Each cleaning product was applied according to the manufacturer's instructions for maximum stain removal.

All of the products removed the coffee, wine, ketchup, and beet stains, but only the spot removers and oxygen-based powders managed to completely remove the tougher stains left by chili, blueberries, chocolate, and mustard. T-shirts tested with the pretreaters and laundry additives came out of the wash with several distinct, if muted, stains.

Spot removers call for brushing or blotting the stain until it is gone, and although this method is the most labor-intensive (in some cases up to seven applications were necessary), even the toughest stains were gone before the garment went into the washing machine. If time is a luxury you can afford and scrubbing and blotting are not your thing, then the oxygen-based powders are the way to go. T-shirts treated with these cleaners—used as concentrated soaking solutions, as per the manufacturers' instructions—needed only a light rubbing to remove the toughest stains. Although the T-shirts did need to soak for up to three hours (with Oxi-Clean working in the shortest amount of time), the process was mostly hands-off.

So if you can't part with that favorite blouse or pair of pants and you don't mind an investment of time but little elbow grease, use an oxygen-based powder.

Rating Stain Removers

WE PURCHASED 16 STAIN REMOVERS AND DIRTIED plain 100 percent cotton T-shirts with the foods most infamous for leaving unrelenting stains: pureed blueberries, pureed beets, black coffee, red wine, ketchup and yellow mustard, melted bittersweet chocolate, and greasy chili. Each cleaning product was applied according to the manufacturer's instructions for maximum stain removal. The 16 products we tested can be divided into four basic categories, which are listed below in order of preference.

RECOMMENDED
Oxygen-Based Powders
With very little work but considerable soaking time, these products removed the toughest food stains. Among the four products tested, Oxi-Clean worked best.

RECOMMENDED WITH RESERVATIONS
Spot Removers
Although labor-intensive—it took up to seven applications in some cases—these products worked well to remove the stains before the shirts were washed.

NOT RECOMMENDED
Pretreaters
These apply-and-wash products couldn't cut through the toughest stains, leaving muted shadows behind on the washed shirts.

NOT RECOMMENDED
Laundry Additives
Not enough boosting power to remove chili, blueberry, chocolate, and mustard stains.

MACARONI AND CHEESE

WHAT WE WANTED: A classic mac 'n cheese recipe that would appeal to everyone, from the finickiest kid to the snobbiest adult.

With the possible exception of meatloaf and fried chicken, few dishes are as personal as macaroni and cheese. Baked or stovetop, custard-based or little more than white sauce and pasta, with or without toasted bread crumbs, there must be a million recipes out there—surely enough to satisfy nearly everyone. Unfortunately, no one of these recipes can satisfy everyone at the same time. Sure, the kids would be fine with the contents of the blue box brand, but for most adults this ready-mix mac and cheese lost its appeal soon after we learned how to boil water. Conversely, decadent recipes replete with cream, eggs, and a who's-who list of pungent cheeses are decidedly adults-only; just try to serve them to the kids and you'll get upturned noses and pushed-back plates.

To get our bearings, we scoured the aforementioned million recipes (or at least 40), starting with our own recipe, published in *Cook's Illustrated* almost 10 years ago. A custard-style macaroni and cheese, this recipe uses eggs and evaporated milk (as opposed to the more traditional whole milk) to prevent the custard from curdling (a common occurrence in recipes with eggs). Although a long-standing test kitchen favorite, this dish is incredibly rich. We wanted something simpler but, as our next test revealed, not too simple. When we layered cooked pasta and cheese into a casserole dish, poured milk over the lot, and put the dish in the oven, the fat from the cheese separated and the result was a greasy mess. We concluded that the cheese needs some sort of binder—either eggs or flour.

We were now left with the path chosen by the vast majority of recipe writers: béchamel sauce. Béchamel is a white sauce made by cooking flour and butter to form a light roux. Milk is gradually whisked in, and the béchamel

is cooked until it thickens. Combined with cheese and partially cooked noodles, the mix is then poured into a casserole dish and baked.

Traditional recipes incorporate the cheese into the béchamel before stirring in parcooked pasta and then baking until the sauce is bubbling hot and thick. It sure sounds easy. But no matter how much attention we paid, we just couldn't pull a great baked macaroni and cheese out of the oven. Sometimes the pasta was overcooked—a result of just one minute too many of boiling on the stovetop. Even worse were the batches made with undercooked noodles. We tried to remedy these by keeping the dishes in the oven longer (anywhere from 20 to 30 minutes), but after a while the bubbling cheese began to separate and the dishes took on an oily, grainy feel.

Frustrated, we pushed the idea of using the oven aside (to heck with tradition) and started working solely on the stovetop. Maybe we could better prevent the overcooking (and undercooking) of the pasta.

We made the next batch of sauce and boiled the pasta on the side. We cooked the pasta until it was a few minutes shy of being done, tossed it in with the sauce and cheese, and simmered it until the pasta was tender, which took a good 10 minutes. To our dismay, this batch had begun to separate, just like our oven-baked experiments, and the parcooked pasta released its starch to the sauce, giving it a gritty feel. Next we cooked the pasta until very tender and quickly mixed it with the cheese and sauce. This time tasters thought that the noodles needed more time to absorb the sauce. We needed to cook the pasta less at the outset. Boiled until just past al dente, the noodles still had enough structure to stand up to the heat of the sauce for a few minutes without turning mushy, and the cheese sauce filled every nook and cranny.

We now decided to work on the correct proportions of butter to flour to milk, reasoning that the winning combination would provide the desired silky sauce. Béchamel recipes that used more butter than flour lacked cohesion. Those using equal parts butter and flour seemed heavy and dull. We had much better luck using slightly more flour than butter (6 tablespoons to 5 tablespoons, respectively). Just this little change cut enough of the richness that we were trying to avoid, and, when we added 5 cups of whole milk, there was a plenitude of sauce with which to smother the noodles.

Technically speaking, as soon as we added cheese to the white sauce, it turned from béchamel to Mornay. We knew that choosing the right cheese (and using the right amount) would affect not only the flavor of the dish but also its texture. Indeed, an unpleasant grainy feel was introduced by hard cheeses such as Parmesan, Gruyère, and some aged cheddars, to say nothing of their overly distinct flavor. On the other hand, incredibly mild, soft cheeses such as mascarpone and ricotta contributed no flavor, and their creamy texture pushed the macaroni and cheese right back into sickly territory. In the end, what worked best was two cheeses—sharp cheddar for flavor and Monterey Jack for creaminess.

How much cheese to use? Many recipes call for twice as much cheese as pasta (we were using 1 pound of pasta). The result was a sticky, stringy macaroni and cheese that was off the charts in terms of richness. More frugal recipes seem designed around an impending cheese shortage, using merely ½ pound of cheese for 1 pound of pasta. The result was more macaroni and milk than macaroni and cheese. We found that 1 pound of cheese was the perfect amount for 1 pound of pasta. Just the right texture and flavor, and easy to remember, too.

We were done, right? Wrong. Many of the tasters wanted at least the option of adding a toasty, golden topping of bread crumbs—a flashback to the baked versions. To keep to our stovetop commitment, we tossed homemade bread crumbs with melted butter and toasted them on the stovetop, then portioned them out over individual servings in generous amounts. But these crumbs seemed more like

an afterthought than part of the dish. We weren't about to go back to baking the macaroni and cheese but wondered if using the broiler instead for a quick blast of heat would work. We placed fresh buttered bread crumbs on top of the next batch of macaroni and cheese and placed it under the broiler. This was it. The broiler concentrated the heat right on the bread crumbs, turning them a deep, golden brown. Better still, the process took only a few minutes—yet it was just enough time to let the bottom of the crumbs sink into the cheese sauce and seem baked right in.

WHAT WE LEARNED: To prevent curdling, keep the macaroni and cheese on the stovetop for as long as possible—and out of the oven. Cook the macaroni just past al dente, then simmer it with a flour-thickened cheese sauce for several minutes so the noodles can absorb some of the sauce. A combination of cheddar and Jack cheese gives the sauce optimal flavor and texture. Finally, don't forget the breadcrumb topping, which should be crisped under the broiler.

CLASSIC MACARONI AND CHEESE

Serves 6 to 8 as a main course or 10 to 12 as a side dish

It's crucial to cook the pasta until tender—that is, just past the al dente stage. Whole, low-fat, and skim milk all work well in this recipe. The recipe may be halved and baked in an 8-inch square, broiler-safe baking dish. If desired, offer celery salt or hot sauce (such as Tabasco) for sprinkling at the table.

bread crumb topping

- 6 slices (about 6 ounces) good-quality white sandwich bread, torn into rough pieces
- 3 tablespoons cold unsalted butter, cut into 6 pieces

pasta and cheese

- 1 tablespoon plus 1 teaspoon salt
- 1 pound elbow macaroni
- 5 tablespoons unsalted butter
- 6 tablespoons all-purpose flour
- 1½ teaspoons powdered mustard
- ¼ teaspoon cayenne (optional)
- 5 cups milk (see note)
- 8 ounces Monterey Jack cheese, shredded (2 cups)
- 8 ounces sharp cheddar cheese, shredded (2 cups)

1. FOR THE BREAD CRUMBS: Pulse the bread and butter in a food processor until the crumbs are no larger than ⅛ inch, ten to fifteen 1-second pulses. Set aside.

2. FOR THE PASTA AND CHEESE: Adjust an oven rack to the lower-middle position and heat the broiler. Bring 4 quarts water to a rolling boil in a stockpot. Add 1 tablespoon of the salt and the macaroni and stir to separate the noodles. Cook until tender, drain, and set aside.

3. In the now-empty stockpot, heat the butter over medium-high heat until foaming. Add the flour, mustard, cayenne (if using), and remaining 1 teaspoon salt and whisk well to combine. Continue whisking until the mixture becomes fragrant and deepens in color, about 1 minute.

Whisking constantly, gradually add the milk; bring the mixture to a boil, whisking constantly (the mixture must reach a full boil to fully thicken), then reduce the heat to medium and simmer, whisking occasionally, until thickened to the consistency of heavy cream, about 5 minutes. Off the heat, whisk in the cheeses until fully melted. Add the pasta and cook over medium-low heat, stirring constantly, until the mixture is steaming and heated through, about 6 minutes.

4. Transfer the mixture to a broiler-safe 13 by 9-inch baking dish and sprinkle with the bread crumbs. Broil until deep golden brown, 3 to 5 minutes. Cool 5 minutes, then serve.

VARIATION

MACARONI AND CHEESE WITH PEAS AND HAM

Cut 8 ounces baked deli ham, sliced ¼ inch thick, into 1-inch squares. Follow the recipe for Classic Macaroni and Cheese, adding the chopped ham and 1 cup frozen peas to the cheese sauce along with the pasta. Proceed as directed.

GETTING IT RIGHT:
Some Failed Experiments

OILY AND SEPARATED   CURDLED AND CLUMPY

RICH AND CLOYING

Some early tests revealed common problems with this recipe. When we layered the noodles, milk, and cheese (without first cooking them together) in the pan, the fat separated from the cheese and the macaroni and cheese was oily (top left). When we added eggs to the recipe, they curdled and produced a lumpy sauce (top right). Too much cheese made the macaroni so rich you could eat only two or three spoonfuls (bottom).

SCIENCE DESK:
Two Cheeses Are Better Than One

IN TESTING VARIOUS CHEESES FOR OUR RECIPE, WE came upon a dichotomy: Monterey Jack could provide appealing texture but only modest flavor, while cheddar brought the best flavor but rough texture. Curious about this, we started digging for answers.

A major distinction between Monterey Jack and cheddar is moisture content. Government regulations allow Jack cheese to have 5 percent more total moisture than cheddar, and more moisture makes a cheese easier to blend into a liquid. Moreover, cheddar cheese has more fat than Jack cheese. Aside from fat and water content, age also has a profound effect on how a cheese behaves when melted. Monterey Jack is never aged for more than a few months, but cheddar can be aged for years. As cheddar ages, casein, the primary protein in cheese, breaks down, and the strong flavor compounds we associate with good cheddar develop.

What does this difference in age mean for cheese sauce? Cheddar, particularly older cheddar, is gritty because the casein structure has been broken down. In contrast, Monterey Jack is creamy because the casein structure is more intact and better able to retain fat and moisture.

GETTING IT RIGHT: How Cheese Melts

When cheddar is melted (right), the fat separates from the cheese. Monterey Jack (left) has a higher moisture content and looks creamier when melted, with less separation.

TASTING LAB: Microwave Popcorn

CHOOSING A MICROWAVE CAN BE EASIER THAN choosing a brand of microwave popcorn. We narrowed the field to nine popular brands. We selected the most basic butter flavor each brand offered; no "butter light" or "butter bonanza." We also threw in some "homemade" microwave popcorn, popping kernels in a paper bag in the microwave and then dousing them with fresh melted butter.

Tasters were asked to give each sample an overall score, as well as to score the popcorns on the following characteristics: buttery, artificial, and corn-y. We discovered what tasters looked for in popcorn: good corn flavor, nothing artificial, and a moderate amount of butter flavor—not too much and not too little. Our top two overall finishers, homemade and Newman's Own, were ranked among the lowest for artificiality and the highest for corniness, and they were right in the middle of the pack when it came to butteriness. Ironically, the two brands deemed the most buttery, Orville Redenbacher and Pop Secret, were also deemed the most artificial and ranked at the bottom of the tasting.

The real surprise of the tasting was the showing of the "homemade" popcorn, which barely squeaked a victory over Newman's Own. Though many tasters praised the real butter flavor of our fresh popped, several described that popcorn as soggy or greasy. Most of the commercial popcorns were flavored with a dry butter powder, which lent a buttery flavor (sometimes) but not a buttery texture. That real butter texture was more appealing when the homemade popcorn was warm, but when the popcorn cooled, it became soft and greasy.

The benefit of popping your own, other than the monetary savings (kernels cost about half as much as packaged microwave popcorn), is that you control the flavor and can add as much butter, salt, or any other seasoning you wish. However, for true convenience and a taste that's almost as good as homemade, choose Newman's Own Butter.

Rating Microwave Popcorns

EIGHTEEN MEMBERS OF THE *COOK'S ILLUSTRATED* STAFF TASTED ALL OF THE POPCORNS AT ROOM TEMPERATURE—IT wasn't possible to taste them hot, so we decided to cool all samples to the same temperature. The popcorns are listed in order of preference based on their scores in this tasting. All brands are available in supermarkets nationwide.

RECOMMENDED
Kernels and Butter **$3.69 for 30 ounces**
We popped our corn in a paper bag and added melted butter. Tasters praised the flavor—"nice toastiness" and "tastes like real butter, yum!"—but weren't wild about the soft texture.

RECOMMENDED
Newman's Own Oldstyle Picture Show Butter Popcorn **$2.49 for 10.5 ounces**
We liked the "good corn flavor" of this popular brand, and most panelists agreed that it was "real tasting."

RECOMMENDED
Shaw's Theater Style Extra Butter Popcorn **$1.59 for 9 ounces**
This inexpensive supermarket brand was described as "quite buttery" and "pretty good, really."

RECOMMENDED
Guiltless Gourmet Butter Popcorn **$3.29 for 10.5 ounces**
Tasters liked the "good corn flavor" but complained that there was "no discernible butter."

RECOMMENDED
Act II Butter Popcorn **$1.99 for 10.5 ounces**
"Average" and "salty" were the best comments this sample could muster.

NOT RECOMMENDED
Healthy Choice Butter Popcorn **$2.49 for 8.55 ounces**
"Dry" and "artificial" was the consensus about this low-fat brand.

NOT RECOMMENDED
Orville Redenbacher's Butter Popcorn **$2.49 for 10.5 ounces**
One taster summed up: "can't taste the corn for all that fake butter."

NOT RECOMMENDED
Pop Secret Butter Popcorn **$2.29 for 10.5 ounces**
"Greasy" and "off tasting" were common complaints.

NOT RECOMMENDED
Newman's Own Pop's Corn (Organic) Butter Popcorn **$2.69 for 10.5 ounces**
The organic version of our winner was deemed "dry and dusty," with one taster complaining that it "tastes like dried shrimp."

NOT RECOMMENDED
Black Jewell Butter Popcorn **$2.99 for 10.5 ounces**
This low-fat sample was "hard and chewy" and tasted "kinda burnt."

Julia demonstrates the classic restaurant method for cutting up a lobster and then pan-roasting and flambéing it.

RESTAURANT COOKING
CHAPTER 9
comes home

Have you ever been tempted to prepare a restaurant recipe only to be disappointed with the results? The recipe sounded great, but once you got to work you realized it was never tested in a home kitchen. Many restaurant recipes require a professional stove, hard-to-find ingredients, and skills that most home cooks simply don't possess.

But there is something awe-inspiring about good restaurant cooking. The combinations of flavors and textures are exciting, and the presentation usually exceeds anything you might ordinarily attempt at home.

Our test kitchen staff eats in a lot of restaurants, and we decided to take some of our favorite chefs' recipes and make them work in a home kitchen. This meant improvising with equipment, ingredients, and techniques, but the results in this chapter will put restaurant creations within reach for the ambitious home cook.

CRAB TOWERS WITH AVOCADO AND GAZPACHO SALSAS

WHAT WE WANTED: To take a stunning appetizer with 35 ingredients and three separate components, plus garnishes, and re-create it at home.

Developing a menu for a large hotel restaurant allows you abundant freedom that you won't find in a standard restaurant, thanks to access to endless ingredients and many able hands to prepare them. A hotel kitchen staff wouldn't break a sweat preparing multi-component appetizers using more than 35 ingredients. The Crab Tower at the Mayflower Park Hotel in Seattle is a prime example of such hotel kitchen exuberance. It is a tidy, striated tower composed of three salads—an avocado–hearts of palm salsa, a crab salad, and a gazpacho salsa—garnished with frisée lightly dressed in a champagne vinaigrette, pea tendrils, grapefruit segments, and minced chives. Although replicating this dish sounds like a huge undertaking, we found a few ways to simplify the recipe without losing either its flavor or its impressive appearance.

Breaking the plate down into its various components, we focused on each component separately before combining them on the plate. All in all, the focus of this dish is on the crab, so we began with the crab salad. In the test kitchen, we prefer Atlantic blue crabmeat. Sold in both lump and backfin forms, the lump offers tender pieces of crab, while the backfin has a more shredded texture. Both types work in this recipe, although tasters preferred the bite-size pieces of lump to the shredded backfin. The cost, however, may make the decision between the two for you—lump can cost up to twice as much as backfin.

To make the crab salad, the Mayflower mixes the crab-meat with a little mayonnaise and a champagne vinaigrette. When preparing the crabmeat, do not rinse it, but rather spread it out on a plate and check for small pieces of shell. Finding that 12 ounces of crabmeat was plenty for six plates, we tossed it with 2 tablespoons of mayonnaise and 3 tablespoons of vinaigrette to produce a flavorful, well-bound salad that highlights crabmeat's naturally sweet flavor.

Next, we focused our attention on the champagne vinaigrette. Because they prepare it in bulk at the hotel, it makes sense that the chefs use it as a flavoring in the crab salad, as well as to dress the frisée garnish. Figuring that we needed a total of 4 tablespoons of vinaigrette, we pared down the Mayflower's 8-cup recipe, which called for two types of oil; we simplified the ingredients to include only olive oil. Other ingredients we included were champagne vinegar, lemon zest, Dijon mustard, salt, and pepper.

Moving on to the avocado–hearts of palm salsa, we figured that our six plates would require a total of 3 cups of salsa. Because we had a hard time finding decent-tasting hearts of palm with any regularity, we decided to omit them, using three avocados and an appropriate amount of the recipe's original seasonings—lime and coriander. Tasters liked the clean, streamlined avocado flavor in combination with the array of other ingredients.

We next turned our attention to the gazpacho salsa, which contained 16 ingredients (eight of which are time-consumingly cut into small dice). We simplified the recipe, which yielded three times more than we needed, by cutting both ingredients and amounts. Although it called for both yellow and red bell peppers, we decided to use just yellow, which contrasts nicely with the red tomato and green cucumber. We also omitted the ⅛-inch dice of lime and orange segments. Not only were they difficult to cut in a tidy fashion, but their juice turned the gazpacho unnecessarily wet. Keeping the sherry vinegar and olive oil, we omitted the other seasonings, including lemon juice, celery salt, and sugar. The result was a crisp, clean flavor and colorful presentation that the tasters liked just as well as the original.

Addressing the last few ingredients used to garnish the plate—dressed frisée, grapefruit segments, pea tendrils, and chives—we omitted both the chives and the hard-to-find,

CRAB TOWERS WITH AVOCADO AND GAZPACHO SALSAS

Serves 6

You can prepare the crabmeat salad and gazpacho salsa several hours ahead of serving, but the avocado salsa should be prepared just before assembly.

crabmeat salad

- 3 tablespoons extra-virgin olive oil
- 1 tablespoon champagne vinegar
- 1 teaspoon minced or grated lemon zest
- ½ teaspoon Dijon mustard
- ½ teaspoon salt
- ⅛ teaspoon ground black pepper
- 2 tablespoons mayonnaise
- 12 ounces lump or backfin Atlantic blue crabmeat, carefully picked over for shell fragments

gazpacho salsa

- 1 small yellow bell pepper, cored, seeded, and cut into ⅛-inch pieces (about ½ cup)
- ½ small cucumber, peeled if desired, seeded, and cut into ⅛-inch pieces (about ½ cup)
- 1 medium plum tomato, cored, seeded, and cut into ⅛-inch pieces (about ½ cup)
- 1 small celery rib, cut into ⅛-inch pieces (about ½ cup)
- ½ small red onion, minced (about ¼ cup)
- ½ small jalapeño chile, stemmed, seeded, and minced
- 1 tablespoon minced fresh cilantro leaves
- ¾ teaspoon salt
- ¼ teaspoon ground black pepper
- 2 tablespoons extra-virgin olive oil
- 1 tablespoon sherry vinegar

avocado salsa

- 3 ripe avocados, cut into ¼-inch dice (see the illustrations on page 115)

sweet-tasting pea tendrils. On their own, the grapefruit segments tasted a bit too tart, so we substituted orange segments, a flavor that we had omitted from the gazpacho salsa.

At the hotel, tall, open-ended metal rings, called timbale rings, are used to build the tall towers of crab and avocado and gazpacho salsas. However, we found that a round biscuit cutter worked just as well after accommodating for its lack of depth (see the illustrations on page 115). Although it sounds a bit fussy, layering the salad into a tall-towered presentation is a simple way to bring the hotel dining experience to the kitchen table.

WHAT WE LEARNED: It's possible to eliminate about a third of the ingredients in the original recipe and still keep the contrasting flavors and textures that make this dish special. And to assemble the towers, biscuit cutters (which most home cooks have on hand) can double for the more traditional timbale rings used in a restaurant.

¼ teaspoon ground coriander
½ teaspoon salt
⅛ teaspoon ground black pepper
2 tablespoons juice from 1 lime

1 cup frisée
2 oranges, peeled using a paring knife and segmented (see the illustrations below), optional

1. FOR THE CRABMEAT SALAD: Whisk the olive oil, champagne vinegar, lemon zest, mustard, salt, and pepper together in a small bowl. Measure 3 tablespoons of the vinaigrette into a medium bowl and mix with the mayonnaise. Add the crabmeat to the mayonnaise mixture and toss to coat. Cover with plastic wrap and refrigerate until needed. Set the remaining vinaigrette aside.

2. FOR THE GAZPACHO SALSA: Toss the yellow bell pepper, cucumber, tomato, celery, red onion, jalapeño, cilantro, salt, pepper, olive oil, and sherry vinegar in a medium bowl and set aside.

3. FOR THE AVOCADO SALSA: Toss the avocado, coriander, salt, pepper, and lime juice in a medium bowl and set aside.

4. TO ASSEMBLE: Place a 3-inch-wide round biscuit cutter in the center of an individual plate. Following the illustrations on page 115, use a slotted spoon to press ⅓ cup of the Avocado Salsa into the bottom of the cutter using the back of a soup spoon. Lift the cutter off the plate slightly to reveal some but not all of the avocado. Holding the cutter aloft, press ⅓ cup of the Crabmeat Salad evenly into the cutter on top of the avocado. Lift the cutter farther to reveal some but not all of the crab salad. Holding the cutter aloft, use a slotted spoon to press ⅓ cup of the Gazpacho Salsa evenly into the cutter on top of the crab. Gently lift the cutter up and away from the plate to reveal the crab tower. Repeat the procedure five more times with the remaining ingredients.

5. Dress the frisée with the remaining champagne vinaigrette. Place a few sprigs of the dressed frisée on top of each crab tower and arrange the orange segments, if using, around the towers. Serve immediately.

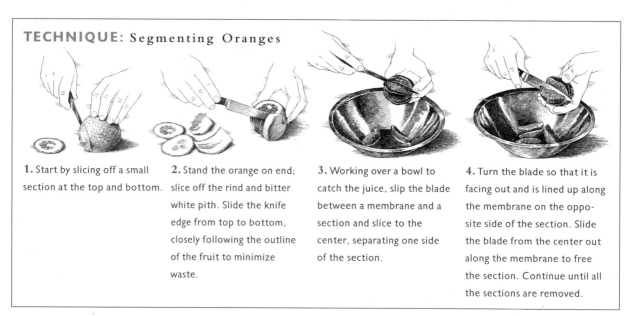

TECHNIQUE: Segmenting Oranges

1. Start by slicing off a small section at the top and bottom.

2. Stand the orange on end; slice off the rind and bitter white pith. Slide the knife edge from top to bottom, closely following the outline of the fruit to minimize waste.

3. Working over a bowl to catch the juice, slip the blade between a membrane and a section and slice to the center, separating one side of the section.

4. Turn the blade so that it is facing out and is lined up along the membrane on the opposite side of the section. Slide the blade from the center out along the membrane to free the section. Continue until all the sections are removed.

TECHNIQUE: Assembling Crab Towers

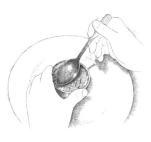

1. Place the biscuit cutter in the center of the plate and, using the back of a soup spoon, press ⅓ cup of the Avocado Salsa evenly into the cutter.

2. Lift the cutter off the plate slightly to reveal some but not all of the avocado.

3. Holding the cutter aloft, press ⅓ cup of the Crabmeat Salad evenly into the cutter, on top of the avocado.

4. Lift the cutter farther off the plate to reveal some but not all of the crab mixture and press ⅓ cup of the Gazpacho Salsa evenly into the cutter, on top of the crab.

5. Gently lift the cutter up and away from the plate to reveal the crab tower.

TECHNIQUE: Dicing Avocado

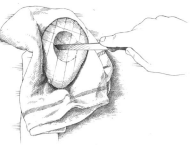

1. Halve and pit the avocado. Hold one half steady in a dish towel. Make ¼-inch crosshatch incisions in the flesh with a dinner knife, cutting down to but not through the skin.

2. Separate the diced flesh from the skin by inserting a soup spoon or rubber spatula between the skin and the flesh, gently scooping out the diced avocado.

FLAMBÉED PAN-ROASTED LOBSTER

WHAT WE WANTED: An alternative to the usual boiled or steamed lobster that would not take much longer to prepare but would deliver tastier results.

When it comes to lobster, most people follow the tried-and-true method and boil it, serving the whole crustacean with a side of drawn butter and a bib. Not that there's anything wrong with tradition, but Jasper White, the renowned New England–based chef and owner of the Summer Shack in Cambridge, Massachusetts, has long applied another practice that we think—at the risk of sounding heretical—produces tastier results. White "pan-roasts" his lobster, employing a combination of high-heat stovetop cooking, broiling, and flambéing. The intense heat yields very rich-flavored, succulent lobster meat—nothing rubbery or bland here. And to replace the side of butter, White whips up a quick pan sauce from the lobster drippings, shallots, bourbon, and tomalley, the lobster's liver. Everything's feasible for the home cook, and we highly recommend that

lobster lovers give this dish a whirl, though be forewarned: the bravura cooking method takes some steely nerves and kitchen confidence.

Progress no further if you are unwilling to cut up a live lobster. Some people—even a few pacifists in the test kitchen—are unwilling to commit the deed, so we fully understand any reticence. The first step in preparing the dish is halving the lobster lengthwise and then crosswise, separating the head from the tail and the claws from the body. The head doesn't contain much meat, but it does lend flavor to the dish, so we include it. The best tool for the job is a large heavy-duty chef's knife or cleaver, which can easily puncture the hard shell without damage to the blade. Center the blade on the lobster's upper portion (that is, the head) and give it a sturdy whack with a mallet. The blade should cleanly cleave the lobster in two. If the knife's blade is short, you may need to finish splitting the tail. The halved lobster may twitch a bit, but it's strictly reflexive—by no means is it alive at this point. The claws can be easily cut at their narrow junction with the body. The legs should be left attached; they don't have much meat inside, but they're great to nibble on.

The lobsters are now ready for cooking. The original recipe specifies heating the skillet on the stovetop over high heat for upward of five minutes before adding the peanut oil and segmented lobsters, but we found this a little dangerous for the home kitchen. Instead, we preferred to heat the oil in the skillet over high heat until smoking. The lobsters are added to the pan shell-side down; otherwise the meat overcooks. The high heat effectively roasts the shells, which imbues the meat with an intense, almost nutty flavor. When the shells are flame red and lightly speckled with browned or blackened spots, the pan is transferred to the broiler to cook the exposed meat.

Now the recipe starts getting really interesting. The skillet is removed from the broiler and returned to the

stovetop, and the lobster is flambéed with a shot of bourbon or cognac. For those who have never flambéed before, it's a little intimidating, but fun, too. And it's for more than just show: In a side-by-side taste test using shrimp and bourbon, we found the flambéed shrimp more fully flavored than those in which the bourbon had simply been reduced. In a restaurant kitchen, there's little worry about setting things alight, but the home kitchen presents a different story. White specifies ¼ cup of bourbon, enough to send a two-foot curtain of flames skyward when ignited—way too dangerous for the home kitchen. For a safer method, we allow the bourbon to reduce for 10 seconds prior to ignition. The flames are lower and the flavor the same. A long fireplace or grill match is the safest bet for lighting the alcohol.

After the lobster is flambéed, it is removed from the pan, and what is essentially a classic pan sauce is quickly "built" in the skillet. Shallots are sautéed and the reserved tomalley and a splash of white wine are added. Despite its unappetizing hue, the tomalley packs an intense flavor and is important to the end result. But if tomalley leaves you cold, exclude it; the sauce will still taste fine. Drizzled with the sauce, the lobster makes for messy eating (and still requires a bib), but it's well worth it.

WHAT WE LEARNED: Pan-roast quartered lobsters in a hot skillet with the shells facing down. Transfer the pan to the broiler to cook the exposed meat. Return the pan to the stovetop to flambé the lobster. Finally, set the lobster aside on a plate while you make a quick pan sauce with shallots, white wine, and herbs.

FLAMBÉED PAN-ROASTED LOBSTER

Serves 2

If you want to prepare more than two lobsters, we suggest that you engage some help. This dish requires close attention, and managing multiple extremely hot pans can be tricky. Before flambéing, make sure to roll up long shirtsleeves, tie back long hair, turn off the exhaust fan (otherwise the fan may pull up the flames), and turn off any lit burners (this is critical if you have a gas stove). For equipment, you will need a large ovensafe skillet, oven mitts, a pair of tongs, and long fireplace or grill matches.

> 2 live lobsters (1½ to 2 pounds each)
> 2 tablespoons peanut or canola oil
> ¼ cup bourbon or cognac
> 6 tablespoons (¾ stick) unsalted butter, cut into 6 pieces
> 2 medium shallots (6 tablespoons), minced
> 3 tablespoons dry white wine
> 1 teaspoon minced fresh tarragon leaves
> 1 tablespoon minced fresh chives
> Salt and ground black pepper
> 1 lemon, cut into wedges (optional)

1. TO QUARTER THE LOBSTERS: Using a large, heavy-duty chef's knife or cleaver, which can easily puncture the hard shell without damage to the blade, center the blade lengthwise on the lobster's upper portion (its head) and give it a sturdy whack with a mallet. Place the blade crosswise behind the lobster's head and split again. Break the claws free from the head and, using a spoon, remove and reserve the green tomalley, if desired. Keep the split lobsters shell-side down. (Don't be put off if the lobsters continue to twitch a little after quartering; it's a reflexive movement.)

2. TO COOK THE LOBSTERS: Adjust an oven rack so it is 6 inches from the broiler element and heat the broiler. Heat the peanut oil in a large ovensafe skillet over high heat until smoking. Add the lobster pieces shell-side down in a single layer and cook, without disturbing, until the shells are bright red and lightly browned, 2 to 3 minutes. Transfer the skillet to the broiler and cook until the tail meat is just opaque, about 2 minutes.

3. Carefully remove the pan from the oven and return it to the stovetop. Off the heat, pour the bourbon over the lobsters. Wait for 10 seconds, then light a long match and wave it over the skillet until the bourbon ignites. Return the pan to medium-high heat and shake it until the flames subside. Transfer the lobster pieces to a warmed serving bowl and tent with foil to keep warm.

4. TO FINISH THE SAUCE: Using tongs, remove any congealed albumen (white substance) from the skillet and add 2 tablespoons of the butter and the shallots. Cook, stirring constantly, until the shallots are softened and lightly browned, 1 to 2 minutes. Add the tomalley and white wine and stir until completely combined. Remove the skillet from the heat and add the tarragon and chives. Stirring constantly, add the remaining 4 tablespoons butter, 1 piece at a time, until fully emulsified. Season with salt and pepper to taste. Pour the sauce over the lobster pieces. Serve immediately, accompanied by the lemon wedges, if desired.

SCIENCE DESK: How a Flambé Works

A FLAMBÉ LOOKS IMPRESSIVE AND IS EASY ENOUGH TO execute, but how does it actually work? Is it just for show or does flambéing make a flavor difference? In tests we have noticed that sauces made with flambéed alcohol usually taste richer and sweeter than sauces made with alcohol that has been simmered. But we wondered why.

A flambé is the ignition of the alcohol vapor that lies above the pan, a reaction that generates significant amounts of heat. To measure this heat, we used an infrared thermometer and discovered that the temperature at the surface of the alcohol quickly climbed past 500 degrees; this

heat would indeed change the chemistry of the bourbon or cognac below. Curious to know whether the high heat served to remove all of the alcohol from the pan, we sent a sample of the completed sauce to the lab for alcohol analysis. The flambé removed most of the alcohol, but what was the high heat doing to the flavor?

Many of the great, flavor-boosting chemical reactions of cooking require high heat. Reactions involving sugar, such as caramelization and browning, occur at temperatures higher than 300 degrees. Because the surface of the sauce had reached above 500 degrees, we noticed some of this type of flavor development. Simmered alcohol, in contrast, maintains a steady heat of about 180 degrees. Another benefit of the flambé is that at very high heat many molecules absorb enough energy to isomerize, or change shape. The consequences of this reconfiguration might include improved solubility and changed flavor perception.

The mystery was solved. A flambéed sauce burns off most of its alcohol but gains flavor from several high-heat cooking reactions. The final result is a sauce with a hint of alcohol and great depth of flavor.

EQUIPMENT CORNER: Meat Cleavers

EVERY GOOD COOK HAS A FAVORITE KNIFE. FOR SOME, it is an impeccably honed chef's knife that can reduce an onion to confetti in a matter of seconds. For others, it is a paring knife so beloved that they do not even own a vegetable peeler. For many of us in the test kitchen, it is a perfectly balanced meat cleaver possessing a blade as sharp as a Lady Bic and as strong as a woodman's axe. But does it matter which brand? We asked five test cooks to evaluate the performance of five brands of meat cleavers based on their comfort, balance, and performance.

A cleaver comes in especially handy when chopping up meat and bones for a stock. It's also great when dealing with lobster. Capitalizing on the opportunity to release some stress, the testers chopped chicken wings, breasts, legs,

and thighs with each cleaver and recorded their conclusions. The best of the lot was the Global 6-Inch Meat Cleaver ($110), which featured a razor-sharp blade and perfectly balanced design that easily finished hacking jobs none of the other cleavers could tackle. For a more reasonable price of $40, the LamsonSharp 7-Inch Meat Cleaver offered a comfortable handle, a sharp blade, and a comparatively light weight, which made it popular among testers with less arm strength.

Of the other models tested, both the J.A. Henckels Professional S 6-Inch Cleaver ($50) and the Wüsthof Trident 6-inch Cleaver ($70) provided good control, though some testers felt the squared-off handles did not provide a secure grip. Other testers, however, praised the Henckels for being substantial without being too heavy.

Bringing up the rear was the Forschner (Victorinox) Fibrox 6-inch Household Cleaver ($71), which had two major strikes against it: It featured a wooden handle whose porous construction could cause cross–contamination, and its thick blade was not sharp enough for many testers, requiring the use of a sawing motion rather than a quick chop.

Although the meat cleaver may not be the go-to knife for carving a turkey or peeling an apple, it is certainly an invaluable tool in the kitchen. Its formidable size and weight make it a formidable adversary to even the toughest bone or shell.

Rating Meat Cleavers

WE TESTED FIVE MEAT CLEAVERS FOR THEIR COMfort, balance, and performance while cutting through meat and bone. The tests were conducted with chicken parts and were performed by five different members of our test kitchen, possessing various hand sizes and arm strengths. The meat cleavers are listed in order of preference. See www.americastestkitchen.com for up-to-date prices and mail-order sources for top-rated products.

HIGHLY RECOMMENDED
Global 6-Inch Meat Cleaver $110
Perfectly balanced, with a razor-sharp blade and a very handsome appearance. Easily handled tasks that stymied other meat cleavers, but this type of performance doesn't come cheap.

RECOMMENDED
LamsonSharp 7-Inch Meat Cleaver $40
This model was lightweight, with a comfortable handle and a thin, sharp blade. It was praised for both performance and value.

RECOMMENDED WITH RESERVATIONS
J.A. Henckels Professional S 6-Inch Cleaver $50
Some testers thought that the small handle on this model was difficult to grip. Did not always chop cleanly through the chicken.

RECOMMENDED WITH RESERVATIONS
Wüsthof Trident 6-Inch Cleaver $70
This cleaver was unbalanced because the handle was heavier than the blade. Additionally, this cleaver tended to shatter the chicken bones.

NOT RECOMMENDED
Forschner (Victorinox) Fibrox 6-inch Household Cleaver $71
Criticized for being too heavy and unwieldy, the blade of this cleaver was also described as thick and dull.

We turned the alley behind the test kitchen into a little bit of Texas as we barbecued beef ribs.

TEXAS rib house

CHAPTER 10

In Texas, good beef ribs are the secret handshake between experienced grillers. With a price tag of roughly $2 a pound and availability at nearly every butcher counter (they are the scrap bones from trimming rib-eye steaks), beef ribs manage to maintain a cool, cult-like obscurity only because their more popular porky brethren hog all the attention. Cost and anonymity aside, it is their huge meaty flavor—combined with spice, smoke, and fire—that epitomizes beef barbecue for many serious Texans.

Could we figure out how to make authentic Texas beef ribs in the alley behind our Boston test kitchen? Could we learn the secret handshake? We knew this recipe would be a challenge to produce, but we think we've succeeded.

And, to our mind, you can't serve ribs without some cornbread. And it better not be the fluffy, cakey, sweet stuff you might see up North. No, we wanted the crusty, baked-in-a-skillet cornbread served throughout the South.

TEXAS BEEF RIBS

WHAT WE WANTED: To re-create authentic Texas barbecued ribs—with their intense beef flavor—at home.

Reckoning that we'd better get a sense of what authentic Texas beef ribs taste like before we fired up the grill, we flew to Texas and spent a hot day driving around Austin and neighboring towns to check out some of the country's best rib joints and roadside stands. Sampling plates of beef ribs throughout the day, we were repeatedly surprised by how much they weren't like what we thought of as barbecued ribs. The meat was not fall-off-the-bone tender but actually required a small toothy tug, and the immense, meaty flavor of the ribs was relatively unadorned by spice rubs and sticky sauces. In fact, if we hadn't been looking for evidence of a spice rub, we might have missed it all together. Served dry with a vinegary dipping sauce on the side, the ribs did not boast a lot of smoke flavor, either; instead, the smoke served as a backdrop for the incredible beefy flavor.

How were these surprisingly flavorful ribs—basically bones lined with juicy steak trimmings—produced? That became our problem. The various barbecue chefs we talked to at each stop simply set dials and pushed buttons on gargantuan, electric smokers outfitted with automated temperature controls. We flew home having learned nothing of value in terms of backyard cooking in a simple kettle-style grill, but at least we knew exactly what we were looking for: potent meat flavor with a bit of honest Texas chew.

Back in Boston, our first task was to track down beef ribs at the local supermarket. Known to butchers as beef back ribs (not to be confused with beef short ribs), they were in fact widely available; we probably had been reaching over them for years. Because these ribs are often considered scrap bones (especially by Yankee butchers), the real challenge is finding any with a decent amount of meat (see "Where's the Beef?" on page 124), and we learned the hard way that skimpy ribs are simply not worth cooking.

There is a membrane with a fair amount of fat that runs along the backside of the bones, and we tested the effects of removing it, scoring it, and leaving it alone. A number of the recipes we had looked at provided detailed instructions on how to remove the membrane using a screwdriver (no joke), but we found this step to be wholly unnecessary, as it resulted in drier meat. Scoring the membrane with a sharp knife also failed to wow tasters; now the ribs presented relatively dry meat as well as a shaggy appearance. The best results—the juiciest meat with the most flavor—were had by means of the easiest route: simply leaving the membrane in place. The fat not only bastes the ribs as they cook but also renders to a crisp, bacon-like texture, which one old local told us is called candy—and a real Texan never trims away the candy.

Moving on to the rub, we remembered the comments of one Austin cook, who said, "It's not about what you put on beef ribs that makes the difference, it's what you leave off." Using a simple mixture of salt, pepper, cayenne, and chili powder, we found that a mere 2 teaspoons rubbed into each rack were all that it took to bring out the flavor of the meat. We then tested the effects of rubbing the slabs and refrigerating them, both wrapped in plastic and unwrapped, on wire racks for two days, one day, and one hour versus the effects of rubbing a slab and cooking it straight away. Surprisingly, we found that the differences in flavor were not the result of the rub's having infiltrated the meat but rather the result of the aging of the beef. Here in the test kitchen, we have generally found that aged beef roasts take on a pleasant hearty flavor. In this case, however, the aged ribs were a bust. They tasted sour and smelled tallowy. We did make one useful discovery, though: Ribs left at room temperature for an hour cooked through more evenly.

The next question was how to turn a kettle grill into a backyard smoker. The first step was choosing the correct

fuel. Hardwood charcoal was out; briquettes burn cooler and longer, making them perfect for barbecue. We had already discovered that cooking the ribs directly over the briquettes didn't work—the ribs burned long before they had cooked through and turned tender. We needed indirect heat, and there were two ways to get it. We could bank all of the coals on one side of the grill, or we could create two piles on opposite sides. A single pile on one side of the grill proved best, providing a slow, even fire that was easy to stoke with fresh coals and left more room for the ribs.

In Texas, barbecue fanatics can be particular about the kind of wood they use to create smoke, so we tested the three most popular varieties: hickory, mesquite, and green oak. The green oak had a clean, gentle smoke that was mild and pleasant, but this wood was hard to find. Dried hickory chunks offered a similar flavor profile and were easy to locate at a hardware store. Mesquite, on the other hand, had a fake, pungent flavor that tasters universally hated. We then wondered if chips (rather than chunks) wrapped in a foil packet were as good. No, they reduced the heat of the charcoal (the aluminum foil acted as a shield), whereas the chunks extended its burning power, acting as a fuel source.

Not wanting the meat to taste too smoky, we then tested the difference among using one, two, and three medium-size (about 2 ounces each) chunks (all soaked in water, as dry chunks burn rather than smoke). One chunk was too little, three were too many, but two were just right. We tried adding both chunks to the fire right at the beginning versus adding just one and letting it burn out before adding the second. Tasters favored the ribs smoked steadily during the entire cooking time, which is how an electric smoker works. These ribs had a more complex flavor than those that were bombarded with lots of smoke at the beginning.

Inspired by the temperature-controlled smokers we saw in Texas, we decided to use an indoor oven to test various cooking temperatures. We would then go back outside to the grill to apply what we'd learned. We tested more than 15 combinations of time and temperature until we got it right. The first thing we learned was that the cooking temperature should never exceed 300 degrees. Higher temperatures render too much fat and turn the meat dry and stringy. Yet the temperature should not dip below 250 degrees. At that temperature the fat won't render, the meat stays tough, and the ribs never achieve that signature roasted beefy flavor. The ideal temperature, then, was a range of 250 to 300 degrees, and the ideal time was about 2½ hours, which causes some, but not all, of the fat to render and makes the ribs juicy, tender, and slightly toothy. When cooked any longer, as is the case with pork ribs, the meat disintegrates into messy shreds, taking on a sticky, pot-roasted sort of texture that any real Texan would immediately reject.

Now we were ready to go back to the grill and add the finishing touches. The first problem was maintaining a constant temperature. The solution was to count out exactly 30 briquettes (and one wood chunk) to start, which brought the grill up to 300 degrees. Over the next hour, the grill cooled to 250 degrees, and it became necessary to add another 20 briquettes along with the second wood chunk. We also found that the top vents should be open two thirds of the way and positioned at the side of the grill opposite from the wood chunk, so that the smoke is drawn across the grill, not straight up and out.

So, yes, you can make authentic Texas ribs at home, with big beef flavor, great chew, and just a hint of smoke and spice. The secret handshake? Confidence. Let the wood and smoke do their work without constant peeking and checking. Don't mess with Texas ribs.

WHAT WE LEARNED: Buy the meatiest ribs you can find, keep the spice rub simple, and barbecue them over a 250- to 300-degree fire with a couple of wood chunks until the ribs are tender but still have some chew.

TEXAS-STYLE BARBECUED BEEF RIBS

Serves 4

It is important to use beef ribs with a decent amount of meat, not bony scraps; otherwise, the rewards of making this recipe are few. For more information about what to look for when buying ribs, see the photos on this page. Because the ribs cook slowly and for an extended period of time, charcoal briquettes, not hardwood charcoal (which burns hot and fast), make a better fuel. That said, do not use Match Light charcoal, which contains lighter fluid for easy ignition. For the wood chunks, use any type of wood but mesquite, which can have an overpowering smokiness. It's a good idea to monitor the grill heat; if you don't own a reliable grill thermometer, insert an instant-read thermometer into the lid vent to spot-check the temperature. Except when adding coals, do not lift the grill lid, which will allow both smoke and heat to escape. When barbecuing, we prefer to use a Weber 22-inch kettle grill.

4 teaspoons chili powder
½ teaspoon cayenne
2 teaspoons salt
1½ teaspoons ground black pepper
3–4 beef rib slabs (3 to 4 ribs per slab, about 5 pounds total)
1 recipe Barbecue Sauce for Texas–Style Beef Ribs (see page 126)

1. Mix the chili powder, cayenne, salt, and pepper in a small bowl; rub the ribs evenly with the spice mixture. Let the ribs stand at room temperature for 1 hour.

2. Meanwhile, cover 2 large wood chunks (see the note above) with water and soak 1 hour; drain. About 20 minutes before grilling, open the bottom grill vents. Using a chimney starter, ignite 30 briquettes (about one third of a large chimney, or 2 quarts) and burn until covered with a thin coating of light gray ash, about 10 minutes. Empty the coals into the grill, then bank the coals against one side of the grill, stacking them 2 to 3 coals high; place 1 soaked wood chunk on top of the coals. Position the grill grate over the coals, cover the grill, and adjust the lid vents two-thirds open. Heat the grate until hot, about 5 minutes (you can hold your hand 5 inches above the grill grate for 2 seconds); scrape the grill grate clean with a grill brush.

3. Position the ribs, meat-side down, on the cool side of the grill (they may overlap slightly); cover, positioning the lid so that the vents are directly above the ribs. (The temperature on a thermometer inserted through the vents should register about 300 degrees.) Cook until the grill temperature

---

GETTING IT RIGHT:
Where's the Beef?

Be careful when shopping for beef ribs—some ribs will yield poor results when barbecued. We prefer partial slabs (with three or four bones) that are very meaty.

TOO SKIMPY
The butcher trimmed too much meat from this slab; you can see the bones.

TOO SMALL
"Shorties" are cut in half and don't offer much meat.

TOO BIG
A whole slab (with seven ribs) is hard to maneuver on the grill.

JUST RIGHT
This partial slab has a thick layer of meat that covers the bones.

drops to about 250 degrees, about 1 hour. (On cold, windy days, the temperature may drop more quickly, so spot-check the temperature. If necessary, add 5 additional briquettes to maintain the temperature above 250 degrees during the first hour of cooking.)

4. After 1 hour, add 20 more briquettes and the remaining wood chunk to the coals. Using tongs, flip the ribs meat-side up and rotate so that the edges once closest to the coals are now farthest away. Cover the grill, positioning the lid so that the vents are opposite the wood chunk. Continue to cook until a dinner fork can be inserted into and removed from the meat with little resistance, the meat pulls away from the bones when the rack is gently twisted, and the meat shrinks ½ to 1 inch up the rib bones, 1¼ to 1¾ hours longer. Transfer the ribs to a cutting board and let rest 5 minutes. Using a chef's knife, slice between the bones to separate into individual ribs. Serve, passing the sauce separately.

VARIATION

TEXAS-STYLE BARBECUED BEEF RIBS ON A GAS GRILL

On a gas grill, leaving one burner on and turning the other(s) off simulates the indirect heat method on a charcoal grill. Use wood chips instead of wood chunks and a disposable aluminum pan to hold them. On a gas grill, it is important to monitor the temperature closely; use an oven thermometer set on the grate next to the ribs and check the temperature every 15 minutes. Try to maintain a 250- to 300-degree grill temperature by adjusting the setting of the lit burner.

1. Follow the recipe for Texas-Style Barbecued Beef Ribs through step 1.

2. Cover 3 cups wood chips with water; soak 30 minutes, then drain. Place the wood chips in a small disposable aluminum pan; set the pan on the gas grill burner that will remain on. Turn all the burners to high, close the lid, and

heat the grill until the chips smoke heavily, about 20 minutes (if the chips ignite, extinguish the flames with a water-filled squirt bottle). Scrape the grill grate clean with a grill brush; turn off the burner(s) without wood chips. Position an oven thermometer and the ribs, meat-side down, on the cool side of the grill. Cover and cook 1¼ hours, checking the grill temperature every 15 minutes and adjusting the lit burner as needed to maintain a temperature of 250 to 300 degrees.

TECHNIQUE:
Soak-Ahead Wood Chunks

Wood chunks are essential when barbecuing, and soaking the chunks ensures that they will smoke slowly, giving food great flavor. If you can never remember to soak the wood in advance (it should stay in cold water for 1 hour), try this tip.

1. Soak as many chunks as you like at the same time. Drain the chunks, seal them in a zipper-lock plastic bag, and store them in the freezer.

2. When ready to barbecue, place the frozen chunks on the grill. They defrost quickly and impart as much flavor as freshly soaked chunks.

3. Using tongs, flip the ribs meat-side up and rotate so that the edges once closest to the lit burner are now farthest away. Cover and continue to cook and check/adjust grill temperature until a dinner fork can be inserted into and removed from the meat with a little resistance, the meat pulls away from the bones when the rack is gently twisted, and the meat shrinks ½ to 1 inch up the rib bones, 1 to 1½ hours longer. Transfer the ribs to a cutting board and let rest 5 minutes. Using a chef's knife, slice between the bones to separate into individual ribs. Serve, passing the sauce separately.

BARBECUE SAUCE FOR TEXAS-STYLE BEEF RIBS

Makes 1¾ cups

Every plate of beef ribs we tasted in Texas was accompanied by a simple, vinegary dipping sauce quite unlike the sweet, thick barbecue sauces found in the supermarket. After more than 30 tries, we figured out that the light flavor of tomato juice was the key.

> 2 tablespoons unsalted butter
> ¼ cup minced onion
> 1 medium garlic clove, minced or pressed through a garlic press (about 1 teaspoon)
> 1½ teaspoons chili powder
> 2 cups tomato juice
> ¾ cup distilled white vinegar
> 2 tablespoons Worcestershire sauce
> ½ teaspoon powdered mustard mixed with 1 tablespoon water
> 1 teaspoon minced chipotle chile in adobo
> 2 tablespoons mild or dark (not blackstrap) molasses
> 1½ teaspoons salt
> ¼ teaspoon ground black pepper

Heat the butter in a small nonreactive saucepan over medium heat until foaming. Add the onion and cook, stirring occasionally, until softened, 2 to 3 minutes. Add the garlic and chili powder and cook, stirring constantly, until fragrant, about 20 seconds. Add the tomato juice, ½ cup of the vinegar, the Worcestershire sauce, mustard, chipotle, molasses, and salt. Increase the heat to high and bring to a simmer, then reduce the heat to medium and continue to simmer, stirring occasionally, until the sauce is slightly thickened and reduced to 1½ cups, 30 to 40 minutes. Off the heat, stir in the pepper and remaining ¼ cup vinegar. Cool to room temperature before serving. (The sauce can be refrigerated in an airtight container for up to 4 days; bring to room temperature before serving.)

SCIENCE DESK:
Best Fire for a Barbecue

BARBECUE EXPERTS HAVE PLENTY OF THEORIES AS TO exactly what goes on inside a covered grill, but agreement is hard to come by. In search of wisdom rather than witchcraft, we wanted to see if we could scientifically determine the best way to lay a fire. What, once and for all, really is the best way to arrange the coals to secure evenly, thoroughly, deeply barbecued meat?

To answer this question, we outfitted a Weber kettle grill with five temperature probes, four around the edges of the grill and one in the center. Through holes drilled in the lid, we attached these probes—or thermocouples—to a computer data recorder that would measure the temperature inside the grill every minute for up to two hours. After running more than a dozen tests over a six-week period, we arrived at some answers.

Because barbecue is by definition slow cooking over low heat, the high temperatures produced by so-called direct heat (cooking directly over a pile of coals) are unacceptable. What's wanted is indirect heat, and, in a kettle grill, you can produce indirect heat in one of two ways: by banking two piles of coals on opposite sides of the grill or by banking one pile on one side.

The computer data showed that splitting the coals between two sides produced worrisome temperature spikes. This was unacceptable if the goal was to maintain a near-constant temperature. Moreover, the temperature at different sites in the grill showed significant variation.

If anything, we expected the variation in heat distribution with the single-banked coals to be even worse. With the exception of the probe placed directly over the fire, however, the probes in this case produced temperature readings that were within a few degrees of each other. This was surprising considering that one probe was about twice the distance from the fire as the other three. This was also good news, as it meant that a large part of the cooking area was being held at a pretty constant temperature. The single-banked method also showed almost no heat spikes and held the temperature between the ideal (for barbecue) 250 and 300 degrees for the longest period of time.

The results of these tests, then, seemed clear: It's best to have a single pile of coals rather than two piles, because one source of heat produced steady, evenly distributed heat, while two sources produced greater temperature variation.

But this wasn't the only thing we learned. Barbecue experts often recommend placing the lid vent (or vents) away from the fire, so this is what we'd been doing during testing. Was it really part of the reason why the pile of banked coals was providing even, steady heat? Sure enough, when we placed the open vent directly over the fire, the fire burned hotter and faster. With the vent in this position, a direct convection current was formed inside the egg-shaped

Weber kettle. When the vent was placed away from the fire, a more diffuse convection current ensured a more even distribution of heat. Also important was the degree to which we opened the lid vent. When the vent was opened up completely, the fire burned much hotter, and the heat was less even throughout the grill. The vent is best kept partially cracked. (Close the vent completely, of course, and you risk snuffing out the fire.)

The final, and most important, thing we learned was also probably the most obvious: When you open the lid to check on the progress of your barbecue, you lose all of the even heat distribution that you have worked so hard to establish. Above all, resist the temptation to peek.

SOUTHERN CORNBREAD

WHAT WE WANTED: A crusty, savory Southern-style cornbread baked in a cast-iron skillet.

Although the two ingredient lists may look similar, the cornbreads of the North and South are as different as Boston and Birmingham. White, not yellow, is the cornmeal of choice for Southern-style cornbread. Unlike Northerners, Southerners use only trace amounts of flour, if any, and if sugar is included it is treated like salt, to be measured out in teaspoons rather than by the cup. Buttermilk moistens, bacon drippings enrich, and a combination of baking powder and soda provides lift.

Classic Southern cornbread batter is poured into a scorching hot, greased cast-iron skillet, which causes it to develop a thin, shattery-crisp crust as the bread bakes. At its best, this bread is moist and tender, with the warm fragrance of the cornfield and the subtle flavor of the dairy in every bite. It is the best possible accompaniment to soups, salads, chilis, stews, and, of course, ribs. So we set out to create a recipe for it that would be foolproof.

We began by testing 11 different cornmeals in one simple Southern cornbread recipe. Before the cornmeal tests, we would have bet that color was a regional idiosyncrasy that had little to do with flavor. But tasting proved otherwise. Cornbreads made with yellow cornmeal consistently had a more potent corn flavor than those made with white cornmeal. Although we didn't want Southern cornbread to taste like dessert, we wondered whether a little sugar might enhance the corn flavor. So we made three batches—one with no sugar, one with 2 teaspoons, and one with a heaping tablespoon. The higher-sugar bread was really too sweet for Southern cornbread, but 2 teaspoons of sugar seemed to enhance the natural sweetness of the corn without calling attention to itself.

Most Southern-style cornbread batters are made with just buttermilk, but we found recipes calling for the full range of acidic and sweet dairy products—buttermilk, sour cream, yogurt, milk, and cream—and made batches with each of them. We still loved the pure, straightforward flavor of the buttermilk-based cornbread, but the batch made with sour cream was actually more tasty and baked into a more attractive shape.

At this point we began to feel a little uneasy about where we were taking this bread. A couple of teaspoons of sugar might be overlooked; yellow cornmeal was a big blow; but the sour cream felt like we were crossing the border, giving up our claim to a recipe for Southern cornbread.

So far all of our testing had been done with a composite recipe under which most Southern cornbread recipes seemed to fall. There were two recipes, however, that didn't quite fit the mold—one very rich and one very lean—and now seemed like the right time to give them a try.

After rejecting the rich version as closer to spoonbread, a soufflé-like dish, than cornbread, we went to the other extreme. In this simple version, boiling water is stirred into the cornmeal, then modest amounts of milk, egg, oil, salt, and baking powder are stirred into the resulting cornmeal mush, and the whole thing is baked. So simple, so lean, so humble, so backwater, this recipe would have been easy to pass over. But given our options at this point, we decided to give it a quick test. Just one bite completely changed the direction of our pursuit. Unlike anything we had tasted so far, the crumb of this cornbread was incredibly moist and fine and bursting with corn flavor, all with no flour and virtually no fat.

We were pleased, but since the foundation of this bread was cornmeal mush, the crumb was actually more mushy than moist. In addition, the baking powder, the only dry ingredient left, got stirred into the wet batter at the end. This just didn't feel right.

After a few unsuccessful attempts to make this cornbread less mushy, we started thinking that this great idea was a bust.

In a last attempt to salvage it, we decided to make mush out of only half the cornmeal and mix the remaining cornmeal with the leavener. To our relief, the bread made this way was much improved. Decreasing the mush even further, from a half to a third of the cornmeal, gave us exactly what we were looking for. We made the new, improved cornbread with buttermilk and mixed a bit of baking soda with the baking powder, and it tasted even better. Finally our recipe was starting to feel Southern again. Although we still preferred yellow cornmeal and a sprinkle of sugar, we had achieved a moist, tender, rather fine-crumbed bread without flour, and a

nicely shaped one at that, without sour cream, thus avoiding two ingredients that would have interfered with the strong corn flavor we wanted.

With this new recipe in hand, we performed a few final tests. Our recipe called for 1 tablespoon of oil, but many Southern cornbreads call for no more fat than is needed to grease the pan. We tried vegetable oil, butter, and bacon drippings, as well as a batch with no fat at all. The cornbread with no added fat was a bit less rich than the other batches—good but not great. The butter burned in the oven, so it was out. Oil was fine, but tasters loved the flavor imparted by bacon drippings. Vegetable oil adds no flavor but is the best substitute if you don't have bacon drippings on hand.

Before conducting these cornbread tests, we didn't think it was possible to bake cornbread in too hot an oven, but after tasting breads baked on the bottom rack of a 475-degree oven, we found that a dark brown crust makes bitter bread. We moved the rack up a notch, reduced the oven temperature to 450 degrees, and were thus able to cook many loaves of bread to golden brown perfection.

One final question: Do you need to heat up the skillet before adding the batter? If you're not a Southerner, the answer is no. Although the bread will not be as crisp in an unheated pan, it will ultimately brown up with a longer baking time. If you are a Southerner, of course, the answer is yes. More than the color of the meal or the presence of sugar or flour, cornbread becomes Southern when the batter hits the hot fat in a cast-iron skillet.

WHAT WE LEARNED : An odd recipe actually makes the best cornbread. Combine part of the cornmeal with boiling water, and then stir the buttermilk and egg into this cornmeal mush before adding it to the remaining cornmeal and other dry ingredients. Pour the batter into a hot, greased cast-iron skillet and bake until crusty.

SOUTHERN CORNBREAD

Serves 8

Though some styles of Southern cornbread are dry and crumbly, we favor this dense, moist, tender version. Cornmeal mush of just the right texture is essential to this bread. Make sure that the water is at a rapid boil when it is added to the cornmeal. Though we prefer to make cornbread in a preheated cast-iron skillet, a 9-inch round cake pan or 9-inch square baking pan, greased lightly with butter and not preheated, will also produce acceptable results if you double the recipe and bake the bread for 25 minutes. For information on the use and care of cast-iron skillets, see page 81.

4	teaspoons bacon drippings or vegetable oil
1	cup (about 5 ounces) yellow cornmeal, preferably stone-ground
2	teaspoons sugar
½	teaspoon salt
1	teaspoon baking powder
¼	teaspoon baking soda
⅓	cup rapidly boiling water
¾	cup buttermilk
1	large egg, beaten lightly

1. Adjust an oven rack to the lower-middle position and heat the oven to 450 degrees. Set an 8-inch cast-iron skillet with the bacon drippings in the heating oven.

2. Measure ⅓ cup of the cornmeal into a medium bowl. Whisk the remaining cornmeal, sugar, salt, baking powder, and baking soda together in a small bowl; set aside.

3. Pour the boiling water all at once into the ⅓ cup cornmeal; stir to make a stiff mush. Whisk in the buttermilk gradually, breaking up lumps until smooth, then whisk in the egg. When the oven is preheated and the skillet is very hot, stir the dry ingredients into the mush mixture until just moistened. Carefully remove the skillet from the oven.

Pour the hot bacon fat from the pan into the batter and stir to incorporate, then quickly pour the batter into the heated skillet. Bake until golden brown, about 20 minutes. Remove from the oven and instantly turn the cornbread onto a wire rack. Cool for 5 minutes, then serve immediately.

TASTING LAB: Cornbread Mixes

MAKING CORNBREAD FROM SCRATCH IS NOT DIFFIcult, but with all the mixes on the market we wondered if we could get from-scratch quality out of a box. We gathered seven brands of cornbread mix, including Southern favorites White Lily and Martha White, supermarket staples Jiffy and Betty Crocker, as well as Washington, Krusteaz, and Hodgson Mills, prepared them in the test kitchen, and held a blind tasting.

As easy as our Southern Cornbread is, nothing can beat the convenience of these mixes—just pour into a bowl, add milk (and sometimes egg), mix, and bake. Within 30 minutes, you can have a hot, steaming cornbread on the table. But can the taste come close to homemade? Not remotely.

All seven of the cornbreads were dismissed by tasters as tremendously inferior to homemade. All received scores that hovered just above or below the "Not Recommended" cutoff; three are barely recommended and four are not recommended.

The problem with all of the cornbreads was summed up by one taster who wrote, "Overall, there is no corn flavor; all have an inexplicable savory flavor." Breads were overwhelmingly dry and bland; none tasted like the corn for which they are named. The better-rated cornbreads rated high for sweetness and moistness.

So what to do if you're looking for easy cornbread with great corn flavor and moist texture? Unfortunately, there just isn't any shortcut; you have to make it yourself.

Rating Cornbread Mixes

FIFTEEN MEMBERS OF THE *COOK'S ILLUSTRATED* STAFF TASTED ALL OF THE PRODUCTS PREPARED ACCORDING to the package instructions. The mixes are listed in order of preference based on their scores in this tasting. All of these mixes are available in supermarkets, although several are regional brands.

RECOMMENDED WITH RESERVATIONS
Betty Crocker Golden Corn Muffin and Bread Mix
$.55 for 6.5 ounces, yielding an 8-inch pan of cornbread

Though one vocal fan called it "pretty darn good," most agreed that it was too "coarse," "crumbly," and "dry." The best of a pretty bad bunch.

RECOMMENDED WITH RESERVATIONS
Jiffy Corn Muffin Mix
$.55 for 8.5 ounces, yielding an 8-inch pan of cornbread

Despite its "buttery" flavor and "rustic" texture, this brand was downgraded for being "sandy" (one taster compared it to "a day at the beach") and "way too dry."

RECOMMENDED WITH RESERVATIONS
Washington Corn Muffin Mix
$.45 for 8 ounces, yielding an 8-inch pan of cornbread

Though there was "not much corn flavor," this brand was "moister than most."

NOT RECOMMENDED
Hodgson Mill Cornbread and Muffin Mix
$1.55 for 7.5 ounces, yielding an 8-inch pan of cornbread

Its "dry" texture and "wheaty" flavor had one taster asking, "Is it made with tree bark?"

NOT RECOMMENDED
Krusteaz Honey Cornbread and Muffin Mix
$1.69 for 15 ounces, yielding an 8-inch pan of cornbread

Most tasters compared this brand unfavorably to dry yellow cake. One taster wrote, "like a sponge—not a sponge cake, a sponge."

NOT RECOMMENDED
Martha White Yellow Cornbread Mix
$1.25 for 6.5 ounces, yielding an 8-inch pan of cornbread

Despite one taster detecting "some corn flavor," most tasters agreed that the flavor of this Southern favorite was "flat" and "salty, salty, salty!"

NOT RECOMMENDED
White Lily White Cornbread Mix
$.67 for 6.5 ounces, yielding an 8-inch pan of cornbread

The "bland, very salty" flavor and "lingering chemical aftertaste" led one taster to remark that this Southern favorite "tastes like the box it came from," though it actually came in a bag.

Television requires an army of charcoal grills,
ready to cook tenderloin and more.

GRILL-ROASTED
CHAPTER 11
beef tenderloin

We don't part easily with money, but we will on occasion break the bank and buy a beef tenderloin. The tender, buttery interior is the big draw, and the combination of a healthy dose of seasoning and the flavor from the charcoal grill is a perfect solution to a rather mild-tasting (boring) piece of meat. Recently, we ordered a whole beef tenderloin from a local supermarket. Six pounds of perfectly trimmed tenderloin later, we had shelled out a jaw-dropping $167.94 (that's $27.99 per pound).

We heated up the grill and gingerly placed our new, most valuable possession over the hot coals. Even though we watched it like a hawk, we couldn't get the tenderloin to cook evenly. The exterior was charred and tough; the interior of the fat butt end was pink, and the thinner tail end was beyond well-done. Worst of all, because we were able to season only the exterior of the tenderloin, the interior was bland.

We wondered if there was a way to take this mammoth and insanely expensive cut of beef and grill it to absolute perfection. And, after having spent nearly $170 on a complete flop, we were determined to find a cheaper alternative to supermarket shopping.

GRILL-ROASTED BEEF TENDERLOIN

WHAT WE WANTED: With a whole tenderloin going for as much as $180, uneven cooking, bland flavor, and a tough outer crust just don't cut it. We wanted it cheaper and better.

Great tenderloin begins at the market. At local supermarkets, we learned, whole beef tenderloin isn't a meat case–ready item. Most butchers we talked to said they keep the tenderloins in the back to be cut for filets, so if you want one, you've got to ask for it. When you do ask for whole tenderloin, it will usually come "peeled," which means the outer membrane of fat and sinew has been removed. These peeled tenderloins run anywhere from $13.99 per pound for Choice grade meat to an even more astounding $32.99 per pound for Prime grade at a high-end butcher—that's $200 dollars for a 6-pound roast. At that price, we expect the butcher to come to our house, grill the meat for us, wash the dishes, and throw in a back rub as well.

A few days later, we found ourselves in a wholesale club. No longer just a place to buy giant cans of beans, most wholesale clubs sell meat as well. We soon found ourselves eye-to-eye with a case full of vacuum-sealed, Choice grade, whole tenderloins. If the mountain of meat hadn't caught our attention, the price sure would have. Weighing in at about $9 per pound, these tenderloins were one third the cost of the roast we had bought from our butcher. We grabbed as many as we could stuff into the giant shopping cart and headed back to the kitchen.

We soon discovered the one downside of using the wholesale club tenderloins. They came "unpeeled," so a fair amount of trimming, tugging, and prying was necessary to rid the meat of its fat, sinew, and silver skin. But we had to be judicious, as we found the trimmings could weigh more than 1½ pounds, including the loss of some valuable meat. The best way to trim one of these tenderloins was to first

peel off as much fat as possible with our hands; the fat came away clean and took very little of the pricey meat with it (see illustrations on page 136). Next, we used a flexible boning knife (a sharp paring knife works well in a pinch) to remove the silver skin, the muscle sheath that would otherwise cause the tenderloin to curl up on the grill. Last, we took the advice of many cookbooks and tucked the narrow tip end of the tenderloin under and tied it securely. This tuck-and-tie step gave the tenderloin a more consistent thickness that would allow it to grill more evenly.

Was this extra 20 minutes of preparatory work worth the effort? We got out our calculators and crunched the numbers. Let's see . . . with a loss of about a pound of trimmings, our $48 roast was now divided by the 5 pounds of remaining meat . . . and that came to around $9.60 per pound. You better believe it was worth it! It still was by no means a "cheap" piece of meat, but it didn't empty our wallet.

While some love beef tenderloin for its "mild" beef flavor, others scoff at it for exactly the same reason. We found ourselves in the latter camp and felt that the tenderloin could use a flavor boost. Many recipes suggested marinades, spice rubs, or herb crusts. Tasters rejected the marinated tenderloins for their weird, spongy texture. Spice rubs made the beef taste too much like barbecue (if we wanted barbecue, we'd buy a cheap rack of ribs), while herb rubs were too powerful for such a tame cut of meat. We were looking for a way to enhance the beef flavor, not to mask it.

Then a colleague suggested a recently heralded technique in which the tenderloin is salted and left to sit overnight in the fridge. The theory goes that the salt penetrates the meat all the way to the center, seasoning the tenderloin throughout. Sure enough, the salted-overnight beef was seasoned through and through, but at quite a cost. The meat had turned a sickly brown-gray (even when the center was cooked to medium-rare), and the texture was webby, like that of an undercooked pot roast (see the photo on page 138). We played around a bit with amounts of salt, going up to ¼ cup of kosher salt and down to 1 tablespoon. But it seemed that time was the villain here—an overnight salting was just too much.

For the next round, we went back to the original 1½ tablespoons of kosher salt and rubbed a couple of tenderloins. We wrapped both in plastic and refrigerated one for four hours, the other for one hour. Although both were markedly better than the overnight-salted tenderloin, the winner was the beef that was salted for only one hour. With just enough time for the salt to season the meat without compromising the texture, the salt brought out a decidedly beefier flavor, one that we greatly appreciated. Even better was letting the salted tenderloin sit on the countertop rather than refrigerating it. The big tenderloin lost some of its chill, and it grilled at a more even rate. After scaling the salt back to 1½ tablespoons, we took our well-seasoned tenderloin in hand and headed for the nearest grill.

Up to this point, we had been grilling the tenderloin directly over the hot fire, an approach that burned the outer crust before the interior had a chance to cook properly. We tried a more moderate heat. Now the exterior was no longer scorched, but the outer inch-thick perimeter of the meat was approaching the well-done mark before the interior was cooked.

In a forehead-slapping moment, it struck us that we were treating (and grilling) the tenderloin as a steak and not as what it was—a roast. For our next test, we set up the grill for grill-roasting, in which indirect heat is used to cook the meat. We piled the coals up on one side of the grill, leaving the other side empty, then placed the tenderloin over the empty side (opposite the coals), covered the grill, and left it alone. About 45 minutes later, we knew that we were onto something. The indirect heat had cooked the tenderloin evenly from tip to tip (OK, so the very ends were more well-done), and the meat had taken on a mild, smoky flavor from spending so much time exposed to the hot coals. But we missed the crust that came with searing the meat. The

solution was to first sear the tenderloin over the hot coals on all sides before switching to the cooler (coal-free) side to finish grilling. This was it: a remarkable, well-browned crust and a rosy pink interior. We tried adding a couple of soaked wood chunks to the pile of hot coals, in hopes of imparting even more smoky flavor to the meat. And smoky was just what we got; there was no denying that this cut of meat had been cooked on the grill. (Some in the test kitchen thought the smoke flavor was too strong for the mild beef. For those in this camp, just omit the wood chunks.)

When we cut into a tenderloin right off the grill, it gave off a lot of juice—not a good idea with such a lean piece of meat. The easy solution was to let the meat rest for 10 to 15 minutes before cutting, but during this rest period the meat rose from medium-rare (about 135 degrees) to medium-well (over 150 degrees). We next removed the tenderloin from the grill when the meat was still rare. After resting, the roast was incredibly juicy, with a rosy pink interior, a beautiful dark brown crust, and a smoky, seasoned flavor—all of which was worth every cent we had paid for it.

WHAT WE LEARNED: Buy an unpeeled tenderloin at a warehouse club, take the 20 minutes to trim the fat yourself, and save $100. Tie the roast up (so it cooks evenly) and then salt the meat an hour before it goes onto the grill. Cook the roast over a two-level fire to achieve a nicely browned crust and perfectly even, rosy interior.

GRILL-ROASTED BEEF TENDERLOIN

Serves 10 to 12

Beef tenderloins purchased from wholesale clubs require a good amount of trimming before cooking. At the grocery store, however, you may have the option of having the butcher trim it for you. Once trimmed, and with the butt tenderloin still attached (the butt tenderloin is the lobe attached to the large end of the roast), the roast should weigh 4½ to 5 pounds. If you purchase an already-trimmed tenderloin without the butt tenderloin attached, begin checking for doneness about 5 minutes early. If you prefer your tenderloin without a smoky flavor, you may opt not to use wood chips or chunks. Serve as is or with Salsa Verde (page 141).

1 beef tenderloin (about 6 pounds), trimmed of fat and silver skin (according to the illustrations below), tail end tucked and tied at 2-inch intervals

1½ tablespoons kosher salt
2 tablespoons olive oil
1 tablespoon ground black pepper

1. About 1 hour before grilling, set the tenderloin on a cutting board or rimmed baking sheet and rub with the salt. Cover loosely with plastic wrap and let stand at room temperature. Cover two 2-inch wood chunks with cold water and soak 1 hour; drain.

2. About 25 minutes before grilling, open the bottom grill vents. Using a chimney starter, ignite about 2½ pounds charcoal briquettes (1 large chimney, or 6 quarts) and burn until covered with a layer of light gray ash, about 15 minutes. Empty the coals into the grill and build a two-level fire by arranging the coals to cover one half of the grill, piling them about 3 briquettes high. Set the wood chunks on the coals. Position the grill grate over the coals, cover the grill,

---

TECHNIQUE: Trimming and Tying a Tenderloin

Although wholesale clubs offer whole beef tenderloins at an affordable price, most come unpeeled, with the fat and silver skin (a tough membrane) intact. Here's how to trim and tie a tenderloin for the grill. Expect to lose between 1 and 1½ pounds during the trimming process. A boning knife is the best tool for this job.

1. Pull away the outer layer of fat to expose the fatty chain of meat.

2. Pull the chain of fat away from the roast, cut it off, and discard the chain.

3. Scrape the silver skin at the creases in the thick end to expose the lobes.

4. Trim the silver skin by slicing under it and cutting upward.

5. Remove the remaining silver skin in the creases at the thick end.

6. Turn the tenderloin over and remove the fat from the underside.

and heat the grate until hot, about 10 minutes (the grill should be medium-hot; you can hold your hand 5 inches above the grill grate for 4 seconds). Scrape the grill grate clean with a grill brush.

3. Uncover the tenderloin, coat with the olive oil, and sprinkle all sides with the pepper. Place the tenderloin on the hot side of the grill directly over the coals. Cook until well browned, about 2 minutes, then rotate one quarter turn and repeat until all sides are well browned, a total of 8 minutes. Move the tenderloin to the cooler side of the grill and cover, positioning the lid vents over the tenderloin. Cook until an instant-read thermometer inserted into the thickest part of the tenderloin registers 120 degrees for rare, 16 to 20 minutes, or 125 degrees for medium-rare, 20 to 25 minutes.

4. Transfer the tenderloin to a cutting board, tent loosely with foil, and let rest 10 to 15 minutes. Cut into ½-inch-thick slices and serve.

VARIATION

GRILL-ROASTED BEEF TENDERLOIN ON A GAS GRILL

If you're using a gas grill, wood chips are a better option than wood chunks.

1. Follow step 1 of the recipe for Grill-Roasted Beef Tenderloin, substituting 2 cups wood chips for the wood chunks and soaking the chips 20 minutes. Drain the chips, place in a small disposable foil pan, and cover with heavy-duty foil; poke 6 holes in the foil and set aside.

2. About 20 minutes before grilling, place the wood chip tray on the primary burner (the burner that will remain on during grilling); position the cooking grates. Turn all the burners to high, close the lid, and heat the grill until the chips smoke heavily, about 20 minutes (if the chips ignite, extinguish the flames with a water-filled squirt bottle). Scrape the grill grate clean with a grill brush.

3. Uncover the tenderloin, coat with the olive oil, and sprinkle all sides with the pepper. Place the tenderloin on the side of the grate opposite the primary burner. Grill the tenderloin over the burner(s) without wood chips until well browned, 2 to 3 minutes, then rotate one quarter turn and repeat until all sides are well browned, for a total of 8 to 12 minutes. Turn off all burners except the primary burner (the tenderloin should be positioned over the extinguished burner[s]). Cover and cook until an instant-read thermometer inserted in the thickest part of the tenderloin registers 120 degrees for rare, 16 to 20 minutes, or 125 degrees for medium-rare, 20 to 25 minutes.

4. Transfer the tenderloin to a cutting board, tent loosely with foil, and let rest 10 to 15 minutes. Cut into ½-inch-thick slices and serve.

SCIENCE DESK:
When Should You Salt Meat?

SALTING MEAT IS NOTHING NEW; IT WAS USED CENTUries before refrigeration as a method of preservation. Recently, though, there has been a renewed chorus of voices singing the praises of the simple salt rub, sometimes applied the night before. One might understand why salt could make a tough cut more palatable, but would this technique improve pricey tenderloin?

We found that salting the meat an hour before cooking gave the roast a beefier flavor. A four-hour salt produced much the same results, but salting the roast the night before cooking was a disaster. The roast turned brown. But why?

Anyone who lives in a cold climate knows that the salting of roadways causes cars to rust. This is due to salt's ability to promote oxidation in iron. Salt can also help to oxidize myoglobin, an iron-containing protein that gives meat its red color. The brown-as-pot-roast color of the tenderloin that had been salted overnight indicated that much of the myoglobin had been oxidized and most of its red color lost.

Perhaps the poor color could be excused if the procedure had produced phenomenal flavor. In fact, the opposite was true; the meat was stringy and the flavor was tired. In addition to oxidizing the myoglobin, the salt had drawn water from the meat, causing it to look thready, as if it had been overcooked. Moreover, little of the mild but juicy beef flavor normally associated with tenderloin was present; instead it tasted dull. In the case of tenderloin, which is beautifully textured and delicately flavored out of the package, there is really no good reason to salt for extended periods—unless, of course, you want to pay $9 a pound for pot roast.

OVERNIGHT SALTING
Looks like overcooked pot roast.

ONE-HOUR SALTING
A tender, juicy, and flavorful roast.

TASTING LAB: Beef Tenderloin

WHEN IT COMES TO BUYING A SPECIAL CUT OF BEEF like tenderloin, more and more cooks are bypassing the supermarket and either seeking bargain prices at wholesale clubs or paying a premium for the "specialty" beef available through mail-order sources. Is there a difference between roasts that cost $9 and $55 per pound?

In a blind tasting, we evaluated a broad selection of tenderloins—one from a local supermarket, three from warehouse clubs, and three from well-known mail-order sources. This last group included several Prime roasts; the roasts from the supermarket and warehouse clubs were either Choice or Select, the next two grades down the quality chain and those commonly found in supermarkets. Given the price differential as well as the various grades of beef in the tasting, we were shocked by the results.

As a whole, our panel found only subtle differences in flavor and texture among the seven tenderloins. None of the mail-order tenderloins managed to stand out from the crowd. The top choice came from the supermarket. And our panel's second choice was a Select roast from a warehouse club. Only the previously frozen Omaha Steaks tenderloin failed to please tasters and is not recommended. So when it comes to tenderloin, you don't have to pay a king's ransom for a princely roast.

SO WHAT DO YOU REALLY GET?

The chart on page 139 indicates the price we paid per pound for our tenderloin. But some tenderloins required much more trimming than others. The figures below indicate the edible portion (as a percentage of the initial weight) we obtained once trimming was complete. We then recalculated the prices to indicate what each pound of edible meat really cost us.

So what did we learn? All of the tenderloins purchased at the supermarket and warehouse clubs required more trimming than the mail-order samples but not enough to really affect overall prices. Even taking into account the extra waste on the tenderloins we purchased at warehouse clubs, they averaged just $13 per pound, compared with $23 per pound for our supermarket sample, and from $41 to $57 per pound for the mail-order samples. Note that the tenderloin from Lobel's required no trimming at all, making this expensive mail-order sample the best choice for lazy cooks with money to burn.

	EDIBLE PORTION (after trimming)	ACTUAL COST (per pound)
Stop & Shop	64%	$23.34
BJ's	67%	$13.24
Lobel's	100%	$54.84
Niman Ranch	76%	$57.50
Costco	70%	$12.60
Sam's Club	64%	$13.87
Omaha	80%	$40.94

Rating Beef Tenderloin

NINETEEN MEMBERS OF THE *COOK'S ILLUSTRATED* STAFF TASTED ALL OF THE TENDERLOINS, WHICH HAD BEEN RUBBED lightly with oil, sprinkled with salt and pepper, and roasted in the oven. The tenderloins are listed in order of preference based on their scores in this tasting. Note that prices for mail-order brands have been adjusted to include shipping and handling. The tenderloins varied significantly in the amount of fat that needed to be trimmed. See the chart on page 138 to see how this affected the actual cost.

RECOMMENDED
Stop & Shop Beef Tenderloin
$14.99 per pound

This roast purchased at our local supermarket won the tasting. "The truest, most pure flavor" raved one taster. The "silky," "almost falling apart" meat was especially tender. One panelist summed up, "best texture, nice flavor."

RECOMMENDED
BJ's Beef Tenderloin
$8.89 per pound

This warehouse club tenderloin finished in a strong second place, with comments such as "rich," "tender," and "beefy." Several tasters thought this roast had more fat than the rest of the pack. A few naysayers complained about a "too soft" texture.

RECOMMENDED
Lobel's Beef Tenderloin Roast
$54.84 per pound

This mail-order sample from a famed New York butcher was the only one to arrive in the test kitchen perfectly trimmed and ready to cook. "Great marbling" with "rich," "meaty" flavor. "Like a good steak," wrote one taster, but look at that price.

RECOMMENDED
Niman Ranch Whole Beef Tenderloin
$43.55 per pound

This mail-order brand is a favorite with chefs. There were several complaints about the "chalky" or "dusty" texture. Panelists were divided about the flavor of this roast, calling it "beefy" and "deep" as well as "too strong" and "strange."

RECOMMENDED
Costco Beef Tenderloin
$8.79 per pound

This warehouse club roast earned decent scores, although it didn't really elicit much strong support. Several tasters objected to the "cottony," "mealy" texture. The flavor was described as either "bland" or "mild."

RECOMMENDED
Sam's Club Beef Tenderloin
$8.87 per pound

This warehouse club tenderloin has a lot of personality. Tasters used adjectives such as "gamey" to "metallic" to describe the flavor. The texture was both "chewy on the outside" and "a bit mushy" in the middle.

NOT RECOMMENDED
Omaha Steaks Chateaubriand Roast
$32.60 per pound

This mail-order sample was the only one deemed unacceptable by tasters. It was shipped frozen, and there were many complaints about the texture of the meat, ranging from "powdery" and "gritty" to "wet cardboard" and "gummy."

SALSA VERDE

WHAT WE WANTED: This all-purpose green sauce made from parsley, olive oil, garlic, and vinegar can be overwhelming and harsh, and it easily separates to boot. We wanted a smooth sauce to accompany grilled tenderloin.

The promise of a brilliant green salsa verde is clear enough. It suggests the possibility of culinary wizardry, transforming a host of bland, forgettable dishes into something memorable. The ingredients are simple enough: parsley, olive oil, lemon juice or vinegar, something pickled or brined (capers, cornichons, and/or green olives), garlic, and sometimes anchovies. Despite its innate simplicity, salsa verde can easily go wrong. In fact, many of the recipes we tested were overly potent and harsh, leaving tasters with puckered lips and raging garlic breath. The texture was problematic, too; all of our initial salsas separated into pools of oil and clumps of parsley. Our intent was to create a balanced yet still bold sauce with a thick, uniform texture.

We started with the parsley. Previous analysis in our test kitchen revealed that Italian, or flat-leaf, parsley is preferable to curly parsley for its fresh, tender flavor, when parsley is a dominant ingredient. Extra-virgin olive oil, red wine vinegar, green olives, a couple of anchovy fillets, and a large clove of garlic completed our starting recipe. The resulting sauce was too tangy and sharp, even in small bites, and the solids collected on the bottom of the bowl, while the oil rested on top. When we reduced the quantity of vinegar, the sauce became dull and flat-tasting. Decreasing the amount of anchovies, garlic, and olives had the same effect. We were at a standstill.

Additional research turned up two possibilities. One recipe called for the addition of hard-cooked egg yolks, while others suggested bread. We assumed that these bland ingredients were included to temper the assertive ones; it was a theory worth testing. The egg yolks did soften the blow of the other flavors, but the sauce tasted fatty and had a mealy texture. (The sauce did not separate, however, which was a major improvement.) Next, we processed chunks of bread with oil and vinegar to create a smooth base, added the remaining ingredients, and crossed our fingers. This sauce was top-notch. The flavors were bright but not aggressive, and the texture was lush and well blended. Further testing proved that airy, moist bread produced gummy sauce. Firm, dry bread with a tight crumb was much better. However, we wanted the option to use whatever bread was on hand. We found that 15 seconds in the toaster dried out even the squishiest bread so that it could be used in this sauce.

We wondered if the parsley should be chopped by hand for maximum flavor. A side-by-side taste test of salsa verde made in the food processor versus finely hand-chopped salsa verde (tasters rejected very roughly chopped sauces) revealed minimal differences; the two were nearly indistinguishable. (Yes, the food processor method won.)

Among olives, capers, cornichons, and combinations thereof, capers alone were the top choice for their salty, pungent bite. As for the acidic component, fresh lemon juice narrowly won out over an array of vinegars. The lemon juice nicely accented the fresh, clean flavor of the parsley. Lemon juice is also less acidic (and less harsh) than most vinegars, which tasters appreciated. When we varied the amount of garlic, tasters favored only one medium clove, preferring to let the flavor of the parsley take center stage. Four anchovy fillets, on the other hand, seemed mandatory, adding a welcome complexity (but not fishiness) to the sauce. A pinch of salt performed its usual work and further improved the sauce.

WHAT WE LEARNED: Start with Italian parsley leaves and add some lightly toasted bread to give the sauce a smooth, well-blended texture. Use lemon juice (rather than vinegar) to keep the sauce from tasting harsh and add garlic sparingly. Finally, capers and anchovies give salsa verde its characteristic piquant flavor.

SALSA VERDE

Makes a generous 1½ cups

Two slices of sandwich bread pureed with the sauce keeps the flavors balanced and gives the sauce texture. Toasting the bread rids it of excess moisture that might otherwise make a gummy sauce. Salsa verde is excellent with grilled or roasted meats, fish, or poultry; poached fish; boiled or steamed potatoes; sliced tomatoes; or as a condiment on sandwiches. It is best served immediately after it is made but can be refrigerated in an airtight container for up to 2 days. If it's refrigerated, bring the sauce to room temperature and stir it to recombine before serving.

    2   large slices white sandwich bread
    1   cup extra-virgin olive oil
    ¼   cup juice from 2 lemons
    4   cups lightly packed fresh Italian parsley leaves,
         washed and dried thoroughly
    4   medium anchovy fillets
    ¼   cup capers, drained
    1   medium garlic clove, minced or pressed through
         a garlic press (about 1 teaspoon)
    ¼   teaspoon salt

1. Toast the bread in a toaster at the low setting until the surface is dry but not browned, about 15 seconds. Cut the bread into rough ½-inch pieces (you should have about 1½ cups).

2. Process the bread pieces, oil, and lemon juice in a food processor until smooth, about 10 seconds. Add the parsley, anchovies, capers, garlic, and salt. Pulse until the mixture is finely chopped (the mixture should not be smooth), about five 1-second pulses, scraping down the bowl with a rubber spatula after 3 pulses. Transfer the mixture to a small bowl and serve.

Q & A

What's the difference between flat-leaf and curly parsley?

Most food professionals use flat-leaf parsley (also called Italian parsley) rather than curly parsley, regarding the latter as pretty but flavorless. To find out if this is true, we chopped up bunches of each and held a taste test. When tossed with hot pasta and garlic, there was little flavor distinction between the two types of parsley. It wasn't until the chopped parsley was tasted alone that we noted differences. On its own, the flat-leaf parsley was preferred for its "fresh," "grassy" flavor and "tender" texture, while some tasters found the curly-leaf parsley to be "bitter" and "tough." The moral of the story? If you're making a dish in which parsley gets star billing, go for flat-leaf. However, if you're sprinkling a little parsley into stew or onto pasta, don't worry if your local supermarket only carries the curly stuff.

VARIATIONS

LEMON-BASIL SALSA VERDE

This variation pairs especially well with fish.

Follow the recipe for Salsa Verde, substituting 2 cups lightly packed roughly chopped fresh basil leaves for 2 cups of the parsley, and adding 1 teaspoon grated lemon zest to the food processor along with the herbs.

SALSA VERDE WITH ARUGULA

Arugula gives this variation a peppery kick that's a nice match for grilled foods.

Follow the recipe for Salsa Verde, substituting 2 cups lightly packed roughly chopped arugula for 2 cups of the parsley.

BROILED ASPARAGUS

WHAT WE WANTED: With tenderloin on the grill, we wanted a simple recipe for cooking asparagus under the broiler that would yield nicely browned, tender spears.

Asparagus presents one main preparation issue—should the spears be peeled, or is it better to discard the tough, fibrous ends entirely? In our tests, we found that peeled asparagus have a silkier texture, but we preferred the contrast between the crisp peel and tender inner flesh. Peeling also requires a lot of work. We prefer to simply snap off the tough ends and proceed with cooking.

The intense dry heat of the broiler concentrates the flavor of the asparagus, and the exterior caramelization makes the spears especially sweet. The result is asparagus with a heightened and, we think, delicious flavor.

The two primary questions related to broiling concerned the thickness of the stalks and the distance they should be kept from the heat sources as they cook. In our tests with thicker asparagus, anywhere from ¾ to 1 inch in diameter, the peels began to char before the interior of the spears became fully tender. When we used thinner spears (no thicker than ⅝ inch), the interior was tender by the time the exterior was browned.

We then focused on how far to keep the spears from the heating element. At 3 inches, the asparagus charred a bit. At 5 inches, the asparagus took a little too long to cook, and they failed to caramelize properly. The middle ground, 4 inches, proved perfect for cooking speed and browning. To encourage browning, toss the asparagus spears with olive oil before cooking them.

WHAT WE LEARNED: Choose medium-thick green asparagus, snap off the tough ends, and then cook the spears under the broiler until lightly browned. Make sure to shake the pan with the asparagus as it cooks so that the spears are turned and cook evenly.

BROILED ASPARAGUS
Serves 6

Broilers vary significantly in intensity, thus the wide range of cooking times in this recipe. Choose asparagus no thicker than ⅝ inch for this recipe.

- 2 pounds thin asparagus spears, tough ends snapped off (see the illustration on page 177)
- 1 tablespoon olive oil
  Salt and ground black pepper

Adjust an oven rack to the uppermost position (about 4 inches from the heating element) and heat the broiler. Toss the asparagus with the oil and salt and pepper to taste, then lay the spears in a single layer on a heavy, rimmed baking sheet. Broil, shaking the pan halfway through to turn the spears, until the asparagus are tender and lightly browned, 6 to 10 minutes. Serve hot or warm.

VARIATIONS
BROILED ASPARAGUS WITH REDUCED BALSAMIC VINAIGRETTE AND PARMESAN

The balsamic glaze will keep in the refrigerator for a week.

- ¾ cup balsamic vinegar
- 1 recipe Broiled Asparagus
- ¼ cup extra-virgin olive oil
- ¼ cup shaved Parmesan cheese (see the illustration on page 173)

Bring the vinegar to a boil in an 8-inch skillet over medium-high heat. Reduce the heat to medium and simmer slowly until the vinegar is syrupy and reduced to ¼ cup, 15 to 20 minutes. Arrange the broiled asparagus on a serving platter. Drizzle the balsamic glaze and olive oil over the asparagus. Sprinkle with the Parmesan and serve immediately.

BROILED ASPARAGUS WITH SOY-GINGER VINAIGRETTE

Putting the garlic through a press ensures that the pieces are very fine. If you don't own a press, mince the garlic to a paste with a knife.

2 medium scallions, white and green parts, minced

1 piece (about 1 inch) fresh ginger, minced (about 1 tablespoon)

2 small garlic cloves, minced or pressed through a garlic press (about 2 teaspoons)

3 tablespoons toasted sesame oil

3 tablespoons soy sauce

¼ cup juice from 2 large limes

1 tablespoon honey

1 recipe Broiled Asparagus

Whisk the scallions, ginger, garlic, sesame oil, soy sauce, lime juice, and honey together in a small bowl. Arrange the asparagus on a serving platter. Drizzle the vinaigrette over the asparagus and serve immediately.

BROILED PROSCIUTTO-WRAPPED ASPARAGUS WITH MASCARPONE

Serves 8 as an appetizer

Mascarpone is an Italian cheese with a consistency similar to cream cheese. It can be found in the specialty cheese section of most large grocery stores. The asparagus will have to be broiled in two batches so the prosciutto can brown properly. Keep the uncooked prosciutto-wrapped asparagus in the refrigerator until they are ready to be broiled.

½ cup mascarpone cheese

12 ounces prosciutto, cut into 4 by 1-inch strips

2 pounds thin asparagus spears, tough ends snapped off (see the illustration on page 177)
Ground black pepper

1. Adjust an oven rack to the uppermost position (about 4 inches from the heating element) and heat the broiler. Smear a scant teaspoon of mascarpone onto each strip of prosciutto. Tightly wrap each asparagus spear in a strip of prosciutto (starting with the tip of the asparagus), securing the end with a toothpick. Place half the spears in a single layer on a heavy, rimmed baking sheet, leaving about ½ inch space between the spears.

2. Broil, turning the spears with tongs halfway through the cooking time, until the asparagus is tender and the prosciutto is lightly browned, 8 to 10 minutes. Transfer the broiled asparagus to a serving platter. Broil the remaining asparagus on the empty baking sheet. Transfer the second batch of broiled asparagus to the platter, season with pepper to taste, and serve warm.

Diane prepares our favorite new chicken recipe with Thai spices.

NEW FLAVORS
CHAPTER 12

from the grill

Even expert grillers can get in a rut. They make the same four or five recipes over and over again. Sure, the steaks are great, but isn't there something a bit more exciting? This chapter looks at two dishes with plenty of sex appeal.

Thai grilled chicken takes boring old chicken parts and adds the potent flavors of Southeast Asia. There's nothing boring about a dish that depends on fish sauce, cilantro, lime juice, hot pepper flakes, and garlic. Our goal for this recipe was simple—develop authentic flavor with ordinary ingredients.

Glazed salmon is a restaurant classic. The fish is coated with a sweet, sticky glaze that turns to a crisp crust over hot coals. The glazes makes basic salmon something special. Although recipes for this dish look simple enough, everyone knows that sticking and burning are constant threats. Sure, a professional can glaze salmon in a restaurant, but will your average Joe and Jane be able to pull this dish off without losing the fish to the grill grate? With a thick marinade, a two-level fire, and a well-oiled grill, the answer is yes.

THAI GRILLED CHICKEN

WHAT WE WANTED: Could we capture the complex flavors and aromas that make this chicken recipe special while keeping the dish practical for the American kitchen?

Thai grilled chicken, or *gai yang,* is classic street food. This herb- and spice-rubbed chicken is served in small pieces and eaten as finger food, along with a sweet and spicy dipping sauce. Thai flavors are wonderfully aromatic and complex, making this dish a refreshing change of pace from typical barbecue fare. But is it possible to bring the flavors of Thailand into the American kitchen (or backyard) without using an ingredient list as long as your arm and making several trips to Asian specialty stores?

An initial sampling of recipes made us wonder if this dish ought to remain as indigenous street food. Among the hard-to-find ingredients were cilantro root and lemon grass, and there was a profusion of odd mixtures, including an unlikely marriage of peanut butter and brown sugar. In the end, the simplest version won out: a rub made only with cilantro, black pepper, lime juice, and garlic. We would use this as our working recipe.

Because tasters preferred white meat, we decided to go with bone-in breasts. Brined chicken was vastly preferred to unbrined, and tasters liked the addition of sugar along with salt, which complemented the sweetness of the sauce. We settled on ½ cup of each in 2 quarts of water.

Tasters liked the working rub recipe, but they wanted more complexity of flavor. Our first step was to reduce the amount of cilantro, as it had been overpowering the other ingredients. Curry powder made the chicken taste too much like Indian food, and coconut milk turned the chicken milky and soggy, with flabby skin. The earthy flavor of coriander was welcome, and fresh ginger worked well in balance with the garlic. Tasters praised this blend as more complex but still lacking bite, so we added more garlic.

The skin on the chicken was now crisp and flavorful, but not much rub was getting through to the meat. Test cooks offered suggestions ranging from slicing pockets in the meat and stuffing them with the rub to butterflying the breasts and placing the rub inside. In the end, the best alternative proved to be the easiest: We took some of the rub and placed it in a thick layer under the skin as well as on top of it. Now it was not only the crisp skin that was flavorful but the moist flesh beneath as well.

Most recipes call for grilling the chicken over a single-level fire, but this resulted in a charred exterior and an uncooked interior. We tried a two-level fire (one side of the grill holds all of the coals; the other side is empty) and, voilà, partial success! We first browned the chicken directly

over the coals and then moved it to the cool side of the grill to finish cooking. This was a big improvement, but the chicken still wasn't cooking through to the middle. Covering the grill—to make it more like an oven—was an obvious solution, but better yet was using a disposable foil pan, which creates a "mini oven." (Charcoal grill covers are home to deposits of smoke, ash, and debris that lend "off" flavors to foods.)

The true Thai flavors of this dish come through in the sauce, a classic combination of sweet and spicy. Most recipes suffered from one extreme or the other. In our working recipe, we had tried to create a balance of flavors: 2 teaspoons of hot red pepper flakes, ⅓ cup of sugar, ¼ cup of lime juice, ¼ cup of white vinegar, and 3 tablespoons of fish sauce. But tasters found even this sauce to be overwhelmingly sweet and spicy.

Reducing the red pepper flakes was a step in the right direction, as it allowed the other flavors to come through. Everyone liked garlic, but not too much; there was already a lot of garlic on the chicken. A decrease in the amount of fish sauce was welcomed, reducing the fishy flavor of the sauce but not its salty complexity. We found it best to mix the sauce right after the chicken goes into the brine, which gives the flavors time to meld.

Traditionally, gai yang is cut into small pieces and eaten as finger food. But our version is just as good (and a whole lot neater) when served whole with a knife and fork. Is this an Americanized dish? Yes. But its flavors are true to its Thai roots, and its ingredients can be found in most supermarkets.

WHAT WE LEARNED: Brine the chicken to keep it juicy, then coat it with a mixture of garlic, fresh ginger, black pepper, ground coriander, fresh cilantro, and lime juice. Grill the chicken over a two-level fire to prevent scorching and serve it with a dipping sauce that is salty, spicy, and tart.

THAI GRILLED CHICKEN WITH SPICY, SWEET, AND SOUR DIPPING SAUCE
Serves 4

For even cooking, the chicken breasts should be of comparable size. The best way to ensure this is to buy whole breasts and split them yourself (see the instructions on page 148). If you prefer to skip this step, try to purchase split bone-in, skin-on breasts that weigh about 12 ounces each. If using a charcoal grill, you will need a disposable aluminum roasting pan to cover the chicken (the lid on a charcoal grill can give the chicken resinous "off" flavors). Some of the rub is inevitably lost to the grill, but the chicken will still be flavorful.

chicken and brine

- ½ cup sugar
- 1 cup Diamond Crystal Salt, ¾ cup Morton Kosher Salt, or ½ cup table salt
- 4 split bone-in, skin-on chicken breasts, about 12 ounces each (see note)

dipping sauce

- 1 teaspoon red pepper flakes
- 3 small garlic cloves, minced or pressed through a garlic press (about 1½ teaspoons)
- ¼ cup distilled white vinegar
- ¼ cup juice from 2 to 3 limes
- 2 tablespoons fish sauce
- ⅓ cup sugar

rub

- 12 medium garlic cloves, minced or pressed through a garlic press (about ¼ cup)
- 1 piece (about 2 inches) fresh ginger, minced (about 2 tablespoons)
- 2 tablespoons ground black pepper
- 2 tablespoons ground coriander

⅔ cup chopped fresh cilantro leaves

¼ cup juice from 2 to 3 limes

2 tablespoons vegetable oil, plus more for the grill grate

1. TO BRINE THE CHICKEN: Dissolve the sugar and salt in 2 quarts cold water in a large container or bowl. Submerge the chicken in the brine and refrigerate at least 30 minutes but not longer than 1 hour. Rinse the chicken under cool running water and pat dry with paper towels.

2. FOR THE DIPPING SAUCE: Whisk the ingredients in a small bowl until the sugar dissolves. Let stand 1 hour at room temperature to allow the flavors to meld.

3. TO MAKE AND APPLY THE RUB: Combine all rub ingredients in a small bowl; work the mixture with your fingers to thoroughly combine. Slide your fingers between the skin and meat of one chicken piece to loosen the skin, taking care not to detach the skin. Rub about 2 tablespoons of the mixture under the skin. Thoroughly rub an even layer of the mixture onto all exterior surfaces, including the bottom and sides. Repeat with the remaining chicken pieces. Place the chicken in a medium bowl, cover with plastic wrap, and refrigerate while preparing the grill.

4. TO GRILL THE CHICKEN: Using a chimney starter, ignite about 2½ pounds charcoal briquettes (1 large chimney, or 6 quarts) and burn until covered with a layer of light gray ash, about 15 minutes. Empty the coals into the grill and build a two-level fire by arranging the coals to cover one half of the grill, piling them about 3 briquettes high. Position the grill grate over the coals, cover the grill, and heat until the grate is hot, about 5 minutes (the grill should

---

GETTING IT RIGHT: Splitting a Chicken Breast

Store-bought split chicken breasts are highly problematic, and we do not recommend that you buy them. Some are so sloppily cut that the tenderloins are often missing, some retain only tattered shreds of skin, and some packages contain wildly divergent sizes. You're better off buying whole breasts and splitting them yourself.

The basic method for splitting a chicken breast is to simply push a chef's knife through the skin, flesh, and bone. While this method is straightforward, sometimes the split breasts are lopsided or both lobes are marred by unruly bits of bone and cartilage around which the knife and fork must eventually navigate. Enter a classic technique to split a chicken breast. It involves the removal of the keel bone and cartilage that divides the breast, thereby making the chicken easier to eat. This method takes a few extra minutes, but we think it's time well spent.

Begin by trimming the rib sections off the split breast (kitchen shears work particularly well for this task). Then, with the breast turned skin-side down on a cutting board, use a chef's knife to score the membrane down the center along the length of the breast. Pick up the breast and, using both hands and some force, bend back the breast lobes, forcing the keel bone to pop free. Put the chicken back on the board, grasp the keel bone, and pull it free. (On occasion, the cartilage breaks—if it does, just dig in with your fingers, grip the remaining piece, and pull it out.) Finally, use the chef's knife to halve the breast down the center at the seam, applying force near the top to cut through the wishbone.

   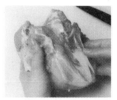 

1. Trim rib sections.   **2.** Score membrane.   **3.** Pop out keel bone.   **4.** Pull out keel bone.   **5.** Halve breast.

be medium-hot; you can hold your hand 5 inches above the grill grate for 4 seconds). Scrape the grill grate clean with a grill brush. Using long-handled grill tongs, dip a wad of paper towels in vegetable oil and wipe the grill grate.

5. Place the chicken, skin-side down, on the hotter side of the grill and cook until browned, about 3 minutes. Using tongs, flip the chicken breasts and cook until browned on the second side, about 3 minutes longer. Move the chicken, skin-side up, to the cool side of the grill and cover with a disposable aluminum roasting pan; continue to cook until an instant-read thermometer inserted into the thickest part of the breast (not touching the bone) registers 160 degrees, 10 to 15 minutes longer. Transfer the chicken to a platter and let rest 10 minutes. Serve, passing the sauce separately.

VARIATION

THAI GRILLED CHICKEN ON A GAS GRILL

1. Follow the recipe for Thai Grilled Chicken with Spicy, Sweet, and Sour Dipping Sauce through step 3.

2. Turn all the burners to high, close the lid, and heat until the grill is very hot, about 15 minutes. Scrape the grill grate clean with a grill brush. Using long-handled grill tongs, lightly dip a wad of paper towels in vegetable oil and wipe the grill grate. Turn all but one burner to low. Place the chicken, skin-side down, on the hotter side of the grill and cook until browned, 4 to 5 minutes. Using tongs, flip the chicken breasts and cook until browned on the second side, 4 to 5 minutes longer. Move the chicken, skin-side up, to the cool side of the grill and close the lid; cook until an instant-read thermometer inserted into the thickest part of the breast (not touching bone) registers 160 degrees, 12 to 15 minutes. Transfer the chicken to a platter and let rest 10 minutes. Serve, passing the sauce separately.

SCIENCE DESK:
Cutting Boards and Bacteria

IN 1994, A RESEARCH REPORT WAS PUBLISHED THAT proved to be the opening salvo in a long battle over which material was more sanitary for cutting boards, wood or plastic. The researchers found that fewer bacteria could be recovered from wooden boards infected with live cultures than from plastic boards treated the same way. These results caused the researchers to question the prevailing view that plastic was more sanitary than wood; some have further interpreted the data to mean that wood is, in fact, a safer material for cutting boards. In a report that followed, researchers at a U.S. Department of Agriculture lab concluded that beef bacteria on polyethylene and wooden cutting boards had statistically similar patterns of attachment and removal. Even so, the idea that wood is more sanitary than plastic persists and was recently reaffirmed in the food section of the *New York Times*.

We wanted to get our own perspective on the problem and so asked four staff members to donate their used boards, two wooden and two plastic. We found very little bacteria growing on these boards when we sampled them, so we took the boards to a local lab to have them artificially inoculated with bacteria. The procedure worked as follows: A drop of the medium was placed on the boards, the boards were left to sit for 40 minutes to allow for absorption of the bacteria, and an attempt was then made to remove the bacteria. In repeated tests, between 6.0 percent and 8.1 percent of the bacteria were recovered from the plastic and between 1.3 percent and 6.2 percent from the wood. Given that the number of bacteria recovered from each type of board was well into the hundreds of thousands, there was little to assure us that one material was much safer than the other. Scrubbing the boards with hot soapy water was a different story. Once the contaminated boards were cleaned, we recovered an average of 0.00015 percent from the plastic and 0.00037 percent from the wood—or fewer than 100 bacteria from each board. In a related test, we were also able to transfer bacteria from contaminated, unwashed boards made from both wood and plastic to a Petri dish using potatoes and onions. But our most surprising discovery by far was that the bacteria could persist on unwashed boards of both types for up to 60 hours!

What, then, is the truth about cutting boards? Both plastic and wooden boards can hold on to bacteria for long periods of time. Both plastic and wooden boards allow for easy transference of bacteria to other foods. Luckily, we found that scrubbing with hot soapy water was quite an effective (though not perfect) way of cleaning both kinds of boards; the USDA also recommends the regular application of a solution of 1 teaspoon bleach per quart of water and then allowing the board to dry. Simply put, maintenance, not material, provides the greatest margin of safety.

Q & A

What are the small green shoots that are sometimes found in garlic cloves?

These green shoots mean that the garlic is old enough to have sprouted. Most experts say these sprouts will give garlic a bitter flavor. To find out if this is true, we used raw garlic in aioli and cooked garlic in pasta with olive oil and tried each recipe with the shoots removed before mincing the garlic as well as with the shoots left in. With the aioli, tasters could clearly identify a more bitter, unpleasant taste in the batch made with the shoots left in. The same thing held true in the pasta test.

When shopping, we suggest that you avoid heads of garlic with green shoots. At home, store garlic in a cool, dark, well-ventilated spot to prolong its freshness. If your garlic does sprout, cut out the green shoots before mincing the cloves.

TASTING LAB: Fish Sauce

AS SOON AS WE OPENED THE FIRST BOTTLE OF FISH sauce, coworkers were off, scattering to the far corners of the office. Why the histrionics? Fish sauce is a very potent Asian condiment based on the liquid from salted, fermented fish—and smells as such. Fish sauce has a very concentrated flavor and, like anchovy paste, when used in appropriately small amounts, lends foods a salty complexity that is impossible to replicate.

We gathered six brands of fish sauce—one from Vietnam (known as *nuoc mam*), one from the Philippines (*patis*), and the rest from Thailand (*nam pla*) from our local supermarket, natural food store, and Asian market. Tasters had the option of tasting the fish sauce straight up (which few could stomach) or in a modified version of the Thai grilled chicken dipping sauce.

There were differences noted immediately among the sauces. Color correlated with flavor; the lighter the sauce, the lighter the flavor. Tasters had preferences among the sauces, but those preferences varied greatly from taster to taster. In the end, all of the sauces were recommended. In fact, there was only one point (out of 10) separating all six sauces.

With such a limited ingredient list—most of the brands contained some combination of fish extract, water, salt, and sugar—the differences among sauces were minimal. And because fish sauce is used in such small amounts, minute flavor differences get lost among the other flavors of a dish.

If you are a fan of fish sauce and use it often, you might want to make a special trip to an Asian market to buy a rich, dark sauce that is suitably pungent. But for most applications, we found that the differences were negligible. Because most supermarkets don't carry a wide selection of fish sauce, we recommend buying whatever is available. That will most likely be Thai Kitchen, an Americanized brand found in most supermarkets, which was the lightest colored (and flavored) brand we tasted.

Rating Fish Sauce

TEN MEMBERS OF THE *COOK'S ILLUSTRATED* STAFF TASTED ALL OF THE FISH SAUCES, EITHER STRAIGHT UP OR IN A modified version of our dipping sauce for Thai grilled chicken. The sauces are listed in order of preference based on their scores in this tasting. Brands are available in supermarkets, natural food stores, and Asian markets.

RECOMMENDED

Tiparos Fish Sauce

Thailand

$2.39 for 23 ounces

This top-rated sauce was described as "really aggressive" as well as "dark and pungent." A favorite among fish sauce aficionados.

RECOMMENDED

Thai Kitchen Fish Sauce

Thailand

$3.25 for 7 ounces

This widely available brand has a "very light flavor" and is "easy to take." The best bet for fish sauce novices.

RECOMMENDED

Golden Boy Brand Fish Sauce

Thailand

$1.09 for 24 ounces

The sauce is intense, with tasters remarking on a "slight smokiness" and saying that it "smells cheesy."

RECOMMENDED

Rufina Fish Sauce

Philippines

$2.09 for 25 ounces

Tasters thought this "very fermented" sauce "tastes like soy." Overall, it was deemed "plain."

RECOMMENDED

Squid Brand Fish Sauce

Thailand

$.95 for 25 ounces

Most panelists thought this sauce was "nicely balanced," and a few called it "a bit sweet."

RECOMMENDED

Three Crabs Brand Fish Sauce

Vietnam

$2.99 for 24 ounces

This sauce provoked strong reactions, with comments such as "musty," "salty," and "acidic."

GRILLED GLAZED SALMON

WHAT WE WANTED: To avoid the burnt, stuck-to-the-grill crust and flavorless interior that plague most glazed salmon. We also hoped to create sweet, crisp, and flavorful salmon.

We have always felt confident in our ability to produce great grilled salmon. With its firm, meaty texture and rich, buttery interior, the salmon on our grill had at least a chance of coming off that hot grate moist and in one piece. Then one day we tried grilled glazed salmon and watched as our dinner (as well as our bravado) went up in smoke. "Sticky" was the operative word here as the glazed salmon gripped the grill grate for dear life and could only be torn off in many tiny pieces. Not that it was actually worth getting off the grill, mind you, because each of those tiny pieces was charred beyond recognition. When it comes to grilled glazed salmon, you can call us chicken.

So why glaze (and inevitably ruin) an otherwise perfect piece of fish? Well, because truly great glazed salmon off the grill is a thing of beauty, both inside and out. Working double duty, the sweet glaze not only forms a glossy, deeply caramelized crust but also permeates the flesh, making the last bite of fish every bit as good as the first. This was the salmon that we wanted to re-create—sweet, crisp, moist, and oh-so-flavorful—and we were willing to ruin a few more fish to get there.

We knew we needed all the help we could get, and we went straight to cookbooks in hopes of direction. The first choice was easy. When confronted with fillets, steaks, and whole sides, we were going with the fillets for ease of grilling (ever try flipping a whole side?) and ease of eating (who wants to eat around all those salmon steak bones, anyway?). The next choice was glazing method, and here things were less clear. We could try using a marinade to flavor the fish. We could try brushing the fish with a thick glaze before throwing it on the grill. Finally, we could simply grill the fish plain and apply the glaze afterward. We fired up the grill and got to work.

After testing, there was no doubt that marinating gave the salmon flavor. Soy sauce was chosen for its ability to season the fish through and through, while vinegar (another standard marinade ingredient) was omitted, as it broke down the salmon until it was too fragile to hold its shape on the grill. In a perfect world, the marinade would also work as a glaze of sorts, with the sugars caramelizing once they hit the hot grill. In fact, tests demonstrated that the marinated salmon failed to produce any kind of crust. Increasing the amount of sugar only served to make the salmon too sweet. Taking a cue from some brush-on glaze recipes, we tested more viscous sweeteners, such as maple syrup, honey, and molasses. While the molasses was rejected for its bitter flavor, the maple syrup and honey worked like a dream. With a thicker marinade, the sweet flavors clung to the salmon rather than dripping through the bars of the grate, and a crust (however thin) was beginning to form.

Using a marinade alone wasn't going to produce the thick crust we wanted, however. The next step was to brush the marinated salmon with a much thicker glaze—a winning combination of soy sauce and maple syrup—very similar to the marinade. Yep, here was a crust—a burnt, stuck-to-the-grill crust; not what we were after. Instead, we basted the salmon with this glaze a few moments after it hit the hot grill. Better. Not as charred, not as sticky, but still not acceptable. Not sure where else to turn at this point, we thought it might be time to examine the fire.

Up to this point, we had been cooking the salmon in a pretty traditional way. We were searing the fish skin-side down, then skin-side up over a hot fire; the superhot grill grate helped to keep the fish from sticking. The problem now was that the hot fire was causing the sweet glazed salmon to burn.

After trying more temperate medium and low fires (both of which failed), we tried a two-level fire. Piling the hot briquettes one-high on one side and two-high on the other, we seared the marinated salmon over the high heat. We then brushed the salmon with some of the glaze and pulled it to the cooler side of the grill to cook through. This was a big improvement, with a decent crust.

But we were still having a problem. When started skin-side down, the fillet buckled, causing the other side to cook unevenly. The solution was to start the salmon skin-side up, flip it to sear the skin side, brush on some glaze, and then flip it again to finish cooking on the cool side of the grill. The downside of this approach was that the grill had to be well oiled to prevent sticking, a step that is not optional. The good news was that we had an incredible crust, built in two layers, that was both sweet and substantial. All that was left to do was to brush the grilled salmon with more glaze before serving. Gilding the lily, perhaps, but with a high-gloss shine and potent flavor within, this fish never looked (or tasted) so good.

WHAT WE LEARNED: Marinate the flesh side of the fish in a mixture of soy sauce and maple syrup. Grill the fish, flesh-side down, then flip, glaze twice, and flip again. When the fish comes off the grill, glaze it again. Needless to say, a well-oiled grill is a must, as is a two-level fire with hotter and cooler cooking areas.

GRILLED GLAZED SALMON

Serves 4

Scraping the grill grate clean will help prevent the salmon from sticking. Also, be sure to oil the grate just before placing the fillets on the grill.

- 1 recipe glaze (recipes follow)
- ⅓ cup soy sauce
- ⅓ cup maple syrup
- 4 salmon fillets (about 8 ounces each), each about 1½ inches at the thickest part
  Ground black pepper
  Vegetable oil for grill grate
  Lemon wedges for serving

1. Measure 2 tablespoons of the glaze into a small bowl and set aside.

2. Whisk the soy sauce and maple syrup in a 13 by 9-inch baking dish until combined. Carefully place the fillets flesh-side down in a single layer in the marinade (do not coat the salmon skin with the marinade). Refrigerate while preparing the grill.

3. Using a chimney starter, ignite about 2½ pounds charcoal briquettes (1 large chimney, or 6 quarts) and burn until covered with a layer of light gray ash, about 15 minutes. Empty the coals into the grill and build a two-level fire by stacking two-thirds of the coals in one half of the grill and arranging the remaining coals in a single layer in the other half. Position the grill grate over the coals, cover the grill, and heat until the grate is hot, about 5 minutes (the grill should be medium-hot; you can hold your hand 5 inches above the grill grate for 4 seconds). Scrape the grill grate clean with a grill brush.

4. Remove the salmon from the marinade and sprinkle the flesh liberally with pepper. Using long-handled grill tongs, dip a wad of paper towels in vegetable oil and wipe the hot side of the grill grate. Place the fillets flesh-side down on the hot side of the grill (at a 45-degree angle to the grate) and cook until grill-marked, about 1 minute. Using tongs, flip the fillets skin-side down, still on the hot side of the grill. Brush the flesh with the glaze and cook until the salmon is opaque about halfway up the thickness of the fillets, 3 to 4 minutes.

5. Using long-handled grill tongs, dip a wad of paper towels in vegetable oil and wipe the cooler side of the grill grate. Brush the flesh again with the glaze, then turn the fillets flesh-side down onto the cooler side of the grill. Cook until a deeply browned crust has formed and the center of the fillet is still translucent when cut into with a paring knife, about 1½ minutes. Transfer the fillets to a platter, brush with reserved 2 tablespoons glaze, and serve with the lemon wedges.

CATCH AND RELEASE

Few things are more frustrating than trying to pull the daily catch off the grill in one piece. But there's no shortage of equipment, gadgets, or plain old advice intended to help you get around this problem. After testing them all, using both sturdy salmon fillets and more fragile flounder, we found that the best method requires equipment that you probably own already. The methods are listed in order of effectiveness.

Tool	Method	Results
Oiled wad of paper towels	Using long-handled tongs, dip the towels in vegetable oil and brush over the heated grill grate.	The most failsafe way to keep fish from sticking to the grill.
Cooking spray	Spray the cold grate before heating.	Worked well, although part of one fillet needed some prodding.
Oil on the fish	Oil the fish before placing on the hot grill.	Mixed reviews. Although the fish released well, flare-ups were a problem.
Lemon slices	Place lemon slices on the grate, then place the fish on top.	Mixed reviews. Although the fish did not stick to the grill, the lemon slices kept the fish from developing exterior color. Works well for fragile fish, though, when browning is not important.
Stainless steel screen material	Place the screen on the grate, then place the fish on top.	Not bad. Worked well when sprayed with vegetable oil spray. The fish must be rapidly removed from the screen after being grilled, as it will begin to stick as it cools.
Fish basket	Place fish in an oiled fish basket.	Not recommended. Salmon stuck to basket. Doesn't work with glazing because one can't get at the caged salmon to brush it.
Grill grate	Tested enameled steel, cast-iron, and stainless steel grates.	When it comes to types of grill grates, fish is nondiscriminatory. It will stick to any surface. It's best to use the oiled grate method with any of these grill grate materials.

VARIATIONS

GRILLED GLAZED SALMON ON A GAS GRILL

1. Follow the recipe for Grilled Glazed Salmon through step 2.

2. Turn all the burners to high, cover, and heat until very hot, about 15 minutes. Scrape the grill grate clean with a grill brush. Turn all but one burner to medium-low. Remove the salmon from the marinade and sprinkle the flesh liberally with pepper. Using long-handled grill tongs, dip a wad of paper towels in vegetable oil and wipe the hot side of the grill grate. Place the fillets flesh-side down on the hot side of the grill and cook until grill-marked, 1 to 2 minutes. Using tongs, flip the fillets skin-side down, still on the hot side of the grill. Brush the flesh with the glaze, cover the grill, and cook until the salmon is opaque about halfway up the thickness of the fillets, 3 to 4 minutes.

3. Again using long-handled grill tongs, dip a wad of paper towels in vegetable oil and wipe the cooler side of the grill grate. Brush the flesh again with the glaze, then turn the fillets flesh-side down onto the cooler side of the grill. Cook until a deeply browned crust has formed and the center of the thickest part of the fillet is still translucent when cut into with a paring knife, about 2 minutes. Transfer the fillets to a platter, brush with the reserved 2 tablespoons glaze, and serve immediately with the lemon wedges.

MAPLE-CHIPOTLE GLAZE

Offer lime wedges instead of lemon when serving.

Stir together 2 tablespoons soy sauce, ¼ cup maple syrup, and 1 teaspoon minced chipotle chile in adobo sauce in a small saucepan. Bring to a simmer over medium-high heat and cook until slightly thickened, 3 to 4 minutes. Off the heat, whisk in 2 tablespoons lime juice.

MAPLE-SOY GLAZE

Stir together 2 tablespoons soy sauce and ¼ cup maple syrup in a small saucepan. Bring to a simmer over medium-high heat and cook until slightly thickened, 3 to 4 minutes.

HONEY-MUSTARD GLAZE

Stir together 2 tablespoons soy sauce and ¼ cup honey in a small saucepan. Bring to a simmer over medium-high heat and cook until slightly thickened, 3 to 4 minutes. Off the heat, whisk in 3 tablespoons Dijon mustard.

GETTING IT RIGHT: The Soft, the Sticky, and the Good

Here's how we solved two common problems that came up during recipe testing.

Too Soft
Salmon that was marinated for more than 30 minutes became mushy and fell apart on the grill.

Too Sticky
When we skipped the step of oiling the grill grate, the salmon stuck terribly.

Just Right
With a short marinating time and a thorough oiling of the grill, our salmon came off the fire intact.

EQUIPMENT CORNER:
Portable Gas Grills

THE GREAT OUTDOORS AND GRILLED MEATS ARE AN indisputable match. Unfortunately, owing to the immense bulk of today's grills, our grilling efforts are almost always confined to the back patio. Many companies are addressing this issue with a new line of portable, propane-powered grills.

There are dozens of portable gas grills on the market, ranging from the inexpensive (about $50) to the truly outrageous ($1,000 or more). We set our ceiling at $200 and gathered five prominent models to test. Our selection included two models that are truly portable and three whose size makes it difficult to venture very far from the back of the SUV. We quickly learned that the smaller models, though very convenient, offered little else of value. The Weber Gas Go Anywhere ($59.99) was extremely easy to carry, but its measly heat output caused us to question whether this model was meant to be a grill or a hand warmer. The Tool Box Gas ($50) grill, as the name implies, is a spitting image of your grandfather's toolbox, but its flimsy grates and inconsistent heat garnered poor marks from the testers. Overall, the portability of these two smaller grills could not make up for their lack of performance.

The three largest models were, predictably, stronger players. The Coleman Road Trip Sport ($170), Weber Q Portable Propane Gas Grill ($159.99), and Thermos Grill-2-Go ($150) all featured large, cast-iron grilling surfaces, high heat outputs, and sturdy designs. These characteristics not only increased the cooking ability of the grills but also added to their heft, and even the strongest among us found it difficult to carry these grills. Although their portability came into question, all three of these grills performed well. The Thermos Grill-2-Go came out on top during testing because of its consistent performance and low price. The Weber Q Portable Propane Gas Grill, a close second, was applauded for its even heating and sturdy construction.

Rating Portable Gas Grills

WE TESTED FIVE PORTABLE GRILLS, GRILLING STEAKS (TO judge searing ability and heat output) and hamburgers (to judge evenness of heating and ability to handle grease). The portable grills were rated for performance as well as design and ease of use. The portable grills are listed below in order of preference. See www.americastestkitchen.com for up-to-date prices and mail-order sources for top-rated products.

RECOMMENDED
Thermos Grill-2-Go #4656110
$150
With an even heating surface and a reasonable price, this model took top honors. Also praised for its handy flat griddle that is perfect for pancakes.

RECOMMENDED
Weber Q Portable Propane Gas Grill #396001
$159.99
The largest and heaviest of the bunch, but also has the most even heating.

RECOMMENDED
Coleman Road Trip Sport
$170
Gets very hot very fast, but the ceramic grill grate is a bit delicate for heavy grilling.

NOT RECOMMENDED
Weber Gas Go Anywhere #1520
$59.99
Very easy to carry, but where's the heat?

NOT RECOMMENDED
Tool Box Gas #112000
$50
Cute concept but weak output.

Julia takes the assembly line approach to fill and roll chicken enchiladas.

MEXICAN favorites

There's a significant disconnect between real Mexican food (as prepared in Mexico) and the food served in "Mexican" restaurants in the United States. The real deal is noted for its bright, intense flavors, rather than the mounds of cheese and sour cream that cover most Americanized dishes served in nacho and salsa joints. Unfortunately, many authentic Mexican dishes require ingredients that can still be hard to find.

For this chapter, we decided to look at two long-time favorites with Americans—enchiladas and Mexican rice. We wanted to make these dishes fresher and livelier—more like the Mexican originals than the bastardized versions most Americans know. Although we didn't want to be slaves to tradition, we wanted dishes that any Mexican cook could proudly serve. We think we've succeeded.

CHICKEN ENCHILADAS

WHAT WE WANTED: Mexican cooking is notoriously time-consuming but delivers rich, deep flavors. We wanted to produce a reasonably authentic chicken enchilada with far less work.

Take a softened tortilla, stuff it with a savory chicken filling, roll it, encase it in a spicy chili sauce, and serve it with an assortment of creamy and crunchy toppings, and you have quite possibly the most popular Mexican dish in the world. And for good reason. Chicken enchiladas are a complete meal that offers a rich and complex combination of flavors, textures, and ingredients. The problem with preparing enchiladas at home is that traditional cooking methods require a whole day of preparation. Could we simplify the process, yet retain the authentic flavor of the real thing?

We began by preparing five simplified recipes, hoping to uncover valuable tips and techniques. All of them produced disappointing results. Mushy tortillas, bland or bitter sauces, uninspired fillings, too much cheese, and lackluster flavor left tasters yearning for something tastier and more authentic.

A side-by-side tasting of corn and wheat flour tortillas came out clearly in favor of the corn, with its more substantial texture. Tasters also preferred the small 6-inch tortillas, with 8-inch tortillas a close second. These sizes provided the best proportion of tortilla to filling and sauce, and both sizes fit neatly into a 9-inch-wide baking pan. Although ingredients and size mattered, we were happy to discover that brand didn't. Given the big flavors from the sauce and filling, flavor differences among various brands of tortillas (which are rather bland-tasting anyway) were not important in the final dish.

Our next task was to figure out how to treat the tortillas so that they would be soft and pliable to roll and toothsome to eat. The traditional approach is to dip each tortilla in hot oil (to create a moisture barrier) and then in the sauce (to add flavor) prior to assembly. Although this technique works well, it is time-consuming, tedious, and messy. We tried rolling chilled corn tortillas straight from the package, but they were tough and cracked easily. Heating a stack of tortillas in the microwave also proved disappointing. The tortillas were soft, but the resulting enchiladas were mushy. Next we tried wrapping the tortillas in foil and steaming them on a plate over boiling water. These tortillas were also easy to roll but were wet and soggy when baked.

Thinking back to the traditional first step of dipping the tortillas in oil gave us an idea. Using the modern-day convenience of oil in an aerosol can, we placed the tortillas in a single layer on a baking sheet, lightly sprayed both sides of the tortillas with vegetable oil, and warmed them in a moderate oven. This proved to be the shortcut we were hoping to find. The oil-sprayed, oven-warmed tortillas were pliable, and their texture after being filled, rolled, and baked was nearly perfect.

Because red chili sauce is the most common sauce used in enchiladas, we decided to prepare a half dozen traditional recipes. The flavors were spicy and complex, the textures smooth and somewhat thick, the colors deep orange-red. The problem was that whole dried chiles played a central role in all of these sauces. Not only are whole chiles difficult to find in some areas, but they require substantial preparation time, including toasting, seeding, stemming, rehydrating, and processing in a blender. Store-bought chili powder would have to be part of the solution.

The obvious question was how to augment the flavor of the usually bland chili powder available in the supermarket. Our first thought was to heat the chili powder in oil, a process that intensifies flavors. We began by sautéing onion and garlic and then added the chili powder to the pan. This indeed produced a fuller, deeper flavor. We enhanced the flavor by adding ground cumin and coriander—ingredients often found in authentic red chili sauce. Tasters gave this combo a thumbs-up.

Many traditional recipes incorporate tomatoes for substance and flavor. With a nod toward convenience, we explored canned tomato products first. We tried adding diced tomatoes and then pureeing the mixture. The texture was too thick and too tomatoey. Canned tomato sauce turned out to be a better option. Focusing on flavor next, we prepared a batch with 2 teaspoons of sugar, which succeeded in expanding and enriching the flavor of the spices.

Next, we were on to the filling and started with how to cook the chicken. We tried the common method of poaching, but tasters said this chicken was dry and bland. We tried roasting both white and dark meat, which was extremely time-consuming, although tasters really liked the dark meat. Obsessed with speed and flavor, we had an idea. Why not use boneless, skinless thighs and cook them right in the sauce? Cutting the thighs into thin strips across the grain, we added them to the pan after the spices were fragrant. The chicken cooked in less than 10 minutes, and it was nicely seasoned. Cooking the chicken in the sauce also lent the sauce a wonderful richness. To separate the chicken from the sauce, we poured the contents of the pot through a medium-mesh strainer.

With the chicken cooked and ready for the filling, we needed to add just a few complementary ingredients. Cheese topped our list. Queso fresco, the traditional choice, is a young, unripened cheese with a creamy color, mild flavor, and crumbly texture. Because it is not readily available in the United States, we tried farmer's cheese. Tasters liked this cheese for its creamy texture and mellow flavor. But it was Monterey Jack and sharp white cheddar that made the top of the list. The Jack is mellow, while the cheddar adds a sharp, distinctive flavor. Our first choice was the cheddar, though certainly the Jack is just fine as well. (Cheese, we discovered, also helps to bind the filling ingredients.) Looking for more heat, we taste-tested the addition of fresh jalapeños, chipotles in adobo sauce, and canned jalapeños. The fresh jalapeños were too mild. Chipotles (smoked jalapeños stewed in a seasoned liquid) added a distinctive, warm heat and smoky flavor that some tasters enjoyed but that most found too spicy and smoky. Everyone was surprised to find that the very convenient canned jalapeños were the favorite. (Because the peppers are pickled in a vinegar solution before being canned, they added spicy, bright, and sour notes.)

Some recipes suggest filling and rolling one enchilada at a time, but we much preferred the efficiency offered by the assembly-line approach. We spread the oil-sprayed, oven-warmed tortillas on the countertop and spread ⅓ cup of filling down the center of each. We rolled them tightly and placed them seam-side down, side by side, along the length of a 13 by 9-inch baking pan that had a little sauce in it. We then poured the rest of the sauce over the enchiladas and sprinkled them with a bit of extra cheese. We experimented with oven temperatures and times before settling on 400 degrees for 20 minutes, at which point the enchiladas were hot and ready to be served.

Enchiladas are traditionally eaten with an array of raw, salad-like garnishes. Tasters passed on chopped tomatoes, saying they did not add much flavor or texture. Raw onions were considered too harsh. Sour cream and avocado were chosen for their cooling qualities, and romaine lettuce was favored for its fresh, crispy crunch. Finally, there were the lime wedges, which gave a nice brightness to the finished dish. Start to finish, our chicken enchiladas now took less than an hour and a half to make: 20 minutes for the sauce, 15 for the filling, 30 to assemble and bake, and 10 to prepare the toppings.

WHAT WE LEARNED: Create a quick red sauce with onions, garlic, spices, and tomato sauce. Cook the chicken right in the sauce (to save time and mess) and then strain it out. For tortillas that will roll without cracking, spray them with oil and bake for several minutes until pliable. Use cilantro, pickled jalapeños, and cheddar cheese to round out the filling and then serve with more cheese, sour cream, avocado, lettuce, and limes.

CHICKEN ENCHILADAS WITH RED CHILI SAUCE

Makes 10 enchiladas, serving 4 or 5 as a main dish

Monterey Jack can be used instead of cheddar, or for a mellower flavor and creamier texture, try farmer's cheese. Be sure to cool the chicken before filling the tortillas, otherwise the hot filling will make the enchiladas soggy.

sauce and filling

1½	tablespoons vegetable or corn oil
1	medium onion, chopped fine (about 1 cup)
3	medium garlic cloves, minced or pressed through a garlic press (about 1 tablespoon)
3	tablespoons chili powder
2	teaspoons ground coriander
2	teaspoons ground cumin
½	teaspoon salt
2	teaspoons sugar
12	ounces boneless, skinless chicken thighs (about 4 thighs), trimmed of excess fat and cut into ¼-inch-wide strips
2	(8-ounce) cans tomato sauce
¾	cup water
½	cup coarsely chopped fresh cilantro leaves
1	(4-ounce) can pickled jalapeño chiles, drained and chopped (about ¼ cup)
8	ounces sharp cheddar cheese, shredded (about 2 cups)

tortillas and toppings

10	(6-inch) corn tortillas
	Vegetable oil cooking spray
3	ounces sharp cheddar cheese, shredded (about ¾ cup)
¾	cup sour cream
1	ripe avocado, diced medium
5	romaine lettuce leaves, shredded
2	limes, quartered

1. FOR THE SAUCE AND FILLING: Heat the oil in a medium saucepan over medium-high heat until hot and shimmering but not smoking. Add the onion and cook, stirring occasionally, until softened and beginning to brown, about 5 minutes. Add the garlic, chili powder, coriander, cumin, salt, and sugar and cook, stirring constantly, until fragrant, about 30 seconds. Add the chicken and cook, stirring constantly, until coated with the spices, about 30 seconds. Add the tomato sauce and water, stir to separate the chicken pieces, and bring to a simmer. Reduce the heat to medium-low and simmer, uncovered, stirring occasionally, until the chicken is cooked through and the flavors have melded, about 8 minutes. Pour the mixture through a medium-mesh strainer into a medium bowl, pressing on the chicken and onions to extract as much sauce as possible; set the sauce aside. Transfer the chicken mixture to a large plate; place in the freezer for 10 minutes to cool, then combine with the cilantro, jalapeños, and cheese in a medium bowl.

2. Adjust the oven racks to the upper- and lower-middle positions and heat the oven to 300 degrees.

3. TO ASSEMBLE: Following the illustrations on page 163, smear the entire bottom of a 13 by 9-inch baking dish with ¾ cup of the chili sauce. Place the tortillas in a single layer on two baking sheets. Spray both sides lightly with cooking spray. Bake until the tortillas are soft and pliable, about 4 minutes. Transfer the warm tortillas to a work surface. Increase the oven temperature to 400 degrees. Spread ⅓ cup of the filling down the center of each tortilla. Roll each tortilla tightly by hand and place, seam-side down, side by side on the sauce in the baking dish. Pour the remaining chili sauce over the top of the enchiladas. Use the back of a spoon to spread the sauce so it coats the top of each tortilla. Sprinkle ¾ cup grated cheese down the center of the enchiladas.

4. TO BAKE: Cover the baking dish with foil. Bake the enchiladas on the lower-middle rack until heated through and the cheese is melted, 20 to 25 minutes. Uncover and serve immediately, passing the sour cream, avocado, lettuce, and lime wedges separately.

VARIATION

CHICKEN ENCHILADAS WITH GREEN CHILI SAUCE

In Mexico, sauce is so central to enchiladas that it often defines them. While the red sauce used in enchiladas rojas is made with dried chiles and is robust and fiery, the green sauce used in enchiladas verdes is prepared with fresh chiles and is more tart and vibrant tasting. Green sauces typically include tomatillos, onions, garlic, and cilantro in addition to fresh chiles. Washing the tomatillos in a bowl of cold water will quickly remove their papery husks.

sauce

2	teaspoons vegetable or corn oil
1	medium onion, chopped (about 1 cup)
3	medium garlic cloves, minced or pressed through a garlic press (about 1 tablespoon)
¾	pound tomatillos, husks and stems removed, each tomatillo quartered (about 1½ cups)
3	large jalapeños, seeded and chopped large (about 1 cup)
1	teaspoon sugar
½	teaspoon salt
⅓	cup water

TECHNIQUE: Assembling Enchiladas

1. Smear the entire bottom of a 13 by 9-inch baking dish with ¾ cup of the chili sauce.

2. Place the tortillas in a single layer on two baking sheets. Spray both sides lightly with cooking spray. Bake until the tortillas are soft and pliable, about 4 minutes.

3. Place the warm tortillas on a work surface. Increase the oven temperature to 400 degrees. Place ⅓ cup of the filling down the center of each tortilla.

4. Roll each tortilla tightly by hand and place, seam-side down, side by side on the sauce in the baking dish.

5. Pour the remaining chili sauce over the top of the enchiladas. Use the back of a spoon to spread the sauce so it coats the top of each tortilla.

6. Sprinkle ¾ cup shredded cheese down the center of the enchiladas.

filling

2	teaspoons vegetable or corn oil
1	medium onion, chopped (about 1 cup)
1	tablespoon ground cumin
12	ounces boneless, skinless chicken thighs (about 4 thighs), trimmed of excess fat and cut into ¼-inch-wide strips
½	cup coarsely chopped fresh cilantro leaves
8	ounces sharp cheddar cheese, shredded (about 2 cups)

tortillas and toppings

10	(6-inch) corn tortillas
	Vegetable oil cooking spray
3	ounces sharp cheddar cheese, shredded (about ¾ cup)
¾	cup sour cream
1	ripe avocado, diced medium
5	romaine lettuce leaves, shredded
2	limes, quartered

1. FOR THE SAUCE: Heat the oil in a medium saucepan over medium-high heat until hot and shimmering but not smoking. Add the onion and cook, stirring occasionally, until softened and beginning to brown, about 5 minutes. Add the garlic, tomatillos, jalapeños, sugar, and salt and cook, stirring constantly, until fragrant, about 30 seconds. Add the water and bring to a simmer. Reduce the heat to medium-low and simmer, uncovered, until the tomatillos are softened, about 8 minutes. Transfer the mixture to a blender and puree until smooth, about 30 seconds; set aside. Rinse out the saucepan.

2. FOR THE FILLING: Heat the oil in the saucepan over medium-high heat until hot and shimmering but not smoking. Add the onion and cook, stirring occasionally, until beginning to soften and brown, about 3 minutes, then reduce the heat to medium and continue to cook until browned, about 3 minutes longer. Add the cumin and cook, stirring constantly, until fragrant, about 15 seconds. Add the chicken and cook, stirring frequently, until the chicken is cooked through, about 5 minutes. Transfer the chicken mixture to a large plate; place in the freezer for 10 minutes to cool, then combine with the cilantro and cheese in a medium bowl and set aside.

3. Follow the recipe for Chicken Enchiladas with Red Chili Sauce from step 2, using the green sauce in place of the red chili sauce.

GETTING IT RIGHT:
Rolling Tortillas Made Easy

Cool and Stiff   **Warm and Pliable**

Straight from the fridge, a corn tortilla is too stiff to roll and will tear at the edges (left). Spraying the tortilla with oil and heating it for 4 minutes in a 300-degree oven makes the tortilla pliable and easy to work with (right).

EQUIPMENT CORNER: Spice Grinders

EVERY ONE OF US IS ACQUAINTED WITH A SPICE SNOB. You know, the neighbor who is constantly bragging about her spice rack that is graced only by whole nutmeg, white peppercorns, and dried chiles. That's right, the bake sale braggart who always hand grinds whole cinnamon for that blue-ribbon Bundt cake. Is all this whole spice hoopla reasonable, or do preground spices measure up to their intact brethren? Well, we are sorry to tell you, but the spice snobs are right—freshly ground spices are far superior to their preground relatives.

To illustrate this fact, we set up a blind tasting of a cardamom pound cake and a savory chutney, both of which pitted preground spices against freshly ground spices. In a unanimous victory, the freshly ground spices were lauded for their superior aroma, vibrancy, and roundness of flavor. With their dominance established, the next question was obvious: How can we enjoy freshly ground spices without driving out to the McCormick's processing plant every morning before work? To find the answer, we set out to identify a spice grinder that is as easy on the arms as it is on the wallet.

The test kitchen standard for grinding spices is an inexpensive blade-type electric coffee grinder (which we use for spices only, reserving a separate unit to grind coffee), but we had never put it up against other devices designed specifically for the task. Could we be missing out on something? To determine the answer to that question, we gathered 13 devices in three basic designs—dedicated spice grinders that are similar to pepper mills, old-fashioned mortars and pestles (and variations), and electric coffee grinders—and used them to reduce mountains of cardamom seeds, toasted whole cumin and coriander seeds, and chipotle chiles to fine powders. We chose these spices because of their varying hardnesses, densities, shapes, and oil content. We were looking for a grinder that would produce the most delicate, uniform powder and that was easy to both use and clean.

First up were the dedicated spice grinders. Like pepper mills, they are torsion-operated, meaning that you twist one part of the device while holding a second part steady. As the device is twisted, internal grooves grind the spices. Because the moving parts on this grinder are largely internal, cleaning the unit was difficult. Additionally, the relentless twisting of these models made testing six of them consecutively seem like an act of masochism.

The next tests revolved around three versions of the age-old mortar and pestle, including a Japanese suribachi with a textured grinding surface to help break down the contents. As a group, these were no more effective than the torsion-operated grinders. To us, using the mortar and pestle was less stressful than the repetitive motion required to work the torsion-operated grinders, but it was still too much effort considering the disappointing piles of bruised, mangled seeds that it produced.

Last up were the electric coffee grinders, which were, in short, like breaths of fresh air. The only physical exertion required to use them was pressing a button. No stress, strain, or sore forearms, and they produced consistently strong results on all of the test spices. And it only got better: The coffee grinders were easy to brush or wipe clean (just mind the blade!), easy to control for texture of grind, and no more expensive than the manual grinders and mortars and pestles. All four blade grinders tested did an equally good job with small and large amounts of all spices tested.

So check your preground spices at the door and join the rest of the spice snobs—freshly ground spices are more flavorful and, thanks to the electric coffee grinder, just as accessible as preground spices. The bright aroma and earthiness of fresh spices can breathe life into your food. From complex dishes to everyday meals, from savory to sweet preparations, a cabinet full of whole spices and an electric coffee grinder are invaluable assets in the kitchen.

Rating Spice Grinders

WE TESTED 13 DEVICES, INCLUDING DEDICATED SPICE GRINDERS, MORTARS AND PESTLES, AND BLADE-TYPE coffee grinders. Grinders are grouped by type and listed in order of preference within their type. See www.americastestkitchen.com for up-to-date prices and mail-order sources for top-rated products.

RECOMMENDED: ELECTRIC COFFEE GRINDERS

Krups Fast-Touch Coffee Mill, Model 203 $19.95
Our top choice produced an exceptionally fine and consistent grind regardless of the amount of spice in the chamber.

Braun Aromatic Coffee Grinder, Model KSM 2B $14.99
This model produced a fine and even grind in small and medium amounts. Also did an impressive job grinding a large amount of each spice.

Mr. Coffee Coffee Grinder, Model IDS55 $14.99
An all-around strong performer that required a bit of extra grinding to break down a small amount of chipotle.

Capresso Cool Grind $19.99
The Capresso required a bit of extra grinding time to fully process large amounts of cumin and coriander but still performed well.

NOT RECOMMENDED: MORTARS AND PESTLES

Mortar & Pestle, Marble $8.99
Did a good job on cardamom and chiles but did not produce a satisfactory grind of cumin or coriander, even after working them for 30 minutes.

Suribachi $16
The chiles broke down completely in this mortar, but not before showering the kitchen floor with partially ground spices.

Creative Home Marble Spice Grinder $11.99
Holy hand strain! The stubby pestle was uncomfortable, especially since you must bear down with considerable pressure to grind anything.

NOT RECOMMENDED: TORSION-OPERATED

Genius Spice Grinder Set $24.99
Did a better job than all other grinders of its kind, but the output was slow compared with that of electric grinders. The grip was relatively comfortable for this type of grinder.

Emsa Würzmühle Spice Mill with Ceramic Grinders $15.95
This model processed chiles very well, albeit slowly. One of our large-handed testers found this narrow model uncomfortable.

WMF Gewürzmühle Ceramill Glass Spice Mill $20
Relatively easy to open, fill, and twist. Did a good job on cardamom but choked on chiles.

Oxo Grind It Spice Grinder $14.99
Good grind quality, but too easy to accidentally pop the grinder housing off the jar while grinding, which sent seeds flying in every direction.

Spice Essentials Grinder with Ceramic Mechanism $27.95
Chiles brought it to a grinding halt. Though not difficult to dismantle, cleaning was a chore.

William Bounds Spice Mill $14.95
The crank was so hard to turn that testers feared onset of carpal tunnel syndrome and tennis elbow! The output was meager as well.

MEXICAN RICE

WHAT WE WANTED: Mexican rice promises bright flavor and a pilaf-style texture, but it rarely delivers. We wanted a rich-tasting side dish—without the usual pools of oil.

A cursory look at Mexican rice reveals a simple pilaf prepared by sautéing raw white rice in oil, then slowly cooking the grains in chicken broth flavored with pureed tomatoes, onion, and garlic. Some cooks finish the dish with a sprinkle of fresh chiles and cilantro. In Mexico, this pilaf is frequently presented as a separate course, in the manner that Italians serve pasta, but on the American table it makes a unique side dish.

Yet for a basic dish with a remarkably short ingredient list, we found it vexing. Variable ingredient quantities and cooking techniques produced disparate results when we put a selection of recipes from respected Mexican cookbook authors to the test. Two of these recipes turned out soupy and greasy, spurring tasters to crack jokes about "Risotto à la Mexicana" and "Mexican Porridge." These descriptions, along with our own taste buds, told us that these supersoggy, oily versions were off-track. Other recipes seemed misguided in terms of ingredient amounts. Some had just a hint of garlic, others tasted of tomato and nothing else, and one was overtaken by pungent cilantro.

To our way of thinking, the perfect version of this dish would exhibit clean, balanced flavors and tender, perfectly cooked rice. It would be rich but not oily, moist but not watery. We returned to the test kitchen with some basic questions in mind: What is the proper ratio of liquid to rice for a moist but not brothy dish? Would canned tomatoes provide for more balanced flavor than fresh? Could we skip the sautéing step and still end up with an agreeable texture?

The liquid traditionally used in this dish is a mixture of chicken broth and pureed fresh tomatoes (plus a little salt); experiments with a variety of ratios helped us to settle on equal parts of each. With too much tomato puree, the rice tasted like warm gazpacho; with too little, its flavor waned. Though past *Cook's* recipes for pilaf have called for less liquid, we found that when pulpy tomatoes make up a portion of the fluid, a 2:1 ratio of liquid to rice produces just the right texture.

Each and every recipe we consulted called for fresh tomatoes, and when we pitted rice made with canned tomatoes against rice made with fresh, the reason for using the latter became clear. Batches made with fresh tomatoes tasted, well, fresh. Those made with canned tomatoes, however eye-catching, tasted overcooked and too tomatoey; the rice should be scented with tomatoes, not overtaken by them. To capture the one benefit of canned tomatoes—an intense, tomato-red color—we stirred in an untraditional ingredient: tomato paste. Mexican rice often appears washed out, and the tomato paste gave it an appealing hue while adding a little flavor to boot.

To further enhance the flavor of the tomatoes, we investigated charring. The technique of blackening fresh tomatoes on a comal (a flat griddle) is often employed for this dish and other Mexican preparations such as salsa. Because it is a rare American cook who owns a comal, we instead charred some tomatoes in a cast-iron skillet. This deeply flavored, complex rice was a hit, but given that the process was time-consuming and we wanted a dish that could serve as a midweek side dish, we relegated charring to a recipe variation.

The usual method for making Mexican rice is to sauté rinsed, long-grain white rice in oil before adding the cooking liquid. Rice that was rinsed indeed produced more distinct, separate grains when compared with unrinsed rice. While some recipes call for only a quick sauté, cooking the rice until it was golden brown proved crucial in providing a mild, toasted flavor and satisfying texture. As for the amount of oil, we experimented with a wide range, spanning from 3 tablespoons to 1¼ cups. When we essentially deep-fried the rice in copious amounts of oil, as more than one recipe suggested, the rice was much too oily; even straining off excess oil from the rice, as directed, didn't help, and it was a messy process. Insubstantial amounts of oil made rice that was dry and lacking richness, while ⅓ cup seemed just right—this rice was rich but not greasy.

We had questions about whether to sauté other components of the recipe, such as the aromatics and the tomato pulp. We tried multiple permutations and landed on a compromise technique of sautéing a generous amount of garlic and jalapeños, then mixing in a puree of raw tomato and onion. This technique produced the balanced yet fresh flavor we were after and allowed us to process the onion in the food processor along with the tomatoes.

We were having trouble achieving properly cooked rice on the stovetop. The grains inevitably scorched and then turned soupy when we attempted a rescue with extra broth. In the past, we've converted rice recipes from finicky to infallible by simply baking the rice, and testing proved that this recipe was no exception. Still, as we baked batch after batch of rice, we were frustrated by cooking times that were inconsistent. Most batches contained a smattering of crunchy grains mixed in with the tender ones. Prolonged cooking didn't solve the problem; what did was stirring the rice partway through cooking to reincorporate the tomato mixture, which had been settling on top of the pilaf. With this practice in place, every last grain cooked evenly.

While many traditional recipes consider cilantro and jalapeño optional, in our book they are mandatory. The raw herbs and pungent chiles complement the richer tones of the cooked tomatoes, garlic, and onions. When a little something still seemed missing from the rice, we thought to offer wedges of lime. A squirt of acidity illuminated the flavor even further.

WHAT WE LEARNED: Rinse the rice to remove excess starch and then fry it in a modest ⅓ cup of oil for a rich but not greasy flavor. Use fresh tomatoes for the best flavor, but add a little tomato paste for color. Bake the rice to ensure even cooking and finish with chiles, cilantro, and lime juice.

MEXICAN RICE

Serves 6 to 8 as side dish

Because the spiciness of jalapeños varies from chile to chile, we try to control the heat by removing the ribs and seeds (the source of most of the heat) from those chiles that are cooked into the rice. It is important to use an ovensafe pot about 12 inches in diameter so that the rice cooks evenly and in the time indicated. The pot's depth is less important than its diameter; we've successfully used both a straight-sided sauté pan and a Dutch oven. Whichever type of pot you use, it should have a tight-fitting, ovensafe lid. Vegetable broth can be substituted for the chicken broth.

2	medium ripe tomatoes (about 12 ounces), cored and quartered
1	medium onion, preferably white, peeled, trimmed of root end, and quartered
3	medium jalapeño chiles
2	cups long-grain white rice
⅓	cup canola oil
4	medium garlic cloves, minced or pressed through a garlic press (about 4 teaspoons)
2	cups low-sodium chicken broth
1	tablespoon tomato paste
1½	teaspoons salt
½	cup minced fresh cilantro leaves
1	lime, cut into wedges for serving

1. Adjust an oven rack to the middle position and heat the oven to 350 degrees. Process the tomatoes and onion in a food processor until smooth and thoroughly pureed, about 15 seconds, scraping down the bowl if necessary. Transfer the mixture to a liquid measuring cup; you should have 2 cups (if necessary, spoon off excess so that the volume equals 2 cups). Remove the ribs and seeds from 2 jalapeños and discard; mince the flesh and set aside. Mince the remaining jalapeño, including the ribs and seeds; set aside.

2. Place the rice in a large fine-mesh strainer and rinse under cold running water until the water runs clear, about 1½ minutes. Shake the rice vigorously in the strainer to remove all excess water.

3. Heat the oil in a heavy-bottomed straight-sided 12-inch ovenproof sauté pan or Dutch oven with a tight-fitting lid over medium-high heat for 1 to 2 minutes. Drop 3 or 4 grains of rice into the oil; if the grains sizzle, the oil is ready. Add the rice and fry, stirring frequently, until the rice is light golden and translucent, 6 to 8 minutes. Reduce the heat to medium, add the garlic and seeded minced jalapeños, and cook, stirring constantly, until fragrant, about 1½ minutes. Stir in the pureed tomato mixture, chicken broth, tomato paste, and salt. Increase the heat to medium-high and bring to a boil. Cover the pan and transfer to the oven. Bake until the liquid is absorbed and the rice is tender, 30 to 35 minutes, stirring well after 15 minutes.

4. Stir in the cilantro and reserved minced jalapeño with seeds to taste. Serve immediately, passing the lime wedges separately.

VARIATION

MEXICAN RICE WITH CHARRED TOMATOES, CHILES, AND ONION

In this variation, the vegetables are charred in a cast-iron skillet, which gives the finished dish a deeper color and a slightly toasty, smoky flavor. A cast-iron skillet works best for toasting the vegetables; a traditional or even a nonstick skillet will be left with burnt spots that are difficult to remove, even with vigorous scrubbing.

- 2 medium ripe tomatoes (about 12 ounces), cored
- 1 medium onion, preferably white, peeled and halved
- 6 medium garlic cloves, unpeeled
- 3 medium jalapeño chiles, 2 halved with ribs and seeds removed, 1 minced with ribs and seeds

- 2 cups long-grain white rice
- ⅓ cup canola oil
- 2 cups low-sodium chicken broth
- 1 tablespoon tomato paste
- 1½ teaspoons salt
- ½ cup minced fresh cilantro leaves
- 1 lime, cut into wedges for serving

1. Heat a large cast-iron skillet over medium-high heat for about 2 minutes. Add the tomatoes, onion, garlic, and halved chiles and toast the vegetables, using tongs to turn them frequently, until softened and almost completely blackened, about 10 minutes for the tomatoes and 15 to 20 minutes for the other vegetables. When cool enough to handle, trim the root ends from the onion and halve each piece. Remove the skins from the garlic and mince. Mince the jalapeños.

2. Adjust an oven rack to the middle position and heat the oven to 350 degrees. Process the toasted tomato and onion in a food processor until smooth and thoroughly pureed, about 15 seconds, scraping down the bowl if necessary. Transfer the mixture to a liquid measuring cup; you should have 2 cups (if necessary, spoon off any excess so that the volume equals 2 cups).

3. Follow the recipe for Mexican Rice from step 2, adding the toasted minced jalapeños and garlic in step 3 along with the pureed tomato mixture.

Basil and onions get ready for their starring role in a quick pasta sauce.

QUICK pasta

Pasta is usually quick, but all too often quick pasta dishes taste like little time or effort was expended during their preparation. But that doesn't mean the only good pasta dishes take forever to prepare. Many Italian recipes are ready in the time it takes to bring a large pot of water to a boil and cook the pasta. The difference between a good quick pasta dish and a mediocre one is details, details, details.

Nothing is faster than a raw tomato sauce for pasta, but if the sauce is watery and bland, who cares if it's fast? Likewise, asparagus can be easily turned into a pasta sauce, but all too often it's bland and boring. And nontraditional pestos can be a hodgepodge of flavors that don't belong together.

Our goal when developing the recipes in this chapter was to keep things simple while avoiding these common problems. Take 20 minutes to make one of these recipes and see if you agree.

PASTA WITH RAW TOMATO SAUCE

WHAT WE WANTED: An easy, not too watery sauce with rich flavor.

Our favorite way to enjoy summer-ripe tomatoes is tossed with pasta, as a fresh and easy summer dinner. In focusing on summer's beefsteak tomatoes, however, we found that they contain excess liquid that results in a watery, bland sauce. One obvious solution was to seed the tomatoes; it is also customary to peel tomatoes intended for sauce, so we thought we'd try that as well. With an armful of tomatoes, we set out to determine the best, most efficient preparation for a light yet satisfying pasta supper.

The process of both peeling and seeding is time-consuming, and the results were only mediocre. Because many of the tomatoes we bought at the farmers market had thin skins, peeling them was particularly difficult. Also, once peeled and added to the pasta, the tomatoes fell apart, the peel having provided structure that was now gone.

Merely seeding the tomatoes produced the better sauce. We cut the tomatoes along their equator, gave the halves a gentle squeeze, and shook them, easily ridding them of their seeds. Moreover, with the skin left on, the tomatoes held their shape and maintained a rich presence; the tomato flavor stayed in the foreground rather than disappearing into the pasta.

While the rich sun-ripened tomatoes were certainly the focus of these sauces, a few more assertive flavors were needed to take them out of the realm of the ordinary. Olive oil is a classic choice. And because these sauces are raw, the robust and complex flavor of a high-quality extra-virgin olive oil was preferred by tasters. In addition to flavor, the oil also provided moisture and helped to coat the pasta, binding the pasta and sauce together.

But we wanted more flavor, so we developed a variety of taste combinations, including the pungent pairing of garlic and scallions, the briny pairing of feta cheese and black olives, and the fragrant crunchiness of fennel with Parmesan. None of these combinations required any cooking—just a quick chop and toss with the tomatoes. All of these combinations brought the acidity and sweetness of the tomatoes into an ideal balance. A word to the wise: Making these tomato sauces in mid-January with supermarket tomatoes will be disappointing. Only the freshest summer-ripe tomatoes are good enough for these sauces.

WHAT WE LEARNED: Seed the tomatoes to rid them of excess moisture but leave the skins on so the chopped tomatoes have some structural integrity. Add extra-virgin olive oil for flavor and moisture and finish with potent ingredients like olives, garlic, and cheese.

FARFALLE WITH TOMATOES, OLIVES, AND FETA

Serves 4

To prevent the feta from melting into the pasta, add it only after the tomatoes have been tossed with the pasta, which gives the mixture the opportunity to cool slightly.

    Salt
1   pound farfalle
1½ pounds ripe tomatoes, cored, seeded, and cut into ½-inch dice
¼   cup extra-virgin olive oil
1   tablespoon chopped fresh mint leaves
½   cup kalamata olives, pitted and chopped coarse
    Ground black pepper
6   ounces feta cheese, crumbled (about 1½ cups)

1. Bring 4 quarts of water to a rolling boil in a stockpot. Add 1 tablespoon salt and the pasta, stir to separate, and cook until al dente. Drain and return the pasta to the stockpot.

2. Meanwhile, combine the tomatoes, oil, mint, olives, ½ teaspoon salt, and ¼ teaspoon pepper in a medium bowl. Add the tomato mixture to the pasta in the stockpot and toss to combine. Add the feta and toss again. Season with salt and pepper to taste and serve immediately.

FUSILLI WITH TOMATOES AND FRESH MOZZARELLA

Serves 4

For maximum creaminess, use fresh mozzarella packed in water rather than the shrink-wrapped cheese sold in supermarkets.

    Salt
1   pound fusilli
1½ pounds ripe tomatoes, cored, seeded, and cut into ½-inch dice
¼   cup extra-virgin olive oil

1   medium garlic clove, minced or pressed through a garlic press (about 1 teaspoon)
3   medium scallions, sliced thin
    Ground black pepper
8   ounces fresh mozzarella, cut into ½-inch cubes

1. Bring 4 quarts of water to a rolling boil in a stockpot. Add 1 tablespoon salt and the pasta, stir to separate, and cook until al dente. Drain and return the pasta to the stockpot.

2. Meanwhile, combine the tomatoes, oil, garlic, scallions, ½ teaspoon salt, and ¼ teaspoon pepper in a medium bowl. Add the tomato mixture and mozzarella to the pasta in the stockpot and toss to combine. Season with salt and pepper to taste and serve immediately.

ORECCHIETTE WITH TOMATOES, FENNEL, AND PARMESAN

Serves 4

See the illustration below for tips on using a vegetable peeler to cut shavings from a wedge of Parmesan.

    Salt
1   pound orecchiette
1½ pounds ripe tomatoes, cored, seeded, and cut into ½-inch dice

---

TECHNIQUE:
Making Parmesan Shavings

Thin shavings of Parmesan can be used to garnish pasta dishes as well as salad. Simply run a sharp vegetable peeler along the length of a piece of cheese to remove paper-thin curls.

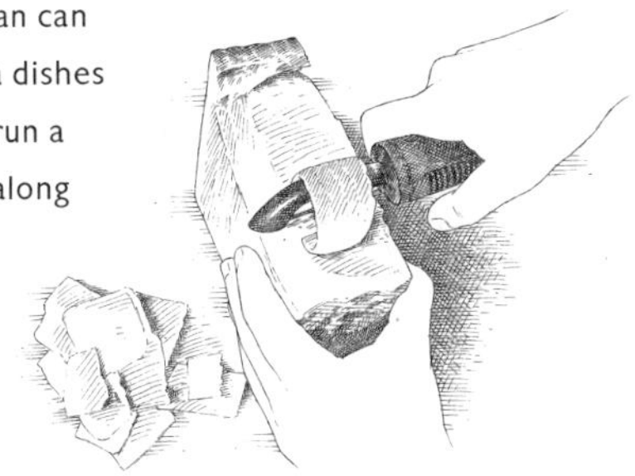

1 small fennel bulb, trimmed of stalks and
   fronds, bulb halved, cored, and sliced thin
   (about 1½ cups)
¼ cup extra-virgin olive oil
¼ cup chopped fresh basil leaves
   Ground black pepper
2 ounces Parmesan cheese, shaved with a
   vegetable peeler

1. Bring 4 quarts of water to a rolling boil in a stockpot.
Add 1 tablespoon salt and the pasta, stir to separate, and cook
until al dente. Drain and return the pasta to the stockpot.

2. Meanwhile, combine the tomatoes, fennel, oil, basil, ½
teaspoon salt, and ¼ teaspoon pepper in a medium bowl.
Add the tomato mixture to the pasta in the stockpot and
toss to combine. Season with salt and pepper to taste and
serve immediately, garnishing individual bowls with the
shaved Parmesan.

GETTING IT RIGHT:
The Effects of Seeding

The tomatoes on the left were not seeded and exuded ¼ cup of
liquid, which would make the pasta sauce watery. The tomatoes
on the right were seeded and exuded just 1 tablespoon of liquid—
not enough to have an adverse effect on the sauce.

Q&A

What is light olive oil?

Light olive oil has been stripped of its characteristic
flavor. It was invented by marketers to appeal to
Americans interested in the heart-healthy properties
of this oil but not its flavor. Light olive oil contains
just as many calories and fat grams as other kinds of
olive oil.

We don't use light olive oil in the test kitchen.
When we want a flavorless oil, we reach for vegetable
or canola oil. When we want the flavor of olive oil in
a salad dressing or pesto, we use extra-virgin olive oil.
When cooking, we choose pure olive oil, which doesn't
have the subtlety of more expensive extra-virgin oils
but is fine for pan-frying or sautéing Italian dishes.

PASTA WITH ASPARAGUS

WHAT WE WANTED: Asparagus sauces for pasta are often bland and boring. We wanted to keep it simple but make this dish livelier.

Asparagus is a natural starting point when trying to make a vegetarian pasta sauce. But more often than not, this dish sounds better than it tastes. Could we create big, intense flavors?

First, we focused on how to cook the asparagus. We ruled out boiling or steaming because the residual water diluted the flavor of the asparagus and made the pasta sauce bland. Grilling added bold and smoky characteristics and broiling also concentrated flavors, but we wanted a simpler method, one that would also allow for the easy introduction of other flavors. We also wanted a cooking method that could be used year-round. The answer, it turned out, was a quick sauté.

We cut the asparagus into 1-inch pieces and sautéed them with other ingredients over high heat. The asparagus caramelized just a bit, and the heat also brought out the flavors of the other ingredients, such as onions, walnuts, garlic, and shallots. To finish off each dish, we tried a variety of additions, including balsamic vinegar, basil leaves, lemon juice, blue cheese, and arugula. The key, we discovered, is not to overpower the asparagus with too much of one bold ingredient. What's wanted instead is a good balance of salty, sweet, and sour ingredients that allow the asparagus flavor to come through.

The bold recipes that follow should forever dispel the myth than pasta and asparagus will be boring.

WHAT WE LEARNED: Cut the asparagus spears into 1-inch pieces and brown them in a hot skillet for a sauce that's both quick and flavorful. And be sure to pair the asparagus with ingredients, like cheese and herbs, that won't overwhelm its delicate, woodsy flavor.

CAMPANELLI WITH ASPARAGUS, BASIL, AND BALSAMIC GLAZE
Serves 4 to 6 as a main dish
Campanelli is a frilly trumpet-shaped pasta that pairs nicely with this sauce. If you cannot find it, fusilli works well, too.

- 1 tablespoon plus ½ teaspoon salt
- 1 pound campanelli
- ¾ cup balsamic vinegar
- 5 tablespoons extra-virgin olive oil
- 1 pound asparagus, tough ends snapped off (see the illustration on page 177), spears halved lengthwise if larger than ½ inch in diameter and cut into 1-inch lengths
- 1 medium-large red onion, halved and sliced thin (about 1½ cups)
- ½ teaspoon ground black pepper
- ¼ teaspoon hot red pepper flakes
- 1 cup chopped fresh basil leaves
- 1 tablespoon juice from 1 lemon
- 2 ounces Pecorino Romano cheese, shaved (about 1 cup) (see the illustration on page 173)

1. Bring 4 quarts of water to a rolling boil in a stockpot. Add 1 tablespoon salt and the pasta, stir to separate, and cook until al dente. Drain and return the pasta to the stockpot.

2. Immediately after putting the pasta in the boiling water, bring the balsamic vinegar to a boil in an 8-inch skillet over medium-high heat; reduce the heat to medium and simmer slowly until reduced to ¼ cup, 15 to 20 minutes.

3. While the pasta is cooking and the balsamic vinegar is reducing, heat 2 tablespoons of the oil in a 12-inch non-stick skillet over high heat until it begins to smoke. Add the asparagus, onion, black pepper, pepper flakes, and remaining

½ teaspoon salt and stir to combine. Cook, without stirring, until the asparagus begins to brown, about 1 minute, then stir and continue to cook, stirring occasionally, until the asparagus is crisp-tender, about 4 minutes longer.

4. Add the asparagus mixture, basil, lemon juice, ½ cup of the Pecorino, and remaining 3 tablespoons oil to the pasta in the stockpot and toss to combine. Serve immediately, drizzling 1 to 2 teaspoons balsamic glaze over individual servings and passing the remaining Pecorino separately.

CAVATAPPI WITH ASPARAGUS, ARUGULA, WALNUTS, AND BLUE CHEESE

Serves 4 to 6 as a main dish

Cavatappi is a short, tubular corkscrew-shaped pasta. Penne is a fine substitute. The grated apple balances the other flavors in this dish.

1	tablespoon plus ½ teaspoon salt
1	pound cavatappi
5	tablespoons extra-virgin olive oil
1	pound asparagus, tough ends snapped off (see the illustration on page 177), spears halved lengthwise if larger than ½ inch in diameter and cut into 1-inch lengths
½	teaspoon ground black pepper
1	cup walnuts, chopped
4	cups lightly packed arugula leaves from 1 large bunch, washed and dried thoroughly
6	ounces strong blue cheese, preferably Roquefort, crumbled (about 1½ cups)
2	tablespoons cider vinegar
1	Granny Smith apple, peeled, for garnish

1. Bring 4 quarts of water to a rolling boil in a stockpot. Add 1 tablespoon salt and the pasta, stir to separate, and cook until al dente. Drain and return the pasta to the stockpot.

2. While the pasta is cooking, heat 2 tablespoons oil in a 12-inch nonstick skillet over high heat until it begins to smoke.

Add the asparagus, pepper, and remaining ½ teaspoon salt and cook, without stirring, until the asparagus is beginning to brown, about 1 minute. Add the walnuts and continue to cook, stirring frequently, until the asparagus is crisp-tender and the nuts are toasted, about 4 minutes longer. Toss in the arugula until wilted.

3. Add the asparagus mixture, blue cheese, vinegar, and the remaining 3 tablespoons oil to the pasta in the stockpot and toss to combine. Serve immediately, grating the apple over individual servings.

FARFALLE WITH ASPARAGUS, TOASTED ALMONDS, AND BROWNED BUTTER

Serves 4 to 6 as a main dish

Watch the butter carefully to make sure it does not burn.

1	tablespoon plus ½ teaspoon salt
1	pound farfalle
2	tablespoons vegetable oil
1	pound asparagus, tough ends snapped off (see the illustration on page 177), spears halved lengthwise if larger than ½ inch in diameter and cut into 1-inch lengths
3	large garlic cloves, sliced thin
2	medium shallots, sliced into thin rings
½	teaspoon ground black pepper
6	tablespoons unsalted butter, cut into 6 pieces
1	cup sliced almonds
¼	cup sherry vinegar
1	teaspoon chopped fresh thyme leaves
2	ounces Parmesan cheese, grated (about 1 cup)

1. Bring 4 quarts of water to a rolling boil in a stockpot. Add 1 tablespoon salt and the pasta, stir to separate, and cook until al dente. Drain and return the pasta to the stockpot.

2. While the pasta is cooking, heat the oil in a 12-inch nonstick skillet over high heat until it begins to smoke. Add the asparagus and cook, without stirring, until beginning to brown, about 1 minute. Add the garlic, shallots, remaining ½ teaspoon salt, and pepper and cook, stirring frequently, until the asparagus is crisp-tender, about 4 minutes. Transfer the asparagus mixture to a large plate and set aside.

3. Return the skillet to high heat and add the butter. When the foaming subsides, add the almonds and cook, stirring constantly, until the almonds are browned and the butter is fragrant, 1 to 2 minutes. Off heat, add the vinegar and thyme. Return the asparagus to the skillet and toss to coat.

4. Add the asparagus mixture and ½ cup of the Parmesan to the pasta in the stockpot and toss to combine. Serve immediately, passing the remaining ½ cup Parmesan separately.

EQUIPMENT CORNER: Pasta Pots

THE NIGHT OWLS KNOW THAT LATE-NIGHT TV OFFERS a plethora of kitchen gadgets. Well, curiosity got the best of us when we saw the pasta pot. We decided to order from TV, as well as round up others from local stores and mail-order sources. In all, we tested five different pasta cooking pots—ranging in price from $7 to $100 (OK . . . the $100 one didn't come from late-night TV) to see if we could retire our trusty stockpot and colander.

These devices come in two basic designs: pots with locking, perforated lids that allow you to drain out the water while keeping the food in the pot in place and pots with fitted perforated inserts that you lift right out of the pot, with the food in it. To test each pot, we cooked a pound each of spaghetti, orzo (small, rice-shaped pasta), potatoes, and frozen corn.

The inserts were a real pain to use. We found that they were sloppy, often drenching the counter or stovetop with water when we pulled them out of the pot. The remedy was to move them into the sink, which is really no easier than transferring a regular pot to the sink with a waiting colander. Worse was the boil-over problem with inserts. Surface tension between the insert and the wall of the pot often caused the water to climb up and boil over where the pot and insert meet at the top, sometimes even extinguishing the gas flame on our test kitchen burners.

By and large, we prefer the locking lids with perforations, but design flaws prevent each model tested from performing perfectly. The lid on the Pasta Pro ($9.95) locks into place and stays put even when we turned the pot fully upside down, but at 6 quarts, the pot itself is too small to comfortably accommodate a gallon of boiling water and one pound of pasta without the danger of overflow. The Ontel Better Pasta Pot ($6.98) was larger, but the locking mechanism for the lid was tricky because it was held in place by the user's hands. You really have to watch how you handle this lid—one adjustment of the hands and the lid can come loose and your pasta will land in the sink.

If you are compelled to purchase a pasta cooking pot, we recommend one with a perforated lid rather than an insert. We didn't find any model with an ideal design though. For now, we'll stick to the trusty stockpot and colander combo.

TECHNIQUE:
Trimming Tough Ends from Asparagus

In our tests, we found that the tough, woody part of the stem will break off in just the right place if you hold the spear the right way. With one hand, hold the asparagus 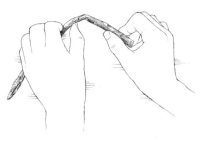 about halfway down the stalk; with the thumb and index fingers of the other hand, hold the spear about an inch up from the bottom. Bend the stalk until it snaps.

Rating Pasta Pots

WE TESTED FIVE DIFFERENT PASTA COOKING POTS BY EVALUATING HOW WELL THEY COOKED AND DRAINED A POUND EACH OF spaghetti, orzo, potatoes, and frozen corn. The results are listed in order of preference. See www.americastestkitchen.com for up-to-date prices and mail-order sources for top-rated products.

HIGHLY RECOMMENDED
Endurance Stainless Steel Footed Colander/Strainer
$25

A colander is still the best way to drain pasta. Our favorite model has a mesh-like perforated bowl that traps even the smallest bits of food.

RECOMMENDED WITH RESERVATIONS
Ontel Better Pasta Pot 5-Piece Set
$6.98

The price is right, but this 8-quart model requires sure hands to secure the lid and a steamy wait for the water to drain.

NOT RECOMMENDED
Pasta Pro Pasta Pot Set
$9.95

The locking lid is secure, but 4 quarts of water and a pound of pasta won't fit in this small 6-quart pot.

NOT RECOMMENDED
Krona Pasta Pot with Strainer Lid
$44.95

A decent 7.5-quart pot, but the perforations in the lid's lip are too few for a pound of pasta to drain in less than 30 seconds.

NOT RECOMMENDED
All-Clad Stainless Steel Multi-Cooker
$99.99

Large space between the bottom of the insert and the 12-quart pot necessitates using the full 12 quarts to boil a pound of pasta. A good pot, but lose the messy insert.

NOT RECOMMENDED
Columbian Home Graniteware Insert
$21.99

Spaghetti gets stuck in the perforations, and orzo falls to the bottom of this 12-quart pot.

PASTA WITH NONTRADITIONAL PESTOS

WHAT WE WANTED: Pesto doesn't have to be made with just basil. We wanted to make quick pestos with a variety of other potent ingredients.

I n the United States, the concept of pesto has moved way beyond basil. Any pureed, highly flavorful oil-based sauce for pasta—including those made from herbs, sun-dried tomatoes, arugula, nuts, or olives—is given the name pesto. Although Italians generally reserve the term pesto for sauces made with basil, they do traditionally use purees of olives and herbs or, perhaps, sun-dried tomatoes and arugula to sauce pasta, especially when fresh basil is out of season.

We found the food processor to be the fastest way to produce a consistently good basil pesto. We found that it's important to use extra-virgin olive oil and a high-quality cheese. When using garlic, we prefer to use it toasted rather than raw. The mellowed and slightly sweetened flavor of toasted garlic allows other flavors to really shine. Unpeeled cloves can be easily toasted in a skillet in less than 10 minutes.

When adding any pesto to cooked pasta, it is important to include some of the cooked pasta water for proper consistency and even distribution. We reserve a portion of the cooking water and stir some of this hot water into the pesto to loosen its consistency and let its flavor bloom. We use more reserved cooking water to moisten the pasta, as necessary, once it has been tossed with the pesto.

Although these pestos will come together very quickly, they can be made in advance. Just store the pestos in an airtight container in the refrigerator for up to 3 days. Press some plastic wrap directly onto the surface of the pesto to prevent discoloration or loss of freshness.

WHAT WE LEARNED: When making pesto, tame the garlic by toasting unpeeled cloves in a hot skillet. And to keep the pasta moist, make sure to reserve some of the pasta cooking water to thin the pesto.

PASTA WITH ARUGULA, GOAT CHEESE, AND SUN-DRIED TOMATO PESTO
Serves 4 to 6

Make sure to rinse the herbs and seasonings from the sun-dried tomatoes. See page 181 for information about buying sun-dried tomatoes.

1   cup drained oil-packed sun-dried tomatoes (one 8½-ounce jar), rinsed, patted dry, and chopped very coarse
6   tablespoons extra-virgin olive oil
¼   cup walnuts, toasted in a small dry skillet over medium heat until browned and fragrant, about 6 minutes
1   small garlic clove, minced or pressed through a garlic press (about ½ teaspoon)
1   ounce Parmesan cheese, grated (about ½ cup)
    Salt and ground black pepper
1   pound campanelli or farfalle
1   medium bunch arugula (about 10 ounces), washed, dried, stemmed, and cut into 1-inch lengths (about 6 cups)
3   ounces goat cheese

1. In a food processor, pulse the sun-dried tomatoes, oil, walnuts, garlic, Parmesan, ½ teaspoon salt, and ⅛ teaspoon pepper until smooth, stopping as necessary to scrape down the sides of the workbowl. Transfer the mixture to a small bowl and set aside.

2. Bring 4 quarts of water to a rolling boil in a stockpot. Add 1 tablespoon salt and the pasta, stir to separate, and cook until al dente. Drain, reserving ¾ cup cooking water, and return the pasta to the stockpot. Immediately stir in the arugula until wilted. Stir ½ cup of the pasta cooking water into the pesto and then stir the pesto into the pasta.

Toss, adding more pasta cooking water as necessary. Serve immediately, dotting individual bowls with ½-inch pieces of the goat cheese.

PENNE WITH TOASTED NUT AND PARSLEY PESTO
Serves 4 to 6
Toasting the unpeeled garlic in a skillet reduces its harshness and gives it a mellow flavor that works well in pesto.

3 medium garlic cloves, unpeeled
1 cup pecans, walnuts, whole blanched almonds, skinned hazelnuts, unsalted pistachios, or pine nuts, or any combination thereof
½ cup packed fresh parsley leaves
7 tablespoons extra-virgin olive oil
1 ounce Parmesan cheese, grated (about ½ cup)
   Salt and ground black pepper
1 pound penne

1. Toast the garlic in a small, dry skillet over medium heat, shaking the pan occasionally, until softened and spotty brown, about 8 minutes; when cool, remove and discard the skins.

2. Toast the nuts in a medium, dry skillet over medium heat, stirring frequently, until golden and fragrant, 4 to 5 minutes. Cool the nuts.

3. In a food processor, process the garlic, nuts, parsley, and oil until smooth, stopping as necessary to scrape down the sides of the workbowl. Transfer the mixture to a small bowl and stir in the Parmesan; season to taste with salt and pepper.

4. Bring 4 quarts of water to a rolling boil in a stockpot. Add 1 tablespoon salt and the pasta, stir to separate, and cook until al dente. Drain, reserving ½ cup cooking water, and return the pasta to the stockpot. Stir ¼ cup of the pasta cooking water into the pesto and then stir the pesto into the pasta. Toss, adding more pasta cooking water as needed. Serve immediately.

SPAGHETTI WITH OLIVE PESTO
Serves 4 to 6
This black pesto is called olivada in Italy. Make sure to use high-quality olives in this recipe. The anchovy adds flavor but not fishiness to the pesto and we recommend its inclusion.

3 medium garlic cloves, unpeeled
1½ cups kalamata olives, pitted
1 medium shallot, chopped coarse
8 large basil leaves
¼ cup packed fresh parsley leaves
1 anchovy fillet, rinsed (optional)
1 ounce Parmesan cheese, grated (about ½ cup), plus extra for serving
6 tablespoons extra-virgin olive oil
1 tablespoon juice from 1 lemon
   Salt and ground black pepper
1 pound spaghetti
1 lemon, cut into wedges

1. Toast the garlic in a small, dry skillet over medium heat, shaking the pan occasionally, until the garlic is softened and

spotty brown, about 8 minutes; when cool, remove and discard the skins.

2. In a food processor, pulse the toasted garlic, olives, shallot, basil, parsley, anchovy, Parmesan, olive oil, and lemon juice, stopping as necessary to scrape down the sides of the workbowl. Transfer the mixture to a small bowl and add salt and pepper to taste.

3. Bring 4 quarts of water to a rolling boil in a stockpot. Add 1 tablespoon salt and the pasta, stir to separate, and cook until al dente. Drain, reserving ½ cup cooking water, and return the pasta to the stockpot. Stir ¼ cup of the pasta cooking water into the pesto and then stir the pesto into the pasta. Toss, adding more pasta cooking water as needed. Serve immediately, passing the lemon wedges and extra Parmesan at the table.

TASTING LAB: Sun-Dried Tomatoes

WHEN SHOPPING FOR SUN-DRIED TOMATOES, YOU HAVE two basic choices. You can buy dried, shelf-stable tomatoes that you reconstitute yourself by soaking them in boiling water, or you can buy ready-to-use tomatoes packed in oil. Is one style of sun-dried tomatoes better than the other? To answer this question, we tested several brands of each style. Tasters were very clear in their preferences. When reconstituted, the dried tomatoes were either mushy or tough. It was very hard to get them just right. The dried tomatoes were also very salty, bitter, or musty. In contrast, the ready-to-use samples packed in oil were pleasantly chewy. However, their flavors were not necessarily good.

We tasted seven samples straight from the jar—Harry's Bazaar, Pastene, Mezzetta, Bella San Luci, Mediterranean Organic, L'Esprit De Campagne, and Trader Joe's. Tasters thought that only the Trader Joe's tomatoes ($3.29 for an 8.5-ounce jar), which are packed in olive oil, garlic, herbs, spices, and sulfur dioxide (to retain color), had the right balance of flavor and sweetness. They were the clear favorite of our tasters. All other brands were thought to have an overpowering musty, herbal flavor, and these tomatoes were indeed noticeably covered in herbs.

Two brands, Mediterranean Organic and L'Esprit De Campagne, were packed in extra-virgin olive oil, which many tasters thought too strong in flavor. Tasters weren't wild about Harry's Bazaar, packed in sunflower oil, or Pastene, packed in a blend of olive and canola oils. We concluded that pure olive oil is the best packing medium for sun-dried tomatoes—it adds just the right amount of flavor without overwhelming the tomatoes. Tasters also noted that brands with brightly colored tomatoes tasted best; darker tomatoes were dull tasting.

Although Trader Joe's tomatoes taste best straight from the jar, we found that we could improve the flavor of the other brands by rinsing away excess herbs and spices. The rinsed tomatoes won't taste as good as our favorite brand, but they won't taste musty, either.

BEST SUN-DRIED TOMATOES
After tasting seven brands, our panel of tasters proclaimed Trader Joe's sun-dried tomatoes the best choice.

Erin is making a list, and checking it twice, before we start shooting our show on Indian cooking.

A PASSAGE to india

Indian food has a reputation for being spicy (most of it is not) and hard to prepare at home (tell that to one billion Indians). However, it is true that many recipes require a long list of spices and other ingredients. Although these ingredients are widely available in most supermarkets, these authentic recipes can be daunting, especially because many of the cooking techniques are unfamiliar to American cooks. Our goal when developing recipes for this chapter was to create dishes with authentic flavors but approachable techniques and ingredient lists.

Mulligatawny is a hearty pureed vegetable soup flavored with coconut, curry powder, ginger, and garlic. It can be thick and gluey or watery and bland. We wanted a rich, aromatic soup that would be hearty but not stodgy. It should also be silky smooth with a good balance of sweet, salty, spicy, and acidic flavors.

Chicken biryani is chicken and rice, Indian style, with saffron-flavored rice, spicy chicken, and a cooling yogurt sauce. Many recipes require a lot of prep time, and the results can be greasy. Our objective was to make this dish lighter, quicker, and better.

MULLIGATAWNY SOUP

WHAT WE WANTED: A mildly spicy and rich soup with a balance of spices and flavors.

Mulligatawny is a pureed vegetable soup that originated in India during the British Raj. The soup is mildly spicy but not hot. There should be some faint sweetness as well, usually from the coconut. The finished soup should be silky and elegant with potent yet balanced spices and aromatics.

We decided to start with the question of the liquid base. Research indicated that chicken stock, lamb stock, beef stock, vegetable stock, and water were possible choices. Tasters found vegetable stock too sweet and vegetal, and beef stock was too strong, even a bit sour. Lamb stock was overpowering, and we ruled it out because of the work involved in making it. In the end, we decided that chicken stock was the ideal base for the competing spices and vegetables. We found that canned broth was fine in this soup. Water made a tasty vegetarian soup that was not quite as rich as the version made with chicken stock.

Curry powder, which is a blend of spices, is a central ingredient in mulligatawny soup. We wondered whether to use a prepackaged blend or to make our own. After experimenting with several homemade curries, we found that the end product was not worth the effort of toasting and grinding our own spices. If we had homemade curry powder on hand, we would use it, but commercial curry powder is just fine with some modifications. We found it best to start with a good-quality curry powder and then boost the flavor with a little additional ground cumin and some cayenne for a bit of heat.

We decided to focus next on the aromatics (garlic and ginger) and coconut. After testing various strategies for adding garlic and ginger flavor to this soup, we found that tasters preferred versions with a small amount of raw garlic and ginger added just before serving and most of the garlic

and ginger sautéed in fat at the outset. To keep tasters from biting into a piece of raw garlic, we adopted a technique common in Indian cooking. We pureed the raw garlic and ginger with water so they could be fully incorporated into the soup for a fresh hit of garlic and ginger.

Coconut gives mulligatawny its distinctive sweet flavor and is authentically Indian along with the curry and ginger. Some recipes call for coconut milk, others for fresh coconut meat, and still others add dried coconut, either sweetened or not. The coconut milk gave the soup a silky consistency but not much coconut flavor. Fresh coconut was not flavorful enough, either, and in any case is much too troublesome to prepare. Dried coconut was the best option, adding enough flavor to the soup without taking over. Sweetened shredded coconut struck many tasters as odd, but unsweetened shredded coconut was delicious.

With our aromatics and spices under control, it was time to test the vegetables, which would give the soup flavor, bulk, and color when pureed. We tested onions, carrots, celery, cauliflower, spinach, peas, potatoes, and bananas. Not surprisingly, we found that onions are a must in the soup. Carrots added color and sweetness, and the celery provided a cool flavor that contrasted nicely with the hot spices. Cauliflower was rejected for the cabbage-like flavor it gave to the soup. Spinach and peas did little to enhance the soup's flavor. In addition, they imparted an undesirable color when pureed.

Potato, which was originally added for flavor, also improved the soup's texture. When pureed, the potato added body to the soup, thickening it slightly. Upon recommendation from several sources, we tried using a banana instead of a potato. The banana produced soup with the same rich body as that made with the potato, but this soup had a richer, slightly sweet flavor that offset the heat from the ginger. Afraid that the banana flavor might be too strong, we held a blind taste test between the banana and the potato.

The tasters unanimously preferred the soup made with the banana, although all were unable to identify the source of the flavor.

A single banana or potato gave the soup some body but did not thicken it quite enough. Adding more banana or potato was the most obvious solution, but more bananas made the soup sweet and the potatoes became gritty in larger amounts. Several recipes suggest using pureed rice or lentils to thicken the soup, but we did not like the thick, porridge-like results. We finally settled on sprinkling flour over the sautéed aromatics to make a roux. One-quarter cup of flour gave the soup the perfect consistency—silky and substantial but not heavy.

Although a few sources say that pureeing is optional, we think that mulligatawny must be smooth. Chunks of meat can float in the finished soup (we developed one variation with chicken, another with lamb), but the soup itself is meant to be refined and smooth. A dollop of yogurt and a shower of cilantro finish the soup. Traditionally, mulligatawny is served over basmati rice or red lentils, although it can stand on its own.

WHAT WE LEARNED: Chicken broth is the best base for this pureed vegetable-laden soup. Shredded unsweetened coconut is the best source for this distinct ingredient. Banana or potato, along with a roux, will give the soup proper body when pureed.

MULLIGATAWNY SOUP

Serves 6 to 8

For freshness, puree some of the garlic and ginger with water in a blender, then leave this mixture in the blender while making the soup. The finished soup is pureed in the same blender, where it will pick up a hit of spicy raw garlic and ginger flavor.

4	medium garlic cloves, 2 peeled and 2 finely minced
1	piece (about 1½ inches) fresh ginger, peeled and grated (about 1½ tablespoons)
¼	cup water
3	tablespoons unsalted butter
2	medium onions, chopped medium
1	teaspoon tomato paste
½	cup shredded unsweetened coconut
1½	tablespoons curry powder
1	teaspoon ground cumin
¼	teaspoon cayenne
¼	cup all-purpose flour
7	cups low-sodium chicken broth
2	medium carrots, peeled and chopped coarse
1	medium celery rib, chopped coarse
1	medium very ripe banana (about 5 ounces), peeled, or 1 small boiling potato (about 5 ounces), peeled and cut into 1-inch pieces
	Salt and ground black pepper
	Plain yogurt
2	tablespoons minced fresh cilantro leaves

1. Place the 2 peeled whole garlic cloves, 2 teaspoons of the grated ginger, and the water in a blender. Blend until smooth, about 25 seconds; leave the mixture in the blender jar and set aside. (You will be pureeing the soup right in the blender with the garlic and ginger.)

2. Heat the butter in a large stockpot or Dutch oven over medium heat until foaming. Add the onions and tomato paste and cook, stirring frequently, until the onions are softened and beginning to brown, about 3 minutes. Stir in the coconut and cook until fragrant, about 1 minute. Add the minced garlic, remaining 2½ teaspoons ginger, curry powder, cumin, cayenne, and flour; stir until evenly combined, about 1 minute. Whisking constantly and vigorously, gradually add the chicken broth.

3. Add the carrots, celery, and whole banana to the pot. Increase the heat to medium-high and bring to a boil. Cover, reduce the heat to low, and simmer until the vegetables are tender, about 20 minutes.

4. Puree the soup in batches in the blender with the garlic and ginger until very smooth. Wash and dry the pot. Return the pureed soup to the clean pot and season to taste with salt and pepper. Warm the soup over medium heat until hot, about 1 minute. (The soup can be refrigerated in an airtight container for up to 3 days. Warm over low heat until hot; do not boil.) Ladle the soup into individual bowls, spoon a dollop of the yogurt over each bowl, sprinkle with the cilantro, and serve immediately.

TECHNIQUE: Grating Ginger

Most cooks who use fresh ginger have scraped their fingers on the grater when the piece of ginger gets down to a tiny nub. Instead of cutting a small chunk of ginger off a larger piece and then grating, try this method: Peel a small section of the large piece of ginger. Grate the peeled portion, using the rest of the ginger as a handle to keep fingers safely away from the grater.

MULLIGATAWNY SOUP WITH CHICKEN
Serves 8
Basmati rice makes a good accompaniment to this soup.

Follow the recipe for Mulligatawny Soup, adding 4 medium (about 1½ pounds) boneless, skinless chicken breasts to the simmering stock in step 3 just before covering the pot. Simmer until cooked through, about 20 minutes. With tongs, transfer the cooked chicken to a cutting board, cool slightly, and cut crosswise into slices ¼ inch wide. Continue with the recipe, adding the reserved chicken to the pureed soup in the pot in step 4. Warm over medium heat until the chicken is hot, about 5 minutes. Garnish as directed.

MULLIGATAWNY SOUP WITH LAMB
Serves 8 to 10
This hearty, stew-like variation is especially good served with red lentils. It's also quite nice with basmati rice.

4	medium garlic cloves, 2 peeled and 2 finely minced
1	piece (about 1½ inches) fresh ginger, peeled and grated (about 1½ tablespoons)
¼	cup water
2	tablespoons olive oil
5	pounds lamb shoulder chops, bone, fat, and gristle discarded; meat cut into 1½-inch pieces
7	cups low-sodium chicken broth
3	tablespoons unsalted butter
2	medium onions, chopped medium
1	teaspoon tomato paste
½	cup shredded unsweetened coconut
1½	tablespoons curry powder
1	teaspoon ground cumin
¼	teaspoon cayenne
¼	cup all-purpose flour
2	medium carrots, peeled and chopped coarse
1	medium celery rib, chopped coarse

1   medium very ripe banana (about 5 ounces),
     peeled, or 1 boiling potato (about 5 ounces),
     peeled and cut into 1-inch pieces
    Salt and ground black pepper
    Plain yogurt
2   tablespoons minced fresh cilantro leaves

1. Place the 2 peeled whole garlic cloves, 2 teaspoons of the ginger, and the water in a blender. Blend until smooth, about 25 seconds; leave the mixture in the blender jar and set aside. (You will be pureeing the soup right in the blender with the garlic and ginger.)

2. Heat a large stockpot or Dutch oven over medium-high heat until very hot. Add 1 tablespoon of the olive oil, swirl to coat the pan bottom, and add half of the lamb pieces. Cook until the lamb is well browned, about 2 to 3 minutes. Transfer the browned lamb to a medium bowl with a slotted spoon. Add the remaining tablespoon of oil to the pot, swirl to coat the pan bottom, add the remaining lamb, and cook until the lamb is well browned on all sides. Return all the lamb to the pot and add the chicken broth, scraping up the browned bits from the pan bottom with a wooden spoon. Bring to a simmer, cover, reduce the heat to medium-low, and simmer until the lamb is tender, about 20 minutes. With a slotted spoon, transfer the lamb to a medium bowl, cover, and reserve. Pour the broth into another bowl and reserve.

3. Heat the butter in a large stockpot or Dutch oven over medium heat until foaming. Add the onions and tomato paste and cook, stirring frequently, until the onions are softened and beginning to brown, about 3 minutes. Stir in the coconut and cook until fragrant, about 1 minute. Add the minced garlic, remaining 2½ teaspoons ginger, curry powder, cumin, cayenne, and flour; stir well until evenly combined, about 1 minute. Whisking constantly and vigorously, gradually add the reserved broth used to cook the lamb.

4. Add the carrots, celery, and whole banana to the stock. Increase the heat to medium-high and bring to a boil. Cover, reduce the heat to low, and simmer until the vegetables are tender, about 20 minutes.

5. Puree the soup in batches in the blender with the garlic and ginger until very smooth. Wash and dry the pot. Return the pureed soup to the clean pot and season to taste with salt and pepper. Add the lamb pieces and warm the soup over medium heat until the lamb is hot, about 5 minutes. Ladle the soup into individual bowls, spoon a dollop of the yogurt over each bowl, sprinkle with the cilantro, and serve immediately.

TASTING LAB: Curry Powder

LIKE CHILI POWDER, CURRY POWDER IS NOT A SINGLE spice but rather a blend of spices. Unlike chili powder, which contains about 80 percent chile pepper, there is no such dominant spice in curry powder. Because of this, flavors vary greatly depending on the blend. Among the spices most commonly used are cardamom, cumin, fenugreek, turmeric (which gives curry its characteristically yellow color), fennel, nutmeg, and chiles. We chose seven mild curry powders (hot curry powder, which contains more red pepper and other hot spices, is also available) and tasted them all in a simple rice pilaf, cooking the curry powder in oil briefly to allow the flavors to bloom.

Overall, tasters leaned toward big, bolder, brighter blends that delivered a lot of color and flavor. First place finisher, Tone's, a darling of the discount club stores, was praised for its "good, heavy spice mix." Distant second place finisher Durkee was also noted for its "shocking color" and "round" flavor. On the other hand, last-place finisher Sun Brand, though praised by some as "nutty and rich," ultimately lost points for its "pale, boring" appearance (in contrast to the bright yellow of the other brands, Sun Brand was very light and almost beige in color).

Unfortunately, some manufacturers consider their exact spice blends to be proprietary information, and they would not share that information with us. Therefore, we cannot speculate on why Tone's dominated over such specialty brands as Penzeys and Kalustyan's.

Rating Curry Powders

HIGHLY RECOMMENDED
Tone's Curry Powder **$7.39 for 16 ounces**

Proprietary Blend

Though there was "nothing exotic" about this brand sold in many warehouse clubs, tasters did praise its "strong" curry flavor.

RECOMMENDED
Durkee Curry Powder **$6.70 for 17 ounces**

Proprietary Blend

Tasters praised this supermarket brand for its "good balance" and deep color. Look for extra-large containers of this brand in warehouse clubs.

RECOMMENDED
Penzeys Sweet Curry Powder **$4.19 for 2.2 ounces**

Contains turmeric, Moroccan coriander, cumin, ginger, fenugreek, nutmeg, fennel, cinnamon, white pepper, cardamom, cloves, Tellicherry black pepper, cayenne red pepper

"Extremely mild" wrote one taster about this mail-order favorite. Seemed "typical" to others.

RECOMMENDED
Spice Islands Curry Powder **$4.75 for 2.1 ounces**

Proprietary Blend

Fans praised this blend's "warmth," but others dismissed it as "flat." Available in supermarkets, especially in the West.

NOT RECOMMENDED
Kalustyan's Imperial Mild Curry Powder **$4.49 for 4 ounces**

Cumin, coriander, black pepper, cinnamon, cloves, cardamom, ginger, nutmeg, turmeric, chili powder

Tasters picked up on the heavy cardamom and clove flavors in this mail-order brand and were not impressed. "No depth or complexity," wrote one taster. "Bland and uninteresting."

NOT RECOMMENDED
McCormick Curry Powder **$5.15 for 1.75 ounces**

Proprietary Blend

Several tasters noted the "strangely vegetal" flavor of this supermarket staple, which many compared unfavorably to celery salt.

NOT RECOMMENDED
Sun Brand Madras Curry Powder **$2.79 for 4 ounces**

Coriander, turmeric, chilies, salt, cumin, fennel, black pepper, garlic, ginger, fenugreek, cinnamon, cloves, anise, mustard

Most tasters were put off by the "pale and brown" color of this curry. They were not impressed by the "burnt," "bland" flavor either.

CHICKEN AND RICE, INDIAN-STYLE

WHAT WE WANTED: Chicken biryani is a complicated (and often greasy) classic Indian dish. Could we make this dish simpler and lighter?

Chicken biryani has about as much in common with American-style chicken and rice as naan does with Wonder bread. They both share the same major ingredients but diverge widely from there. In biryani, long-grain basmati rice takes center stage, enriched with butter, saffron, and a variety of fresh herbs and pungent spices. Pieces of tender chicken and browned onions are layered with the rice and baked until the flavors have mingled. This is India in a pot.

But it comes at a stiff price. Traditional biryani recipes are long in both ingredients and labor. The chicken is rubbed with spices and marinated before being browned; the rice is soaked, blanched, and mixed with a complex masala, or blend, of innumerable spices; the onions are deep-fried. Finally everything is layered (rice, onions, chicken, repeat) into a cooking vessel and baked or steamed until the flavors have blended. In addition, most biryani recipes we tested were made greasy by the deep-fried onions, and the rice had overcooked by the time the chicken was done. We set out to find a middle path between the extremes of dull simplicity and epicurean complexity.

We prepared a few classic biryani recipes to better acquaint ourselves with the dish, a task that required a full day in the test kitchen and produced a huge pile of dirty dishes. We made three time-saving discoveries. First, we learned that we could skip the step of marinating the chicken (too much time, too little flavor enhancement). Second, we could prepare the whole recipe on the stovetop, eliminating the need for an oven. Third, it was possible to cook the onions and the chicken in the same large skillet, saving a pan. The streamlined recipe, although still not a 30-minute supper, now consisted of cooking the onions, browning the chicken, parboiling the rice, and then simmering/steaming the layered biryani until done.

The best-tasting biryani from our recipe tests was made with two abundant layers of deep-fried onions, but they inevitably turned the dish greasy. Onions sautéed in a tablespoon of fat (oil or butter) failed to brown properly. More fat was clearly necessary, but how much could we add without turning the dish greasy? We started with ½ cup of fat for two sliced onions and reduced it 1 tablespoon at a time. In the end, 3 tablespoons proved sufficient. Butter prevailed over oil, adding more flavor and color.

Tasters preferred dark meat chicken—it was more flavorful and juicy than white meat, which ended up dry. Bone-in thighs are the test kitchen favorite because they are so meaty. Having already eliminated marinating, we followed test kitchen protocol for braising chicken pieces. (Biryani is, in essence, a braise because it uses moist, low heat for cooking.) To eke out as much flavor as we could, we browned the chicken deeply, with the skin on for protection. Before layering the pieces with the rice, we stripped off the skin. With this last step, the greasiness issue was finally put to rest.

Biryani's subtle, delicate flavor and aroma are largely derived from the masala of whole spices blended into the rice. (Ground spices—we tested these as well—tasted raw.) Cardamom and cinnamon are essential, but too much of

either easily overwhelmed other flavors. Tasters quickly ruled out nutmeg and cloves as overpowering. Coriander, too, was excluded, because it was too mild. In the end, tasters approved of cardamom, cinnamon, cumin seed, and fresh ginger sliced into coins. Sweet, earthy, sharp, and musky, the spices paired well together. Lightly smashing the cardamom and ginger with a chef's knife intensified their flavor.

Before serving, we diligently fished out the spices from the rice as tasters strongly objected to unexpectedly biting down on whole cardamom pods, but this nitpicky task grew tiresome. We began thinking of ways to isolate the spices. In French cooking, herbs and spices are often bundled together in cheesecloth and added to soups. The liquid flows through the permeable bundle, and the soup is flavored. We decided to try a little fusion cooking and give the bundle idea a whirl. We tied the spices together and added the bundle to the layered biryani before steaming, but that accomplished little. In the end, an even easier solution delivered big flavor. We simply simmered the bundle in the water used to parboil the rice. We also found that adding a portion of this flavored liquid to the layered biryani—sort of like adding pasta cooking water to a pasta dish—further intensified the spice flavor. Now we had included both French and Italian technique in streamlining a classic Indian dish.

Saffron is mixed with the rice as both a coloring and a flavoring agent. Any more than a pinch turned the rice Day-Glo orange and made it taste medicinal. Tasters demanded a fair amount of garlic and jalapeño, as well as some seeds from the chiles for additional fire. A little sweetness from currants (or raisins, in a pinch) helped to temper the heat and accent the warm spices. Cilantro and mint, both standard biryani ingredients, found favor with tasters.

WHAT WE LEARNED: Sauté the onions in just 3 tablespoons of butter for extra flavor without greasiness. Brown the chicken and then remove the skin, again to keep greasiness under control. Use a spice-flavored broth to cook the rice and perfume the dish with the flavors of cardamom, cinnamon, ginger, and cumin.

CHICKEN BIRYANI

Serves 4

This recipe requires a 3½- to 4-quart saucepan about 8 inches in diameter. Do not use a large, wide Dutch oven, as it will adversely affect both the layering of the dish and the final cooking times. Begin simmering the spices in the water prior to preparing the remaining ingredients; the more time the spices have to infuse the water (up to half an hour), the more flavor they will give to the rice. Biryani is traditionally served with a cooling yogurt sauce; ideally, you should make it before starting the biryani to allow the flavors in the sauce to meld, but no longer than a day ahead, otherwise the garlic flavor will become overpowering.

yogurt sauce

- 1 cup whole milk or low-fat plain yogurt
- 1 medium garlic clove, minced or pressed through a garlic press (about 1 teaspoon)
- 2 tablespoons minced fresh cilantro leaves
- 2 tablespoons minced fresh mint leaves
  Salt and ground black pepper

chicken and rice

- 10 cardamom pods, preferably green, smashed with a chef's knife
- 1 cinnamon stick
- 1 piece (about 2 inches) fresh ginger, cut into ½-inch-thick coins and smashed with a chef's knife
- ½ teaspoon cumin seed
- 3 quarts water
  Salt
- 4 bone-in, skin-on chicken thighs (about 1½ pounds), trimmed of excess skin and fat and patted dry with paper towels
  Ground black pepper
- 3 tablespoons unsalted butter
- 2 medium onions, sliced thin (about 4 cups)
- 2 medium jalapeño chiles, one seeded and chopped fine, the other chopped fine with seeds

4 medium garlic cloves, minced or pressed through a garlic press (about 1 generous tablespoon)

1¼ cups basmati rice

½ teaspoon saffron threads, lightly crumbled

¼ cup dried currants or raisins

2 tablespoons chopped fresh cilantro leaves

2 tablespoons chopped fresh mint leaves

1. FOR THE YOGURT SAUCE: Combine the yogurt, garlic, cilantro, and mint in a small bowl; season to taste with salt and pepper. Let stand at least 30 minutes to blend flavors or cover and refrigerate up to 1 day before serving.

GETTING IT RIGHT: The Layered Look

Layering the ingredients into a saucepan is the secret to the mingling of flavors in chicken biryani. Here's the assembly method that works best: Return half of the parboiled rice to the saucepan, top with half the onions, followed by the chicken pieces, the rest of the onions, and then the rest of the rice. Moisten everything with the spice-infused cooking liquid from the rice, cover, and steam over medium-low heat until the chicken is done and the rice is tender.

---

2. FOR THE CHICKEN AND RICE: Wrap the cardamom pods, cinnamon stick, ginger, and cumin seed in a small piece of cheesecloth and secure with kitchen twine. In a 3½- to 4-quart heavy-bottomed saucepan about 8 inches in diameter, bring the water, spice bundle, and 1½ teaspoons salt to a boil over medium-high heat. Reduce the heat to medium and simmer, partially covered, until the spices have infused the water, at least 15 minutes (but no longer than 30 minutes).

3. Meanwhile, season both sides of the chicken thighs with salt and pepper and set aside. Heat the butter in a 12-inch nonstick skillet over medium-high heat until the foaming subsides; add the onions and cook, stirring frequently, until soft and dark brown about the edges, 10 to 12 minutes. Add the jalapeños and garlic and cook, stirring frequently, until fragrant, about 2 minutes. Transfer the onion mixture to a bowl, season lightly with salt, and set aside. Wipe out the skillet with paper towels, return the heat to medium-high, and place the chicken thighs skin-side down in the skillet; cook, without moving the chicken, until well browned, about 5 minutes. Flip the chicken and brown the second side, 4 to 5 minutes longer; transfer the chicken to a plate and remove and discard the skin. Tent with foil to keep warm.

4. If necessary, return the spice-infused water to a boil over high heat; stir in the rice and cook 5 minutes, stirring occasionally. Drain the rice through a fine-mesh strainer, reserving ¾ cup of the cooking liquid; discard the spice bundle. Transfer the rice to a medium bowl; stir in the saffron and currants (the rice will turn splotchy yellow). Spread half of the rice evenly in the bottom of the now-empty saucepan using a rubber spatula. Scatter half of the onion mixture over the rice, then place the chicken thighs, skinned-side up, on top of the onions; add any accumulated chicken juices. Sprinkle evenly with the cilantro and mint, scatter the remaining onions over the herbs, then cover with the remaining rice; pour the reserved cooking liquid evenly over the rice.

Several American rice growers now sell their own basmati. Unfortunately, the two products we tasted couldn't compare with the real thing. Their flavor was not nearly as aromatic as Indian-grown basmati, and the cooked grains were soft and stubby. We later learned that American-grown basmati is not aged and hence doesn't expand as much as Indian-grown rice. Luckily, Indian rice is available in most supermarkets and costs about the same as domestic basmati. Make sure that the label indicates that the rice has been aged; otherwise your biryani might be uncharacteristically mushy.

5. Cover the saucepan and cook over medium-low heat until the rice is tender and the chicken is cooked through, about 30 minutes (if a large amount of steam is escaping from the pot, reduce the heat to low). Run a heatproof rubber spatula around the inside rim of the saucepan to loosen any affixed rice; using a large serving spoon, spoon the biryani into individual bowls, scooping from the bottom of the pot and serving 1 chicken thigh per person.

CALIFORNIA DREAMIN'
This California rice lacked the aroma and flavor of the Indian original, and tasters found the cooked grains "mushy" and broken.

TASTING LAB: Basmati Rice

BASMATI IS A VARIETY OF VERY LONG-GRAIN RICE most commonly grown in northern India and Pakistan. It is aged for a minimum of a year, though often much longer, before being packaged. Aging dehydrates the rice, which translates into grains that, once cooked, expand greatly—more so than any other long-grain rice.

TROUBLE IN TEXAS
Comments on this rice were nearly identical to those about the California rice, including "gummy," "soft," and "chewed-up looking."

THE ORIGINAL AND THE BEST
Tasters' comments on Indian-grown, aged rice included "great texture," "great grain separation," "something to chew on," and "toasty."

SCIENCE DESK:
Where's the Chile Heat?

Chiles get their "heat"—or "pungency," as the experts like to say—from a group of chemical compounds called capsaicinoids, the best known of which is capsaicin. To figure out where most of these compounds reside, we donned rubber gloves and separated the colored green flesh, whitish pith (also called membranes or ribs), and seeds from 40 jalapeños. We then sent the lot to our food lab. It turned out there were just 5 milligrams of capsaicin per kilogram of green jalapeño flesh (not enough to really make much impact on the human tongue), 73 mg per kg of seeds, and an impressive 512 mg per kg of pith.

According to the Chile Pepper Institute, a research and education center housed at New Mexico State University, capsaicin is produced in the pith, not by the seeds. The reason why the seeds registered more heat than the flesh is simply because they are embedded in the pith; they are essentially guilty—or hot—by reason of association. From now on, then, when we want to carefully mete out the fire in our salsa or biryani, we'll do it by means of the pith. The seeds will just be along for the ride.

TASTING LAB: Saffron

While most cooks know that saffron is the world's most expensive spice, few are aware that it is grown in many locations and that price and quality can vary considerably. Though the bulk of commercially produced saffron comes from Spain and Iran, it is also harvested on a small scale in India, Greece, France, and, closer to home, in Lancaster County, Pennsylvania.

We decided to toss saffron from different places purchased at different prices into a few pots and set up a test. We prepared three batches of risotto alla Milanese and flavored one with Spanish saffron, one with Indian, and one with American. (Chicken biryani is so complex that we worried it would not provide a neutral background against which to taste the delicate flavor of the saffron.)

The finished risottos were similar in hue, though the Indian Kashmir saffron threads were darkest prior to cooking. Surprisingly, no one cared for the Indian saffron, although it was almost twice as costly as the other two and is generally regarded as one of the best in the world. Despite its heady aroma, floral tones, and earthy scent, many tasters found it "tinny" and "bland" when cooked. The risotto made with the Spanish saffron was better, but we overwhelmingly favored the risotto made with the Pennsylvania-grown saffron, judging it the "most potent" and "perfumed" of the three samples.

Our conclusion: Just because saffron has an expensive pedigree doesn't mean it will taste good. Shop carefully, buying only saffron threads, not ground saffron. And, if you find domestic saffron, it can be an excellent—and relatively inexpensive—alternative.

TECHNIQUE:
Crumbling Saffron Threads

To extract as much flavor as possible from saffron, crumble the threads between your fingers just before adding them to recipes. Crumbling the threads releases flavorful oils and helps the saffron dissolve quickly in liquid.

Chicken Biryani **page 191**

Thai Grilled Chicken with Spicy, Sweet, and Sour Dipping Sauce **page 147**

196

Glazed Carrots **page 60**

Eggplant Parmesan **page 225**

Pasta e Fagioli **page 25**

Crab Towers with Avocado and Gazpacho Salsas **page 113**

Grilled Glazed Salmon **page 153**

Grill-Roasted Beef Tenderloin **page 136**

Southern Cornbread **page 130**

Sticky Buns with Pecans **page 272**

Nut Crescent Cookies **page 301**

Classic Brownies **page 283**

Chocolate Sour Cream Bundt Cake **page 307**

Spiced Pumpkin Cheesecake **page 320**

208

Glazed Butter Cookies, Jam Sandwiches, Lime-Glazed Coconut Snowballs, and Chocolate-Cherry Bar Cookies with Hazelnuts **page 295**

Pissaladière **page 214**

PISSALADIÈRE

CHAPTER 16

Pissaladière is Provençal street food, a fragrant, pizza-like tart prized for its contrast of salty black olives and anchovies against a backdrop of sweet caramelized onions and thyme. Supporting this rough and rustic flavor combination is a wheaty crust with a texture that is part chewy pizza and part crisp cracker. Commonly eaten as an appetizer or even a light supper alongside a salad, this classic French favorite is still something of a foreigner to most Americans—darkly handsome but a bit difficult to understand.

But the ingredients are simple enough. The crust is basically pizza dough, and the toppings are caramelized onions, herbs, anchovies, and olives. The key is to balance all of these strong flavors so that they work together. We knew we could figure out how to make a great version of this French classic.

PISSALADIÈRE

WHAT WE WANTED: The classic olive, anchovy, and onion pizza from Provence is easy enough to prepare, but each ingredient must be handled just so. We wanted a recipe worthy of the finest bakery in Nice.

When coming up with our version of pissaladière, we had to start with a series of "get acquainted" tests to fully comprehend the range of possibilities. Most recipes produced a crust in the style of a pizza, others called for savory pie dough fit into a fluted tart pan, and we even found a few that used squares of store-bought puff pastry. All of them called for caramelized onions, black olives, thyme, and anchovies, but additional sources of flavor, such as Parmesan, sun-dried tomatoes, basil, and oregano, were not uncommon. As for the basic flavor ingredients, almost all of the caramelized onions were underdone, while the bullish flavor of anchovies overran the olives and thyme. Anchovies, we thought, should not rule but rather act as a counterpoint to the sweet onions, briny olives, and fragrant thyme.

As for the crust, the test kitchen quickly eliminated puff pastry and pie dough. Unfortunately, the more authentic pizza-like crusts weren't very good, either. Textures were too short (think shortbread) and crackery or overly soft and doughy. Tasters thought that good pissaladière should have a dual-textured crust that is crisp on the outside (like a cracker) and chewy on the inside.

Although they are not exactly right for pissaladière, we whipped up three different pizza crusts to see if any could be used as a jumping-off point. The thin crust wasn't sturdy enough and the deep-dish crust was too doughy, but the traditional crust was the right thickness (about half an inch) and had the right flavor. Knowing that we wanted it to be chewier, with a more cracker-like exterior, we took a closer look at each of its four major ingredients—bread flour, oil, water, and yeast—to see where we could make adjustments.

We replaced various amounts of bread flour with all-purpose flour but made zero headway. Bread flour has more protein than all-purpose, and that translates into a more substantial chew. Testing amounts of olive oil ranging from none at all up to 6 tablespoons, we again found that the original recipe (which called for 1 tablespoon) produced the best balance of crisp to tender without causing the dough to be brittle (a problem when the amount of oil dropped below 1 tablespoon) or greasy (a problem when the amount of oil exceeded 1 tablespoon).

Next on the list of ingredients to tinker with was water. The original recipe called for ¾ cup of water to 2 cups of flour. Less water made the crust drier (no surprise) and tougher. More water made the dough chewier, but we soon learned that there was such a thing as too chewy. When we increased the water to 1¼ cups, the crust baked up with huge holes and was as chewy as bubble gum. The crust made with 1 cup of water proved to be a happy medium—chewier than the original pizza crust but not over the top.

When we varied the amount of yeast, the flavor changed (as did the rising time), but not the texture. Less yeast and an overnight rise—a common flavor-enhancing technique—did produce a crust with a slightly more complex flavor, but it was awfully hard to detect once it came up against the onions, olives, and anchovies. One teaspoon of yeast pumped the dough through the first rise in a convenient 75 minutes (give or take 15 minutes, depending on the humidity and the kitchen temperature), during which there was ample time to prepare and caramelize the onions.

Doughs made in a standing mixer, a food processor, and by hand showed substantial differences and, surprisingly, tasters preferred the method most professional bakers would scoff at. Doughs made by hand and in the mixer were tough and snappy after being baked, requiring a full set of well-rooted molars. To achieve the best texture, this dough apparently would accept only minimal handling. We knew

that bread dough could be kneaded in a food processor in a two-step process. Step 1 is to whiz the ingredients for a mere 15 seconds until they come together; step 2 is to wait for two minutes and then knead the dough in the food processor an additional 30 seconds. It turned out that the secret to perfect pissaladière dough was to complete step 1 and simply ignore step 2! This crust was a winner, unanimously favored for its cracker-like exterior and decently chewy crumb. (We eventually figured out how to make the dough by hand and in a standing mixer, but the process for both was more time-consuming and difficult, and the timing and results were never as consistent.) The best part of the food processor technique is that it's foolproof. You know that the dough has been processed properly when it comes together in a ball. Nothing could be simpler.

Dough pressed onto a rimmed baking sheet didn't brown nearly as well as a free-form oval baked directly on a preheated baking stone at 500 degrees. Pressing the dough out on parchment paper made for an easy transfer to the oven. Tasters also preferred the rustic texture of dough that was pressed out by hand as opposed to the uniform consistency of dough flattened by a rolling pin.

A key problem with this recipe is the stickiness of the dough. We had been using plenty of flour when shaping the dough, until, on a whim, we tried oil instead. Good idea. Not only was it a snap to shape the dough on the parchment, but the extra oil pressed into the bottom of the crust made it even crisper. Brushing the dough with yet more olive oil before adding the toppings further ensured a cracker-like exterior, officially turning this crust from pizza to pissaladière.

Most recipes for caramelized onions subscribe to one of two methods—low and slow or fast and furious—yet neither works. Low and slow dries out the onions before

they have a chance to get dark, while fast and furious leaves the onions crunchy and burnt tasting. Taking a cue from our caramelized onion recipe, we used a combination of high and low heat, starting the onions on high to release their juices and soften them, then turning the heat to medium-low to let the juices caramelize.

A nonstick skillet works best for caramelizing onions. The low sides of a skillet (as opposed to the high sides of a Dutch oven) allow the steam to evaporate rather than interfere with browning, while the nonstick surface ensures that the caramelization sticks to the onions, not the pan. Once the onions were cooked, though, we had problems sprinkling them over the pizza, as they tended to clump. The solution? We stirred in just a bit of water once we removed the onions from the heat.

Whereas most recipes call for whole black olives, we found that they roll around and occasionally fall off the crust. In addition, the intense heat of the oven dries them to a leathery texture. A better method is to chop the olives coarsely and layer them underneath the onions, where they are protected from overcooking. This same trick also works with the leaves of fresh thyme.

It's traditional to arrange anchovies across the top of a pissaladière in a crosshatch pattern. This was too much anchovy for the test kitchen staff, so we focused on how to incorporate their strong flavor without offending anyone. As with the olives, we found it best to chop and spread them underneath the onions. Just four anchovies per tart was perfect, and rinsing them first made sure they weren't too salty or fishy. (Still, several fish lovers missed the crosshatching, so we included it as an option.) The only untraditional flavors that passed our relatively strict code of authenticity were fennel seeds and freshly minced parsley, and both are optional.

WHAT WE LEARNED: Make the dough in a food processor and knead it as little as possible to create a crust with a crisp exterior and chewy crumb. Bury the anchovies and olives under the caramelized onions to protect them from burning in the oven.

PISSALADIÈRE

Makes 2 tarts, serving 8 to 10 as a first course

If your food processor includes a plastic dough blade attachment, use it; its short blades and dull edges make kneading easier on the motor. If not, the regular metal blade works almost as well. For best flavor, use high-quality oil-packed anchovies; in a recent tasting, Ortiz was our favorite brand. The dough in this recipe rises for 1 to 1½ hours. If a longer or overnight rise is more convenient, make the dough with ½ teaspoon of instant yeast and let it rise in the refrigerator for 16 to 24 hours. The caramelized onions can also be made a day ahead and refrigerated.

dough

- 2 cups (11 ounces) bread flour, plus more for dusting the work surface
- 1 teaspoon instant yeast
- 1 teaspoon salt
- 1 tablespoon olive oil, plus more for brushing the dough and greasing hands
- 1 cup warm water (about 110 degrees)

caramelized onions

- 2 tablespoons olive oil
- 2 pounds yellow onions, sliced ¼ inch thick
- ½ teaspoon salt
- 1 teaspoon brown sugar
- 1 tablespoon water

olives, anchovies, and garnishes

- Olive oil
- ½ teaspoon ground black pepper
- ½ cup niçoise olives, pitted and chopped coarse
- 8 anchovy fillets, rinsed, patted dry, and chopped coarse (about 2 tablespoons), plus 12 fillets, rinsed and patted dry for garnish (optional)
- 2 teaspoons minced fresh thyme leaves
- 1 teaspoon fennel seeds (optional)
- 1 tablespoon minced fresh parsley (optional)

1. FOR THE DOUGH: In the workbowl of a food processor fitted with the plastic dough blade (see note), pulse the flour, yeast, and salt to combine, about five 1-second pulses. With the machine running, slowly add the oil, then the water, through the feed tube; continue to process until the dough forms a ball, about 15 seconds. Generously dust the work surface with flour. Using floured hands, transfer the dough to the work surface and knead lightly, shaping the dough into a ball. Lightly oil a 1-quart measuring cup or small bowl, place the dough in the measuring cup (see the photo below), cover tightly with plastic wrap, and set aside in a draft-free spot until doubled in volume, 1 to 1½ hours.

2. FOR THE CARAMELIZED ONIONS: While the dough is rising, heat the oil in a 12-inch nonstick skillet over high heat until shimmering but not smoking. Stir in the onions, salt, and brown sugar and cook, stirring frequently, until the moisture released by the onions has evaporated and the onions begin to brown, about 10 minutes. Reduce the heat to medium-low and cook, stirring frequently, until the onions have softened and are medium golden brown, about 20 minutes longer. Off the heat, stir in the water; transfer to a bowl and set aside. Adjust the oven rack to the lowest position, set a baking stone on the rack, and heat the oven to 500 degrees.

GETTING IT RIGHT: Rising the Dough

Just Mixed

Fully Risen

A quart-size liquid measuring cup is good for more than just holding liquid. We let the pissaladière dough rise in a measuring cup covered with plastic wrap. The lines on the measuring cup make it easy to tell when the dough has doubled in size.

3. TO SHAPE, TOP, AND BAKE THE DOUGH: When the dough has doubled, remove it from the measuring cup and divide into two equal pieces using a dough scraper. Working with one piece at a time, form each piece into a rough ball by gently pulling the edges of the dough together and pinching to seal (see illustration 1, at right). With floured hands, turn the dough ball seam-side down. Cupping the dough with both hands, gently push the dough in a circular motion to form a taut ball (illustration 2). Repeat with the second piece. Brush each piece lightly with oil, cover with plastic wrap, and let rest 10 minutes. Meanwhile, cut two 20-inch lengths of parchment paper and set aside.

4. Coat your fingers and the palms of your hands generously with oil. Using a dough scraper, loosen one piece of dough from the work surface. With well-oiled hands, hold the dough aloft and gently stretch it to a 12-inch length (illustration 3). Place the dough on a parchment sheet and gently dimple the surface of the dough with your fingertips (illustration 4). Using oiled palms, push and flatten the dough into a 14 by 8-inch oval (illustration 5). Brush the dough with oil and sprinkle with ¼ teaspoon pepper. Leaving a ½-inch border around the edge, sprinkle ¼ cup of the olives, 1 tablespoon of the chopped anchovies, and 1 teaspoon of the thyme evenly over the dough, then evenly scatter with half of the onions (illustration 6). Arrange 6 whole anchovy fillets, if using, on the tart and sprinkle with half of the fennel seeds, if using. Slip the parchment with the tart onto a pizza peel (or inverted rimless baking sheet), then slide it onto the hot baking stone. Bake until deep golden brown, 13 to 15 minutes. While the first tart bakes, shape and top the second tart.

5. Remove the first tart from the oven with a peel or pull the parchment onto a baking sheet. Transfer the tart to a cutting board and slide the parchment out from under the tart. Cool 5 minutes; sprinkle with 1½ teaspoons of the parsley, if using. Cut the tart into 8 pieces; serve immediately. While the first tart cools, bake the second tart.

TECHNIQUE: Shaping Pissaladière

1. Pull the dough edges together.

2. Roll the dough into a taut ball.

3. Hold the dough aloft and stretch it.

4. Dimple the dough with your fingers.

5. Push the dough into an oval.

6. Add the toppings.

GETTING IT RIGHT:
Understanding the Dough

We found that the same basic ingredients—flour, water, yeast, salt, and oil—can yield doughs that bake up quite differently, depending on the ratio of ingredients as well as the shaping technique and baking temperature. Here are the characteristics and differences of four of our dough recipes.

Focaccia Dough

Focaccia is made with a lot of olive oil and is baked in a pan in a moderate oven. As a result, it bakes up thick, chewy, and very soft.

Thin-Crust Pizza Dough

This dough is rolled with a rolling pin until very thin and baked directly on a heated stone in a superhot oven. It bakes up crisp and brittle.

Deep-Dish Pizza Dough

This dough is baked in a pan set on a preheated stone. Adding olive oil to the pan ensures a crisp bottom. However, because the dough is so thick, the top and interior are fairly soft.

Pissaladière Dough

This recipe combines attributes of all the other doughs. A moderate amount of olive oil is rubbed into the exterior to crisp the crust, and, because the dough is not stretched thin, the interior remains chewy.

EQUIPMENT CORNER: Baking Stones

BAKING STONES (ALSO CALLED PIZZA STONES) ARE prized for their ability to retain heat and lessen the effects of hot spots and temperature fluctuations in home ovens. Usually made of clay or ceramics (although soapstone and composite cement stones are also available), baking stones, when coupled with extreme heat, absorb moisture, thus producing crispier, drier pizzas and breads.

We tested seven stones in different shapes, sizes, and materials, ranging in price from $20 to $80. We judged the stones on two main criteria: design (including ease of use, installation, and storage) and performance (including heat conductivity, evenness of browning, and crispness of baked goods). There was little issue with heat conductivity. We took the surface temperature of each stone, and each one exceeded 500 degrees after 60 minutes of preheating. Also, with little variance, all seven stones produced evenly colored and crisp crusts on pizzas.

Although performance was similar in all the models we tested, some designs were much easier to work with. Lipped edges inhibited easy placement and removal of food from a peel, and stones with this feature were downgraded, as were stones that were extremely heavy (one weighed a whopping 19 pounds). We did not like clay tiles (they seemed easy to lose and were hard to install), and stones that were either too big to fit in most home ovens or too small to handle a large pizza received low marks. Our recommendation is to choose a good-size stone (14 by 16 inches is ideal) with smooth edges.

Rating Baking Stones

WE TESTED SEVEN STONES IN DIFFERENT SHAPES, SIZES, AND MATERIALS. STONES WERE EVALUATED ON DESIGN (including ease of use, installation, and storage) and performance (including evenness of browning, crispness of baked goods, and heat conductivity). The stones are listed in order of preference. See www.americastestkitchen.com for up-to-date prices and mail-order sources for top-rated products.

HIGHLY RECOMMENDED
The Baker's Catalog Baking Stone (Manufactured by Old Stone Oven)
$34.95
We like this ceramic stone for its moderate weight and good size (14½ inches by 16½ inches).

RECOMMENDED
Handmade Pizza/Bread Stone
$38.50
This 15¼-inch round clay stone is just a tad smaller than our winner. Very light and easy to maneuver.

RECOMMENDED
Exeter Round Pizza Stone
$19.99
This 16-inch ceramic stone is another good choice, and the price is right.

RECOMMENDED WITH RESERVATIONS
Sur la Table Pizza Stone with Copper Handles
$79.95
The appearance of this 14-inch soapstone stone was intriguing, but its steep price tag and lipped edge were not. The handles are convenient for this very heavy stone, but they get extremely hot in the oven.

RECOMMENDED WITH RESERVATIONS
FibraMent Rectangular Oven Stone
$59.99
This cement stone lost points for its incredible heft (19 pounds) and large size (20 by 15 inches), which won't work in many ovens. A slight cement odor was also detected each time the stone was heated, though it did not transfer to the food.

RECOMMENDED WITH RESERVATIONS
Old Stone Oven Baking Tiles
$29.99
When these ceramic tiles are installed correctly (which takes some work), they approximate the size of a baking stone. The pieces might be easy to lose if you don't store them in your oven.

RECOMMENDED WITH RESERVATIONS
Sassafras Baking and Pizza Stone
$23.95
The small size (12 by 15 inches) and lipped edge on this clay stone landed it at the bottom of our ratings.

TASTING LAB: Black Olives

PRIZED IN PROVENCE FOR THEIR NUTTY, SMOKY FLAVOR, tiny niçoise olives are a staple of the region's cuisine and the traditional olive of choice for topping a pissaladière. These brine-cured olives are generally sold loose or packed in deli containers, and they cost a pretty penny—usually $11 per pound or more (and most of that weight is pit!). On a pizza already packed with the powerful flavors of caramelized onions and anchovies, would other types of readily available black olives make acceptable substitutes? After ruling out canned black "California" olives (which are really green olives colored black with a chemical additive), we gathered eight varieties of jarred and fresh black olives.

Sampled plain, most other black olives, with the exception of kalamatas, made poor substitutes for the niçoise. Buried beneath a layer of onions and anchovies, however, most of the olives were hard to distinguish from the niçoise, although there were two exceptions. Salt-cured black olives (often erroneously labeled "oil-cured" and known for their wrinkled exterior) were far too salty and bitter in combination with the anchovies. The other loser was the oversized cerignola, which was so mild that the pissaladière was left with almost no olive flavor at all.

BEST OLIVES FOR PISSALADIÈRE
Niçoise olives (left) are our first choice for this recipe. They have a smoky, nutty flavor that works well with the onions. Kalamatas (right) are the best substitute. They are fruitier and brinier than niçoise olives.

Q&A

In yeasted breads, can whole-wheat flour be substituted for all-purpose flour or bread flour?

We generally do not recommend a wholesale substitution because the whole wheat will compromise the structure and texture of the original recipe. But a partial substitution is often possible. In general, you can replace one quarter to one third of the white flour with whole-wheat flour. The texture will be slightly heartier but still good. However, if you use more whole-wheat flour, many loaves will be dense and tough.

Q&A

Can I make pizza crust, freeze it, and then add toppings at a later date?

We found that pizza crusts, including pissaladière, can be parbaked and then frozen. Here's what to do. Make and shape the dough as directed. Brush the crust liberally with oil and then bake as directed, just until the crust has set, about 2 to 3 minutes if making our pissaladière. Remove the crust from the oven, cool, wrap in plastic, and freeze for up to two months. When ready to serve, preheat the oven and baking stone and defrost the crust for about one hour. Add the toppings and bake, shaving a couple of minutes off the baking time in the original recipe.

EQUIPMENT CORNER: Pizza Cutters

HOMEMADE PIZZA CAN BE THE MOST REWARDING OF comfort foods, but all too often you end up with uneven, half-cut slices because you don't have a knife big enough to cut through the thick crust and extra cheese. Purchasing a pizza cutter is a natural solution, but our local kitchen store offered more pizza cutter models than Domino's has toppings. A shoddy pizza cutter drags melted cheese and toppings out of place, sprays hot grease, and fails to cut through crispy crust cleanly, leaving you to finish the job by tearing loose a slice by hand. A good pizza cutter gets the job done quickly, cleanly, and safely (and also makes an excellent tool for trimming the edges of rolled-out pastry dough). But with so many different options, how do you know which brand to choose? We decided to line up 10 different models ranging from double-wheeled pizza cutters to straight-edged pizza choppers to see which model would stand supreme.

The basic wheel cutter is the most common variety with dozens of models to choose from, priced from $3 to $25. Pre-testing eliminated the flimsiest models from further consideration, leaving eight sturdy wheels to test on thin- and thick-crust pizzas, evaluating them on price, cutting ability, ease of use, and safety. All of the pizza wheels cut through crisp thin-crust pies without a problem, but thick-crust, deep-dish pizzas overloaded with gooey cheese and toppings quickly thinned the pack. Cutters with large, 4-inch diameter wheels were able to plow through the pies without a problem, while those with smaller wheels were quickly mired in the mess and left us with greasy knuckles. Of the large-wheel cutters, the clear winner was the Oxo Good Grips 4-inch ($10). Testers liked its rubberized, non-slip handle, protective thumb guard, and angled neck, which made cutting easier on the wrist. The large KitchenAid cutter ($15) also performed well and was the only cutter to come with a protective sheath, but it was heavy (almost 1 pound) and testers with smaller hands found it hard to grip

the oversized handle, which was made from hard plastic and tended to get slippery.

Instead of a wheel cutter, professional pizzerias often employ a large rocking knife to cut clean through the pie in one stroke without dragging any hot cheese out of place. A few home versions of these knives are available, though usually by mail order. VillaWare's 14-inch Stainless Pizza Chopper ($14) cuts cleanly through crusts both thick and thin, but its size makes it doubly awkward: It's a bit too short to cut through a larger diameter pizza, but still too large for easy storage. LamsonSharp makes a similar size rocker ($25), but its wooden handles are trouble in the dishwasher, and its ultra-sharp edge curves up toward the grips, posing a serious hazard to exposed pinkies. Although these models managed to cleave the pizzas with relative ease, their oversized, machete-like blades seemed a bit over the top—not only difficult to store but just flat-out dangerous.

As the tests concluded, the superior performance of the pizza wheel means that we can finally have handsome homemade pizza. So save your money (and your fingers) and go with our champion—the Oxo Good Grips.

Rating Pizza Cutters

WE TESTED 10 WIDELY AVAILABLE MODELS AND RAN THEM THROUGH THIN-CRUST AND DEEP-DISH PIZZAS. THE PIZZA CUTTERS were rated for their cutting ability, ease of use, price, and safety and are listed in order of preference. See www.americastestkitchen.com for up-to-date prices and mail-order sources for top-rated products.

RECOMMENDED
Oxo Good Grips 4-inch Pizza Wheel
$10

The large wheel and comfortable handle on this cutter took home the trophy. It plowed through thin-crust and deep-dish pies alike.

RECOMMENDED WITH RESERVATIONS
Farberware Nonstick Pizza Wheel
$6

This model's large wheel rolled over even the deepest-dish pies with ease, but the straight handle made for an uncomfortable arm angle while cutting. The nonstick wheel is a nice touch, but testers thought it was extraneous.

RECOMMENDED WITH RESERVATIONS
VillaWare 14-inch Pizza Chopper
$14

This model was very effective, particularly on personal size pizzas. It lost some points for being heavy, awkward, and dangerous—there is a lot of sharp metal on this model.

RECOMMENDED WITH RESERVATIONS
KitchenAid Pizza Wheel
$15

Both powerful and substantial, this model made quick work of the pizzas, but its hard plastic handle got greasy during testing. Some testers also considered this model too heavy.

NOT RECOMMENDED
Henckels Twin Select Pizza Wheel
$15

With a small wheel, straight grip, and uncomfortable handle, this model seemed to be designed for form not function. The wheel guard made for tough cleanup and was considered unnecessary.

NOT RECOMMENDED
Oxo Good Grips Pizza Wheel
$8

Even though this model's big brother took the blue ribbon, we found the small wheel and slightly canted, small handle to be unsatisfactory. It performed especially poorly with deep-dish pizza.

NOT RECOMMENDED
WMF Double Wheel
$29.99

This model was flashy for sure, but its small wheels and flimsy construction prove that aesthetics aren't everything.

NOT RECOMMENDED
Zyliss Pizza Wheel
$10

The lack of a handle made it very difficult to control, particularly on straight cuts. Cleaning was also a pain.

NOT RECOMMENDED
LamsonSharp Pizza Rocker
$25

Bulky and sharp, and deemed unsafe due to its unprotected, curved blade. The wooden handles are not dishwasher safe.

NOT RECOMMENDED
Stelton Pizza Knife
$48

Possessing a design similar to a pie wedge, this model was the clear loser in the group. Testers blasted this model for its cost (which was by far the highest), its uncomfortable handle, its poor design, and its inexcusably dull serrated cutting edge.

Our eggplant Parmesan uses oven-fried slices of breaded eggplant for a less greasy take on this perennial favorite.

IN AN ITALIAN-
american
kitchen

CHAPTER 17

In the test kitchen, we enjoy authentic Italian dishes such as pasta all'amatriciana (chapter 18) and osso buco and polenta (chapter 19). But we also like to prepare Italian-American dishes. These recipes may have their inspiration in Italy, but they are decidedly American in their execution. This is the kind of food you are more likely to encounter at a chain "Italian" restaurant, such as Olive Garden, than at a traditional Italian restaurant run by a Roman, Tuscan, or Sicilian chef.

So what kind of food are we talking about? Eggplant Parmesan, with its layers of breaded eggplant, tomato sauce, and cheese, is a classic example of this exuberant cooking. It's hearty (some might say heavy) and tasty. Pasta with chicken and broccoli in a creamy sauce is another Italian-American creation. This pasta is a one-dish meal, with carbohydrates, protein, and vegetables all in one bowl.

While this food is great when done correctly, more often than not eggplant Parmesan is a soggy, oily mess and pasta with chicken and broccoli is heavy and bland. But after many tests in the kitchen, we feel we've come up with recipes that give these simple, honest dishes the respect they deserve.

EGGPLANT PARMESAN

WHAT WE WANTED: A fresher, lighter take on this classic but often greasy Italian dish. Could we eliminate the frying, streamline the dish, and make it taste better than the original?

The main objection we have to most eggplant Parmesan recipes is their requirement to fry the eggplant in four or five batches. It takes an attentive eye to keep the oil at just the right temperature, making the risk of greasy eggplant great. And even if things go right with the breading, frying, and sauce-making steps, most versions are oily and dense. We decided to reinvent this dish by baking the eggplant rather than frying it.

Most recipes for eggplant Parmesan begin by purging (salting) the eggplant to expel bitter juices and prevent the porous flesh from soaking up excess oil. To double-check this theory, we baked some unsalted eggplant. Oil absorption wasn't a problem, but the eggplant did taste bitter, and it had a raw, mealy texture. Thirty minutes of salting remedied the problem. For efficiency's sake, we chose good-size globe eggplants; we didn't want to multiply the number of slices we'd have to prepare. For the best appearance, taste, and texture, we settled on unpeeled ¼-inch-thick crosswise slices, not lengthwise planks.

In our first effort to sidestep deep-frying, we dispensed with the breading altogether, baking naked, salted eggplant slices on a baking sheet coated with cooking spray. (This method is often employed in low-calorie recipes for eggplant Parmesan.) The resulting eggplant earned negative comments from tasters. We concluded that breading was essential and ticked off a list of possibilities. Flour alone wasn't substantial enough. Eggplant swathed in mayonnaise and then bread crumbs turned slimy. Eggplant coated in a flour and egg batter and then bread crumbs was thick and tough. A standard single breading (dipping the eggplant first in egg, then bread crumbs) was too messy—the egg slid right off the eggplant, leaving the crumbs with nothing to adhere to.

A double, or bound, breading proved superior. Dipping the eggplant first in seasoned flour, then egg, then bread crumbs created a substantial (but not heavy) and crisp coating that brought the mild flavor and tender, creamy texture of the eggplant to the fore. The initial coating of flour in a bound breading creates a dry, smooth base to which the egg can cling. We seasoned the bread crumbs with generous amounts of Parmesan, salt, and pepper.

We'd been using fresh bread crumbs and wondered whether we could get away with using store-bought crumbs. The answer was no. Store-bought crumbs were so fine that they disappeared under the blankets of tomato sauce and cheese.

After considerable experimentation, we found that the best way to achieve a crisp coating is to bake the breaded slices on two preheated baking sheets, each coated with a modest 3 tablespoons of vegetable oil (olive oil tasted sour), rotating the pans and flipping the slices partway through. At 425 degrees, the slices sizzled during cooking and became fully tender in 30 minutes. Using this technique, we turned out crisp, golden brown disks of eggplant, expending a minimum of effort (and using very little oil). And now, seeing that we weren't busy frying up four batches of eggplant in hot oil, we had time to grate cheese and whip up a quick tomato sauce while the eggplant baked.

Eggplant Parmesan couldn't be called such without Parmesan cheese, so that was a given. We'd already used some for breading the eggplant, and a little extra browned nicely on top of the casserole. Mozzarella is another standard addition. A modest amount (8 ounces) kept the casserole from becoming stringy.

A few cloves of minced garlic, a sprinkling of red pepper flakes, and some olive oil started off a quick tomato sauce, followed by three cans of diced tomatoes, with just

EGGPLANT PARMESAN

Serves 6 to 8

Use kosher salt when salting the eggplant. The coarse grains don't dissolve as readily as the fine grains of regular table salt, so any excess can be easily wiped away. It's necessary to divide the eggplant into two batches when tossing it with the salt. To be time-efficient, use the 30 to 45 minutes during which the salted eggplant sits to prepare the breading.

eggplant

- 2 pounds globe eggplant (2 medium eggplants), cut crosswise into ¼-inch-thick rounds
- 1 tablespoon kosher salt
- 8 slices high-quality white sandwich bread (about 8 ounces), torn into quarters
- 2 ounces Parmesan cheese, grated (about 1 cup)
  Salt and ground black pepper
- 1 cup all-purpose flour
- 4 large eggs
- 6 tablespoons vegetable oil

tomato sauce

- 3 (14.5-ounce) cans diced tomatoes
- 2 tablespoons extra-virgin olive oil
- 4 medium garlic cloves, minced or pressed through a garlic press (about 1 generous tablespoon)
- ¼ teaspoon red pepper flakes
- ½ cup coarsely chopped fresh basil leaves
  Salt and ground black pepper

- 8 ounces whole-milk or part-skim mozzarella, shredded (about 2 cups)
- 1 ounce Parmesan cheese, grated (about ½ cup)
- 10 fresh basil leaves, torn, for garnish

two of them pureed in the food processor to preserve a chunky texture. A handful of fresh basil leaves (we reserved some basil for garnish, too) plus salt and pepper were the final flourishes.

Because breading softens beneath smothering layers of sauce and cheese, we left most of the top layer of eggplant exposed. This left us with about one cup of extra sauce, just enough to pass at the table. Another benefit of this technique was that without excess moisture, the casserole was easy to cut into tidy pieces. With the eggplant fully cooked, the dish needed only a brief stay in a hot oven to melt the cheese.

In the end, we had drastically reduced the amount of oil and attention required to make this dish, and we had done it without compromising flavor.

WHAT WE LEARNED: Salt the eggplant to remove some bitterness and improve its texture. The best coating is a double breading of flour, eggs, and fresh bread crumbs. Baking the breaded eggplant on a preheated, oiled baking sheet yields crisp, golden brown disks. Finally, leaving the top layer of eggplant unsauced keeps it crisp in the oven.

1. FOR THE EGGPLANT: Toss half of the eggplant slices and 1½ teaspoons of the kosher salt in a large bowl until combined; transfer the salted eggplant to a large colander set over a bowl. Repeat with the remaining eggplant and kosher salt, placing the second batch on top of the first. Let stand until the eggplant releases about 2 tablespoons liquid, 30 to 45 minutes. Spread the eggplant slices on a triple thickness of paper towels; cover with another triple thickness of paper towels. Press firmly on each slice to remove as much liquid as possible, then wipe off the excess salt.

2. While the eggplant is draining, adjust the oven racks to the upper- and lower-middle positions, place a rimmed baking sheet on each rack, and heat the oven to 425 degrees. Pulse the bread in a food processor to fine, even crumbs, about fifteen 1-second pulses (you should have about 4 cups). Transfer the crumbs to a pie plate and stir in the Parmesan, ¼ teaspoon salt, and ½ teaspoon pepper; set aside. Wipe out the workbowl (do not wash) and set aside.

3. Combine the flour and 1 teaspoon pepper in a large zipper-lock bag; shake to combine. Beat the eggs in a second pie plate. Place 8 to 10 eggplant slices in the bag with the flour; seal the bag and shake to coat the slices. Remove the slices, shaking off the excess flour, dip into the eggs, let the excess egg run off, then coat evenly with the bread crumb mixture; set the breaded slices on a wire rack set over a baking sheet. Repeat with the remaining eggplant.

4. Remove the preheated baking sheets from the oven; add 3 tablespoons oil to each sheet, tilting to coat evenly with the oil. Place half of the breaded eggplant slices on each sheet in a single layer; bake until the eggplant is well browned and crisp, about 30 minutes, switching and rotating the baking sheets after 10 minutes, and flipping the eggplant slices with a wide spatula after 20 minutes. Do not turn off the oven.

GETTING IT RIGHT: The Crumbs

We prepared eggplant in nearly a dozen ways. Here are some failed samples, with tasters' harsh comments.

Baked Naked
"Nasty"

Flour Alone
"Insubstantial"

Mayo & Crumbs
"Slimy"

Batter & Crumbs
"Thick and tough"

Eggs & Crumbs
"Too messy"

A WINNING COMBINATION

Flour, Eggs, & Crumbs
Dipping the eggplant into flour, then egg, then bread crumbs created a substantial (but not heavy) and crisp coating.

5. FOR THE SAUCE: While the eggplant bakes, process 2 cans of the diced tomatoes in the food processor until almost smooth, about 5 seconds. Heat the olive oil, garlic, and red pepper flakes in a large heavy-bottomed saucepan over medium-high heat, stirring occasionally, until fragrant and the garlic is light golden, about 3 minutes; stir in the processed and remaining can of diced tomatoes. Bring the sauce to a boil, then reduce the heat to medium-low and simmer, stirring occasionally, until slightly thickened and reduced, about 15 minutes (you should have about 4 cups). Stir in the basil and season with salt and pepper to taste.

6. TO ASSEMBLE: Spread 1 cup of the tomato sauce in the bottom of a 13 by 9-inch baking dish. Layer in half of the eggplant slices, overlapping the slices to fit; distribute 1 more cup of the sauce over the eggplant; sprinkle with half of the mozzarella. Layer in the remaining eggplant and dot with 1 more cup of the sauce, leaving the majority of eggplant exposed so it will remain crisp; sprinkle with the Parmesan and the remaining mozzarella. Bake until bubbling and the cheese is browned, 13 to 15 minutes. Cool 10 minutes, scatter the basil over the top, and serve, passing the remaining tomato sauce separately.

PASTA WITH CHICKEN AND BROCCOLI

WHAT WE WANTED: This Italian-American favorite makes a complete meal but is often bland and heavy. Could we take this appealing concept and turn it into a light yet flavorful one-dish meal with tender chicken, crisp broccoli, and toothsome pasta?

Italian chain restaurants known for cheap wine and doughy breadsticks almost always list pasta with chicken and broccoli on the menu. Unfortunately, the broccoli is mushy and drab, the pasta has no bite, and the chicken tastes tough and generic. The whole mess is drowned in a fatty cream sauce whose only flavor is garlic. Our goal was obvious: We wanted to reclaim this dish with fresh, crisp broccoli, tender chicken, and a flavorful sauce. We also wanted a recipe that was easy and healthy enough to appear as a regular on the supper table at home.

A quick sampling of existing recipes turned up the obvious issues of overcooking and blandness as well as a few others. Many recipes called for very small amounts of chicken and broccoli, treating them more as garnishes to the pasta rather than as major elements of the dish. Most of the recipes also required far too many pots and pans for a simple, midweek meal. Lastly, a few casseroles cropped up, but they took a long time to put together and didn't solve any of the overcooking problems. In order to figure this dish out, we needed to tear it apart into its four components—chicken, sauce, broccoli, and pasta—and tackle each individually.

Right off the bat, we decided that boneless, skinless chicken breasts were the best choice for this recipe and tested various cooking methods, including broiling, sautéing, microwaving, and poaching (simmering in a liquid). Microwaving produced bland chicken, and the timing was tricky—one minute too long and the chicken was completely dry. Broiling and sautéing produced meat with the most flavor; however, the nicely seared edges of the chicken seemed tough and stringy after being tossed with the pasta

and sauce. Poaching the chicken, either in the pasta water or simmering sauce, produced meat that was tender and juicy; however, the flavor was badly washed out.

Wanting the flavor of the sautéed chicken yet the tenderness of the poached chicken, we wondered if we could combine the two methods. First we lightly cooked the chicken with a little butter in a skillet until it just began to turn golden, then we removed it from the pan while still partly raw. Building a sauce using the residual drippings left in the skillet, we then returned the chicken to the sauce and let it simmer until fully cooked. Bingo—the chicken was perfectly cooked, tender, and flavorful. Throughout all this testing, we realized that cutting the chicken into bite-size pieces before cooking was best because it eliminated the last-minute rush of having to slice or shred it into fork-friendly pieces. We also noted that a nonstick skillet made cleanup a breeze, and that 1 pound of chicken and half a pound of pasta was an ample amount for four people for dinner.

With the chicken cooked properly, it was time to focus on the broccoli. We tried multiple ways to cook the florets, including simmering them in the sauce, steaming, blanching (a quick dunk in boiling water), and microwaving. Simmering them in the sauce was a disaster—the broccoli gave the sauce both an off flavor and a dirty color. Steaming on the stovetop and in the microwave both worked OK, but neither was as easy as blanching, especially since there was already a pot of boiling water going for the pasta. Cooking the broccoli florets in the pasta water first, we simply scooped them from the water using a slotted spoon, then returned the water to a boil before adding the pasta.

We ran into the problem of broccoli with an army green color and slightly mushy texture when we simply let the florets sit in a bowl after being blanched—they continued to steam as they sat in a big pile. Dunking them in a bowl of ice water prevented this, but then we had a hard time warming them up again before tossing them with the

pasta and sauce (they always remained a bit chilled). Finally, we tried spreading the blanched florets out over a large plate as the pasta cooked. This allowed them to cool off enough so as not to turn an ugly color, yet they were easily warmed through by the hot pasta and sauce. The key, then, was to slightly undercook the florets in the boiling water and let them continue to cook a little as they waited for everything to be done.

Finally, we turned our attention to the sauce. Using a classic base of cream thickened with a roux (a flour and butter combination), we determined that garlic, pepper flakes, fresh herbs, and white wine were all critical components. Tasters were still unimpressed, commenting that the sauce tasted lifeless. We then tried omitting the roux and simply letting the cream simmer and thicken on its own, but this produced a very fatty sauce. Using milk or half-and-half instead of cream didn't work either—the sauces tasted watery and dull.

Having exhausted all our cream sauce options, we wondered how tasters would react to a broth-based sauce that was finished with butter. We simmered store-bought chicken broth with the aromatics before whisking in some butter and were relieved to see the tasters nod their heads with approval. The flavor of the aromatics now jumped out, and there was a significant boost in chicken flavor. The sauce still needed a final kick of flavor, and tasters cheered over the addition of sun-dried tomatoes along with a handful of Asiago cheese. The sauce now had serious flavor and when it was tossed with the perfectly cooked broccoli and tender chicken, we had a dish that is worth staying home for.

WHAT WE LEARNED: Partially cook the chicken in a hot pan with butter, build a quick broth-based sauce from the drippings, and then finish the sauce with a bit more butter and the chicken. The broccoli should be blanched in the pasta pot and then removed so the pasta can be cooked.

PASTA WITH CHICKEN AND BROCCOLI
Serves 4

Use low-sodium chicken broth in this recipe; regular chicken broth will make the dish unpalatably salty. The broccoli is ready to be removed from the boiling water when it's tender at the edges but still crisp at the core; it will continue to cook with residual heat.

4   tablespoons (½ stick) unsalted butter
1   pound boneless, skinless chicken breasts, trimmed of excess fat and prepared according to the illustrations on page 230
     Salt and ground black pepper
1   small onion, chopped fine (about ⅔ cup)
6   medium garlic cloves, minced or pressed through a garlic press (about 2 tablespoons)
¼   teaspoon red pepper flakes
1   tablespoon chopped fresh thyme leaves
2   teaspoons unbleached all-purpose flour
1   cup dry white wine
2   cups low-sodium chicken broth
1   large bunch broccoli (about 1½ pounds), florets cut into 1-inch pieces, stems discarded
½   pound penne, ziti, campanelli, or cavatappi
2   ounces Asiago cheese, grated fine (about 1 cup), plus extra for serving
2   tablespoons minced fresh parsley leaves or chives
1   (8½-ounce) jar oil-packed sun-dried tomatoes, drained, rinsed, patted dry, and sliced into ¼-inch strips (about 1 cup)
1   lemon, cut into wedges (optional)

1. Bring 4 quarts of water to a rolling boil in a stockpot.

2. Meanwhile, melt 1 tablespoon of the butter in a 12-inch nonstick skillet over high heat until just beginning to brown, about 1 minute. Add the chicken in a single layer and sprinkle with salt and pepper to taste. Cook for 1 minute without stirring, then stir the chicken and continue to cook until most, but not all, of the pink color has disappeared and the chicken is lightly browned around the edges, about 2 minutes longer. Transfer the chicken to a clean bowl; set aside.

3. Return the skillet to high heat and melt 1 more tablespoon of the butter. Add the onion and ¼ teaspoon salt and cook, stirring occasionally, until browned around the edges, 2 to 3 minutes. Stir in the garlic, red pepper flakes, thyme, and flour; cook, stirring constantly, until fragrant, about 30 seconds. Add the wine and chicken broth. Bring to a simmer, then reduce the heat to medium and continue to simmer, stirring occasionally, until the sauce has thickened slightly and is reduced to 1¼ cups, about 15 minutes.

4. While the sauce simmers, add 1 tablespoon salt and the broccoli florets to the boiling water. Cook until the broccoli is bright green and tender but still crisp at the center, about 2 minutes. Using a slotted spoon, transfer the broccoli to a large paper towel–lined plate and set aside. Return the water to a boil, stir in the pasta, and cook until al dente. Drain, reserving ½ cup pasta cooking water, and return the pasta to the stockpot.

5. A minute or so before draining the pasta, stir in the remaining 2 tablespoons butter, the Asiago, parsley, sun-dried tomatoes, and chicken into the sauce in the skillet. Cook until the chicken is hot and cooked through, about 1 minute. Off the heat, season the sauce with pepper to taste. Pour the chicken-and-sauce mixture over the pasta and add the broccoli. Toss gently to combine, adding the reserved pasta cooking water as needed to adjust the sauce consistency. Serve immediately, passing additional Asiago and the lemon wedges (if using) separately.

TECHNIQUE:
Preparing the Chicken

1. Separate the tenderloin from the breast. Starting at the thick end, cut into ¼-inch slices. Stop slicing when you reach the tapered triangle end.

2. With the flat side of the knife, press each slice to an even ¼ inch thickness and then cut the slices into 1-inch squares.

3. Use the same technique for the tenderloin, flattening it with the side of the knife and then cutting it into 1-inch pieces.

Sautéing mushrooms in a skillet and folding them into the rice at the last minute is the key to great mushroom risotto.

ITALIAN classics

There seems to be an endless supply of "classic" Italian dishes. Just when we think we've mastered the canon, we realize there are more seminal Italian dishes to learn—recipes as important as pesto, steak fiorentina, or pasta with garlic and oil. The depth of classic recipes is testament to the genius of the Italian cook. There are dozens of core recipes, known by almost every Italian cook, and almost all of these recipes are appropriate and appealing for American cooks.

Risotto is a basic Italian recipe, and with mushrooms this dish becomes hearty enough to serve as a main course. Besides cooking the rice right, the key challenge here is getting intense mushroom flavor. Spending a fortune on fancy mushrooms is one route. Instead, we wanted to coax great flavor from everyday mushrooms.

Pasta all'amatriciana is perhaps Rome's most famous dish. Despite the fancy name, it's nothing more than long-strand pasta sauced with tomatoes, onion, bacon, and hot pepper flakes and dusted with cheese. This simple dish is about the details, and we knew they could be mastered.

IN THIS CHAPTER

THE RECIPES
Mushroom Risotto
Mushroom Risotto with Pancetta
    and Sage

Pasta with Tomato, Bacon,
    and Onion
    (Pasta all'Amatriciana)

EQUIPMENT CORNER
Rotary Cheese Graters

TASTING LAB
Rice for Risotto
Jarred Pasta Sauces

MUSHROOM RISOTTO

WHAT WE WANTED: To make risotto with potent mushroom flavor without turning to pricey foraged fungi.

A favorite main-course risotto dish of ours is one packed with earthy robust flavor courtesy of myriad wild mushrooms—the puffball, hen-of-the-woods, trompette de la mort. These are mushrooms with fanciful names to match their exotic flavor. The trouble is, these exotically flavored wild mushrooms are both elusive and expensive. We wondered if we could approximate (even surpass) that paragon of risottos with supermarket mushrooms and a bit of test-kitchen determination.

Simply put, risotto is medium-grain, Italian-grown rice cooked in such a manner that some of the grains' starch renders into a creamy sauce, the mechanics of which we have previously tested. Our technique eschews what most recipes consider sacrosanct: feverish stirring and small, frequent additions of broth. We found that half the liquid can be added at the beginning and the rice stirred infrequently until the liquid is absorbed (about halfway through the cooking process). At that point, we return to standard protocol and add the remaining broth in modest amounts and stir often until the rice is both creamy and al dente. While our method doesn't expedite matters, it does allow some freedom from the tedium of constant attention. With our tested method in hand, then, we could focus our attention on flavor.

Most of the mushroom risotto recipes we found were divided into two camps: authentic recipes using wild mushrooms and workaday ones using cultivated mushrooms. But there was a small third group of recipes that relied largely on dried porcini mushrooms for flavor. Sold by the ounce and packing a punch, dried porcini are both robustly flavored and aromatic—just the thing for that earthy edge we craved. We prepared several of these recipes to mixed reviews. Tasters appreciated the porcini flavor but missed the firm texture and visual presence of fresh mushrooms. Some combination of the two, then, looked to be the best tack to take.

We knew that corralling the bullish flavor of the porcini was our first order of business. Using our basic Parmesan risotto as a baseline (flavored with onion, garlic, white wine, chicken broth, and Parmesan cheese), we made batches laced with dried porcini, each varying in content by ¼ ounce. We prepared the mushrooms according to standard procedure: reconstituted in hot water and chopped fine (if left large, they're rubbery). We also added the porcini-infused soaking liquid to the chicken broth, after straining it to filter out any debris. A scant ¼ ounce lent little flavor, as did ½ ounce. But 1 ounce suffused the rice with a forceful flavor and aroma.

As far as fresh mushrooms go, experience has taught us that they are at their best when cooked in the dry, intense heat of a smoking skillet or a fiery oven. Moist cooking, such as simmering in risotto, renders them rubbery and bland. A preliminary test of roasted mushrooms versus sautéed showed little difference, so we opted for the skillet to keep things on the stovetop. We sautéed the three most common supermarket mushrooms—the standard button, the brown-capped, meaty cremini, and the cremini's larger though similarly flavored sibling, the portobello—and added them to separate batches of the porcini-flavored risotto.

Tasters found the button mushrooms mild and better appreciated the fuller flavor and meatier texture of the cremini and portobellos. Cremini were easier to prepare than portobellos, as the latter's feathery gills must be trimmed before cooking lest they stain the risotto inky black. Over medium-high heat and lightly sprinkled with salt, the mushrooms first shed their liquid, then browned deeply. To preserve their texture and flavor, we didn't add the mushrooms to the risotto until the rice was fully cooked.

The hot skillet and a knob of butter (which tasters preferred to olive oil) did wonders for the mushrooms' flavor, but we wanted more. With onions prepped for the rice, we purloined a portion to sauté with the mushrooms.

This step proved successful, as the onions lent both sweetness and piquancy. On a roll, we added a couple of cloves of minced garlic and scored again: These mushrooms were good enough to eat on their own.

The risotto's flavor was emphatically mushroomy but one-dimensional and in need of refinement. We added ½ cup more wine to bring some much-needed acidity to the fore. As for herbs, thyme pairs well with mushrooms, so we added a minced teaspoon and then, heeding tasters' demands, minced parsley as well. We kept the Parmesan cheese to 1 cup.

Even with these changes, though, the risotto still fell short of our expectations, being milder and less dynamic than we wanted. We wondered if we were missing obvious flavor enhancements, hemmed in by the confines of Italian cooking. Throwing tradition out the window, we turned to a cuisine known for its deft touch with mushrooms: Chinese. A quick thumbing through several Chinese cookbooks inspired us to try replacing the chicken broth with mushroom broth. We combined the dried porcini with bundled herbs and chicken broth cut with water and simmered the mixture until the mushrooms were tender, about 15 minutes (time enough to prepare the other ingredients). We then strained the fungi from the broth and finely minced them before returning them to the rice. The results were promising: The risotto was much fuller-flavored than before and we had cut preparation time.

Borrowing again from the Chinese palette, we added soy sauce to the broth. Sweet, salty, and earthy, soy sauce has a galvanizing effect on the flavor of mushrooms that we sensed might pay off in the risotto. The scantest splash rounded out the broth's flavor and gave it indescribable depth. Tasters couldn't detect the soy sauce in the finished risotto, but everyone commented on the dish's fuller, earthier flavor.

WHAT WE LEARNED: Combine dried porcini with fresh cremini mushrooms for an inexpensive but potent flavor base. Brown the mushrooms in a separate skillet and then fold them into the finished risotto to maintain their texture. Add soy sauce for meaty intensity.

MUSHROOM RISOTTO

Serves 6 as a main course, 8 as a first course

Cremini mushrooms are sometimes sold as baby bella mushrooms. If they're not available, button mushrooms make a fine though somewhat less flavorful substitute. Toward the end of cooking, judge the doneness of the rice by tasting it.

2   bay leaves
6   sprigs fresh thyme
4   sprigs fresh parsley, plus 2 tablespoons minced parsley leaves
1   ounce dried porcini mushrooms, rinsed in a mesh strainer under running water
3½   cups low-sodium chicken broth
2   teaspoons soy sauce
6   tablespoons (¾ stick) unsalted butter
1¼   pounds cremini mushrooms, wiped clean with a paper towel, stems discarded, and caps cut into fourths if small or sixths if medium or large
2   medium onions, chopped fine (about 2 cups)
     Salt
3   medium garlic cloves, minced or pressed through a garlic press (about 1 tablespoon)
1   pound (2⅛ cups) Arborio rice

GETTING IT RIGHT:
An Unusual Broth for Risotto

Soy Sauce   Dried Porcini

Our search for a better cooking medium for the rice led us to an unusual culinary pairing: soy sauce and dried porcini mushrooms.

1 cup dry white wine or dry vermouth
2 ounces Parmesan cheese, grated fine
(about 1 cup)
Ground black pepper

1. Tie the bay leaves, thyme sprigs, and parsley sprigs together with kitchen twine. Bring the bundled herbs, porcini mushrooms, broth, soy sauce, and 3½ cups water to a boil in a medium saucepan over medium-high heat; reduce the heat to medium-low and simmer until the dried mushrooms are softened and fully hydrated, about 15 minutes. Remove and discard the herb bundle and strain the broth through a fine-mesh strainer set over a medium bowl (you should have about 6½ cups strained liquid); return the liquid to the saucepan and keep warm over low heat. Finely mince the porcini and set aside.

2. Adjust an oven rack to the middle position and heat the oven to 200 degrees. Heat 2 tablespoons of the butter in a 12-inch nonstick skillet over medium-high heat. When the foaming subsides, add the cremini mushrooms, 1 cup of the onions, and ½ teaspoon salt; cook, stirring occasionally, until the moisture released by the mushrooms evaporates and the mushrooms are well browned, about 7 minutes. Stir

in the garlic until fragrant, about 1 minute, then transfer the mushrooms to an oven-safe bowl and keep warm in the oven. Off the heat, add ¼ cup water to the now-empty skillet and scrape with a wooden spoon to loosen any browned bits on the pan bottom; pour the liquid from the skillet into the saucepan with the broth.

3. Heat 3 more tablespoons of the butter in a large saucepan over medium heat. When the foaming subsides, add the remaining 1 cup onions and ¼ teaspoon salt; cook, stirring occasionally, until the onions are softened and translucent, about 9 minutes. Add the rice and cook, stirring frequently, until the edges of the grains are transparent, about 4 minutes. Add the wine and cook, stirring frequently, until the rice absorbs the wine. Add the minced porcini and 3½ cups of the broth and cook, stirring every 2 to 3 minutes, until the liquid is absorbed, 9 to 11 minutes. Stir in an additional ½ cup broth every 2 to 3 minutes until the rice is cooked through but the grains are still somewhat firm at the center, 10 to 12 minutes (the rice may not require all of the broth). Stir in the remaining 1 tablespoon butter, then stir in the mushrooms (and any accumulated juices), the cheese, and reserved chopped parsley. Season with salt and pepper to taste; serve immediately in warmed bowls.

VARIATION

MUSHROOM RISOTTO WITH PANCETTA AND SAGE

Follow the recipe for Mushroom Risotto through step 2, omitting the thyme from the broth. Cook 2 ounces finely chopped pancetta and 1 tablespoon butter in a large saucepan over medium heat, stirring frequently, until the pancetta has rendered some fat, about 5 minutes. Add the remaining 1 cup onions, cooking the onions until softened and translucent, about 7 minutes; continue with the recipe, adding and cooking the rice as in step 3 and adding 1 tablespoon minced fresh sage leaves along with the chopped parsley.

TASTING LAB: Rice for Risotto

VARIETIES OF RICE ARE ROUGHLY GROUPED AS LONG grain, medium grain, or short grain according to their cooked length and width. Long-grain rice is about four times as long as it is wide, medium grain is twice as long, and short grain is almost round. The manner in which they cook is largely defined by the ratio of two starches that (in part) constitute rice: amylose and amylopectin. The former does not break down (gelatinize) when heated; the latter does. Rice with a high percentage of amylose, then, is long, firm, and discrete when cooked; rice with a lower percentage (and thus more amylopectin) is shorter and starchy, or "sticky." For comparison's sake, long-grain rice contains between 23 and 26 percent amylose, and medium-grain rice contains between 18 and 26 percent amylose. Italian Arborio rice, the classic choice for risotto, contains roughly 19 to 21 percent amylose.

But say a hankering for risotto hits and you can't find Italian rice. Will any other type of rice do? We made Parmesan risotto with four types of rice: standard long grain, converted par-cooked long grain, regular medium grain (we chose Goya brand from the supermarket), and short grain (sushi-style rice). The two long-grained varieties bombed, turning mushy and lacking the creaminess essential to risotto. The par-boiled rice—Uncle Ben's, in this case—also had the jarring, unmistakable flavor of pre-cooked rice. Medium- and short-grain rice fared much better, earning passing grades from most tasters, who agreed that these batches possessed all the creaminess of risotto made with Arborio, though not its al dente bite.

That desirable "bite" is due to a defect in Arborio and other Italian-grown superfino-grade rices called chalk. During maturation, the starch structures at the grain's core deform, making for a firm, toothy center when cooked. An aberration in other varieties of rice, chalk is a sought-after attribute in Italian medium-grain rices, a category that includes Arborio as well as Carnaroli and Vialone Nano.

So the long and short of it? If you're in a pinch and can't find Arborio, look for medium- or short-grain rice for an acceptable—but not perfect—batch of risotto.

LONG-GRAIN RICE
Discrete, firm grains and no creaminess.
Good for pilaf; bad for risotto.

MEDIUM-GRAIN RICE
Creamy sauce, but rice is a bit soft.
Acceptable for risotto in a pinch.

SHORT-GRAIN RICE
Very creamy, but rice is a bit mushy.
Acceptable for risotto in a pinch.

PASTA ALL'AMATRICIANA

WHAT WE WANTED: An easy version of this Roman pasta dish with tomatoes, bacon, and onion.

Pasta all'amatriciana is arguably Rome's most famous dish. This lusty pasta dish starts with bucatini, an extralong tube pasta that looks like a drinking straw. The sauce contains tomato, bacon, onion, dried chile, and pecorino cheese. Like most Roman cooking, this dish is bold and brash.

What makes Amatriciana so popular? First, most cooks have all the ingredients on hand. Second, the sauce can be made in the time it takes to boil the water and cook the pasta. Third, although the recipe is simple, the flavors are complex and perfectly balanced—acidity from the tomatoes, sweetness from the sautéed onions, heat from the dried chile, meatiness and salt from the bacon, and tangy dairy from the cheese. Our goals in developing our version were to stay faithful to the traditional recipes but to use ingredients available to Americans. The biggest challenge was the bacon. Romans use guanciale, which is bacon made from pork jowls. In the rest of Italy, pancetta (bacon made from pork belly) is used.

We tested pancetta, American bacon, Canadian bacon, Irish bacon (the latter two are cured pork loin), and salt pork (unsmoked pork belly). Tasters preferred the pancetta, which was the meatiest. The pure pork and salt flavors of the pancetta worked best with the sauce.

All three bacons were good, but most tasters felt that the smoke flavor and sweetness were distracting. The Canadian bacon and the Irish bacon (also called Irish back bacon) were meatier than the American bacon, although both were deemed a bit "ham-like." Regular American bacon was excessively fatty. If using it, you will need to drain off the rendered fat (up to ⅓ cup), an unnecessary step when using pancetta, Canadian bacon, or Irish bacon.

The only product we don't recommend is the salt pork. Although it comes from the belly and is not smoked, it is much too fatty to use in a pasta sauce.

Whatever kind of bacon you use, make sure it is sliced thick. When we used thinly sliced pancetta or regular American bacon, the meat nearly disappeared in the sauce.

About half of the recipes we consulted called for sautéing the bacon and onion together, then building the tomato sauce on top of them. In the remaining recipes, the bacon was fried until crisp and removed from the pan, and then the onion was cooked in the bacon fat. Once the onion softened, it was time to make the tomato sauce. The crisped bacon was added back just before tossing the sauce with the pasta.

When we simmered the bacon with the tomatoes, the bacon was leathery and lacking in flavor. We much preferred bacon that was fried and then removed from the pan. It was crisp, flavorful, and chewy when tossed with the pasta.

The next issue was the tomato. Crushed tomatoes made the worst sauce—the tomato flavor was weak, and the consistency of the sauce was too thin. We missed the chunks of tomato, which give this sauce some character. Fresh tomatoes were good, but tasters liked canned diced tomatoes even better. They were a tad juicier, and the preparation was certainly easier—no peeling, seeding, or chopping.

We tried simmering a small dried red chile in the sauce as an alternative to hot red pepper flakes. The red pepper flakes won out, as they provide a more consistent heat level and are more likely to be on hand.

Some Amatriciana recipes call for Parmesan cheese, although pecorino is traditional. We found the taste of Parmesan too subtle to stand up to the chile's heat. Sharp, robust pecorino works better.

WHAT WE LEARNED: The pork flavor of thickly sliced pancetta (unsmoked Italian bacon) is the best choice for this recipe. Once the pancetta is crisp, remove it from the pan and build the sauce in the remaining fat. Toss the crisp pancetta with the tomato sauce and pasta.

PASTA WITH TOMATO, BACON, AND ONION (PASTA ALL'AMATRICIANA)

Serves 4

This dish is traditionally made with bucatini, also called perciatelli, which appear to be thick, round strands but are actually thin, extralong tubes. Linguine works fine, too. When buying pancetta, ask the butcher to slice it ¼ inch thick; if using bacon, buy slab bacon and cut it into ¼-inch-thick slices yourself. If the pancetta that you're using is very lean, it's unlikely that you will need to drain off any fat before adding the onion. Use 1½ small (14½-ounce) cans of diced tomatoes, or dice a single large (28-ounce) can of whole tomatoes packed in juice.

- 2 tablespoons extra-virgin olive oil
- 6 ounces ¼-inch-thick sliced pancetta or bacon, cut into strips about 1 inch long and ¼ inch wide
- 1 medium onion, chopped fine
- ½ teaspoon red pepper flakes, or to taste
- 2½ cups canned diced tomatoes
  Salt
- 1 pound bucatini, perciatelli, or linguine
- ⅓ cup grated pecorino cheese

1. Bring 4 quarts of water to a rolling boil in a stockpot.

2. Meanwhile, heat the oil in a large skillet over medium heat until shimmering but not smoking. Add the pancetta and cook, stirring occasionally, until lightly browned and crisp, about 8 minutes. Transfer the pancetta with a slotted spoon to a paper towel–lined plate; set aside. If necessary, drain all but 2 tablespoons of fat from the skillet. Add the onion to the skillet; sauté over medium heat until softened, about 5 minutes. Add the pepper flakes and cook to release their flavor, about 30 seconds. Stir in the tomatoes and salt to taste; simmer until slightly thickened, about 10 minutes.

3. While the sauce is simmering, add 1 tablespoon salt and the pasta to the boiling water. Stir to separate and cook until the pasta is al dente; drain and return the pasta to the stockpot.

4. Add the pancetta to the tomato sauce and adjust the seasonings with salt. Add the sauce to the pot with the pasta and toss over low heat to combine, about 30 seconds. Add the pecorino and toss again; serve immediately.

TASTING LAB: Jarred Pasta Sauces

JARRED PASTA SAUCES CONSTITUTE A BOOMING $1.4 billion market. They are certainly popular, but are they any good? In a past tasting, held back in 1999, we were not very impressed. Even the winner of that tasting, Barilla, didn't exactly sweep tasters off their feet. It won for being the freshest tasting of a not-very-fresh-tasting lot. Fast forward five years and we wanted to find out if any of the new players could do better.

Because there are just too many nationally available brands to include in a blind tasting, we narrowed the lineup to the following: the winner of the last jarred pasta sauce tasting (Barilla), the nation's three top-selling brands (Prego, Classico, and Ragú, respectively), and five of the most widely available newcomers since the 1999 tasting. All of the sauces were either marinaras or the brand's most basic tomato and herb–style sauce.

From our perspective, the challenge of making a good-tasting jarred pasta sauce is to preserve a fresh tomato flavor. In the 1999 tasting, we learned that the pervasive lack of freshness among jarred sauces can be credited to the common practice of using tomato paste, reconstituted with water, as the primary tomato ingredient instead of a fresher product, such as canned diced tomatoes. Made from tomatoes that are cooked for several hours until reduced to a thick, spreadable consistency, tomato paste is a highly concentrated product. In the test kitchen, we typically buy tomato paste in toothpaste-sized tubes because it's the kind of ingredient we use just a tablespoon or two at a time, typically to add depth of flavor or body to a sauce or stew.

Why do most jarred pasta sauce manufacturers prefer to use tomato paste—and in relatively large quantities? Robert Graf, president of the California League of Food Processors, helped to clear this up. (He ought to know; California grows 11 million tons of tomatoes in a typical year, supplying 35 percent of the world's processed tomatoes.) His explanation was simple enough: Most jarred pasta sauces are manufactured east of the Rockies, and fresher-tasting products, such as diced or crushed tomatoes, contain a lot of water. "Water," he said, "is very expensive to ship." It is therefore much cheaper to ship tomato paste and reconstitute the paste with water at the manufacturing plant as a first step in making the jarred sauce.

The good news is that some manufacturers, such as Patsy's, Bertolli, and Barilla, do use fresher tomato products. Each of them uses some fresher form of canned tomatoes, such as diced or freshly pureed, as their main tomato ingredient (although some tomato paste may be used as a secondary ingredient). This difference delivered not only winning flavor but a pleasant chunky consistency instead of the smooth, ketchup-like texture of most other sauces.

To get a better handle on the differences between a "tomato paste" sauce and one made with less processed tomatoes, we ran a small experiment in the test kitchen. We took a portion of each sauce and rinsed it with water in a fine-meshed sieve until all of the soluble ingredients were rinsed away. A reputable portion of tomato chunks remained in the sieves with the favored sauces (see photo at near right). But the tomato paste sauces displayed only meager bits of tomato flesh (see photo at far right). With one sauce, we could see little besides flecks of herbs, tomato skin, and dehydrated onion.

Another key to a good jarred pasta sauce turned out to be balanced flavor. Many sauces couldn't get it right, over-dosing on the dried herbs or loading up on sweetener (sugar or corn syrup) and salt. When comparing the amount of sodium and sugar in the sauces, it was readily apparent that the top three contained only moderate amounts of both. Colavita was the perfect example of a potentially good sauce that missed its mark by way of unbalanced flavor. It was the

only other sauce in the tasting that wasn't made primarily of tomato paste—containing whole and crushed canned tomatoes—but it also contained absolutely no added salt or sugar. Tasters felt that it tasted incomplete, more like canned tomatoes than pasta sauce.

There has not, then, been a revolution underway in the making of jarred sauces. What has happened is that the options for a half-decent jarred sauce have broadened, albeit slightly. Given this finding, we continue to plead the case—as we did in 1999—that a quick homemade marinara remains a far better option.

Finally, we wondered if kids would agree with the assessment made by the adults in our tasting panel. To find out, we brought in a group of 19 fifth and sixth graders from the Atrium School in Watertown, Mass., who were happy to take the job seriously. Their favorite, as predicted, was the sauce with nearly twice as much sugar (from corn syrup) as the others, Prego, which had 13 grams per serving versus an average 7 grams among the other sauces. But there is good news for parents who prefer not to buy such sugary tomato sauces. The kids' second choice (third place for the adults) was Barilla, which they appreciated for its "tomatoey" chunky texture.

GETTING IT RIGHT: Where Are the Tomatoes?

Sauce made with diced tomatoes	Sauce made with tomato paste

We spooned equal amounts of each sauce into a strainer and then rinsed the sauce under running water to see what would be left. Our top-rated sauces, including Bertolli (left), showed off nice chunks of tomatoes, even after rinsing for about 45 seconds. In contrast, the low-rated sauces washed away to almost nothing. After rinsing the Ragú (right), we were left with nothing but tomato skin, herbs, and bits of diced vegetables.

Rating Jarred Pasta Sauces

TWENTY-FOUR MEMBERS OF THE *COOK'S ILLUSTRATED* STAFF TASTED ALL OF THE SAUCES, WHICH WERE SERVED warm with cooked ziti on the side. The sauces are listed in order of preference based on their scores in this tasting. All brands are available in supermarkets.

RECOMMENDED
Patsy's Marinara
$8.49 for 24 ounces

Garlic lovers rallied around this marinara, said to be the very same sauce served at the popular Patsy's Italian Restaurant in New York City. In addition to the garlic, which is added fresh (not in a powder), the sauce had an equally strong herbal punch and an "OK balance of acid, sweetness, and salt." The chunky tomato texture was deemed appealing. But talk about sticker shock: Patsy's was more than three times the price of most other sauces.

RECOMMENDED
Bertolli Tomato & Basil Pasta Sauce
$2.49 for 26 ounces

Tasters thought that this sauce had the freshest flavor. As one taster summed it up, "bright, zesty, tomatoes, with some depth of flavor." The texture was "meaty," with an agreeable balance of tomato chunks and puree. Herbs and spices were evident but not assertive.

RECOMMENDED
Barilla Marinara Tomato & Onion
$2.79 for 26 ounces

The top jarred sauce in our 1999 tasting, Barilla held its own among sauces new to the market for being one of the freshest in flavor. Many tasters indicated that they would like the sauce more if it wasn't so heavily seasoned with oregano. The oregano not-withstanding, it had good balance and a pleasant chunky texture.

RECOMMENDED WITH RESERVATIONS
Emeril's Home Style Marinara
$4.29 for 25 ounces

More than one taster likened this famed chef's marinara to pizza sauce. There was no "Bam!" This was instead a balanced, "plain and simple" sauce that some found "not very interesting" and even "kinda boring." The texture was that of a smooth puree.

RECOMMENDED WITH RESERVATIONS
Prego Traditional Pasta Sauce
$2.19 for 26 ounces

As America's top-selling jarred pasta sauce, Prego was the favorite in our kids' tasting. Its heavy oregano taste was popular with many tasters but a "dried-herb nightmare" for others.

RECOMMENDED WITH RESERVATIONS
Classico Sweet Basil Marinara
$2.50 for 26 ounces

This familiar-tasting national top seller wasn't a favorite but was ranked among those considered decent enough. A cooked tomato paste flavor contributed to a noted sweetness and thick, paste-like texture. It "tastes like nondescript pasta sauce from a jar," noted one taster.

RECOMMENDED WITH RESERVATIONS
Buitoni Marinara Pasta Sauce
$2.99 for 26 ounces

Another sauce that was strong on oregano and likened to pizza sauce. It did have a relatively good balance of flavors, but the flavorless, crunchy bits of something unidentifiable were troubling to munch on.

NOT RECOMMENDED
Ragú Traditional Old World Style Pasta Sauce
$2.19 for 26 ounces

More than one taster said that this sauce tasted as if it came from a tin can. The absence of favorable comments was striking: "might as well be tomato paste," "extremely salty," and tastes "heavily cooked/cooked for days," "like V-8," and "more like tomato soup." It had a texture like ketchup.

NOT RECOMMENDED
Colavita Marinara Sauce
$4.69 for 26 ounces

A little doctoring with salt and sugar (neither of which is listed in the ingredients) might have saved this ultrabland sauce that tasted "like a can of crushed tomatoes." The herbs were also too understated.

EQUIPMENT CORNER:
Rotary Cheese Graters

"SOME CHEESE, SIR?" AS UBIQUITOUS AS A SALTSHAKER in many Italian restaurants, the rotary cheese grater is the waiter's sidearm. Tirelessly descending upon table after table and showering pastas, risottos, and salads with wonderfully earthy wisps of Parmesan cheese, the grater-laden waiter will not take "no" for an answer. It is almost impossible to refuse the touch of class (and flavor) that the rotary grater brings to the restaurant table. But do these graters have a place at home? To find out, we tested eight models by grating Parmesan, cheddar, mozzarella, and even chocolate. To ensure the validity of the results, these tests were performed by a variety of test cooks with different hand sizes and strengths.

As we began testing, one point was immediately obvious—this was deceptively difficult work! Most of the handles were tiny and slippery, and even the most comfortable of the lot became painful after extended use. All but the Pedrini ($14.99) and KitchenAid ($19.99) struggled with the mozzarella and cheddar cheeses; these two were more successful because of their larger grating drums, which kept the cheese from sticking. Additionally, none of the grater hoppers could accommodate more than 1 or 2 ounces of cheese at a time, and each grater gave us hand fatigue after just a few moments of use. The rotary grater is adept at providing a light dusting of cheese, but it is much too slow for use in the kitchen. If you are making a recipe that calls for more than a few tablespoons of grated cheese, get out a box or rasp grater; your arm will thank you.

On the positive side, having an internal grating plate, the rotary grater eliminates the risk of raking your knuckles—a common occurrence with a box or rasp grater. (Do use caution when cleaning the grater, however, as the internal blades are very sharp.) A rotary grater also produces a much finer grind of cheese than traditional graters. This provides a more subtle texture to the grated cheese that is particularly appropriate for dusting bowls of pasta. Lastly, a rotary grater offers a taste of the restaurant experience at home. Guests have the option of grating their own cheese at the table.

Overall, the rotary grater is a fairly inexpensive and reasonably useful tool for the table. Half showpiece and half functional equipment, a rotary grater will, at the very least, bring some excitement to your dining room. So while rotary graters are not a kitchen necessity, they certainly do offer a sprinkle of charm to your everyday meals.

Q&A

How can I prevent pasta from sticking to the pot and boiling over?

First of all, don't skimp on water. You need a lot of water so the pasta has room to swell. Also, there must be enough water to dilute the starches released by the pasta. We found that 1 pound of pasta should be cooked in 4 quarts of water. Waiting to add the pasta until the water is at a rolling boil will also reduce the likelihood of pasta sticking together or to the pot. Finally, make sure to stir the pasta often, especially during the first few minutes of the cooking time, when the noodles are most likely to fuse to each other and the pot.

Given what we just said about using a lot of water to prevent sticky pasta, you should not use less water thinking you will reduce the likelihood of boil-overs. Pasta must be cooked in a big pot. You might be able to get away with a 6-quart Dutch oven or stockpot, but we prefer to use an 8-quart pot.

EQUIPMENT CORNER:
Rotary Cheese Graters

"SOME CHEESE, SIR?" AS UBIQUITOUS AS A SALTSHAKER in many Italian restaurants, the rotary cheese grater is the waiter's sidearm. Tirelessly descending upon table after table and showering pastas, risottos, and salads with wonderfully earthy wisps of Parmesan cheese, the grater-laden waiter will not take "no" for an answer. It is almost impossible to refuse the touch of class (and flavor) that the rotary grater brings to the restaurant table. But do these graters have a place at home? To find out, we tested eight models by grating Parmesan, cheddar, mozzarella, and even chocolate. To ensure the validity of the results, these tests were performed by a variety of test cooks with different hand sizes and strengths.

As we began testing, one point was immediately obvious—this was deceptively difficult work! Most of the handles were tiny and slippery, and even the most comfortable of the lot became painful after extended use. All but the Pedrini ($14.99) and KitchenAid ($19.99) struggled with the mozzarella and cheddar cheeses; these two were more successful because of their larger grating drums, which kept the cheese from sticking. Additionally, none of the grater hoppers could accommodate more than 1 or 2 ounces of cheese at a time, and each grater gave us hand fatigue after just a few moments of use. The rotary grater is adept at providing a light dusting of cheese, but it is much too slow for use in the kitchen. If you are making a recipe that calls for more than a few tablespoons of grated cheese, get out a box or rasp grater; your arm will thank you.

On the positive side, having an internal grating plate, the rotary grater eliminates the risk of raking your knuckles—a common occurrence with a box or rasp grater. (Do use caution when cleaning the grater, however, as the internal blades are very sharp.) A rotary grater also produces a much finer grind of cheese than traditional graters. This provides a more subtle texture to the grated cheese that is particularly appropriate for dusting bowls of pasta. Lastly, a rotary grater offers a taste of the restaurant experience at home. Guests have the option of grating their own cheese at the table.

Overall, the rotary grater is a fairly inexpensive and reasonably useful tool for the table. Half showpiece and half functional equipment, a rotary grater will, at the very least, bring some excitement to your dining room. So while rotary graters are not a kitchen necessity, they certainly do offer a sprinkle of charm to your everyday meals.

Q&A

How can I prevent pasta from sticking to the pot and boiling over?

First of all, don't skimp on water. You need a lot of water so the pasta has room to swell. Also, there must be enough water to dilute the starches released by the pasta. We found that 1 pound of pasta should be cooked in 4 quarts of water. Waiting to add the pasta until the water is at a rolling boil will also reduce the likelihood of pasta sticking together or to the pot. Finally, make sure to stir the pasta often, especially during the first few minutes of the cooking time, when the noodles are most likely to fuse to each other and the pot.

Given what we just said about using a lot of water to prevent sticky pasta, you should not use less water thinking you will reduce the likelihood of boil-overs. Pasta must be cooked in a big pot. You might be able to get away with a 6-quart Dutch oven or stockpot, but we prefer to use an 8-quart pot.

Rating Jarred Pasta Sauces

TWENTY-FOUR MEMBERS OF THE *COOK'S ILLUSTRATED* STAFF TASTED ALL OF THE SAUCES, WHICH WERE SERVED warm with cooked ziti on the side. The sauces are listed in order of preference based on their scores in this tasting. All brands are available in supermarkets.

RECOMMENDED
Patsy's Marinara
$8.49 for 24 ounces

Garlic lovers rallied around this marinara, said to be the very same sauce served at the popular Patsy's Italian Restaurant in New York City. In addition to the garlic, which is added fresh (not in a powder), the sauce had an equally strong herbal punch and an "OK balance of acid, sweetness, and salt." The chunky tomato texture was deemed appealing. But talk about sticker shock: Patsy's was more than three times the price of most other sauces.

RECOMMENDED
Bertolli Tomato & Basil Pasta Sauce
$2.49 for 26 ounces

Tasters thought that this sauce had the freshest flavor. As one taster summed it up, "bright, zesty, tomatoes, with some depth of flavor." The texture was "meaty," with an agreeable balance of tomato chunks and puree. Herbs and spices were evident but not assertive.

RECOMMENDED
Barilla Marinara Tomato & Onion
$2.79 for 26 ounces

The top jarred sauce in our 1999 tasting, Barilla held its own among sauces new to the market for being one of the freshest in flavor. Many tasters indicated that they would like the sauce more if it wasn't so heavily seasoned with oregano. The oregano notwithstanding, it had good balance and a pleasant chunky texture.

RECOMMENDED WITH RESERVATIONS
Emeril's Home Style Marinara
$4.29 for 25 ounces

More than one taster likened this famed chef's marinara to pizza sauce. There was no "Bam!" This was instead a balanced, "plain and simple" sauce that some found "not very interesting" and even "kinda boring." The texture was that of a smooth puree.

RECOMMENDED WITH RESERVATIONS
Prego Traditional Pasta Sauce
$2.19 for 26 ounces

As America's top-selling jarred pasta sauce, Prego was the favorite in our kids' tasting. Its heavy oregano taste was popular with many tasters but a "dried-herb nightmare" for others.

RECOMMENDED WITH RESERVATIONS
Classico Sweet Basil Marinara
$2.50 for 26 ounces

This familiar-tasting national top seller wasn't a favorite but was ranked among those considered decent enough. A cooked tomato paste flavor contributed to a noted sweetness and thick, paste-like texture. It "tastes like nondescript pasta sauce from a jar," noted one taster.

RECOMMENDED WITH RESERVATIONS
Buitoni Marinara Pasta Sauce
$2.99 for 26 ounces

Another sauce that was strong on oregano and likened to pizza sauce. It did have a relatively good balance of flavors, but the flavorless, crunchy bits of something unidentifiable were troubling to munch on.

NOT RECOMMENDED
Ragú Traditional Old World Style Pasta Sauce
$2.19 for 26 ounces

More than one taster said that this sauce tasted as if it came from a tin can. The absence of favorable comments was striking: "might as well be tomato paste," "extremely salty," and tastes "heavily cooked/cooked for days," "like V-8," and "more like tomato soup." It had a texture like ketchup.

NOT RECOMMENDED
Colavita Marinara Sauce
$4.69 for 26 ounces

A little doctoring with salt and sugar (neither of which is listed in the ingredients) might have saved this ultrabland sauce that tasted "like a can of crushed tomatoes." The herbs were also too understated.

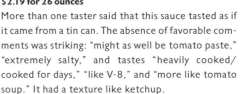

Rating Rotary Graters

WE RATED EIGHT MODELS BASED ON DESIGN, EASE OF USE, AND PERFORMANCE. TESTERS WITH DIFFERENT HAND SIZES and strengths rated each model for its ability to grate Parmesan cheese, cheddar cheese, mozzarella cheese, and chocolate. The rotary graters are listed in order of preference. See www.americastestkitchen.com for up-to-date prices and mail-order sources for top-rated products.

RECOMMENDED
Pedrini Rotary Grater
$14.99

An Italian-made grater with a large hopper, sharp grating teeth, and well-designed handle, the Pedrini took top honors.

RECOMMENDED
KitchenAid Rotary Grater
$19.99

Similar to the Pedrini, this model also had a large hopper, sharp grating teeth, and a fairly comfortable grip. One issue—this model was not designed for the left-handed.

NOT RECOMMENDED
Cuisipro Rotary Cheese Grater
$20

This stainless steel grater was very sturdy and made quick work of the cheese and chocolate. However, testers repeatedly noted that this model was uncomfortable in their hands.

NOT RECOMMENDED
Microplane Revolutionary Rotary Grater
$16.95

Turns out the fluffiest, finest shreds, but it was the slowest model tested.

NOT RECOMMENDED
Oxo Good Grips Seal & Store Rotary Grater
$14.99

Likable rubberized handle, but the hopper is rather small. Not designed for lefties.

NOT RECOMMENDED
Hoffritz Stainless Steel Rotary Grater
$15.99

Awkward design hurt testers' hands. Not designed for lefties.

NOT RECOMMENDED
Norpro Stainless Steel Commercial Drum Grater
$15.99

This heavy-duty stainless steel grater quickly caused hand fatigue.

NOT RECOMMENDED
Zyliss Transparent Cheese Grater
$14.99

Downgraded for its small handle, which becomes slippery with use.

A heavy, enameled cast-iron Dutch oven is the perfect vessel for a slow-simmering braise.

WINTER supper

Stew and starch is a familiar and comforting winter combination. Stew-and-starch pairings include everything from beef stew and mashed potatoes to chicken paprikash and egg noodles. Our favorite Italian stew-and-starch combo is osso buco and polenta.

Osso buco, literally "bone with a hole," is the Italian term for veal shanks. This meaty cut, akin to beef shanks or lamb shanks, becomes meltingly tender when stewed for several hours in a covered pot. Because veal is so delicate, the stewing liquid usually starts with white wine, rather than the red wine used with most beef stews, and also includes tomatoes. Our goal was to create a recipe that guaranteed perfectly tender meat with rich flavor.

Polenta is Italian for cornmeal mush. Nothing more than cornmeal cooked in salted water, good polenta should burst with corn flavor. It is the perfect base for many stews, including osso buco. But getting the texture just right is a challenge. Not-so-tiny lumps often mar the polenta. To avoid this problem, most recipes suggest constant stirring for a half hour or more. We found a way to get good results with a lot less work.

OSSO BUCO

WHAT WE WANTED: Meltingly tender veal shanks cooked in a rich broth for spooning over polenta, potatoes, or noodles.

Osso buco, or Italian braised veal shanks, is too venerable a recipe to fiddle with. With humility, we headed into the kitchen. We decided the best way to approach the dish was to perfect (and simplify, if possible) the cooking technique and to extract the most flavor from the simple ingredients: veal shanks (which are browned), aromatics (onions, carrots, and celery, all sautéed), and liquids (a blend of wine, stock, and tomatoes).

To start, we gathered three classic recipes and prepared each in the test kitchen. At the tasting, there was little consensus about the recipes, although white wine was clearly preferred to red wine. Tasters did, however, offer similar ideas as to what constitutes the perfect osso buco; it should be rich in flavor and color and somewhat brothy but not stewy. This first goal is the reason why we prefer osso buco to veal stews made with boneless shoulder meat. While shoulder meat can be a bit wan, the shank is robust, and the bone adds tremendous flavor to the stewing liquid. With these traits in mind, we created a rough working recipe and set out to explore the two main components in this dish—the veal shanks and the braising liquid.

Most recipes we reviewed call for shanks from the upper portion of the hind leg, cut into pieces between 1 and 1½ inches thick. We found that purchasing shanks is tricky, even when we special-ordered them. From one market, we received stunning shanks with a lovely pinkish blush, which were ideal except for the weight. Each shank weighed between 12 and 16 ounces—too large for individual servings. Part of the charm of osso buco is receiving an individual shank as a portion. We concluded that shanks should weigh 8 to 10 ounces (with the bone) and no more. At another market, the shanks were generally in the ideal weight range,

but the butchering job was less than perfect. In the same package, shank widths varied from 1 to 2½ inches and were occasionally cut on an extreme bias, making it difficult to tie them (see the explanation below) and sear them evenly.

The first step, then, is to shop carefully. We found a thickness of 1½ inches and a weight of 8 ounces ideal. Make sure all the shanks you buy are close to these specifications. Each shank should have two nicely cut, flat sides to facilitate browning.

Preparing the meat for braising was the next step. Most recipes call for tying the shanks and dredging them in flour before searing. We found that tying a piece of butcher's twine around the equator of each shank does prevent the meat from falling apart and makes for a more attractive presentation. When we skipped this step, the meat fell off the bone and floated about in the pot.

Although we do not generally dredge meat in flour before browning, we felt we should at least try it, considering that the majority of osso buco recipes include this step. Tasters felt that the meat floured before searing was gummy and lacked depth. The flour on the meat browns rather than the meat itself, and the flour coating may peel off during the long braising time.

To develop the best flavor in the shanks, we seasoned them heavily with salt and pepper and seared them until a thick, golden brown crust formed. We seared the shanks in two batches (even if they could all fit in the pan at the same time) so that we could deglaze the pan twice with wine, thereby enriching the braising liquid doubly.

The most difficult part of developing this recipe was attaining an ideal braising liquid and sauce. Braising, by design, is a relatively inexact cooking method because the rate at which the liquid reduces can vary greatly. Some of the initial recipes we tried yielded far too much liquid, which was thin in flavor and texture. In other cases, the liquid nearly evaporated by the time the meat was tender. We needed to create a foolproof, flavorful braising liquid and cooking technique that produced a suitable volume of rich sauce and did not need a lot of last-minute fussing.

We experimented with numerous techniques to attain our ideal liquid, including reductions before braising and after braising (with the aromatics and without) and a reduction of the wine to a syrup during the deglazing process. In the end, we settled on the easiest method: natural reduction in the oven. The seal on most Dutch ovens is not perfectly tight, so the liquid reduces as the osso buco cooks. We found further simmering on the stovetop unnecessary as long as we started with the right amount of liquid in the pot.

The braising liquid traditionally begins with meat stock and adds white wine and tomatoes. As few cooks have homemade meat stock on hand and canned versions are often unappealing, we knew that canned chicken broth would be our likely starting point. Two cups (or one can) seemed the right amount, and tests confirmed this. To enrich the flavor of the broth, we used a hefty amount of diced onions, carrots, and celery. Tasters liked the large amount of garlic in one recipe, so we finely minced about five cloves and added them to the pot prior to the broth. We rounded out the flavors with two bay leaves.

We hoped to write the recipe in even amounts, using whole vegetables, one can of broth, one bottle of wine, and so on. But an entire bottle of wine proved overwhelming. The resulting sauce was dominated by acidity. Some testers also felt that the meat was tougher than in previous batches with less wine. We scaled the wine back to 2½ cups, about two thirds of a bottle, and were happy with the results. More than half of the wine is used to deglaze the pot between searing batches of veal shanks and thus the final dish is not as alcoholic or liquidy as it might seem.

With the wine and broth amounts settled, we needed to figure out how to best incorporate the tomatoes. Most tasters did not like too much tomato because they felt it easily overwhelmed the other flavors in the sauce. Fresh tomatoes are always a gamble outside of the summer months, so we chose canned diced tomatoes, thoroughly strained of their juice. This approach worked out well, and the strained tomatoes did not overwhelm the sauce.

We still needed to determine the ideal braising time. Several sources suggest cooking osso buco almost to the consistency of pulled pork. Tasters loved the meat cooked this way, but it was less than attractive—broken down and pot roast–like. We wanted compact meat firmly attached to the bone, so we cooked the meat until it was just fork-tender but still clinging to the bone. Two hours in the oven produced veal that was meltingly soft but still attached to the bone. With some of the larger shanks, the cooking time extended to about 2½ hours.

We experimented with oven temperature and found that 325 degrees reduced the braising liquid to the right consistency and did not harm the texture of the meat. While beef stews are best cooked at 300 degrees, veal shanks have so much collagen and connective tissue that they can be braised at a slightly higher temperature.

Just before serving, osso buco is sprinkled with gremolata, a mixture of minced garlic, parsley, and lemon zest. We were surprised to find variations on this classic trio. A number of recipes include orange zest mixed with lemon zest or on its own. Other recipes include minced anchovies. We tested three gremolatas: one traditional, one with orange zest mixed in equal part with lemon zest, and one with anchovies. Tasters liked all three dishes but favored the traditional version.

In some recipes the gremolata is used as a garnish, and in others it is added to the pot just before serving. We chose a compromise approach, stirring half the gremolata into the pot and letting it stand for five minutes so that the flavors of the garlic, lemon, and parsley permeated the dish. We sprinkled the remaining gremolata on individual servings for a hit of freshness.

WHAT WE LEARNED: Choose medium-size shanks, tie them to keep the meat attached, and brown them in two batches to develop maximum flavor from this mild-tasting meat. Use a mix of chicken broth, white wine, and canned tomatoes as the braising liquid. Stir half of the gremolata (minced garlic, lemon, and parsley) into the stew and sprinkle the rest over individual portions.

OSSO BUCO

Serves 6

To keep the meat attached to the bone during the long simmering process, tie a piece of twine around the thickest portion of each shank before it is browned. Use a zester, vegetable peeler, or paring knife to remove the zest from a single lemon, then mince it with a chef's knife. With the lid on the pot cracked, the braising liquid should reduce to a sauce-like consistency in the oven. Just before serving, taste the liquid and, if it seems too thin, simmer the liquid on the stovetop as you remove the strings from the osso buco and arrange them in individual bowls.

osso buco

- 4   tablespoons vegetable oil
- 6   veal shanks, 1½ inches thick (8 to 10 ounces each), patted dry with paper towels and tied around the equator with butcher's twine
       Salt and ground black pepper
- 2½   cups dry white wine
- 2   medium onions, cut into ½-inch dice (about 2 cups)
- 2   medium carrots, cut into ½-inch dice (about 1½ cups)
- 2   medium celery ribs, cut into ½-inch dice (about 1 cup)
- 6   medium garlic cloves, minced or pressed through a garlic press (about 2 tablespoons)
- 2   cups low-sodium chicken broth
- 2   small bay leaves
- 1   (14.5-ounce) can diced tomatoes, drained

gremolata

- 3   medium garlic cloves, minced or pressed through a garlic press (about 1 tablespoon)
- 2   teaspoons minced zest from 1 lemon
- ¼   cup minced fresh parsley leaves

1. FOR THE OSSO BUCO: Adjust an oven rack to the lower-middle position and heat the oven to 325 degrees. Heat 1 tablespoon of the oil in a large ovenproof Dutch oven over medium-high heat until shimmering. Meanwhile, sprinkle both sides of the shanks generously with salt and pepper to taste. Swirl to coat the pan bottom with the oil. Place 3 shanks in a single layer in the pan and cook until they are golden brown on one side, about 5 minutes. Using tongs, flip the shanks and cook on the second side until golden brown, about 5 minutes longer. Transfer the shanks

---

Q&A

What exactly is a simmer, and how does it differ from a boil?

Simmering is a key technique used to make stews, soups, sauces, and stocks. The idea is to cook foods slowly but gently. For instance, if stews boil, the meat will fall apart. Boiling also causes fat to break down into small globules that are harder to remove. The end result is a greasy boiled stew or stock.

So how do you distinguish a boil from a simmer?

A rapid boil occurs at 212 degrees (at sea level) and is characterized by large bubbles bursting all over the surface of the liquid. The bubbles appear to be rolling over each other—hence the term "a rolling boil." A steady simmer occurs between 206 and 211 degrees. Bubbles break over the surface of the liquid, but they do not roll over each other. More bubbles are found along the edges of the pot. Finally, a gentle simmer occurs between 198 and 205 degrees. Very few bubbles break the surface, and all of these bubbles are confined to the edges of the pot.

to a bowl and set aside. Off the heat, add ½ cup of the wine to the Dutch oven, scraping the pan bottom with a wooden spoon to loosen any browned bits. Pour the liquid into the bowl with the browned shanks. Return the pot to medium-high heat, add 1 more tablespoon of the oil, and heat until shimmering. Brown the remaining shanks, about 5 minutes for each side. Transfer the shanks to the bowl. Off the heat, add 1 cup of the wine to the pot, scraping the bottom to loosen the browned bits. Pour the liquid into the bowl with the shanks.

2. Set the pot over medium heat. Add the remaining 2 tablespoons oil and heat until shimmering. Add the onions, carrots, celery, ¼ teaspoon salt, and ⅛ teaspoon pepper and cook, stirring occasionally, until soft and lightly browned, about 9 minutes. Add the garlic and cook until lightly browned, about 1 minute longer. Increase the heat to high and stir in the broth, remaining 1 cup wine, accumulated veal juices in the bowl, and bay leaves. Add the tomatoes; return the veal shanks to the pot (the liquid should just cover the shanks). Bring the liquid to a full simmer. Cover the pot, cracking the lid just slightly, and transfer the pot to the oven. Cook the shanks until the meat is easily pierced with a fork but not falling off the bone, about 2 hours. (Can be refrigerated for up to 2 days. Bring to a simmer over medium-low heat.)

3. FOR THE GREMOLATA: Combine the garlic, lemon zest, and parsley in a small bowl. Stir half of the gremolata into the pot, reserving the rest for garnish. Season with salt and pepper to taste. Let the osso buco stand, uncovered, for 5 minutes.

4. Using tongs, remove the shanks from the pot, cut off and discard the twine, and place 1 veal shank in each of 6 bowls. Ladle some of the braising liquid over each shank and sprinkle each serving with the remaining gremolata. Serve immediately.

TASTING LAB: Bottled Water

IT IS RATHER BAFFLING THAT A SUBSTANCE AS FUNDA-mental and as abundant as water can form the basis of an astonishingly large business. In 2003, bottled water sales ballooned to $8.3 billion in the United States alone. Per capita consumption was more than 22 gallons, nearly double what it had been only a decade earlier, and sales and consumption of bottled water are only expected to grow further. To meet the demand, retailers have stocked their shelves with a multitude of brands, both domestic and foreign, many wearing labels that suggest pristine alpine springs or crisp, clean mountain air. That the bottles differ in labeling is clear; what is less apparent is the extent to which they differ in taste. To better understand what—if anything—distinguishes one bottled water from another, we conducted a blind tasting.

We collected nine brands that covered the still-water spectrum—both domestic and imported. We also included a water not expressly meant for drinking, ultrapure plasma-grade water. Used in sensitive chemistry applications, this water is double-distilled and virtually free of all minerals and impurities. We reasoned that by including in the tasting water in its near-purest form, we might gain some insight into what makes water taste good—its purity or its impurities, in a manner of speaking.

There are several types of bottled water, but three categories stand out: spring water, artesian water, and purified water. A bottle labeled "spring water" must contain water that came from an underground water source that flows naturally to the earth's surface. The location of the source must be identified. The water is collected either at the spring or through a hole that has been made to tap the source that feeds the spring. Spring water is sometimes bottled without additional treatment (this is true particularly of European bottled waters), but domestic bottlers often use carbon filtration to remove odors, micro- or ultrafiltration to remove fine particles and impurities, and/or ultraviolet light or ozonation to disinfect the water.

Some producers tap several springs, bottle each separately, yet sell all under the same brand name. This means that a bottle of brand X purchased on the East Coast may not be from the same source as a bottle of brand X purchased on the West Coast. This practice is common among domestic producers and allows suppliers to better meet demand and minimize the cost of transport. But it also means that the flavor profiles of the same brand may differ from one region of the country to another. Many European and foreign producers bottle water from a single source—and are proud of it. Of the nine brands we assembled for our tasting, six were spring waters—Arrowhead, Crystal Geyser, Dannon, Evian, Poland Spring, and Volvic.

Artesian water differs from spring water in that its source must be an underground formation known as a confined aquifer. The water is sandwiched between—or confined by—a top and bottom layer of impermeable rock. When the aquifer is tapped, natural internal pressure causes the water to flow. Is artesian water better than

"regular" spring water? Not necessarily. While the U.S. Environmental Protection Agency says that water from artesian aquifers is often cleaner because the confining layers of rock and clay impede the movement of contaminants, there is no guarantee that artesian water is any more pure—or otherwise better—than spring water. The only artesian water in the tasting was Fiji, which is indeed imported from the Fiji Islands in the Pacific and is the second-best-selling imported brand.

Spring water and artesian water both contain dissolved solids (or minerals) such as calcium, magnesium, sulfates, silica, and chlorides. Mineral water is spring or artesian water that naturally contains at least 250 parts per million (ppm) of total dissolved solids (TDS). Evian was the only mineral water in the tasting, although it is not marketed as such. (A laboratory analysis we conducted did show that our sample of Fiji had TDS of more than 250 ppm, but to qualify as a mineral water, the water must, through repeated analysis, be shown to consistently contain 250 ppm of TDS. According to Fiji, its water has TDS of 210 ppm.)

Two purified waters, Pepsi-Cola's Aquafina and Coca-Cola's Dasani, were part of our tasting. Aquafina is the best-selling brand of bottled water in this country, and Dasani is number two. What is purified water? The simple definition is that purified water has been processed to remove contaminants and minerals before bottling. The source is often a municipal water supply. Pepsi and Coke tap municipal water sources in various parts of the country and filter the water in a process called reverse osmosis. Reverse osmosis removes most of the impurities, and the water is left nearly bereft of minerals. Such a tight filtration process means that no matter what the source, the taste of purified water is likely to be consistent from bottle to bottle.

Purified water is frequently criticized for being merely a highly filtered version of what flows when you open the home tap. Coke claims, however, that consumers are much more concerned about taste than source. For that reason, after reverse-osmosis processing, Coke adds minerals back to the purified water to obtain a particular flavor profile. Pepsi does not add minerals to Aquafina.

By contrast, a spring water's flavor profile is organically derived. As the water journeys from its origin as rainwater or snowmelt to the spring, a process that can take years, it travels through layers of rock, clay, gravel, and/or sand that filter out impurities. As the impurities are filtered out, the water also acquires dissolved minerals that in their specific combinations give the water its signature flavor.

The only water in the tasting that tasters unanimously rejected was the ultrapure plasma-grade water, which earned the lowest possible score because of its flat, vapid flavor. Though this water is of course unavailable to consumers, it did teach us something. Ostensibly, when it comes to water, absolute purity is a liability, not an asset. Some mineral content makes water likable and palatable.

Is spring water better than purified municipal water? The two purified waters we sampled, Aquafina and Dasani, earned respectable scores, coming in fourth and fifth, respectively, and beat out four spring waters. But they were not in the winners' circle. Two spring waters and the one artesian water in the tasting swept the pack, with win, place, and show. Volvic, a spring water from France, was the clear winner, with Fiji, the artesian water, close behind.

What should you buy? While most of our tasters will now purchase Volvic or Fiji when given the option, our results show that the flavor differences between bottled waters are not great. Unlike the differences between brands of chocolate or barbecue sauce, the distinctions between brands of bottled water are so modest that you are unlikely to be disappointed with any of those that we tasted.

TASTING LAB: Bottled versus Tap Water

WE WERE CURIOUS TO SEE HOW THE HIGHEST- AND lowest-rated bottled waters would fare against tap water, so we organized a second tasting in which we sampled Volvic (first place), Poland Spring (last place), Boston tap water, samples of water from the Metropolitan Water District (MWD) of Southern California in Los Angeles (because it has won awards in its category at international water tastings), and tap water from a residence in Los Angeles County.

Volvic and the MWD water were equally well liked, earning identical scores and accolades such as "fresh" and "clean." Poland Spring came in next, besting Boston tap water, which tasters described as metallic, musty, and stale. Residential Los Angeles County water was so chlorinated that it stopped tasters in their tracks. Why would the MWD water be so good and the residential water so bad? The MWD is a water wholesaler, and the water it has to offer is not necessarily the water that flows from area faucets. A phone call to the MWD revealed that it was, in fact, not the source of the residential tap water that we tasted.

What, then, did we learn from this tasting? That tap water can rival even the best bottled water (at least in theory), but that even our least-favorite bottled water was superior to water culled straight from two not-so-excellent taps in Boston and Los Angeles.

Rating Bottled Waters

TWENTY-THREE MEMBERS OF THE *COOK'S ILLUSTRATED* STAFF SAMPLED NINE DIFFERENT BRANDS OF STILL BOTTLED WATER. The waters were tasted at room temperature, which allows odors and flavors to be more perceptible than when tasted chilled. Total dissolved solids (TDS) analysis was conducted by an independent laboratory; the amounts listed below (in parts per million) may not be identical to amounts given by producers. The waters are listed in order of preference. Unless otherwise noted, the waters are available in supermarkets nationwide.

RECOMMENDED
Volvic Natural Spring Water
$1.29 for 1 liter
Source: Clairvic Spring, Volvic, France
TDS: 137 ppm

Tasters had a clear preference for this water, calling it very fresh, pure, and clean, with slight mineral flavors. One taster wrote, "smooth and velvety," while another declared it a favorite because it "tastes like water."

RECOMMENDED
Fiji Natural Artesian Water
$1.59 for 1 liter
Source: Viti Levu, Republic of Fiji
TDS: 260 ppm

Tasters appreciated the "nice and clean," "incredibly drinkable," "unadulterated" quality of this water. One taster hailed it as "perfect." It was also described as having a hint of sweetness and mineral flavor. A few detractors called it "dull."

RECOMMENDED
Dannon Natural Spring Water
$0.53 for 25 ounces
Source: Springs in Bellefonte, Pa.; Grand Prairie, Texas; Anaheim, Calif.; High Springs, Fla.; Mount Shasta, Calif. (sample tasted was from Bellefonte, Pa.)
TDS: 200 ppm

"Pure," "clean," "fresh," and "smooth" were the accolades. A couple tasters noted a sweetness. Negative comments included "stale" and "flat."

RECOMMENDED
Aquafina Purified Drinking Water
$0.99 for 1 liter
Source: Multiple municipal water supplies
TDS: 30 ppm

Most tasters found this water to be sweet, but there agreement ended. Comments like "fresh" and "lively" were countered with criticisms like "metallic" and "artificial."

RECOMMENDED
Dasani Purified Water
$1.19 for 1 liter
Source: Multiple municipal water supplies
TDS: 80 ppm

Nearly half of the tasters found this water to have distinct mineral flavors ("like licking a geode," said one). Though it was described as "clean," some found it "harsh."

RECOMMENDED
Arrowhead Mountain Spring Water
$1.09 for 1 liter
Source: Multiple springs in the U.S. and Canada
TDS: 120 ppm

Comments about this water, available in the West, ranged from positive ("nice taste" and "silky") to moderate ("not bad") to decidedly negative ("yuck, tap water"). Some tasters commented that this water had an aftertaste, and one said that the flavor "lingers on and on."

RECOMMENDED
Evian Natural Spring Water
$1.69 for 1 liter
Source: Cachat Spring, Evian, France
TDS: 360 ppm

This was a controversial water. "Soft, smooth, and supple" and "very refreshing" were the praises. "Heavy," "creamy," and "yuck" were criticisms. Most tasters agreed that this water had a notable sweetness and strong mineral flavors.

RECOMMENDED
Crystal Geyser
$0.69 for 1.5 liters
Source: Springs in Benton, Tenn., and Mount Shasta, Calif. (sample tasted was from Benton, Tenn.)
TDS: 180 ppm

Tasters mustered little excitement—positive or negative—about this water. "Pretty neutral and clean" and "a bit dull, but relatively clean" typified comments.

RECOMMENDED
Poland Spring
$0.89 for 1 liter
Sources: Springs in Hollis, Fryeburg, Poland Spring, and Poland, Maine (sample tasted was from Hollis)
TDS: 50 ppm

This water, which is widely available in the Northeast, was criticized for tasting "unnatural" and having "off flavors." More temperate tasters commented that it was "basic" but uninteresting. Several tasters noted a saltiness.

POLENTA

WHAT WE WANTED: Creamy, smooth polenta, achieved without lumps or constant stirring.

If your mother ever complained about slaving over a hot stove, she was probably talking about making polenta. Nothing more than cornmeal mush, polenta is made from dried, ground corn cooked in liquid until the starches in the corn hydrate and swell into soft, balloon-like structures. For many purposes, this soft stage is the most delicious way to serve polenta.

The stiff polenta you often see in restaurants starts out as a soft mass but is spread into a thin layer on a baking sheet or marble surface, cooled until firm, sliced, and then sautéed, fried, or grilled until it resembles a crouton. These crisp rectangles are rarely more than a garnish. However, a smooth, piping-hot mound of soft polenta can be a meal. More commonly, soft polenta is used as a filler to stretch out meager game birds like quail or to cut the richness of sausages. Most stews and braised dishes—everything from osso buco to braised rabbit—can be ladled over a bowl of soft polenta.

Although making polenta sounds easy, the traditional Italian method for cooking it is a lot of work. The polenta must be slowly added to boiling salted water and stirred constantly (to prevent scorching) during the entire 30- to 40-minute cooking time. Within five minutes, you'll feel like you've been arm-wrestling Arnold Schwarzenegger. Thirty minutes of such constant stirring can seem like an eternity.

Of course, this assumes that you have avoided the biggest pitfall of all, the seizing problem at the beginning of the cooking process. Cornmeal is a starch, and starch thickens when mixed with water and heated. If this happens too quickly, the cornmeal seizes up into a solid, nearly immovable mass.

We tested adding cornmeal to cold water, using more water, using less water, and using different grinds of cornmeal, all to no avail. Yes, we learned to prevent seizing (add the cornmeal very slowly), but we still needed to stir constantly for at least 30 minutes to prevent scorching.

This testing did, however, reveal some important information. We found that medium-grind cornmeal makes the best polenta. (For more information about cornmeal, see page 255.) Finely ground cornmeal, such as the Quaker brand sold in many supermarkets, is too powdery and makes gummy polenta. Cornmeal with a texture akin to granulated sugar, not table salt, makes the best polenta. We also discovered that a ratio of 4 parts water to 1 part cornmeal delivers the right consistency. As for salt, 1 teaspoon is the right amount for 1 cup of cornmeal.

At this point in our testing, we started to explore alternative cooking methods. The microwave was a bust, yielding sticky, raw-tasting polenta. The pressure cooker was even worse; the polenta took a long time to cook and then stuck firmly to the pot. We finally got good results when we prepared polenta in a double boiler. The polenta was cooked over simmering water so it didn't scorch or seize up the way it can when cooked over direct heat. It emerged with a soft, light texture and sweet corn flavor. There is only one drawback to this method, and it is a big one: time.

While a double boiler produced undeniably rich, creamy polenta, the cooking time was prohibitively long. Even with the minimum attention that the technique required, 1½ hours of cooking was simply impractical. We wondered whether we could produce similar results via more conventional methods. The double boiler method proved to us that slow, very gentle heat was the key to unlocking cornmeal's smooth texture, not vigilant stirring. Could we approximate a double boiler's low heat with a conventional saucepan?

Luckily, we could. A heavy-bottomed saucepan on the stove's lowest possible setting (or in conjunction with a flame tamer; see the recipe note) shielded the polenta from cooking too rapidly and allowed the starches to be released and the flavor of the cornmeal to develop. Keeping the cover on the pot held in moisture and reduced the risk of scorching the polenta, even when we stirred infrequently rather than constantly. Within ½ hour, a third of the time it took in the double boiler, we had creamy polenta ready for the table. We did find, however, that with the slightly higher temperature, stirring was a more significant issue. When we left the polenta unheeded for more than seven minutes, it tended to stick to the pot bottom and corners, where it remained immovably until washing. Stirring vigorously every five minutes prevented such mishaps.

WHAT WE LEARNED: Start with one part medium-grind cornmeal and four parts water for polenta with the right consistency. Slowly add the cornmeal to simmering water and then turn the heat down very low and cover so that the polenta can cook slowly without scorching or constant stirring.

BASIC POLENTA

Serves 4 to 6

If you do not have a heavy-bottomed saucepan, you may want to use a flame tamer to manage the heat. A flame tamer can be purchased at most kitchen supply stores, or one can be fashioned from a ring of foil (see the illustration on page 255). It's easy to tell whether you need a flame tamer or not. If the polenta bubbles or sputters at all after the first 10 minutes, the heat is too high, and you need one. Properly heated polenta will do little more than release wisps of steam. When stirring the polenta, make sure to scrape the sides and bottom of the pan to ensure even cooking. Use this polenta as the base for any stew or braise, especially osso buco (page 248). Cooked leafy greens also make excellent toppings for soft polenta.

6 cups water
    Salt
1½ cups medium cornmeal, preferably stone-ground
3 tablespoons unsalted butter, cut into large chunks
    Ground black pepper

1. Bring the water to a rolling boil in a heavy-bottomed 4-quart saucepan over medium-high heat. Reduce the heat to the lowest possible setting, add 1½ teaspoons salt, and pour the cornmeal into the water in a very slow stream from a measuring cup, all the while whisking in a circular motion to prevent lumps.

2. Cover and cook, vigorously stirring the polenta with a wooden spoon for about 10 seconds once every 5 minutes and making sure to scrape clean the bottom and corners of the pot, until the polenta has lost its raw cornmeal taste and becomes soft and smooth, about 30 minutes. Stir in the butter, season with salt and pepper to taste, and serve immediately.

VARIATIONS

POLENTA WITH PARMESAN AND BUTTER

Serves 4 to 6 as a first course or side dish

Follow the recipe for Basic Polenta, stirring in ¾ cup grated Parmesan cheese along with the butter. Divide the polenta among individual bowls and top each with a small pat of butter. Sprinkle generously with more grated Parmesan to taste and serve immediately.

POLENTA WITH GORGONZOLA

Serves 4 to 6 as a substantial first course or light entrée

Choose a Gorgonzola dolce or other mild, creamy blue cheese such as Saga Blue. Do not use an aged Gorgonzola for this dish. Other aged blue cheeses will also be too salty, crumbly, and pungent.

Follow the recipe for Basic Polenta, dividing the finished polenta among individual bowls. Top each bowl with a 1-ounce slice of Gorgonzola cheese and serve immediately.

TASTING LAB: Cornmeal

LARGE COMMERCIAL MILLS USE HUGE STEEL ROLLERS TO grind dent corn (a hard, dry corn) into cornmeal. This is how Quaker cornmeal, the leading supermarket brand, is produced. But some smaller mills scattered around the United States grind with millstones; this product is called stone-ground cornmeal. (If water is used as an energy source, the cornmeal may be labeled water-ground.) Stone-ground cornmeal is usually a bit coarser than cornmeal processed through steel rollers. The difference is like that between granulated sugar (which is a tiny bit coarse) and table salt (which is smooth and fine).

In addition, smaller millers often choose not to degerm, or remove all the germ, cleanly. This makes their product closer to whole-grain cornmeal. If the color is uniform, the germ has been removed. A stone-ground cornmeal with some germ has flecks that are both lighter and darker than the predominant color, whether yellow or white.

In our tests, we found the texture of polenta made with stone-ground meal more interesting, as the grind of the cornmeal was not uniform. More important, we found that polenta made with stone-ground cornmeal tasted much better than that made with the standard Quaker cornmeal. Stone-ground cornmeal gives polenta a sweeter, more intense corn flavor. Yellow cornmeal is traditional for polenta making and was the first choice among our tasters.

The higher moisture and oil content of stone-ground cornmeal causes it to go rancid rather quickly. Wrap stone-ground cornmeal tightly in plastic or put it into a moisture-proof container, then refrigerate or freeze it to prolong freshness. Degerminated cornmeals, such as Quaker, keep for a year if stored in a dry, cool place.

TECHNIQUE: Flame Tamer

A flame tamer is a metal disk that can be used as a buffer between a burner and a pot to maintain a gentle, low level of heat. A flame tamer is especially useful when trying to cook a stew or soup at the barest simmer for a long time. If you don't own a flame tamer, aluminum foil can be fashioned into a thick, slightly flattened ring and placed right on top of a gas burner.

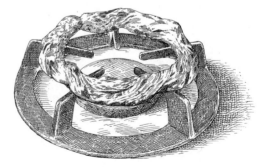

Cut a 3-foot length of foil and squeeze it into a ¾-inch-thick rope. Roll one end to form a ring the size of the burner. Twist the remaining foil rope around the ring to form a flame tamer. Set the ring on the burner, then place the pot on top.

Ceramic crocks are filled with onion soup and ready for their crusty cheese topping and a quick trip under the broiler.

BISTRO Classics

CHAPTER 20

Who doesn't like bistro food? It offers the panache of fine French cooking but in a casual setting. The dishes are rustic, hearty, and satisfying. And unlike so much restaurant cooking, bistro food makes sense at home. Most recipes rely on inexpensive, easy-to-find ingredients and basic techniques.

That doesn't always mean that bistro food is great. Casualness can sometimes translate as sloppiness. Who hasn't been served a bowl of watery French onion soup with crunchy onions and way too much gooey cheese? Or maybe the onions were cooked properly but the broth was way too salty?

A baked goat cheese salad is a delicate balance of textures (crunchy greens and creamy cheese), temperatures (cool lettuce and warm cheese), and flavors (sweet, tangy, bitter, and acidic) that is often out of kilter. Our goal for this chapter was simple. Take French onion soup and baked goat cheese salad and make stellar versions of these bistro favorites.

BAKED GOAT CHEESE SALAD

WHAT WE WANTED: To make this bistro classic at home with warm but not fluid goat cheese, tasty greens, and the right dressing.

Warm goat cheese salad has been a fixture of restaurant menus for years, featuring artisanal cheeses, organic baby field greens, barrel-aged vinegars, and imported oils. Marketing being what it is, the jargon is often more intriguing than the execution: tepid, crumb-dusted cheese on overdressed designer greens at a price that defies reason. When we've tried to prepare this salad at home, the results have been equally disappointing, albeit less expensive. We've usually ended up with flavorless warm cheese melted onto the greens. What we wanted was quite different: creamy cheese rounds infused with flavor and surrounded by crisp, golden breading, all cradled in lightly dressed greens.

Coating and heating the cheese is clearly the major challenge of this recipe. Techniques uncovered in the recipes we researched included pan-frying, broiling, and baking. We began by coating portions of goat cheese in herbs (thyme and chives), then dipping the goat cheese rounds in beaten egg (with a little Dijon mustard added for bite), and finally fresh bread crumbs (the most common option for coating). We tried pan-frying (the most frequent method in cookbook recipes and the classic restaurant technique). Although the bread crumbs crisped up nicely after a short stay in the hot oil, several problems arose. The worst problem was that the interior of the cheese rounds began to melt while the first side was browning, which made turning the disks a nightmare.

Nevertheless, we continued to pursue this method, chilling the rounds in the refrigerator for 30 minutes before they hit the oil, which we hoped would prevent the centers from overheating before the crust had crisped, but this, too, failed. One recipe suggested broiling the goat cheese rounds, but the rounds simply melted under the intense heat of the broiler.

It was time to try baking. Baking the cheese at temperatures ranging from 300 to 400 degrees for 4 to 7 minutes resulted in pallid, soggy crusts across the board, with varying degrees of unpleasant melting. Curious whether higher temperatures would yield the crust we were searching for, we turned the oven up to 475 degrees and ended up with goat cheese fondue.

Logic (or stubbornness) had persuaded us that higher temperatures had the potential to produce a crisp crust, but reality had shown that we needed a more durable breading. Then we hit upon the idea of using Melba toasts—perhaps these extremely dry (and extremely hard) crackers would work. We pulverized them, dunked the cheese in beaten egg, and then coated the rounds in the sandy crumbs. Appearing to fuse with the egg, the Melba crumbs formed a cohesive, shell-like barrier in the oven. Finally, our crust was crisp, although there still was some oozing of the cheese.

Theorizing that if the oven were blistering hot and the cheese arctic cold we would get a crispy crust and no oozing cheese, we placed our goat cheese rounds in the freezer rather than the refrigerator for 30 minutes. Baking our "frozen" cheese at 475 degrees for 7 minutes, we struck gold. Although a few kitchen naysayers found the Melba crust a bit dry, we found that a quick brush of olive oil onto the exterior of the breaded and chilled rounds solved this problem.

It was time to add the baked goat cheese rounds to a salad. Most tasters preferred a mix of heartier greens, such as arugula and frisée, and all tasters preferred a classic vinaigrette, as this dressing echoed and complemented the flavors of the goat cheese rounds. Given the fat in the cheese, we found that it's important to dress the greens lightly.

WHAT WE LEARNED: Ground Melba toasts make the crispest crust for the goat cheese, which should be frozen and then baked in a very hot oven to brown the exterior without causing the rounds to lose their shape.

SALAD WITH HERBED BAKED GOAT CHEESE AND VINAIGRETTE

Serves 6

The baked goat cheese should be served warm. Prepare the salad components while the cheese is in the freezer, then toss the greens and vinaigrette while the cheese cools a bit after baking.

goat cheese

3	ounces white Melba toasts (about 2 cups)
1	teaspoon ground black pepper
3	large eggs
2	tablespoons Dijon mustard
1	tablespoon chopped fresh thyme leaves
1	tablespoon chopped fresh chives
12	ounces firm goat cheese
	Extra-virgin olive oil

salad

2	tablespoons red wine vinegar
1	tablespoon Dijon mustard
1	teaspoon finely minced shallot
¼	teaspoon salt
6	tablespoons extra-virgin olive oil
	Ground black pepper
18	ounces (about 14 cups) mixed hearty greens, washed and dried

1. FOR THE CHEESE: In a food processor, process the Melba toasts to fine, even crumbs, about 1½ minutes; transfer the crumbs to a medium bowl and stir in the pepper. Whisk the eggs and mustard in another medium bowl until combined. Combine the thyme and chives in a small bowl.

2. Using dental floss or kitchen twine, divide the cheese into 12 equal pieces (see the photograph on page 260). Roll each piece of cheese into a ball; roll each ball in the combined fresh herbs to coat lightly. Transfer 6 pieces to the egg mixture and turn each piece to coat; transfer to the Melba crumbs and turn each piece to coat, pressing the crumbs into the cheese. Flatten each ball gently with your fingertips into a disk about 1½ inches wide and 1 inch thick and set on a baking sheet. Repeat with the remaining 6 pieces of cheese. Transfer the baking sheet to the freezer and freeze the disks until firm, about 30 minutes. (The cheese may be wrapped tightly in plastic wrap and frozen up to 1 week.) Adjust an oven rack to the uppermost position; heat the oven to 475 degrees.

3. FOR THE SALAD: Meanwhile, combine the vinegar, mustard, shallot, and salt in a small bowl. Whisking constantly, drizzle in the olive oil; season with pepper to taste. Set aside.

4. Remove the cheese from the freezer and brush the tops and sides evenly with olive oil. Bake until the crumbs are golden brown and the cheese is slightly soft, 7 to 9 minutes (or 9 to 12 minutes if the cheese is completely frozen). Using a thin metal spatula, transfer the cheese to a paper towel–lined plate and cool 3 minutes.

5. Place the greens in a large bowl, drizzle the vinaigrette over them, and toss to coat. Divide the greens among individual plates; place 2 rounds of goat cheese on each salad. Serve immediately.

VARIATION

SALAD WITH APPLES, WALNUTS, DRIED CHERRIES, AND HERBED BAKED GOAT CHEESE

Plump 1 cup dried cherries in ½ cup hot water in a small bowl, about 10 minutes; drain. Quarter and core 2 medium Granny Smith apples and cut into ⅛-inch-thick slices. Follow the recipe for Salad with Herbed Baked Goat Cheese and Vinaigrette, replacing the red wine vinegar with 2 tablespoons cider vinegar and adding ¼ teaspoon sugar to the dressing. Proceed as directed, dividing cherries, apples, and ½ cup toasted and chopped walnuts among individual salad plates.

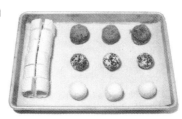
TASTING LAB: Goat Cheese

THE FRENCH ONCE HAD A CORNER ON THE GOAT cheese (or chèvre) market, but that's no longer the case. We conducted a tasting of three domestic and four readily available imported fresh goat cheeses. All were sold in log form ranging in size from 3.5 to 5 ounces.

Our tasters concluded that American producers have mastered the craft of making goat cheese. All of the domestic cheeses were well liked, but the clear favorite was Vermont Chèvre, from the Vermont Butter and Cheese Company. It was creamy and tangy but not overpowering.

Reviews of the imported cheese were mixed. Tasters were enthusiastic about Le Biquet from Canada, but many of the French cheeses were described as gamey or muttony, with a chalky, Spackle-like texture. A few adventurous tasters appreciated the assertive flavors of the imported cheeses, but the overall feeling was that the domestic cheeses were cleaner tasting, more balanced, and better suited for use in a baked goat cheese salad. (A head-to-head tasting of our favorite domestic and imported cheeses bore this out.)

Whether you like a mild or assertive goat cheese, when using goat cheese for salad look for a firm log with a relatively dry exterior. Softer cheeses are more difficult to portion evenly and don't lend themselves well to rolling and breading.

GETTING IT RIGHT: Cooking the Cheese

| Pan-Fried | Baked at 350 Degrees | Baked at 475 Degrees |

Pan-fried goat cheese develops a crisp crust, but it's very tricky to turn the rounds over without crushing the melting interior and causing the cheese to ooze out (left photo). Goat cheese coated with bread crumbs and baked in a 350-degree oven (center photo) is soggy and pale. Goat cheese coated with ground Melba crumbs, partially frozen, and baked at 475 degrees is crisp; it doesn't ooze; and it maintains its shape (right photo). It has all the benefits of pan-frying with none of the disadvantages.

Rating Goat Cheeses

TEN MEMBERS OF THE *COOK'S ILLUSTRATED* STAFF TASTED ALL OF THE CHEESES AS IS, WITH CRACKERS AND WATER offered to cleanse palates. The cheeses are listed in order of preference based on their scores in this tasting. Look for these cheeses in supermarkets and specialty markets.

HIGHLY RECOMMENDED

Vermont Butter & Cheese Company Chèvre

Websterville, Vermont **$3.59 for 4 ounces**

The clear favorite was described by tasters as "creamy," "tangy," and "buttery."

HIGHLY RECOMMENDED

Le Biquet Plain Goat Cheese

Chesterville, Quebec **$5.99 for 3.5 ounces**

The best imported goat cheese in the tasting. This cheese was well liked by tasters, who called it "well balanced" and "tangy."

RECOMMENDED

Capri, Westfield Farm Goat Cheese

Hubbardston, Massachusetts **$5.49 for 5 ounces**

This cheese had a slightly "chalky" texture but a nice "nutty" flavor.

RECOMMENDED

Belmont Goat Cheese

Belmont, Wisconsin **$3.59 for 4 ounces**

Tasters described this cheese as "lemony" and "tangy" with a texture "like thick cream cheese."

RECOMMENDED WITH RESERVATIONS

Chevron Goat Cheese

France **$3.99 for 4 ounces**

This cheese had a quite strong flavor that was compared to feta cheese. Comments ranged from "tangy" to "sour."

RECOMMENDED WITH RESERVATIONS

Couturier Fresh Goat Cheese

France **$3.99 for 4 ounces**

Tasters described this cheese as "bitter," and there were several complaints about the "Spackle-like" texture.

RECOMMENDED WITH RESERVATIONS

Montrachet Chèvre

France **$3.79 for 5 ounces**

The texture of this cheese was deemed "chalky" and "starchy," and the flavor was described as either "grassy" or "like mutton."

FRENCH ONION SOUP

WHAT WE WANTED: French onion soup should have a dark, rich broth, intensely flavored by an abundance of seriously cooked onions and covered by a slice of French bread that is broth-soaked beneath and cheesy and crusty on top.

Making traditional French onion soup is easily a two-day affair, with one day spent making the beef stock and the next toiling over the onions to finish the soup. And there's no guarantee that it will turn out right. Over the years, we have consumed many crocks of flavorless onions floating in hypersalty beef bouillon and topped with globs of greasy melted cheese. We've also eaten weak, watery soups. We set out to develop a soup to obliterate these bad memories.

The first obstacle to success is the base. This soup is most commonly made with homemade beef stock. If the right stock is used, the results can be delicious. But making beef stock takes at least three hours. We wondered if there was a way to get around this step.

We tested soups made with homemade chicken stock (which takes considerably less time to prepare than beef stock) and canned broth. Both were too chickeny and just not right. Soups made with canned beef broth were terrible. Commercial beef broth does not have enough flavor to carry the day alone. After experimentation, we devised a formula for what we call "cheater" broth. By combining canned beef and chicken broths with red wine (the secret ingredient here), we came up with a broth that has enough good, rich flavor to make an excellent soup base.

The next obvious step was to examine the choice of onions. We found Vidalias to be disappointingly bland and boring, white onions to be candy-sweet and one-dimensional, and yellow onions to be only mildly flavorful, with just a slight sweetness. Red onions ranked supreme in our tests. They were intensely oniony and sweet but not cloying, with subtle complexity and nuance.

It was exasperating that the onions took so long—nearly an hour—to caramelize. On top of that, they required frequent stirring to keep them from sticking to the bottom of the pot and burning. We found that adding salt to the onions as they began to cook helped draw out some of the water in the onions and shaved about 10 minutes off the cooking time, but this didn't seem to be our answer. We also tried roasting the onions, thinking that the even, constant heat of the oven might be the answer. Wrong again. Opening and closing the oven door to stir the onions is an incredible hassle.

It was inattentiveness that caused us to let the drippings in the pot of a batch of onions go a little too far. The onions themselves weren't thoroughly caramelized, but all the goo stuck on the pot was. We were sure that the finished soup would taste burnt, but we were surprised to find that it was, in fact, as sweet, rich, and flavorful as the soups we had been making with fully caramelized onions. To refine the technique we had stumbled on, we decided that medium-high heat was the way to go and that the drippings should be very, very deeply browned. There's no way around frequent stirring, but this method cut about another 10 minutes off the onion-cooking time, bringing it down to just over 30 minutes.

With all those wonderful, tasty drippings stuck on the bottom of the pot, the deglazing process of adding the liquid and scraping up all the browned bits is crucial. Once the broth is added to the onions, we found that a simmering time of 20 minutes is needed to allow the onion flavor to permeate the broth and for the flavors to meld.

Many French onion soup recipes call for herbs. A couple of sprigs of fresh parsley, some thyme, and a bay leaf simmered in the soup rounded out the flavors and imparted freshness. Having arrived at a soup that was rich, well-balanced, and full of fabulous onion flavor, it was time to move on to the bread and the cheese.

Some recipes call for placing the bread in the bottom of the bowl and ladling the soup over it. We disagree. We opt to set the bread on top, so that only the bottom of the slice is moistened with broth while its top is crusted with cheese. The bread can then physically support the cheese and prevent it from sinking into the soup. To keep as much cheese as possible on the surface, we found it best to use two slices of bread to fill the mouth of the bowl completely. A baguette can be cut on the bias as necessary to secure the closest fit in the bowl.

Traditionally, French onion soup is topped with Swiss, Gruyère, or Emmentaler. We also ventured across the border to try Asiago. Plain Swiss cheese was neither outstanding nor offensive. It was gooey, bubbly, and mild in characteristic Swiss flavor. Both Gruyère and Emmentaler melted to perfection and were sweet, nutty, and faintly tangy, but they also were very strong and pungent, overwhelming many tasters' palates.

We surprised ourselves by favoring the subdued Italian Asiago. Its flavor, like that of Gruyère and Emmentaler, was sweet and nutty, but without the pungent quality.

Asiago is a dry, not a "melting," cheese, so although we were leaning toward it in flavor, we were left wanting in texture. The obvious answer was to combine cheeses. We tried a layer of Swiss topped with a grating of Asiago. A winning combination, hands down, of chewy goodness and nutty sweetness.

The final coup that weakens knees and makes French onion soup irresistible is a browned, bubbly, molten cheese crust. The quickest way to brown the cheese is to set the bowls on a baking sheet under the broiler, making heat-safe bowls essential. Bowls or crocks with handles make maneuvering easier. This is no soup for fine china.

WHAT WE LEARNED: Start with lots of red onions and cook them until very well browned. Use canned beef and chicken broth along with red wine to create a flavorful soup. Finish with a cheesy crouton (covered with Swiss and Asiago cheeses) that floats on top of individual bowls.

FRENCH ONION SOUP

Serves 6

Tie the parsley and thyme sprigs together with kitchen twine so they will be easy to retrieve from the soup pot. Slicing the baguette on the bias will yield slices shaped to fill the mouths of the bowls.

soup

2	tablespoons unsalted butter
5	medium red onions (about 3 pounds), halved and sliced thin
	Salt
6	cups low-sodium chicken broth
1¾	cups low-sodium beef broth
¼	cup dry red wine
2	sprigs fresh parsley
1	sprig fresh thyme
1	bay leaf
1	tablespoon balsamic vinegar
	Ground black pepper

cheese-topped crusts

1	baguette, cut on the bias into ½-inch slices (2 slices per serving)
4½	ounces Swiss cheese, sliced ¹⁄₁₆ inch thick
1½	ounces Asiago cheese, grated (about ¾ cup)

1. FOR THE SOUP: Melt the butter in a large stockpot or Dutch oven over medium-high heat; add the sliced onions and ½ teaspoon salt and stir to coat the onions thoroughly with the butter. Cook, stirring frequently, until the onions are reduced and syrupy and the inside of the pot is coated with a very deep brown crust, 30 to 35 minutes. Stir in the chicken and beef broths, red wine, parsley, thyme, and bay leaf, scraping the pot bottom with a wooden spoon to loosen the browned bits, and bring to a simmer. Simmer to blend the flavors, about 20 minutes, and discard the herbs. Stir in the balsamic vinegar and season with salt and pepper. (The soup can be cooled to room temperature and refrigerated in

an airtight container up to 2 days; return to a simmer before finishing the soup with the croutons and cheese.)

2. FOR THE CRUSTS: Adjust an oven rack to the upper-middle position and heat the oven to 350 degrees. Spread the bread out on a rimmed baking sheet and bake, flipping once, until lightly browned, about 15 minutes. Remove the bread from the oven. Turn the oven to broil.

3. Set heat-safe soup bowls or crocks on a rimmed baking sheet; fill each with about 1½ cups of the soup. Top each bowl with 2 toasted baguette slices and divide the Swiss cheese slices, placing them in a single layer, if possible, on the bread. Sprinkle each serving with about 2 tablespoons of the grated Asiago and broil until well browned and bubbly, 7 to 10 minutes. Cool 5 minutes and serve.

SCIENCE DESK: Blue Onion Soup?

RED ONIONS MAY BE THE BEST CHOICE IN TERMS OF flavor, but they can turn onion soup an unappetizing bluish-gray color. This is because they contain anthocyanin, a water-soluble pigment that also causes red cabbage to discolor when cooked. This pigment is present in some other reddish fruits and vegetables as well, such as cherries and radishes.

When the fruit or vegetable is cooked in liquid, the anthocyanin leaches out. If the liquid is alkaline (as is the case with our soup), the anthocyanin turns blue. Adding some acid, either lemon juice or vinegar, to the soup at the end helps it to regain its reddish color. This may sound improbable, but when we stirred in 1 tablespoon of balsamic vinegar, the soup returned to a deep reddish brown. The vinegar also brightens the flavors in the soup. So, whenever the color of cooked red onions becomes dull looking, add a little citrus juice or vinegar to restore their naturally vibrant color.

TECHNIQUE: Bouquet Garni

A bouquet garni is a classic French combination of herbs and spices used to flavor soups, stocks, and stews. Traditional recipes call for wrapping the herbs in cheesecloth for easy removal. A paper coffee filter works just as well. (Another option is a tea ball; see page 193.)

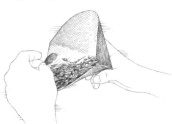

1. Place the herbs (usually bay leaves and thyme, either dried or fresh, and fresh parsley) and spices (usually black peppercorns) in the coffee filter.

2. Tie the end of the filter closed, catching the stems of the herbs as you do so.

3. Tie the other end of the string to the handle of the pot so you can easily retrieve the bouquet garni once the herbs and spices have given up their flavor.

EQUIPMENT CORNER: Santoku Knives

THE SANTOKU HAS LONG BEEN THE JAPANESE EQUIVALENT of a chef's knife—an all-purpose blade capable of performing any task in the kitchen. But only recently has this knife gained America's attention, as the darling of celebrity chefs such as Ming Tsai and Rachel Ray. With the popularity of Japanese minimalism in the culinary world at its apex, could this be a case of media hype, or were we missing something? We set out to see if the santoku could supplant our kitchen's workhorse, the classic 8-inch chef's knife.

What is a santoku knife? Compared with a classic chef's knife, the santoku, sometimes labeled in stores as an Asian or oriental chef's knife, is typically shorter and has a thinner blade, a stubbier tip, and a straighter edge. The santoku's slight size, believed to have evolved from the narrow, rectangular Japanese vegetable knife, equates to a great amount of blade control.

To fully evaluate the santoku, we bought 10 models, ranging in price from $30 to $100, with blades made from a variety of materials, from the conventional high-carbon stainless steel to the exotic, including ceramic and a titanium silver alloy. To be as thorough as possible, we ran them through a series of tests, using the Forschner (Victorinox) chef's knife (the winning model from an earlier test of chef's knives) for comparison. The tests included preparing onions, garlic, carrots, tomatoes, and boneless chicken breasts. We assessed each knife for precision, control, sharpness of blade, efficiency, comfort, price, and finally size, which proved to be very significant in these tests.

During the first test we conducted, mincing and chopping onions, the size of the santoku blade came into play. All of the santoku blades ranged in size from 6 to 7 inches, but the larger blades significantly outperformed their smaller counterparts. The 6-inch blade was so short that most of the testers ended up knuckle-deep in onions after just a few strokes. The larger-bladed santokus, on the other hand, performed very well during the onion test, with the Kershaw Shun ($99.95) taking home top honors over the Forschner chef's knife.

Where the Santokus really excelled was in more precise or delicate tasks. Julienned carrots rifled off the blade, and the chicken breasts practically butterflied themselves under the accurate blade of the santokus. Most testers found the santokus superior in these situations because their thin, short blades reduced friction and felt more exact against the dense flesh of the carrots and the chicken.

During mincing evaluations, the curve of the blade was the main factor mentioned by our testers. Because of the rocking motion used during mincing, the santokus with straighter edges tended to feel more jarring than those with more rounded edges. The straight-edged santokus seemed to be geared more toward slicing, and in fact, they performed very well while slicing tomatoes. A very telling test, slicing tomatoes calls for only the sharpest of blades. High-carbon stainless steel knives performed best in this test, followed by the ceramic-bladed Kyocera Ming Tsai ($99.95) that was adequately sharp, but not weighty enough to take top honors. Bringing up the rear in the tomato test was the titanium silver alloy Boker Cera-Titan I ($63.95) that was at once too thin, overly flexible, and disappointingly dull.

While most of the testers appreciated the performance and quality of many of the santoku knives, only two

EQUIPMENT CORNER:
Hollowed-Edge Santoku Knives

MANY SANTOKUS ARE AVAILABLE WITH EITHER A standard or a granton blade, the latter being hollow-ground and incorporating oval recesses along the blade. (This design was originally intended to make slicing meat easier.) Granton blades are often advertised as "nonstick."

Unfortunately, we quickly learned that these knives are not exactly nonstick. Minced garlic and cucumber slices will still cling vigilantly to the sides of a granton-style blade. However, as master bladesmith Robert Kramer explained to us, the hollows do help break the surface tension between the food and the blade surface. The hollows create air pockets between the breadth of the blade and the food, thus reducing the drag or friction between the two. So it was no coincidence that the two knives with the tallest hollows, the Mac and the Kershaw Shun, seemed to show the biggest decrease in friction when tested against their standard-edge versions. Even then, the differences didn't bowl us over.

A santoku with a granton edge typically costs $10 to $20 more than one with a standard edge. Knives with granton edges can be sharpened, although it takes a little more care because once sharpened into the hollows, the blade becomes slightly thinner. Given the less-than-eye-opening differences, we prefer santokus with the cheaper standard edge.

knives—the Mac Superior ($55) and the Kershaw Shun Classic—were consistently preferred to the Forschner chef's knife in the tests. Now, although this fact speaks highly of santoku knives in general, it could be argued that the tests we performed were geared toward the lightweight santokus. In preliminary tests, we attempted tasks such as butchering a whole chicken or halving acorn squash. In most cases, the santokus were deemed too small or lightweight for these operations, while the chef's knife tackled them with ease.

So should you run out to the nearest cutlery dealer and purchase the latest celebrity-endorsed santoku? Not necessarily. The santoku would certainly be a reliable addition to any kitchen—its lightweight and lightning quick blade feels right at home with vegetable preparations. However, due to its smaller size and delicate blade, the santoku comes up short in its ability to function as an all-purpose blade. A good santoku can complement—but not replace—a trusted chef's knife.

A BETTER EDGE?
A granton-style blade with oval recesses reduces friction ever so slightly. But this minor perk is not worth the higher price tag.

Rating Santoku Knives

SEVEN TEST COOKS AND ONE KITCHEN INTERN EVALUATED EACH KNIFE ACCORDING TO PERFORMANCE AND design. The knives were used to chop and dice onions, mince and slice garlic, thinly slice and julienne carrots, slice tomatoes, and butterfly boneless, skinless chicken breasts. The testers ran the gamut in terms of knife skills—from beginner to advanced—as well as hand size and strength. Only one tester was left-handed. Knives are listed in order of preference. See www.americastestkitchen.com for up-to-date prices and mail-order sources for top-rated products.

HIGHLY RECOMMENDED
MAC Superior Santoku **$55**

An ideal bridge between the cramped, smaller santokus and the larger chef's knife. Admired for being the most sharp and responsive, this knife was especially nimble, easy to control, and precise. As one tester gushed, "great with everything."

RECOMMENDED
Kershaw Shun Classic Santoku model DM-0702 **$99.95**

Praised as the Cadillac of the group, this knife felt "sturdy" and "solid." The curvature of the blade made it good at rocking while mincing, and the tip was sharp and decisive. We docked points for a handle that was uncomfortable for the left-handed tester.

RECOMMENDED
Wüsthof Grand Prix Oriental Cook's Knife **$70**

This model excelled at thin slicing and fine mincing. Its straight blade created a "see-saw" effect when rocking to mince or chop. Some testers applauded the Wüsthof's light feel as a smaller, quicker chef's knife. Others deemed it flimsy.

RECOMMENDED
Global Oriental Cook Knife **$81.99**

This could have been a perfect knife if not for a narrow, sleek stainless steel handle that made the grip feel unsteady. The sharp blade with a markedly curved edge and the tapered tip were useful—more like a chef's knife than a santoku.

RECOMMENDED
Zwilling Henckels Four Star Santoku **$65**

A sharp, relatively thick blade made this knife a strong, substantial slicer, but the blade's flat curve made its rocking motion shallow and somewhat jarring. This knife generally had an awkward, less maneuverable feel.

RECOMMENDED
Oxo Good Grips MV55-Pro Santoku **$30**

This model possessed decent sharpness and maneuverability but was best suited to slicing. The stubby, cleaver-shaped blade felt somewhat dead while mincing and coarse chopping. The fat handle on the Oxo was liked by many for its soft, grippy feel.

NOT RECOMMENDED
Kyocera Ming Tsai Santoku **$99.95**

This knife's notably sharp, short blade performed delicate knife work respectably but didn't have the weight behind it to handle all tasks. The white ceramic blade made it tricky to see light-colored foods (such as garlic) when working on a white plastic board. Overall, too small to be of much use.

NOT RECOMMENDED
Furi Pro East/West Santoku **$70**

This knife's blade was dull, fat, stubby, and clumsy—more like a cleaver. It had a decent rocking motion but lacked the capacity for delicate and precise work. The molded stainless steel handle was deemed too large and cumbersome.

NOT RECOMMENDED
Boker Cera-Titan I Santoku **$63.95**

Feather-light, flimsy, short, and cheap in feel was the overall consensus on this knife. Difficult control and a shallow, abrupt rocking motion were common complaints.

NOT RECOMMENDED
Forschner Santoku **$35**

Most testers found the Forschner's teeny, hobbit-size handle uncomfortable and difficult to control. Not enough clearance under the handle, so even those with small hands banged their knuckles when the blade came in full contact with the cutting board.

Best-ever sticky buns rise to the occasion.

ULTIMATE sticky buns

CHAPTER 21

Sticky buns are things of breakfast-time debauchery. In bakeries, they are often plate-size buns, warm and glistening, heady with brown sugar and spices. In our opinion, anything less than a great one is not worth its calories.

A sticky bun should be neither dense nor bready, neither saturated with butter nor so sugary that it makes your heart race. The crumb should be tender and feathery and the sticky glaze gently chewy and gooey; the flavor should be warm and spicy, buttery and sweet—but just enough so that devouring one doesn't feel like a feat.

Home bakers rarely attempt them, probably because sticky buns, like many other sweet yeasted breads, are a project, requiring a substantial time commitment. But we think that's a shame. Sticky buns are worth the effort. We set out to develop a recipe that would be irresistible.

STICKY BUNS

WHAT WE WANTED: These bakery favorites are often too sweet, too big, too rich, and just too much. We wanted sticky buns that were impressive, not excessive.

In our search for the ultimate sticky bun, we looked at dozens of recipes. Our research turned up all manner of sticky buns. Of those that we tried, one was too lean—like a sugar-soaked baguette. One was cakey, with an insubstantial crumb, and it had a meager amount of sticky goo; another was doughy and had a hard sugar veneer. The most laborious recipe resulted—some 18 hours later—in overly rich sticky buns that weren't worth the time or the effort. Those recipes that contained nuts, which were baked beneath the buns, had in common soggy, steamy pecans or walnuts that contributed little to either flavor or texture.

The basic MO for sticky buns starts with a sugary glaze mixture that is put into a baking dish. The dough, after its first rise, is rolled, filled, and cut into buns. The buns are set on top of the glaze mixture, allowed a second rise, then baked, inverted, and devoured.

We began this multi-component preparation with the dough. From the start we knew that a lean dough, made with only flour and water, was out. It was an anomaly anyway. Most recipes involved fairly rich doughs with milk, butter, eggs, and sugar in addition to the requisite flour, yeast, and salt. First off, we tried different liquids. Water, milk, and buttermilk all worked, but the buttermilk dough was vastly superior to the others. In the baked buns, the tanginess of the buttermilk translated into a flavor complexity that the others simply lacked; its acidity, though not overt, made a nice counterpoint to the sugary sweetness. Both flavor and texture were rich without being heavy, and the crumb was tender and light. Nonfat and low-fat buttermilk succeeded equally, as did, to our surprise, powdered buttermilk (which is added as a dry ingredient, with water being substituted for the buttermilk).

For the four or so cups of flour in the dough, we tested varying quantities of butter and finally settled on 6 tablespoons. It turned out that melted, rather than softened, butter was not only easier to use but yielded superb results to boot. Next we experimented with eggs, starting with no eggs and going up to three whole eggs. With too few eggs, the texture of the buns lacked substance; the crumb was too soft and yielding, like a squishy sandwich bread. Egg-rich versions—namely, those made with three eggs—were the favorite. These were moist, with a nice, light, open crumb. They were also tender and yet had substantial structure and chew.

The rest of the dough fell into place. One-quarter cup of sugar gave it a light sweetness, and a hit of salt boosted flavor. One packet of instant yeast (2¼ teaspoons) worked to get the dough rising in a timely manner without leaving a distinct yeastiness in its wake (as an overabundance of yeast would). Bread flour didn't outperform all-purpose flour, so all-purpose it was.

After the dough's first rise, or fermentation, it is rolled out into a rectangle and filled. The spiced sugar filling, which creates the swirl in the shaped buns, was quickly settled. Brown sugar beat out granulated because it has more presence; its color is darker and its flavor more assertive. A healthy dose of ground cinnamon and a dash of ground cloves added warmth and fragrance. We were making quick progress.

Most recipes specify dark brown sugar for use in the glaze as well as the filling, but before too long we dropped dark brown sugar in favor of light brown for the glaze. During baking, dark brown sugar took on too much color, and, though it tasted fine, it made the buns look unattractive . . . just shy of singed.

At this point, progress slowed. In the batches we baked, the glaze invariably cooked up treacherously sticky and far too firm—ideal for ripping out dental work (which it did in fact do to one unfortunate taster). In combination with ¾ cup of brown sugar, we tried different amounts of

butter—2, 4, 6, 8, and even 10 tablespoons. We increased and decreased the brown sugar. We tried adding water to the glaze mixture. We shortened baking times and lowered oven temperatures so that the glaze faced less heat (heat is what causes it to cook and harden). All to no avail. We tried adding a dose of corn syrup. The glaze showed some improvement—it had a softer, chewier texture—but it was still rather stiff and taffy-like, and it lacked fluidity. With a thick, unctuous, but pourable, classic caramel sauce in mind (one made from caramelized sugar and heavy cream), we tried adding heavy cream—just 2 tablespoons—and it worked like magic. The topping was now sticky, gooey, and just a bit sauce-like. The downside to the cream was that it had a slight dulling effect on the flavor of the caramel, but tasters—and their fillings, bridges, and crowns—could live with that.

We tried different oven temperatures, and a 350-degree oven worked best, as did a 13 by 9-inch baking pan. Yet the buns were still far from perfect. They had a tacky, doughy, underdone surface, and the caramel glaze was a couple shades too light. One cookbook author suggested placing the baking dish on a preheated baking stone, a step that vastly improved the evenness of browning and allowed the bottoms of the buns (which, bear in mind, later become the tops) to bake through in spite of all the goo that they sat in. With

the baking stone in play, though, the baking pan's material became important. A nonstick metal pan proved the best choice (see page 275 for details). At first, we were inverting the hot sticky buns out of the pan as soon as they were done. After a few batches, though, we finally realized the merits of allowing them to cool for about 10 minutes before inversion. When hot, the caramel glaze was so molten that it quickly ran off the buns and pooled on the platter. Cooled for just a bit, however, the glaze was viscous enough to generously blanket the surface.

According to tasters, the sticky buns were close to being great, but they were missing something—nuts, pecans in particular. Instead of sprinkling chopped toasted pecans over the glaze in the baking dish, where we knew they would turn soggy, we introduced them to the filling. No good. Encased in the dough rather than sitting beneath it, the once toasty, crisp pecans still turned soft and soggy. The sticky buns were hardly better off for having them.

We recalled a recipe that had included an unusual postbake glaze. At first the idea of still more glaze seemed superfluous (enough sugar already!), but then we realized that it could form a sort of base for a topping . . . a toasted pecan topping. We formulated a mixture of more glaze ingredients—butter, light brown sugar, and corn syrup for fluidity—to which we added toasted chopped pecans and some vanilla for good measure. The relatively small amount of sugar in this topping gave the nuts some cohesion without oversweetening matters. We poured/spread the nut topping over the buns as soon as we turned them out of the pan. Crowned with pecans, the sticky buns had achieved greatness.

WHAT WE LEARNED: Start with an egg-rich, buttery dough, coat the pan with a caramel-like glaze made fluid by the addition of heavy cream, and then fill the dough with a simple mixture of brown sugar, cinnamon, cloves, and butter. For proper browning, use a nonstick metal pan placed on a preheated baking stone. To keep nuts crisp, use them in a second glaze to coat the baked buns, rather than adding them to the dough.

STICKY BUNS WITH PECANS

Makes 12 buns

This recipe has four components: the dough that is shaped into buns, the filling that creates the swirl in the shaped buns, the caramel glaze that bakes in the bottom of the baking dish along with the buns, and the pecan topping that garnishes the buns once they're baked. Although the ingredient list may look long, note that many ingredients are repeated; for example, butter is called for in all four components (for a total of 16 tablespoons, or 2 sticks), light brown sugar is called for in three (for a total of 1¾ cups, or about 12 ounces), and corn syrup in two (for a total of 6 tablespoons). If not using a baking stone or nonstick baking dish, see "Baking the Buns" on page 275. Leftover sticky buns can be wrapped in foil or plastic wrap and refrigerated for up to 3 days, but they should be warmed through before serving. They reheat quickly in a microwave oven (for 2 buns, about 2 minutes at 50 percent power works well).

dough

- 3   large eggs, at room temperature
- ¾   cup buttermilk, at room temperature
- ¼   cup (1¾ ounces) granulated sugar
- 1¼   teaspoons salt
- 2¼   teaspoons (1 envelope) instant yeast
- 4¼   cups (21¼ ounces) unbleached all-purpose flour, plus more for dusting the work surface
- 6   tablespoons (¾ stick) unsalted butter, melted and cooled until warm

caramel glaze

- 6   tablespoons (¾ stick) unsalted butter
- ¾   cup (5¼ ounces) packed light brown sugar
- 3   tablespoons light or dark corn syrup
- 2   tablespoons heavy cream
     Pinch salt

cinnamon–sugar filling

- ¾   cup (5¼ ounces) packed light brown sugar
- 2   teaspoons ground cinnamon

- ¼   teaspoon ground cloves
     Pinch salt
- 1   tablespoon unsalted butter, melted

pecan topping

- 3   tablespoons unsalted butter
- ¼   cup (1¾ ounces) packed light brown sugar
- 3   tablespoons light or dark corn syrup
     Pinch salt
- 1   teaspoon vanilla extract
- ¾   cup (3 ounces) pecans, toasted in a small, dry skillet over medium heat until fragrant and browned, about 5 minutes, then cooled and coarsely chopped

1. FOR THE DOUGH: In the bowl of a standing mixer, whisk the eggs to combine; add the buttermilk and whisk to combine. Whisk in the sugar, salt, and yeast. Add about 2 cups of the flour and the butter; stir with a wooden spoon or rubber spatula until evenly moistened and combined.

GETTING IT RIGHT: Problem Buns

We tested dozens of recipes and found that several recurring problems plagued most of them.

RUNAWAY GOO
Immediately after baking, the glaze is molten and will run off the buns if the pan is inverted too soon.

UNDERBROWNED
When baked in a glass Pyrex baking dish, the surface of the buns appears underbaked in color and texture.

SEEMINGLY BURNT
Using dark brown sugar in the glaze results in dark, almost burnt-looking sticky buns.

Add all but about ¼ cup of the remaining flour and knead with a dough hook at low speed 5 minutes. Check the consistency of the dough (the dough should feel soft and moist but should not be wet and sticky; add more flour, if necessary); knead at low speed 5 minutes longer (the dough should clear the sides of the bowl but stick to the bottom). Turn the dough out onto a lightly floured work surface; knead by hand about 1 minute to ensure that the dough is uniform (the dough should not stick to the work surface during hand kneading; if it does, knead in additional flour 1 tablespoon at a time).

2. Lightly spray a large bowl or plastic container with non-stick cooking spray. Transfer the dough to the bowl, spray the dough lightly with cooking spray, then cover the bowl tightly with plastic wrap and set in a warm, draft-free spot until doubled in volume, 2 to 2½ hours.

3. FOR THE GLAZE: Meanwhile, combine all the ingredients for the glaze in a small saucepan; cook over medium heat, whisking occasionally, until the butter is melted and the mixture is thoroughly combined. Pour the mixture into a nonstick metal 13 by 9-inch baking dish; using a rubber spatula, spread the mixture to cover the surface of the baking dish; set the baking dish aside.

4. TO ASSEMBLE AND BAKE THE BUNS: For the filling, combine the brown sugar, cinnamon, cloves, and salt in a small bowl and mix until thoroughly combined, using your fingers to break up any sugar lumps; set aside. Turn the dough out onto a lightly floured work surface. Gently shape the dough into a rough rectangle with a long side nearest you. Lightly flour the dough and roll to a 16 by 12-inch rectangle. Brush the dough with the 1 tablespoon melted butter, leaving a ½-inch border along the top edge; brush the sides of the baking dish with the butter remaining on the brush. Sprinkle the filling mixture over the dough, leaving a ¾-inch border along the top edge; smooth the filling in an even layer with your hand, then gently press the mixture into the dough to adhere. Beginning with the long edge nearest you, roll the dough into a taut cylinder. Firmly pinch the seam to seal and roll the cylinder seam-side down.

TECHNIQUE: Assembling Sticky Buns

1. Spread the hot glaze in a baking dish.

2. Sprinkle the dough with the filling mixture.

3. Roll the dough into a taut cylinder.

4. Firmly pinch the seam to seal.

5. Cut the cylinder into 12 buns.

6. Arrange the buns in the prepared baking dish.

Very gently stretch to form a cylinder of even diameter and 18-inch length; push the ends in to create an even thickness. Using a serrated knife and gentle sawing motion, slice the cylinder in half, then slice each half in half again to create evenly sized quarters. Slice each quarter evenly into thirds, yielding 12 buns (the end pieces may be slightly smaller).

5. Arrange the buns cut-side down in the prepared baking dish; cover tightly with plastic wrap and set in a warm, draft-free spot until puffy and pressed against one another, about 1½ hours. Meanwhile, adjust an oven rack to the lowest position, place a baking stone (if using) on the rack, and heat the oven to 350 degrees.

6. Place the baking pan on the baking stone; bake until golden brown and the center of the dough registers about 180 degrees on an instant-read thermometer, 25 to 30 minutes. Cool on a wire rack 10 minutes; invert onto a rimmed baking sheet, large rectangular platter, or cutting board. With a rubber spatula, scrape any glaze remaining in the baking pan onto the buns; cool while making the pecan topping.

7. FOR THE TOPPING: Combine the butter, brown sugar, corn syrup, and salt in a small saucepan and bring to a simmer over medium heat, whisking occasionally to

thoroughly combine. Off heat, stir in the vanilla and pecans until the pecans are evenly coated. Using a soup spoon, spoon a heaping tablespoon of nuts and topping over the center of each sticky bun. Continue to cool until the sticky buns are warm, 15 to 20 minutes. Pull apart or use a serrated knife to cut apart the sticky buns; serve.

VARIATIONS

HAND-KNEADED METHOD FOR STICKY BUNS

1. Using same ingredient list as for Sticky Buns with Pecans, in a large bowl, whisk the eggs to combine; add the buttermilk and whisk to combine. Whisk in the sugar, salt, and yeast. Add about 2 cups of the flour and the butter; stir with a wooden spoon or rubber spatula until evenly moistened and combined. Add all but about ¼ cup of the remaining flour and stir until the mixture forms a shaggy dough. Turn the dough out onto a lightly floured work surface and knead by hand 10 to 15 minutes, adding more flour as needed (after about 5 minutes, the dough should feel soft and moist but should not stick to the work surface).

2. Continue with the recipe from step 2.

OVERNIGHT STICKY BUNS

If you'd like to serve freshly baked sticky buns for a late breakfast or for a brunch and want to minimize early morning preparation, they can be made and shaped the night before and then refrigerated. The next morning, to help the buns rise in a timely manner, they should be set in a warm-water bath for 20 minutes and then allowed to complete their rise at room temperature.

1. Follow the recipe for Sticky Buns with Pecans; after forming and arranging the buns in the baking pan, cover the pan tightly with plastic wrap and refrigerate 10 to 14 hours.

2. Place the baking pan in a warm-water bath (about 120 degrees) in a kitchen sink or large roasting pan for 20

Q&A

What's the best way to clean up a sticky bowl lined with bits of dough?

Never wash bowls that have been used to make bread dough with hot water. The heat swells the starches in the flour, and they begin to harden. Cold water is a much better choice. To keep sponges from becoming clogged with dough, we save the mesh bags that onions are sold in and use them to scrub doughy bowls. Once the bowl is cleaned, we simply discard the mesh bag and all the dough attached to it.

minutes. Remove the baking dish from the water bath and let stand at room temperature until the buns look slightly puffy and are pressed against one another, about 1½ hours. About an hour before baking, adjust an oven rack to the lowest position, place the baking stone on the rack (if using), and heat the oven to 350 degrees.

3. Continue with the recipe from step 6.

SCIENCE DESK: Designer Yeast

LESAFFRE, THE PRODUCER OF RED STAR YEAST, MAKES a line of yeast called Nevada Gold Label ($6.50 for 15.85 ounces, available from www.bakerscatalogue.com)that is specifically designed for high-sugar doughs, and we thought that our sweet sticky buns would be an ideal candidate on which to test it. After baking two batches of rolls, we found that this designer yeast worked, decreasing the time required for the first rise by 33 percent and the second rise by 45 percent when compared with the standard SAF instant yeast. In total, this saved us more than an hour in rising time. Our curiosity was piqued.

It's not easy being unicellular yeast. Precious little separates their insides from the harsh world at large—no skin, no fat, just a membrane. Most bakers consider sugar food for yeast, but sugar in too high a concentration can be a killer. Yeast placed in a high-sugar dough can undergo osmotic stress, in which water wants to flow out of the yeast and into the dough, causing the yeast to dry out.

Nevada Gold Label yeast is designed to withstand this stress better than regular yeast. The dough we made with it performed particularly well in the second rise, when the rolls were shaped, cloaked in sugar, and exposed to the air—definitely a harsh environment for a moisture-loving organism. If you bake a lot of sweet breads, you may want to keep some Nevada Gold Label on hand.

TASTING LAB: Supermarket Coffees

IT WASN'T TOO LONG AGO THAT IF YOU WANTED A CUP of coffee, you had two choices: brew it yourself at home with a supermarket brand or buy a watery, tasteless cup at your local convenience store or diner. Today, specialty coffees abound, with boutique shops in every town selling "premium" beans so that quality coffee can be had at home. But what about those old stalwarts, the supermarket brands of yore? At just one-quarter the price of premium beans and widely available, there's no beating the cost or the convenience. Are any of these dinosaurs of an era past worth drinking?

After sampling eight brands of ground coffee from the supermarket (including Starbucks, a supposedly premium brand that is now available in supermarkets already ground), we can safely say no. The best anyone could say about our "winner" was that it was the "least offensive" of the lot.

We brewed all the coffees to the strength recommended by the Specialty Coffee Association, which is 1.6 grams of coffee per ounce of water, and used the same model of electric drip coffee maker for all of them. We tasted the coffees plain, without sugar or milk.

Only one coffee is recommended, and even that one received mostly negative comments from tasters, though a few found it palatable. The problem most of the tasters had with the coffees was the lack of depth; the overriding flavor in almost all of the samples was bitterness, with no floral, fruity, or chocolatey flavors that you would find in a good coffee. Chock Full o' Nuts (which also performed well in a previous tasting of French roast coffees) was less the most liked of the brands than the least hated of them. As for the rest of the pack—well, let's just say that no one wanted to save the leftovers for iced coffee.

So is this just a case of money buying quality? Will the $12-a-pound coffee you buy at the coffee shop always be better than the coffee you buy in the supermarket? Well, yes and no. Starbucks, a premium brand that is sold in most major supermarkets (as well as in dedicated coffee shops), placed second-to-last in our tasting, yet it costs more than three times as much as our top finisher, Chock Full o' Nuts. Our reasons for not liking Starbucks, however, are different than those for not liking the other supermarket brands. In our opinion, Starbucks tends to overroast their beans, which can lead to overtly bitter tones in the coffee, something our tasters didn't like.

There are two likely reasons we didn't like the supermarket brands, both having to do with the beans. The beans used by supermarket brands are of a lower quality than those used at coffee shops. The second factor is the grind; when you buy coffee at a coffee shop, the beans are ground when you purchase them (or shortly before). With supermarket coffee, the beans are ground far in advance of when you buy them. And with freshness goes much of the flavor.

Money, then, is not necessarily the best judge of coffee; rather, you should go for freshness first and always buy high-quality beans.

Rating Supermarket Coffees

TWENTY-THREE MEMBERS OF THE *COOK'S ILLUSTRATED* STAFF PARTICIPATED IN THE TASTING. WE BREWED THE COFFEES TO THE same strength (1.6 grams of coffee per ounce of water, the ratio recommended by the Specialty Coffee Association) and in the same model of electric drip coffee maker. The coffees were tasted plain—no sugar, no milk. The coffees are listed in order of preference based on their scores in this tasting. All brands are available in supermarkets.

RECOMMENDED WITH RESERVATIONS

Chock Full o' Nuts Original **$2.69 for 13 ounces**

No one got very excited by this brand, which was deemed the "least offensive." "Tastes like diner coffee," wrote one taster.

NOT RECOMMENDED

Melitta Traditional Roast **$3.99 for 11.5 ounces**

This brand costs more than other basic options and wasn't any better. "Very sour" and "no aroma" were typical comments.

NOT RECOMMENDED

Folgers Classic Roast **$2.79 for 13 ounces**

"Bursting with charcoal flavors, and nothing else," summed up the general reaction to this coffee.

NOT RECOMMENDED

Hills Bros. Original Blend Medium Roast **$2.79 for 13 ounces**

This sample had very little flavor. "Tastes like hot water, but at least the bitterness is in check."

NOT RECOMMENDED

Nescafé Taster's Choice (Instant) **$5.49 for 4 ounces**

Lack of flavor was the most common criticism of this instant coffee. "Sour," "greasy," and "tastes like nothing."

NOT RECOMMENDED

Maxwell House Original **$2.79 for 13 ounces**

"No depth" and "highly bitter" were typical criticisms of this familiar brand. So much for drinking the last drop.

NOT RECOMMENDED

Starbucks House Blend **$8.39 for 12 ounces**

Too much flavor—rather than too little—was the problem with this coffeehouse favorite, which is now sold in many supermarkets. "Smells like a forest fire," quipped one taster.

NOT RECOMMENDED

Chase & Sanborn Special Roast **$2.49 for 11.5 ounces**

The worst of the worst. "Tastes like something . . . dirt, maybe?"

EQUIPMENT CORNER:
New Generation Coffee Makers

IN OUR EXPERIENCE, AUTOMATIC-DRIP COFFEE MACHINES make coffee easily, but rarely well—often producing a burnt and bitter liquid reminiscent of stale truck stop coffee. Recently, appliance makers have introduced machines with improved technologies aimed at brewing better tasting coffee. The three main categories are: grind-and-brew machines, electric vacuum machines, and single-cup brewers similar to espresso machines. We selected seven of these machines, which range in price from $50 to $250, and rated them according to their price, coffee flavor, convenience, full pot brew time, and full pot temperature (when fresh, 30 minutes, and 60 minutes old).

According to the Specialty Coffee Association of America, the quality of a cup of coffee is affected by 10 primary variables, from the chemistry of the beans to the composition of the water and the method used to hold the finished beverage. Automatic brewers, whether drip or another type, should control at least four of the 10 variables. Those are brewing time (four to six minutes for a full pot using medium-grind coffee, optimally), temperature (195 to 205 degrees for brewing and 155 to 175 degrees for serving), delivery of water and resulting agitation of the grounds (large filter basket to provide room for grounds to swell without compacting), and holding conditions (assuming that you brew a partial or entire pot, as opposed to a single cup).

The first three machines that we tested, the grind-and-brew models, attempted to produce a better cup of coffee by grinding the beans immediately before brewing. Ideally, this would enhance the coffee by limiting the dissipation of flavorful chemical compounds caused by premature grinding. This would be an effective approach, but unfortunately, the 10- to 12-minute brewing cycles of these machines seemed to have an adverse effect on the coffee's aroma. Even so, tasters rated the Cuisinart ($149.99) and the Capresso ($199.99) coffee well. Where they did not impress was in convenience—both

were difficult to clean and the latter lacked a thermal carafe that would preserve the brewed coffee.

The next style of machine, the electric vacuum brewer, has predecessors dating back to the mid-1800s. Consisting of two bowls sitting one on top of the other, this machine exploits the vacuum produced when steam forces boiling water from the bottom to the top bowl. From there, the water and coffee mix and drip back down through a filter to the bottom bowl. We tested two of these machines, a Black & Decker ($69.99) and a Bodum ($99.99) and found that they both produced a very hot and distinctly robust brew, which will appeal to many (but not all) coffee drinkers. The brew cycles on both machines were, respectably, in the four- to six-minute range, but neither model featured a thermal carafe. We gave top honors for the vacuum machines to the Black & Decker because it was easier to clean.

The final category, the espresso-method single-cup brewers, trumpeted a very intriguing development in the java world. Each time that you want a cup of coffee, you brew a fresh one—in less than one minute. These machines work much like an espresso machine; the units use pumps (typically air or steam powered) to force hot, pressurized water through packaged coffee grounds to extract maximum flavor in seconds. These machines also produced a distinct style of coffee. It was mild with a light body, basically what we think of as classic American coffee. The only drawback to these machines is that they only accept coffee cartridges, or pods, provided by the machine's manufacturer. The Keurig ($249.99), in all fairness, does offer almost 80 varieties of coffee, but the Melitta ($49.99) offers only six selections.

If you are a fan of a light, American-style coffee, we suggest the single-cup brewers over the grind-and-brew machines, largely because of the design idiosyncrasies among the latter. Because we like our coffee strong and full-bodied, we prefer the electric vacuum brewers, despite their lack of thermal carafes. If the R & D people were to produce a vacuum brewer that incorporated a thermal carafe, we'd buy it in a second. For now, we'll simply pour the brewed coffee into a separate thermal carafe.

Rating New Generation Coffee Makers

OUR TEST INCLUDED SEVEN ELECTRIC COFFEE MAKERS (OF WHICH THREE WERE PROTOTYPES BECAUSE PRODUCTION models were not available at testing time), each with designs or features aimed at improving the flavor of the coffee, ease of use, or both. Whenever possible, we chose models with a thermal carafe, which we prefer over a traditional glass carafe on a hot burner plate for keeping coffee hot and fresh tasting over time. For all of the machines except the single-cup brewers, we brewed three full pots and evaluated the coffee when fresh, after 30 minutes, and after 60 minutes. With the single-cup machines, we evaluated the coffee only when fresh. The machines are listed by type and in order of preference within each type. See www.americastestkitchen.com for up-to-date prices and mail-order sources for top-rated products.

GRIND AND BREW

RECOMMENDED WITH RESERVATIONS
Cuisinart Grind & Brew Thermal 10-Cup Coffee Maker, Model DGB-600
$149.99

Though the coffee was good, the unit was a nuisance to clean. It lacks a grind adjustment feature and maximum fill mark in the carafe. The grinder chamber is small.

RECOMMENDED WITH RESERVATIONS
Melitta Automatic Mill & Brew with Thermal Carafe, Model MEMB10T
$95

This model was very easy to use, and it features a large grinder/filter assembly that was easy to clean. Some tasters found this coffee to be bitter unless the grind was set to coarse.

RECOMMENDED WITH RESERVATIONS
Capresso CoffeeTEAM Luxe, Model 453th
$199.99

Although it brews a good pot of coffee, testers found this machine to be temperamental. You must change two settings to brew a partial pot, and the carafe must be positioned perfectly to prevent condensation from building in the coffee feeder channel.

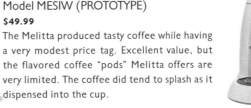

VACUUM

RECOMMENDED
Black & Decker InFuze 10-Cup Vacuum-Brew Coffeemaker (PROTOTYPE)
$69.99

The Black & Decker was praised for its ease of use and cleaning. It brewed the hottest coffee of all the machines, but it lost points for not having a thermal carafe.

RECOMMENDED WITH RESERVATIONS
Bodum Santos Electric Vacuum Coffee Maker
$99.99

This model was easy to set up and use, but its narrow carafe made cleaning it a bit of a chore. Lost points for not having a thermal carafe.

SINGLE CUP

RECOMMENDED
Melitta One:One Java-Pod Coffee Maker, Model MESIW (PROTOTYPE)
$49.99

The Melitta produced tasty coffee while having a very modest price tag. Excellent value, but the flavored coffee "pods" Melitta offers are very limited. The coffee did tend to splash as it dispensed into the cup.

RECOMMENDED
Keurig B-100 Single-Cup Brewing System (PROTOTYPE)
$249.95

This was the sexiest of the machines—quick brewing, easy to clean, and a lovely design. The downside? This model lacks the ability to adjust the brew strength, and it was the most expensive of the coffee makers tested.

Erika whips up a batch of her all-American brownies.

BAKE SALE favorites

Every afternoon around three, editors come sniffing around the test kitchen looking for cookies fresh from the oven. Given how many cookies we make, our test cooks appreciate bar cookies. There's no measuring or shaping of the dough. Just spread the entire batter into the pan, bake, cool, and cut into squares. Bar cookies are understandably popular items at bake sales. They are easy to make and are always a hit.

But brownies and other bar cookies can be disappointing. Many brownies are rather dull, and blondies (as well as Congo bars, their coconut-flavored cousins) can be even worse, since they are even plainer. So when we created recipes for these favorite bake sale items, we kept the recipes simple (a bar cookie that required exotic ingredients or difficult techniques just wouldn't do) while developing superior flavor and texture. The result is brownies, blondies, and Congo bars so good that you'll want to bake two batches—one for the bake sale at school or church and one to keep at home.

CLASSIC BROWNIES

WHAT WE WANTED: A chewy, not over-the-top, yet chocolatey brownie. It should have intense flavor without being overly rich or candy-like.

These days, if you go to a bakery and order a brownie, chances are you'll end up with a heavy chunk of pure confection. While there's no denying that such brownies are sumptuous, they are also most often overwhelming. More candy than cake, such brownies are fine as infrequent treats, but many of us can look back to a time when the brownie was a much simpler affair, more chocolate bar than chocolate truffle, more bake sale than upscale café.

Our initial recipe testing was not a success. Either pale and dry or cloyingly sweet, all of the brownies we baked lacked substantial chocolate flavor. We wanted an old-fashioned brownie, but we also wanted serious chocolate flavor.

Before we embarked on our testing, there was one thing about all of the research recipes that we knew we wanted to change: the size. The recipes called for baking the brownies in skimpy 8-inch square pans. We wanted big brownies, and a lot of them, so a 13 by 9-inch baking pan was the size of choice. We then constructed a recipe with 4 ounces of unsweetened chocolate, two sticks of butter, 2 cups of sugar, four eggs, and 1¼ cups of all-purpose flour.

Our working recipe yielded brownies that were dense and a bit greasy. Cutting back on the butter seemed like an obvious way to make them less greasy. Going from two sticks to 1½ sticks did the trick, but it also produced an unanticipated side effect—an unpleasantly gritty texture. We suspected that the source of the problem might be in the starch in the recipe, not just from the all-purpose flour we'd been using but from the chocolate, which also contains starch. Not wanting to alter the amount of chocolate (our brownies needed more chocolate flavor, not less), we decreased the flour. The brownies were still too gritty. Next, we tried substituting cake flour for the entire amount of all-purpose flour. This solved the problem, producing nicely tender brownies. (Cake flour is milled from softer wheat than all-purpose flour and contributes less protein, or gluten, to a recipe. The result is a finer-textured product, which, in the case of these brownies, was preferred.) Here was our first big revelation: Cake flour makes tender brownies with a delicate chew.

Though tender, the brownies were still too compact. We thought an extra egg might provide more structure, but it made the brownies too cakey. Maybe baking powder would lighten the crumb. Well, too much baking powder produced a dry and cakey brownie, but a modest ¾ teaspoon was just right. The texture of the brownies was now nearly perfect, right in the middle between cakey and fudgy.

Our brownies now had the right texture—neither fudgy nor cakey, with a tender chew—but the flavor was a bit insipid. Although we didn't want the decadent texture of fudgy brownies, we did appreciate their assertive chocolate flavor. In search of a similar chocolate intensity, we added a little high-quality bittersweet chocolate to the unsweetened chocolate in our working recipe. These brownies were too sweet, too greasy, and too heavy. When we cut back on the sugar, the brownies were less sweet, but they remained heavy and soggy. In addition, tasters felt that the flavor was more reminiscent of milk chocolate (that is, very mild) than bittersweet chocolate. When we used considerably more bittersweet chocolate, the flavor was more intense but the texture now decidedly confection-like. Ounce for ounce, unsweetened chocolate has more chocolate flavor than bittersweet or semisweet chocolate (which are one third to one half sugar). To get enough flavor from these chocolates, you have to use a lot, and that made the brownies fudgy and rich—exactly what we did not want.

We tried adding cocoa, but in small amounts; it did nothing to pump up the chocolate flavor in our brownies.

Using ¼ cup cocoa in place of an equal amount of flour started to help, but now the texture was dense and pasty. We crossed cocoa off our list.

We wondered what would happen if we increased the amount of unsweetened chocolate in our working recipe. Using 6 ounces of unsweetened chocolate (rather than 4 ounces) gave us the desired flavor we were after—not too sweet, with profound chocolate notes. Although we had performed a lot of unnecessary tests, we now realized why most recipes call for unsweetened chocolate. We just needed to use more to make our recipe taste better. We also found that we needed a generous amount of salt and vanilla to enhance the chocolate flavor and give the brownies more depth.

Many recipes call for creaming the butter (beating it until light-textured), but our tests showed that this produced a light, dry texture. Much to our relief, the easiest method worked best: Melt the chocolate and butter, add the sugar, eggs, and vanilla, and then fold in the flour.

As simple as they are to mix, these brownies need to be baked just right to guarantee the perfect texture. An even temperature of 325 degrees baked them through without drying the edges, a problem when the oven temperature was higher. Close attention near the end of the baking time proved beneficial as well. Underbaking by just a couple of minutes resulted in a gummy (undercooked) center, and overbaking quickly dried them out. Because home ovens are notoriously fickle and poorly calibrated, the baking times in this recipe should be used only as a general guide.

When we mixed nuts into the batter before baking the brownies, they steamed and became soft. Sprinkling the nuts on top just before baking kept the nuts dry and crunchy; toasting them first made them even crunchier while also enhancing their flavor. That said, we decided to make the nuts—not everyone's preference in brownies—optional.

WHAT WE LEARNED: Use unsweetened chocolate—and a lot of it—for a potent chocolate punch. Cake flour and a little baking powder give the brownies a nice chew. Melt the butter, rather than creaming it, for a dense texture.

CLASSIC BROWNIES

Makes 24 brownies

Be sure to test for doneness before removing the brownies from the oven. If underbaked (the toothpick has batter clinging to it), the texture of the brownies will be dense and gummy; if overbaked (the toothpick comes out completely clean), the brownies will be dry and cakey.

- 1 cup pecans or walnuts, chopped medium (optional)
- 1¼ cups (5 ounces) plain cake flour
- ½ teaspoon salt
- ¾ teaspoon baking powder
- 6 ounces unsweetened chocolate, chopped fine
- 12 tablespoons (1½ sticks) unsalted butter, cut into six 1-inch pieces
- 2¼ cups (15¾ ounces) sugar
- 4 large eggs
- 1 tablespoon vanilla extract

1. Adjust an oven rack to the middle position and heat the oven to 325 degrees. Line a 13 by 9-inch baking pan with two pieces of foil (see the illustration on page 288). Spray the foil-lined pan with nonstick cooking spray.

2. If using nuts, spread the nuts evenly on a rimmed baking sheet and toast in the oven until fragrant, 5 to 8 minutes. Set aside to cool.

3. In a medium bowl, whisk the flour, salt, and baking powder together until combined; set aside.

4. Melt the chocolate and butter in a large heatproof bowl set over a saucepan of almost-simmering water, stirring occasionally, until smooth. (Alternatively, in a microwave, heat the butter and chocolate in a large microwave-safe bowl on high for 45 seconds, then stir and heat for 30 seconds more. Stir again and, if necessary, repeat in 15-second increments; do not let the chocolate burn.) When the chocolate mixture is completely smooth, remove the bowl from the saucepan and gradually whisk in the sugar. Add the eggs, one at a time, whisking after each addition until thoroughly combined. Whisk in the vanilla. Add the flour mixture in 3 additions, folding with a rubber spatula until the batter is completely smooth and homogeneous.

5. Transfer the batter to the prepared pan; using a spatula, spread the batter into the corners of the pan and smooth the surface. Sprinkle the toasted nuts (if using) evenly over the batter. Bake until a toothpick or wooden skewer inserted into the center of the brownies comes out with a few moist crumbs attached, 30 to 35 minutes. Cool on a wire rack to room temperature, about 2 hours, then remove the brownies from the pan by lifting them out using the foil overhangs. Cut the brownies into 2-inch squares and serve. (Store leftovers in an airtight container at room temperature up to 3 days.)

CHOCOLATE-GLAZED MINT-FROSTED BROWNIES

These brownies have both a mint frosting and a chocolate glaze.

1. Follow the recipe for Classic Brownies, omitting the optional nuts; when the brownies are cool, leave them in the pan.

2. In the bowl of a standing mixer or with a handheld mixer, beat 8 tablespoons (1 stick) softened unsalted butter and 2 cups (8 ounces) confectioners' sugar at low speed until just incorporated, then increase the speed to medium and beat until smooth and fluffy, about 1½ minutes. Add 1 tablespoon milk and 1 teaspoon mint extract and continue to beat until combined, about 30 seconds, adding up to 1 additional tablespoon milk if necessary to achieve a soft spreadable consistency. Using an offset spatula, spread the mint frosting evenly onto the cooled brownies, cover with foil, and refrigerate until firm, about 1 hour.

3. Melt 4 ounces chopped bittersweet or semisweet chocolate and 4 tablespoons (½ stick) unsalted butter in a medium heatproof bowl set over a saucepan of barely simmering water, stirring occasionally, until smooth; set aside to cool slightly, about 10 minutes.

4. Pour the chocolate glaze on the frosted brownies; using an offset spatula, spread the glaze into an even layer. Cover with foil and refrigerate until firm, about 1 hour. Remove the brownies from the pan by lifting the foil overhang, cut into 2-inch squares, and serve. (Store leftovers in an airtight container in the refrigerator.)

CLASSIC BROWNIES WITH COCONUT-PECAN TOPPING

These brownies have the flavors of German chocolate cake.

1. Follow the recipe for Classic Brownies, toasting only ¾ cup pecans in step 2 and reserving the pecans for the topping (do not sprinkle the pecans over the batter before baking); when the brownies are cool, leave them in the pan.

2. Whisk 2 large egg yolks, ½ cup (3½ ounces) sugar, and ⅛ teaspoon salt in a small nonreactive saucepan until combined. Whisk in 4 tablespoons (½ stick) softened unsalted butter, then gradually whisk in ½ cup heavy cream and ½ teaspoon vanilla extract. Cook over low heat, stirring constantly, until the mixture is fluffy, begins to thicken, and registers about 180 degrees on an instant-read thermometer, 8 to 12 minutes. Off the heat, stir in the pecans and 1 cup lightly packed sweetened flaked coconut. Spread the topping evenly onto the cooled brownies, cover with foil, and refrigerate until set, about 2 hours. Remove the brownies from the pan by lifting the foil overhang, cut into 2-inch squares, and serve. (Store leftovers in an airtight container in the refrigerator.)

GETTING IT RIGHT: Developing a Brownie to Please Everyone

Seemingly minor changes in brownie recipes can yield quite different results.

Too Cakey	**Too Fudgy**	**Just Right**
This recipe called for creaming the butter and sugar and for lots of baking powder, yielding brownies with a fluffy, cakey texture.	This recipe called for a lot of chocolate and no baking powder and produced a confection-like brownie that was extremely rich and dense.	With a moderate amount of chocolate and a little baking powder, our brownie has good flavor and a moist texture that is neither cakey nor fudgy.

TASTING LAB: Boxed Brownie Mixes

ADMIT IT. IN A MOMENT OF DESPERATION YOU'VE reached for a boxed brownie mix. Maybe you forgot about tomorrow's school bake sale, or in a moment of haste you volunteered to make something for an office party. Why not use one of the countless pre-packaged comestibles available on supermarket shelves?

You know why not—most boxed brownies are not very good. But we wondered which brands were better than the others—and thought maybe one could rival homemade. (OK, that was a bit optimistic.) We purchased six brands, prepared each according to the instructions on the package, and rated them according to their texture, moistness, and chocolate flavor.

We came away with only one boxed brownie mix to halfheartedly recommend: Ghirardelli Double Chocolate Premium Brownie Mix. No one loved these brownies, but they had a decent amount of chocolate flavor (they are made with both cocoa and semisweet chips) and were the least offensive of the bunch. Tasters complained, loudly, about artificial flavors and excessive sweetness in the Pillsbury, Betty Crocker, and Duncan Hines mixes.

The two remaining brands were a bit different. In place of the typical water, vegetable oil, and egg additions that most mixes require, No-Pudge calls for nonfat yogurt and vanilla extract, and Dr. Oetker uses melted butter and eggs. Tasters felt both lacked chocolate flavor and had undesirable textures.

In the end, we can't be too enthusiastic about any of these choices, especially since homemade brownies are so easy to prepare. But if you must use a mix, at least now you know they're not all the same.

Rating Brownie Mixes

TWELVE MEMBERS OF THE *COOK'S ILLUSTRATED* STAFF tasted all of the brownie mixes, which were prepared and baked according to the package directions. Some packages come with directions for using the mix in pans of various sizes. If more than one option was listed on the package, we have listed the largest pan size below. The mixes are listed in order of preference based on their scores in this tasting. All the brands are available in supermarkets.

PASSABLE IN A PINCH
Ghirardelli Double Chocolate Brownie Mix
$2.79 for 20 ounces, yielding an 8-inch pan of brownies
These brownies were twice as thick as other brands and had the "best chocolate flavor." However, they were on the sweet side and "somewhat mushy."

NOT RECOMMENDED
Pillsbury Rich & Moist Fudge Brownie Mix
$1.79 for 19.5 ounces, yielding a 13 by 9-inch pan of brownies
These brownies were "bitter" with a "mild, fake chocolate flavor."

NOT RECOMMENDED
Betty Crocker Traditional Chewy Fudge Brownie Mix
$1.89 for 19.8 ounces, yielding a 13 by 9-inch pan of brownies
Tasters deemed these brownies "artificial" and said eating them was "like chewing on a chocolate chamois."

NOT RECOMMENDED
Duncan Hines Family-Style Chewy Fudge Brownies
$1.89 for 21 ounces, yielding a 13 by 9-inch pan of brownies
"Tastes totally commercial," said one taster about these brownies. Others called them "dry" and "chalky."

NOT RECOMMENDED
Dr. Oetker Simple Organics Organic Brownie Mix
$3.19 for 13.1 ounces, yielding an 8-inch pan of brownies
"Leaden," "tough," and "no flavor" was the consensus on these brownies.

NOT RECOMMENDED
No-Pudge Fat-Free Fudge Brownie Mix
$3.69 for 13.7 ounces, yielding an 8-inch pan of brownies
Tasters said these brownies were "like chewing gum" and had "no chocolate flavor."

BLONDIES

WHAT WE WANTED: Bakers like blondies because they are so simple to prepare, but many recipes are pretty flavorless. Is there a way to make a great blondie that's still quick and easy?

Blondies are first cousins to both brownies and chocolate chip cookies. Although blondies are baked in a pan like brownies, the flavorings are similar to those in chocolate chip cookies—vanilla, butter, and brown sugar, otherwise known as butterscotch. Blondies are sometimes laced with nuts and chocolate chips or butterscotch chips. Most of the time, blondies are pretty bland and need all the help they can get from additional ingredients. Dry, floury, flavorless—we have eaten them all. What does it take to make a good blondie?

The majority of the recipes we found had essentially the same ingredients but in different proportions that yielded blondies with dramatically different textures—from light and cakey to dense and buttery. Tasters preferred the latter, but with reservations. They felt that blondies could be too dense, as were some of the ones we tried. Super-dense blondies tasted of little more than raw flour and butter.

After baking a variety of blondie recipes, we found that the key to dense blondies that did not taste raw lay in how the butter was incorporated into the batter and the amount of flour in the batter. Melted butter produced a much denser blondie than creamed butter because the creaming process incorporates air into the batter. Melting the butter also meant that we could make the batter by hand rather than dirtying a food processor or electric mixer.

While we knew all-purpose flour would give us the chewiest, densest texture, the exact amount of flour was tricky to determine. Too much flour resulted in a dense, flavorless cookie, and too little produced a greasy cookie that oozed butter. After a dozen batches with the slightest variations in the amounts of flour, we finally settled on 1½ cups of all-purpose flour leavened with a small amount of baking powder. These bar cookies were definitely dense and very chewy, but they had risen just enough to prevent them from being gooey.

For sweetening and flavor, tasters favored light brown sugar, which lent the right amount of earthy, molasses flavor; dark brown sugar was overpowering. And combined with a substantial amount of vanilla extract and salt (to sharpen the sweetness), the light brown sugar developed a rich butterscotch flavor.

To add both texture and flavor to the cookies, we included chocolate chips and pecans. While the chips are traditional, pecans are not. Most recipes suggest walnuts, but tasters thought the pecans better complemented the butterscotch flavor.

We also tried butterscotch chips, but most tasters found that they did little for this recipe. On a whim, we included white chocolate chips with the semisweet chips, and we were surprised that they produced the best blondie yet. While white chocolate does not have cocoa, it does have cocoa butter, which highlighted both the vanilla and caramel flavors. These blondies now had a significantly deeper and richer flavor.

WHAT WE LEARNED: Use melted rather than creamed butter to create dense, chewy blondies. Light brown sugar (rather than dark brown sugar) and vanilla are the keys to creating a rich butterscotch flavor. A combination of semisweet and white chocolate chips adds a big boost of chocolate flavor.

BLONDIES

Makes 36 bars

If you have trouble finding white chocolate chips, chop a bar of white chocolate into small chunks.

1½	cups (7½ ounces) unbleached all-purpose flour
1	teaspoon baking powder
½	teaspoon salt
12	tablespoons (1½ sticks) unsalted butter, melted and cooled
1½	cups (10½ ounces) packed light brown sugar
2	large eggs
1½	teaspoons vanilla extract
½	cup semisweet chocolate chips
½	cup white chocolate chips
1	cup pecans, toasted and chopped coarse

1. Adjust an oven rack to the middle position and heat the oven to 350 degrees. Line a 13 by 9-inch baking pan with two pieces of foil (see the illustration on this page). Spray the foil-lined pan with nonstick cooking spray.

2. Whisk the flour, baking powder, and salt together in a medium bowl; set aside.

3. Whisk the melted butter and brown sugar together in a medium bowl until combined. Add the eggs and vanilla and mix well. Using a rubber spatula, fold the dry ingredients into the egg mixture until just combined. Do not overmix. Fold in the semisweet and white chocolate chips and the nuts and turn the batter into the prepared pan, smoothing the top with a rubber spatula.

4. Bake until the top is shiny and cracked and feels firm to the touch, 22 to 25 minutes. Place the pan on a rack and cool completely. Cut into 1½ by 2-inch bars.

VARIATION
CONGO BARS

Despite their name, Congo bars have nothing at all to do with Africa. In fact, they are little more than blondies enriched with coconut—an ingredient that was exotic in years past perhaps but is far from it these days. We tried adding both sweetened, flaked coconut and unsweetened, shredded coconut to our blondies, and tasters unanimously preferred the unsweetened. Sweetened coconut did little but make the bars overly sweet and unpleasantly chewy. We were able to extract a bit more flavor from the unsweetened coconut by toasting it golden brown before adding it to the blondie dough. If you have trouble locating unsweetened shredded coconut, try a natural food store or an Asian market. Keep a close eye on the coconut when toasting as it can burn quickly.

Toast 1½ cups unsweetened, shredded coconut on a rimmed baking sheet on the middle oven rack at 350 degrees, stirring 2 to 3 times, until light golden, about 4 to 5 minutes. Transfer to a small bowl to cool. Follow the recipe for Blondies, adding the toasted coconut with the chocolate chips and nuts in step 3.

TECHNIQUE:
Removing Bar Cookies from the Pan

1. Place two sheets of aluminum foil or parchment paper perpendicular to each other in the pan, pushing the foil or paper into the corner.

2. After the bars have baked and cooled, use the foil or paper to transfer them to a cutting board, then slice into individual portions.

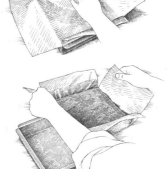

What is the difference between margarine and shortening?

Margarine is a manufactured product made with vegetable oil; it was developed in France in 1869 as a butter substitute when butter was scarce and more expensive. In order to make the oil solid at room temperature, it is hydrogenated (extra hydrogen atoms are added to unsaturated fat, a process that creates trans-fatty acids and converts the mixture to saturated fat). Regular margarine must contain 80 percent fat; the other 20 percent is liquid, coloring, flavoring, and other additives. There are many varieties, including butter-margarine blends, cholesterol-lowering blends, soft margarine, and whipped margarine. When used in baked goods in place of butter, margarine often compromises both flavor and texture.

Shortening is also a solid fat made from vegetable oils through the process of hydrogenation. Unlike margarine, shortening is 100 percent fat and is virtually flavorless. Shortening can be more stable than butter and therefore can help a less experienced baker work with certain doughs at room temperature. It can be especially helpful when making pie crust. Shortening generally won't compromise texture (in fact, it makes very flaky pie crust), but it can have a detrimental effect on the flavor of many baked goods.

EQUIPMENT CORNER: Baking Pans

HERE IN CAKE-AND-CASSEROLE-CRAZED AMERICA, THE shallow, rectangular 13 by 9-inch baking dish is a kitchen workhorse. As expected, there is a huge variety of options from which to choose, many with new designs, materials, finish colors, and baking surface textures, all taking aim at the tried-and-true pans of old—Pyrex and stoneware. These "improvements," of course, come at a cost.

Would our grandparents have spent nearly $100 on a baking pan? En route to determining the true value of these pans, we found ourselves knee-deep in cornbread, lasagna, raspberry squares, and gingerbread, all baked in each of 12 pans representing the major designs and materials, both old and new.

Though no longer common, rough stoneware and earthenware pans have been around since the days of communal bread ovens in the village square. Ovensafe glass, represented by the Pyrex brand, came to market in 1915 and in the years since has become a standard kitchen item familiar to almost every home cook.

Pans made from both materials performed well in our tests, browning cornbread deeply and evenly. (We put a high value on the enhanced flavor and texture of deeply browned exterior surfaces. Pans that did not brown well were marked down.) Like a trusty cast-iron skillet, stoneware has a huge capacity to absorb and retain heat. The story is similar for glass. Although it heats up slowly, once glass is hot, it stays that way. In both cases, that's good news for fans of deeply browned crusts.

Our group included six pans with nonstick surfaces. All but the Wearever CushionAir ($22.99), which is also insulated (more on this later), browned cornbread deeply. Previous bakeware tests have shown—and the cornbread baked in this test confirmed—that when it comes to browning, a dark surface color is more important than the material of the pan. Dark-colored surfaces absorb heat in the oven; bright surfaces do, too, but they also reflect it.

The nonstick pans did, however, present a serious practical consideration. Many dishes baked in a 13 by 9-inch pan, including the lasagna we tested, are customarily cut and served right from the pan. With a nonstick pan that's a problem, because the use and care recommendations usually advise against cutting in the pan to protect the nonstick coating. Though not officially part of this test, some old, poorly cared for pieces of nonstick bakeware brought in from home by several editors were scarred, chipped, and rusted, proving that it pays to follow the manufacturer's guidelines in this respect. In our view, not being able to cut in a pan is a strike against it.

In the last couple of years, some manufacturers, including Doughmakers and Emerilware, have introduced heavy-gauge aluminum pans with textured baking surfaces that are supposed to increase airflow beneath the baked good to improve browning and release. Although pure aluminum is known to conduct heat efficiently, previous tests of bakeware have shown that this advantage is offset by its shiny surface, which reflects some of the oven's radiant heat. (The crusts of cornbread baked in these pans were on the light side.) Also, when you grease a textured pan, excess lubricant clings to the ridges, which in our tests caused the bottom of the gingerbread cake to turn soggy.

In addition to subpar browning, aluminum pans have another limitation. Manufacturers recommend against preparing acidic foods (such as tomato-based products) in them because acid and aluminum can react, causing off flavors.

The Rolls-Royce of the aluminum group was the All-Clad. Though it was solid as a rock, this wallet-wilting $95 pan didn't brown cornbread or raspberry squares as well as some of its darker competitors. Yes, it's nonreactive, and, yes, you can put it under the broiler and use metal utensils with it, but this pan just costs too much for us to recommend it over less expensive alternatives that performed better.

Another design innovation that has surfaced in recent years is insulated bakeware, which incorporates an air layer between two sheets of metal. Although this pan has a dark nonstick finish on the cooking surface, it did a lousy job of browning. Part of the problem was the reflective, shiny exterior surface of the pan. The pan's main selling point, its insulating air layer, was the second problem. We found that it also prevents baked goods from browning—not a good thing.

The newest and most unexpected design in our group was the Kaiser Backform Noblesse springform ($31.99), which brings the removable sides of a classic round cheesecake pan to a 13 by 9-inch size. This unique pan had both pros and cons. Removal of baked goods intact couldn't have been easier, but the seal between the sides and bottom was not tight enough to prevent some lasagna juices from leaking out and burning in the oven.

It turns out that our story ends almost right where it began, with Pyrex. This pan may not be perfect, but it did have five distinct advantages over the newcomers. First, it browned on a par with the dark-colored nonstick pans. Second, it is compatible with metal utensils. Third, it is nonreactive. Fourth, while it's no stunning beauty, most people we asked were perfectly willing to set it on a dining table at dinnertime, which allows it to pull double duty in sweet and savory baking. Last, at $8.95 it's inexpensive; only two other pans in the lineup cost less. The stoneware pan offers the same virtues but costs more. Of course, if your baking is usually of the sweet variety and you are willing to forgo cutting foods right in the pan, any of the recommended nonstick models will also serve you well.

Rating Baking Pans

WE TESTED TWELVE 13 X 9-INCH CAKE/BAKING PANS BY BAKING CORNBREAD, RASPBERRY SQUARES, GINGERBREAD, AND A simple lasagna. The pans were evaluated by a number of criteria, including price, performance, and pan restrictions. Performance differences among the pans that did well were minor enough to let us recommend any of them. Within the Recommended and Not Recommended categories, pans are listed in ascending order by price. See www.americastestkitchen.com for up-to-date prices and mail-order sources for top-rated products.

HIGHLY RECOMMENDED
Pyrex Bakeware 13 x 9
Baking Dish
$8.95

Produced deep and evenly golden brown cornbread and slightly dark edges on raspberry squares and gingerbread. The clear glass makes it easy to monitor browning.

RECOMMENDED
Baker's Secret Non-Stick
Oblong Cake Pan
$6.29

Browns deeply and evenly, cleans up easily, and is inexpensive. Not the sturdiest pan but cheap enough to replace if need be.

RECOMMENDED
Chicago Metallic Professional
Bake N' Roast Pan
$10.57

Produced handsome dark golden brown cornbread and raspberry squares but difficult to wash and dry.

RECOMMENDED
KitchenAid Sheet
Cake Pan 13 x 9
$24.99

The oversized rims/handles on this pan make for especially easy handling.

RECOMMENDED
Calphalon Commercial Non-stick
Bakeware Rectangular
Cake Pan
$25.99

The absence of rims or handles made it a bit tricky to grab this model with oven mitts.

RECOMMENDED
Pampered Chef Family Heritage
Stoneware Rectangular
Baker
$30.75

Surprisingly, this pan did not retain food odors; however, it does require initial seasoning and cannot be washed with soap or detergents.

RECOMMENDED
Kaiser Backform Noblesse Quadro
13 x 9 Springform
Pan
$31.99

Despite its super-easy release owing to the springform design, we wouldn't use this pan for dishes that might produce juices, for fear of leakage.

NOT RECOMMENDED
Wilton Performance Pan
13 x 9 Sheet
$7.69

This pan cooked raspberry squares less thoroughly than other pans and was not as easy to clean as nonstick pans.

NOT RECOMMENDED
Doughmakers
13 x 9 Cake Pan
$19.99

The crust of the cornbread and the base of the raspberry squares were lighter than examples baked in darker nonstick pans.

NOT RECOMMENDED
Wearever CushionAir
Covered Oblong
Baking Pan
$22.99

This pan produced pale, spongy cornbread, raspberry bars ranging from pale to raw, and leaden, underbaked gingerbread. Cannot be soaked in water—a minus for sure.

NOT RECOMMENDED
Emerilware 13 x 9
All Purpose Pan
$24.99

Cornbread crusts and raspberry square bottoms were lighter than we prefer, and the bottom of the gingerbread was soggy.

NOT RECOMMENDED
All-Clad Rectangular Cake Pan
13 x 9, #9004
$94.99

Browning of the cornbread crust and raspberry squares was acceptable but not stellar. Given the price, this pan should slice and butter your cornbread for you.

Chris knows which cookie recipes have been naughty and which have been nice.

HOLIDAY cookies

CHAPTER 23

Making cookies is a favorite holiday activity. Many people who bake infrequently during the year throw themselves into marathon cookie projects. These occasional bakers need reliable recipes. Dough that sticks to the rolling pin, cookies that melt together in the oven, and glazes that refuse to set up just won't do. The holidays are stressful enough. You certainly don't need suspect cookie recipes.

We set out to create a foolproof rolled butter cookie dough that tasted great and could be turned into an array of different cookies. Could we create lots of cookies, with distinct flavors and shapes, from the same basic dough? And could we do it easily?

Nut crescents go by a variety of names, including Viennese crescents, butterballs, and Mexican wedding cakes. Whatever the name, these cookies always have two things in common—a melt-in-your-mouth texture and an attractive coating of powdered sugar. But they also can be dry, bland, and soggy. We aimed to avoid these pitfalls and create nut crescents that would taste as good as they looked.

IN THIS CHAPTER

THE RECIPES

Glazed Butter Cookies
Jam Sandwiches
Lime-Glazed Coconut Snowballs
Chocolate-Cherry Bar Cookies
   with Hazelnuts

Pecan or Walnut Crescent
   Cookies
Almond or Hazelnut Crescent
   Cookies

EQUIPMENT CORNER

Handheld versus Standing Mixers

SCIENCE DESK

Why Does Mixing Method
   Matter?

HOLIDAY ROLLED COOKIES

WHAT WE WANTED: A roll-and-cut holiday cookie that is almost as easy as the slice-and-bake tubes of cookie dough in the supermarket—but without the glue-like flavor or pasty texture.

When we started our recipe development process, we knew what we wanted, but we didn't know how to get there. We wanted a buttery cookie dough that doesn't cling to the rolling pin or rip and tear. We wanted a simple one-hour process, not a half-day project. We wanted to develop a simple recipe that would yield a forgiving, workable dough and produce cookies that would be sturdy enough to decorate yet tender enough to be worth eating. And, to save even more time, we wanted a chameleon-like dough that could be transformed into distinctly different cookies with just a few additional ingredients.

We started our investigation by testing five recipes that called for similar ratios of flour to fat and followed the standard butter-and-sugar creaming method of cookie making. These recipes did vary slightly in their choice of ingredients. One used a combination of shortening and butter, one called for all confectioners' sugar, and another used all light brown sugar. Some added an egg or dairy component, while others utilized a leavener. Although these cookies were certainly edible, we still found ourselves in a sticky situation. Only one batch had been easy to handle, but that batch also tasted like powdery cardboard because it used so much confectioners' sugar. We realized that if we wanted the perfect holiday cookie dough, we would have to go back to basics.

The most important issue was the ratio of butter to flour. After extensive testing, we ended up with 2½ cups of flour to two sticks of butter. (Shortening adds no flavor to cookies and is not an option.) This was just enough butter to stay true to the nature of a butter cookie but not so much

that the dough would be greasy. Although the dough was not perfect (it still had a tendency to stick when rolled), we at least had a good jumping-off point for the rest of our recipe development.

Next we experimented with flour, first testing cake flour, which produced delicate cookies with a chalky texture. We got similar results when we tried replacing different amounts of all-purpose flour with equal parts of cornstarch, another common tenderizing technique. These cookies were also very fragile—not ideal when it's time to decorate. We came to the conclusion that a little bit of structure-providing gluten (the combination of proteins found in greater amounts in all-purpose flour than in cake flour or cornstarch) wasn't necessarily a bad thing.

Because these cookies would play host to glazes or sweet fillings, we did not want to add too much sugar to the dough—just enough to enhance their flavor. Confectioners' sugar was out because of its bland flavor and powdery texture, while brown sugar made the cookies too soft and chewy. But when we tried superfine sugar, we were surprised at the difference it made. Cookies made with regular granulated sugar had a crumb with larger holes and a flaky texture. The cookies made with superfine sugar, on the other hand, had a fine, even crumb and were compact and crisp—very definitely positive attributes. Liking these thin and crisp cookies, we ruled out the use of a leavener (which would make them puff in the oven) and eggs (which would add both moisture and chewiness). But we still needed to enrich the flavor of the cookies, so we tried adding flavorful dairy components to the dough: buttermilk, sour cream, and cream cheese. The buttermilk produced a crisp yet overly tangy cookie, and the sour cream made the dough far too wet. But the cream cheese—a surprise ingredient to be sure—was just right. It gave the cookies flavor and richness without altering their texture. With a pinch of salt and a dash of vanilla, we had obtained

a simple but top-notch flavor for our holiday cookies.

We had come a long way in terms of improving the flavor (rich but direct) and texture (fine and crisp) of the baked cookies, but we were still having trouble rolling out the dough. It was less sticky than the doughs we had made from other recipes, but we wanted a dough that was even easier to work with—something foolproof. All the recipes we had tested called for the creaming method, wherein butter and sugar are beaten into a fluffy union. What if we creamed the butter with the sugar and the flour? The dough came together in two minutes and was incredibly easy to handle: soft, pliable, and easy to roll. Even with less chilling time than before, the dough was easily rolled to a slight thickness of ⅛ inch, cut out into different shapes, and maneuvered to a baking sheet. (For more on why this technique works so well, see "Why Does Mixing Method Matter?" on page 298.)

As far as oven temperature goes, 375 degrees was best, as was using only one rack placed in the center of the oven. In the amount of time it took to cut out a second sheet of cookies, the first sheet was finished. But the final selling point was the baked result: thin, flat cookies that were both crisp and sturdy. They tasted great and were foolproof— what more could a holiday baker want?

WHAT WE LEARNED: Superfine sugar makes rolled cookies especially crisp, and all-purpose flour gives them some structure. Cream cheese makes them rich, and vanilla adds flavor. And to make the dough easy to roll out, add the butter to the dry ingredients rather than creaming it with the sugar alone.

GLAZED BUTTER COOKIES
Makes about 38 cookies

If you cannot find superfine sugar, you can obtain a close approximation by processing regular granulated sugar in a food processor for about 30 seconds. If desired, the cookies can be finished with sprinkles or other decorations immediately after glazing.

butter cookie dough

- 2½ cups (12½ ounces) unbleached all-purpose flour
- ¾ cup (5½ ounces) superfine sugar (see note)
- ¼ teaspoon salt
- 16 tablespoons (2 sticks) unsalted butter, cut into 16 pieces, softened but still cool
- 2 teaspoons vanilla extract
- 2 tablespoons cream cheese, at room temperature

glaze

- 1 tablespoon cream cheese, at room temperature
- 3 tablespoons milk
- 1½ cups (6 ounces) confectioners' sugar

1. FOR THE COOKIES: In the bowl of a standing mixer, or with a handheld mixer, mix the flour, sugar, and salt at low speed until combined, about 5 seconds. With the mixer running on low, add the butter 1 piece at a time; continue to mix until the mixture looks crumbly and slightly wet, about 1 minute longer. Add the vanilla and cream cheese and mix on low until the dough just begins to form large clumps, about 30 seconds.

2. Knead the dough by hand in the bowl for 2 to 3 turns to form a large, cohesive mass. Turn the dough out onto a work surface; divide it in half, pat each half into a 4-inch disk, wrap the disks in plastic, and refrigerate until they begin to firm up, 20 to 30 minutes. (The disks can be refrigerated up to 3 days or frozen up to 2 weeks; defrost in the refrigerator before using.)

3. Adjust an oven rack to the middle position and heat the oven to 375 degrees. Roll out 1 dough disk to an even ⅛-inch thickness between 2 large sheets of parchment paper; slide the rolled dough, still on the parchment, onto a baking sheet and refrigerate until firm, about 10 minutes. Meanwhile, repeat with the second disk.

4. Working with the first portion of rolled dough, cut into desired shapes using cookie cutters and place the shapes on a parchment-lined baking sheet, spacing them about 1½ inches apart. Bake until the cookies are light golden brown, about 10 minutes, rotating the baking sheet halfway through the baking time. Repeat with the second portion of rolled dough. (The dough scraps can be patted together, chilled, and rerolled once.) Cool the cookies to room temperature on a wire rack.

5. FOR THE GLAZE: Whisk the cream cheese and 2 tablespoons of the milk in a medium bowl until combined and no lumps remain. Whisk in the confectioners' sugar until smooth, adding the remaining milk as needed until the glaze is thin enough to spread easily. Drizzle or spread a scant teaspoon of glaze with the back of a spoon onto each cooled cookie, as desired.

VARIATIONS
JAM SANDWICHES
Makes about 30 cookies
See the illustrations on page 297 to prepare these cookies.

- 1 recipe Butter Cookie Dough, prepared through step 3
- 2 tablespoons turbinado, Demerara, or white decorating sugar
- 1¼ cups (12 ounces) raspberry jam, strained, simmered until reduced to 1 cup, and cooled to room temperature

1. Using a 2-inch fluted round cookie cutter, cut rounds from 1 piece of rolled dough and bake on a parchment-lined baking sheet in a 375-degree oven, rotating the baking sheet halfway through the baking time, until the cookies are light golden brown, 8 to 10 minutes.

2. Sprinkle the second piece of rolled dough evenly with the sugar.

3. Using a 2-inch round cookie cutter, cut out rounds of sugar-sprinkled dough and place them on a parchment-lined baking sheet. Using a ¾-inch fluted round cookie cutter, cut out the centers of the rounds. Bake, rotating the baking sheet halfway through the baking time, until the cookies are light golden brown, about 8 minutes.

4. When the cookies have cooled, spread 1 teaspoon jam on the top of each solid cookie, then cover with a cut-out cookie. Let the filled cookies stand until set, about 30 minutes.

LIME-GLAZED COCONUT SNOWBALLS
Makes about 40 cookies
See the illustrations on page 297 to prepare these cookies.

- 1 recipe Butter Cookie Dough, with 1 teaspoon grated lime zest added with the dry ingredients and prepared through step 1
- 1 recipe Glaze, with 3 tablespoons lime juice substituted for the milk
- 1½ cups sweetened shredded coconut, pulsed in a food processor until finely chopped, about fifteen 1-second pulses

1. Use your hands to roll the dough into 1-inch balls. Place the balls on parchment-lined baking sheets, spacing them about 1½ inches apart. Bake, one batch at a time, in a 375-degree oven until lightly browned, about 12 minutes. Cool to room temperature.

TECHNIQUE: One Dough, Many Cookies

Our butter cookie dough is not only foolproof but also the perfect vehicle for a number of different flavorings, shapes, and sizes. One easy-to-handle dough can be the basis for a wide assortment of holiday cookies. Here's how to make three of our favorite cookies with this dough.

Cutting and Filling Jam Sandwiches

1. Using a 2-inch fluted round cookie cutter, cut rounds from 1 piece of rolled dough.

2. Sprinkle the second piece of rolled dough evenly with turbinado sugar.

3. Cut out 2-inch rounds of sugar-sprinkled dough and place on a parchment-lined baking sheet. Using a ¾-inch fluted round cookie cutter, cut out the centers.

4. When the cookies have cooled, spread 1 teaspoon jam on the tops of each solid cookie, then cover with a cut-out cookie.

Shaping and Coating Lime-Glazed Coconut Snowballs

1. Use your hands to roll the dough into 1-inch balls. Place the balls on parchment-lined baking sheets.

2. Dip the tops of the baked and cooled cookies into the glaze and scrape away the excess, then dip them into the coconut. Set the cookies on a rack until the glaze dries.

Making Chocolate-Cherry Bar Cookies with Hazelnuts

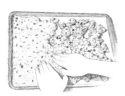   

1. Press the dough evenly into a 17 by 12-inch rimmed baking sheet that has been lined with parchment paper.

2. Immediately after removing the baking sheet from the oven, sprinkle evenly with the chocolate chips; let stand to melt, about 3 minutes.

3. Using an offset icing spatula, spread the chocolate into an even layer, then sprinkle the chopped hazelnuts evenly over the chocolate.

4. When the cookies have cooled slightly, use a pizza wheel to cut on the diagonal into 1½-inch diamonds.

2. Dip tops of the cookies into the glaze and scrape away the excess, then dip them into the coconut. Set the cookies on a rack and let stand until the glaze sets, about 20 minutes.

CHOCOLATE-CHERRY BAR COOKIES WITH HAZELNUTS

Makes about 50 cookies

See the illustrations on page 297 to prepare these cookies.

1	recipe Butter Cookie Dough, 1 cup chopped dried cherries added with the dry ingredients, prepared through step 1
1½	cups semisweet chocolate chips
1½	cups hazelnuts, toasted, skinned, and chopped

1. Press the dough evenly into a 17 by 12-inch rimmed baking sheet that has been lined with parchment paper. Bake on the lower-middle rack in a 375-degree oven until golden brown, about 20 minutes, rotating the baking sheet halfway through the baking time.

2. Immediately after removing the baking sheet from the oven, sprinkle evenly with the chocolate chips; let stand to melt, about 3 minutes.

3. Using an offset icing spatula, spread the chocolate into an even layer, then sprinkle the chopped hazelnuts evenly over the chocolate. Cool on a wire rack until just warm, 15 to 20 minutes.

4. Using a pizza wheel, cut on the diagonal into 1½-inch diamonds. Transfer the cookies to a wire rack to cool completely.

SCIENCE DESK:
Why Does Mixing Method Matter?

CREAMING IS A COMMON METHOD USED IN BAKING. Butter and sugar are whipped until light and fluffy, eggs are added, and then dry ingredients are incorporated gradually. This method delivers good results when making most cookies, but we found that it did not work well for rolled butter cookies, and we wondered why.

Our recipe has two striking features: It contains no leavener (we did not want the cookies to puff) and no liquid. Because the dough is somewhat dry, the flour did not incorporate well when added at the end of the mixing process. As a result, the dough was unevenly mixed, with

---

GETTING IT RIGHT: Chasing the Perfect Holiday Cookie

If your rolled cookies look like the three sorry samples on the left, we've figured out why. It's not your technique but your dough. If the dough is too sticky, the cookies will be misshapen (far left). If the dough contains too much butter, the cookies will bake up very fragile (second from left). If the dough contains too much sugar, the cookies will spread in the oven and look bloated (second from right). If you follow our "reverse creaming" method for making the dough, the cookies will roll out easily and bake up perfectly (far right).

Misshapen

Fragile

Bloated

Perfect

---

streaks of butter, which became sticky when handled. This streaking also had negative effects on the final baked product, as the pockets of butter led to puffed, uneven cookies. Butter is about 18 percent water, and when its temperature reaches 212 degrees Fahrenheit, this water turns to steam and expands dramatically, producing bubbles.

When we reversed the order of mixing and added the butter to the flour, the dough was much more uniform, without streaks of butter. Thus, the dough was neither sticky when rolled nor puffy when baked. The baked cookies had flat tops, ready for decorating.

STANDARD CREAMING   "REVERSE" CREAMING

An enormous bubble formed where the butter had not been mixed in completely using the standard creaming method (left). The cookie made using our "reverse" creaming method (right) was uniform throughout, indicating that the butter was evenly distributed.

Q & A

Can waxed paper be used in place of parchment paper?

Waxed paper cannot be substituted for parchment paper in many cases. Parchment can withstand temperatures up to 425 degrees without burning, while waxed paper will smoke when subjected directly to heat. So, for lining a cake pan, waxed paper will do. The batter will cover the paper and prevent burning. But for lining a baking sheet, waxed paper will smoke and parchment is the only choice.

Q & A

Can wet and dry measuring cups be used interchangeably?

First of all, 1 cup in a "dry" measuring cup is exactly the same volume as 1 cup in a "wet" measuring cup. The choice, then, of how to measure dry ingredients and wet ingredients comes down to convenience and accuracy.

Let's start by defining what we mean by "dry" and "wet" cups. Dry measuring cups are made from metal or plastic and can be leveled off with a straight edge. Wet measuring cups are made of heatsafe glass (such as Pyrex) or plastic and have a pouring spout. Whereas dry measures usually come in sizes from ⅛ or ¼ cup up to 1 cup, wet measures are available in sizes of 1, 2, 4, and 8 cups.

When using both dry and wet measuring cups to weigh dry ingredients—sugar and flour—we found the dry cups to be much easier to use. It is nearly impossible to get an accurate measure of 1 cup of flour in a liquid measure of any size (even 1 cup) because the top can't be leveled off. Dry ingredients, then, ought to be measured in dry measuring cups.

Wet ingredients, on the other hand, ought to be measured in wet measuring cups. Measuring liquids in a dry measuring cup is a messy business. You must fill the cup right up to the rim, and spills are likely. It is also important that a wet measuring cup be transparent. To get an accurate reading of an amount of liquid, you have to stoop down so that the measuring cup is at eye level and look through the cup at the surface of the liquid.

Finally, we are often asked what is the best way to measure honey, molasses, peanut butter, and other sticky, thick ingredients. The answer is the push-up style measuring cup (see page 49), which looks like a wide syringe. You pull out the plunger to set the proper quantity (say, ½ cup), fill the device with the item to be measured, and then simply push it out of the cup. Nothing is left behind (a problem with sticky ingredients in "regular" dry and wet measuring cups), so you can be sure that the measurement is accurate.

NUT CRESCENT COOKIES

WHAT WE WANTED: Nut crescents with a rich, nutty, buttery flavor and a delicate, melt-in-your-mouth texture.

Nut crescents, coated in a pasty layer of melting confectioners' sugar, can taste like stale, dry, floury, flavorless little chokeballs. They often fall short of the buttery, nutty, slightly crisp, slightly crumbly, melt-in-your-mouth nuggets they should be. But that is a shame. When they are well made, they are delicious. Their snowy white appearance also makes them festive enough for the holiday cookie platter.

We gathered recipe after recipe from large, authoritative books and small, pamphlet-size publications in our quest for the best nut crescent cookies. These cookies, round or crescent-shaped, go by different names: Viennese crescents, butterballs, and Mexican wedding cakes, as well as almond, pecan, or walnut crescents. All the recipes are surprisingly similar, differing mainly in the amount and type of sugar and nuts. The standard ratio of butter to flour is 1 cup to 2 cups, with the amount of flour in a few instances going as low as 1¾ cups or as high as 2½ cups. Across the board, the ingredients are simple: flour, sugar, butter, and nuts. Some add vanilla extract and salt. We chose four recipes and, with the input of a few tasters, formed a composite recipe to serve as the springboard for our testing.

Flour was our starting point. We certainly didn't need to go very far. Cookies made with 2 cups of all-purpose flour to 1 cup of butter were right on. The dough was easy to shape and handle, and the baked cookies were tender, delicate, and shapely. Any less flour and the rich cookies spread and lost some form in the oven; any more and they were dry and floury. We tried cake flour and cornstarch in place of some of the all-purpose flour, thinking that one or another would provide extra tenderness. Both were failures. The resulting cookies disintegrated unpleasantly in the mouth.

Next we zeroed in on sugar. Granulated sugar yielded a cookie that was tasty but coarse in both texture and appearance. Cookies made with confectioners' sugar were very tender, light, and fine-textured. Superfine sugar, however, proved superior, producing cookies that were delicate, lightly crisp, and superbly tender, with a true melt-in-your-mouth quality. In a side-by-side tasting, the cookies made with superfine sugar were nuttier and purer in flavor, while the cornstarch in the confectioners' sugar bogged down the flavor and left a faint pastiness in the mouth.

As we tinkered with the amount of sugar, we had to keep in mind that these cookies are coated in confectioners' sugar after they are baked. One-third cup gives them a mildly sweet edge when they're eaten plain, but it's the roll in confectioners' sugar that gives them their finished look and just the right amount of extra sweetness.

When to give the baked cookies their coat of confectioners' sugar is a matter of some debate. Some recipes say to dust or dip them while they're still hot or warm. The sugar melts a bit, and then they're usually given a second coat to even out their appearance and form a thicker coating. But we didn't like the layer of melting moistened confectioners' sugar, concealed or not. It formed a thin skin that was pasty and gummy and didn't dissolve on the tongue with the same finesse as a fine, powdery coat. We found it better to wait until the cookies had cooled to room temperature before coating them with confectioners' sugar.

Sifting sugar over the cooled cookies was tedious, and we weren't able to achieve a heavy enough coating on the tops, or any at all on the bottoms. What worked much better was simply rolling them in confectioners' sugar. One roll resulted in a rather thin layer that was a bit spotty, but a second coat covered any blemishes, giving them an attractive, thick, powdery white coating. If not served immediately, the cookies may lose a little in looks due to handling and storage. This problem can be easily solved by reserving the second coat of confectioners' sugar until just before serving.

While testing the nuts, we concluded that what affected the cookies most was not the taste of the nuts but whether they were oily or dry. We found that when they were ground, the two types of nuts affected the cookies in different ways.

The flavor of oily nuts like walnuts and pecans is strong and distinct. These nuts are easier to chop and grind and, when finely ground, become quite oily. This is a definite advantage when making nut crescents, because the dough becomes softer and the resulting cookies are incredibly tender and delicate. Dry nuts like almonds and hazelnuts taste rather subdued by comparison. Toasting brings out their maximum flavor and crunchiness. Although nut crescents made with almonds or hazelnuts are delicious, they just don't melt in your mouth with the same abandon as the pecan and walnut ones.

Chopped nuts were too coarse for the fine texture of the crescents and were quickly dismissed. Ground nuts, on the other hand, warranted further investigation. Ground nuts were flavorful, and because grinding really brought out the oils, they actually tenderized the cookies. We thought, though, that using a combination of ground and finely chopped nuts might tenderize, be flavorful, and add a pleasant crunch. Hands down, a combination of 1 cup of finely chopped and ¾ cup of ground nuts was the tasters' choice.

Recipes suggested baking temperatures ranging from a ridiculously low 300 degrees to a hot 400. At 400 degrees, the cookies browned too quickly, while at 300, they never achieved a nice golden hue, even after nearly half an hour of baking. Cookies baked at 350 degrees were good, but those baked at 325 degrees had a smoother, finer appearance and were more tender and evenly textured and colored.

WHAT WE LEARNED: Use superfine sugar for a delicate, melt-in-your-mouth texture. Pecans and walnuts give these cookies a stronger flavor than almonds or hazelnuts, although toasting can enhance the flavor of the milder nuts. As for the exterior coating of powdered sugar, wait until the cookies have cooled and roll them twice in the sugar for even coverage.

PECAN OR WALNUT CRESCENT COOKIES
Makes about 48 cookies

You can buy superfine sugar in most grocery stores. You can also process regular granulated sugar to superfine consistency in about 30 seconds in a food processor.

2	cups whole pecans or walnuts, chopped fine
2	cups (10 ounces) unbleached all-purpose flour
½	teaspoon salt
16	tablespoons (2 sticks) unsalted butter, softened but still cool
⅓	cup (2½ ounces) superfine sugar
1½	teaspoons vanilla extract
1½	cups confectioners' sugar for rolling cooled cookies

1. Adjust the oven racks to the upper- and lower-middle positions and heat the oven to 325 degrees. Line 2 large baking sheets with parchment paper.

2. Mix 1 cup of the chopped nuts, the flour, and salt in a medium bowl; set aside. Place the remaining chopped nuts in a food processor and process until they are the texture of coarse cornmeal, 10 to 15 seconds (do not overprocess); stir into the flour mixture and set aside. (To finely grind chopped nuts by hand, roll them between 2 large sheets of plastic wrap with a rolling pin, applying moderate pressure, until broken down to a coarse cornmeal-like texture.)

3. Either by hand or with an electric mixer, cream the butter and sugar until light and fluffy, about 1½ minutes; beat in the vanilla. Scrape the sides and bottom of the bowl with a rubber spatula; add the flour mixture and beat at low speed until the dough just begins to come together but still looks scrappy, about 15 seconds. Scrape the sides and bottom of the bowl again with the rubber spatula; continue beating at low speed until the dough is cohesive, 6 to 9 seconds longer. Do not overbeat.

4. Working with about 1 tablespoon of dough at a time, roll the dough in 1¼-inch balls. Following the illustrations on this page, roll each ball between your palms into a rope that measures 3 inches long. Place the ropes on the parchment-lined baking sheet and turn up the ends to form a crescent shape. Bake until the tops are pale golden and the bottoms are just beginning to brown, 17 to 19 minutes, rotating the baking sheets front to back and top to bottom halfway through the baking time.

5. Cool the cookies on the baking sheets about 2 minutes; remove with a wide metal spatula to a wire rack and cool to room temperature, about 30 minutes. Working with 3 or 4 cookies at a time, roll the cookies in the confectioners' sugar to coat them thoroughly. Gently shake off the excess. (They can be stored in an airtight container up to 5 days.) Before serving, roll the cookies in the confectioners' sugar a second time to ensure a thick coating and tap off the excess.

VARIATION
ALMOND OR HAZELNUT CRESCENT COOKIES

Choosing almonds for your cookies automatically presents you with a second choice: whether to use them raw for traditional almond crescent cookies that are light in both color and flavor or to toast them to enhance the almond flavor and darken the crescents. Toast the almonds or hazelnuts in a preheated 350-degree oven until very lightly browned, stirring twice during baking, 12 to 14 minutes. The hazelnuts should be skinned after they are toasted.

Follow the recipe for Pecan or Walnut Crescent Cookies, substituting a scant 1¾ cups whole blanched almonds (toasted or not) or 2 cups toasted, skinned hazelnuts for the pecans or walnuts. If using almonds, add ½ teaspoon almond extract along with the vanilla extract.

TECHNIQUE:
Making Nut Crescent Cookies

1. Working with 1 tablespoon of dough each time, roll the dough in 1¼-inch balls. Roll each ball between your palms into a rope that measures 3 inches long.

2. Place the ropes on a parchment-lined baking sheet and turn up the ends to form a crescent shape.

3. Rolling the cooled crescents in a bowl of confectioners' sugar creates a thicker, more attractive coating than sifting the sugar over the cookies.

EQUIPMENT CORNER:
Handheld versus Standing Mixers

CURIOUS ABOUT THE PERFORMANCE DIFFERENCES between our favorite handheld and standing mixers (both made by KitchenAid), we conducted side-by-side tests to establish general guidelines for their use. We whipped cream, beat egg whites for meringue, and made cookies, cakes, and buttercream frosting.

Although it took the handheld mixer 40 to 60 seconds longer than the standing mixer to whip cream and beat egg whites, it did just as good a job (both were fitted with the whisk attachment). When making oatmeal cookie dough, the standing mixer (with the paddle attachment) produced more volume in the batter, but the baked cookies were identical in number, texture, and flavor. Neither mixer had trouble mixing oatmeal and nuts into the stiff dough at low speed.

Our favorite yellow layer cake recipe baked up the same when made with both mixers, although the standing mixer created a slightly more voluminous batter. The same was true with génoise, a cake leavened by whole-egg foam, although the handheld mixer took nearly twice as long to beat the eggs to the right volume. For those partial to buttercream frostings, we found that the handheld mixer actually worked better than the standing mixer because it was easier to keep the hot sugar syrup from clinging to the beaters.

OUR CONCLUSION: The standing mixer does offer greater flexibility and versatility. (Its dough hook is ideal for kneading bread, something a handheld mixer can't do.) Also, the solid base leaves your hands free to accomplish other tasks. We found, however, that with some adjustments for time and technique, the handheld mixer generally yields baked goods that are identical to those prepared in a standing mixer.

After performing these side-by-side kitchen tests with both standing and handheld mixers, we found some pointers to help ensure good results with both kinds of mixers.

When using a handheld mixer:
• Use a deep, narrow bowl to avoid flinging batter around your kitchen.
• Continuously move the beaters around the circumference of the bowl and through its center to incorporate all ingredients.
• Remove batter stuck to beaters by lifting the beaters out of the batter—but still keeping them below the lip of the bowl—and (very carefully) turning the mixer on medium for several seconds.
• Stabilize the mixing bowl by resting it within a damp towel twisted in a circle or on a piece of rubber shelf-liner.

When using a standing mixer:
• Avoid overbeating egg whites or cream by turning off the mixer, detaching the whisk attachment, removing the bowl from the mixer, and using the whisk attachment to make the last few strokes by hand.

• Prevent overbeating by resisting the impulse to push the speed lever all the way to the end when a recipe says, "Beat at high speed." To prevent overbeating on our powerful KitchenAid mixers, we rarely go above 8.
• Use the paddle attachment to cream butter and mix batters.
• Use the whisk attachment to whip heavy cream and egg whites.
• Use the hook attachment to knead bread dough.

No matter which mixer you use:
• Scrape down the sides and bottom of the bowl frequently with a rubber spatula to ensure that all the ingredients are incorporated.
• Start on low speed when adding ingredients and gradually increase the speed as necessary to avoid pushing the contents out of the bowl.

Chocolate Bundt cake might have a hole in the center, but when it comes to flavor it's not missing a thing.

THERE'S A HOLE
in your cake

Cakes baked in Bundt pans and tube pans are popular for a variety of reasons. First of all, these pans make cakes that are especially attractive. Second, the cakes made in these pans are pretty simple to prepare; no complicated arrangement of layers or frosting. Most Bundt cakes require just a dusting of confectioners' sugar. Angel food cake, the recipe we prepare most often in our tube pan, is even simpler to decorate. Just cool and serve, adding some fresh berries or perhaps a scoop of ice cream.

Bundt pans and tube pans work with especially thick or heavy batters. The center tube conducts heat and helps the batter to rise. This promotes even cooking and ensures a moist texture.

In addition to angel food cake, we decided to develop a recipe for chocolate Bundt cake. With their short ingredient lists and easy preparation, these recipes are perfect for novice bakers. But that doesn't mean they always turn out right. Angel food cakes can be dry and cottony (or worse, they can fall), and chocolate Bundt cakes are often bland. We set out to perfect these cakes with the hole in the center.

CHOCOLATE BUNDT CAKE

WHAT WE WANTED: A cake that's not only attractive but moist and rich with chocolate flavor.

A Bundt cake is the pinnacle of cake-baking simplicity. With its decorative shape, this cake doesn't require frosting or fussy finishing techniques. What chocolate Bundt cakes do require, it turns out, is a major boost in flavor. Despite their tantalizing looks, most of these cakes have at best a muted chocolate presence. We wanted a cake that would deliver that moment of pure chocolate ecstasy when the first bite stops time. A chocolate Bundt cake should taste every bit as good as it looks, with a fine crumb, moist texture, and rich flavor.

Unfortunately, these sweet masters of disguise disappointed us so often in our initial taste tests that we almost relegated this recipe to the dustbin. Moist but pale, many of the cakes were devoid of any chocolate flavor. Others looked appealingly dark and mysterious but managed to capture only flat, bitter nuances of chocolate. An overly sweet, walnut-studded "tunnel of fudge" cake with a gummy, underbaked center was hardly worth the calories. A cake similar to a pound cake had great texture—dense and moist owing to the addition of sour cream—but the only thing that told tasters it was chocolate was its brown color.

Because the pound cake made with sour cream had come closest to our textural ideal, we started with a working recipe using roughly the same proportions of butter, sugar, eggs, and flour and using the traditional method of creaming the butter and sugar (beating them together) before adding the other ingredients. We then focused on boosting the virtually nonexistent chocolate flavor. The recipe included a small amount of cocoa powder, so we thought that a good dose of melted chocolate would be in order. We started with unsweetened chocolate, which has the most intense flavor. The resulting cake tasted bitter, and its texture was chalky, reminiscent of third-rate brownies. Trying both semisweet

and bittersweet chocolates, we noticed an improvement in texture, as both of these chocolates have added sugar and stabilizers that make them smoother and creamier than unsweetened. Tasters found the semisweet chocolate too sweet; the bittersweet added the right chocolate edge.

Now we had more chocolate flavor, but we wanted a deeper, more complex taste. This time, more cocoa powder seemed like a logical solution. We replaced a portion of the flour in our recipe with an equal amount of cocoa powder. We had to choose between Dutch-processed cocoa powder and natural cocoa powder. (The first is "alkalized"—treated so as to reduce acidity—and is thought to provide a smoother chocolate flavor with an intensely dark color. The second, natural or regular cocoa powder, is slightly acidic and has a lighter, reddish hue.) Tasters preferred the cakes made with natural cocoa. Its assertive flavor with fruity undertones stood up better to the sour cream in the recipe.

We came upon the real trick to developing the chocolate flavor of this cake, however, when we tried a technique that the test kitchen had earlier developed for devil's food cake. We poured boiling water over the cocoa and chocolate to dissolve them, a step that not only disperses the cocoa particles throughout the batter but also blooms the flavor.

Now we had great, complex chocolate flavor, but we also had a new problem—the cake was too dry. To remedy this, we first tried decreasing the flour by ½ cup. The resulting cake was more moist but still not moist enough, and we could not remove more flour without compromising its structure. We tried increasing the butter, but this merely made the cake greasy. We added an extra egg (most recipes call for just four; we went up to five), and that helped. Finally, we switched from granulated to light brown sugar, which not only added moistness but dramatically improved the flavor.

But even after all of these amendments to the recipe, we were still falling short of our goal of a really moist cake.

We decided to review the quantity of sour cream. When we increased it, the cake became greasy and overly acidic. We went back to the original recipes and found that many of them used either milk or buttermilk, which have a higher water content than sour cream. This tipped us off to a simple way to solve the problem: increasing the amount of boiling water added with the cocoa powder and chocolate. The resulting batter was looser and the baked cake significantly more moist—moist enough to finally satisfy our goal.

To finish the recipe, we dissolved a small amount of espresso powder along with the chocolate and cocoa and also added a healthy tablespoon of vanilla extract. Both flavors complemented the floral nuances of the chocolate. With the right pan and a ready batter, we baked cakes at temperatures of 325, 350, and 375 degrees. The cake baked at the highest temperature developed a thick upper crust and an uneven crumb. Finding little difference in the cakes baked at the other two temperatures, we opted for the quicker baking time at 350. At long last, we had reached chocolate heaven.

WHAT WE LEARNED: Use both bittersweet chocolate and cocoa powder and intensify their flavor by melting them with boiling water. Sour cream makes the cake rich, dense, and moist, as does brown sugar.

CHOCOLATE SOUR CREAM BUNDT CAKE
Serves 12 to 14

Natural (or regular) cocoa gives the cake a fuller, more assertive chocolate flavor than does Dutch-processed cocoa. In addition, Dutch-processed cocoa will result in a compromised rise. The cake can be served with just a dusting of confectioners' sugar but is easily made more impressive with Tangy Whipped Cream and Lightly Sweetened Raspberries (recipes follow). The cake can be made a day in advance; wrap the cooled cake in plastic and store it at room temperature. Dust with confectioners' sugar just before serving.

cake release
- 1 tablespoon unsalted butter, melted
- 1 tablespoon cocoa

cake
- ¾ cup (2¼ ounces) natural cocoa (see note)
- 6 ounces bittersweet chocolate, chopped
- 1 teaspoon instant espresso powder (optional)
- ¾ cup boiling water
- 1 cup sour cream, at room temperature
- 1¾ cups (8¾ ounces) unbleached all-purpose flour
- 1 teaspoon salt
- 1 teaspoon baking soda
- 12 tablespoons (1½ sticks) unsalted butter, at room temperature
- 2 cups (14 ounces) packed light brown sugar
- 1 tablespoon vanilla extract
- 5 large eggs, at room temperature
- Confectioners' sugar for dusting

1. FOR THE PAN: Stir together the butter and cocoa in a small bowl until a paste forms. Using a pastry brush, coat all the interior surfaces of a standard 12-cup Bundt pan. (If the mixture becomes too thick to brush on, microwave it for 10 to 20 seconds, or until warm and softened.) Adjust an oven rack to the lower-middle position and heat the oven to 350 degrees.

2. FOR THE CAKE: Combine the cocoa, chocolate, and espresso powder (if using) in a medium heatproof bowl. Pour the boiling water over and whisk until smooth. Cool to room temperature; then whisk in the sour cream. Whisk the flour, salt, and baking soda in a second bowl to combine.

3. In a standing mixer fitted with the flat beater, or with a handheld mixer, beat the butter, brown sugar, and vanilla on medium-high speed until pale and fluffy, about 3 minutes. Reduce the speed to medium and add the eggs one at a time, mixing about 30 seconds after each addition and scraping down the bowl with a rubber spatula after the first 2 additions. Reduce to medium-low speed (the batter may appear separated); add about one third of the flour mixture and half of the chocolate/sour cream mixture and mix until just incorporated, about 20 seconds. Scrape the bowl and repeat using half of the remaining flour mixture and all of the remaining chocolate mixture; add the remaining flour mixture and beat until just incorporated, about 10 seconds. Scrape the bowl and mix on medium-low until the batter is thoroughly combined, about 30 seconds.

4. Pour the batter into the prepared Bundt pan, being careful not to pour the batter on the sides of the pan. Bake until a wooden skewer inserted into the center comes out with a few crumbs attached, 45 to 50 minutes. Cool in the pan 10

minutes, then invert the cake onto a parchment-lined wire rack; cool to room temperature, about 3 hours. Dust with confectioners' sugar, transfer to a serving platter, and cut into wedges. Serve with Tangy Whipped Cream and Lightly Sweetened Raspberries, if desired.

TANGY WHIPPED CREAM

Makes about 2½ cups

This garnish is good either on its own or with the raspberries.

1	cup cold heavy cream
¼	cup sour cream
¼	cup packed light brown sugar
⅛	teaspoon vanilla extract

With an electric mixer, beat all the ingredients, gradually increasing the speed from low to high, until the cream forms soft peaks, 1½ to 2 minutes.

LIGHTLY SWEETENED RASPBERRIES

Makes about 3 cups

The berries are best served with the whipped cream garnish.

3	cups fresh raspberries, gently rinsed and dried
1–2	tablespoons granulated sugar

Gently toss the raspberries with the sugar, then let stand until the berries have released some juice and the sugar has dissolved, about 15 minutes.

TECHNIQUE:
Filling Tube and Bundt Pans

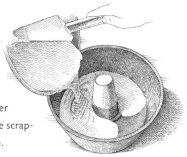

Batter can run down into the hole in the center of a tube or Bundt pan and burn. To prevent this, place a small paper cup over the center tube just before scraping the batter into the pan.

Q&A

Why do some baking recipes call for flour by weight?

Professional bakers measure all ingredients by weight rather than volume. As long as the scale is accurate, you can rest assured that 5 ounces of flour is always 5 ounces of flour.

Because of the different ways cooks use dry measuring cups, volume measures are far less accurate. If you spoon flour into a measuring cup then sweep off the excess, you will end up with about 25 percent less flour than if you dip the measuring cup into a container of flour and sweep off the excess. Even with the so-called dip-and-sweep method (which we use in the test kitchen), different cooks can obtain different amounts of flour. (We tested our staff and found the variance was about 10 percent.) Weighing flour and other dry ingredients, especially sugar, eliminates this problem and ensures consistent results.

According to our test kitchen standards, 1 cup of all-purpose flour should weigh 5 ounces. An equal amount of cake flour weighs 4 ounces. Granulated sugar and packed brown sugar weigh 7 ounces per cup.

TASTING LAB: Chocolate Ice Cream

IT'S HARD TO IMAGINE "BAD" CHOCOLATE ICE cream. But as any ice cream lover knows, some brands are a lot better than others. We tested seven leading brands to find out which ones have the scoop on the competition.

We found two clear winners—Häagen-Dazs and Double Rainbow, both of which were praised for their "intense" chocolate flavor and rich, creamy, dense texture. Both of these brands have a low overrun, a technical term that indicates how much air has been pumped into the ice cream during processing. Kids may want something sweeter and fluffier, but our adult tasters were in chocolate heaven.

The rest of the field ranged from "pretty good" to "barely decent." Tasters generally panned the fluffy-style ice creams sold in half-gallon containers. Yes, they are a lot cheaper than the good stuff that comes in small pint or quart containers, but then again you're paying for a lot of air. More important, brands at the bottom of our rankings did not pack enough chocolate flavor. If you want something cold and sweet, buy vanilla. But we think if you're going to buy chocolate ice cream, you'd better be able to taste the chocolate.

Rating Chocolate Ice Creams

TWENTY-EIGHT MEMBERS OF THE *COOK'S ILLUSTRATED* STAFF TASTED ALL SEVEN ICE CREAMS. THE ICE CREAMS ARE LISTED in order of preference based on their scores in this tasting. All brands are available in supermarkets.

RECOMMENDED

Häagen-Dazs Chocolate Ice Cream

$5.29 for 1 quart

Tasters responded to the "intense bittersweet chocolate" flavor and smooth, "dense" texture of this familiar premium brand. Several panelists praised the "lovely, fresh milk" flavor.

RECOMMENDED

Double Rainbow Ultra Chocolate Ice Cream

$3.49 for 1 quart

"Dark" chocolate flavor with a "clean" finish was the general consensus about this brand. The texture was described as "eggy" and "creamy." Not as potent as Häagen-Dazs but still an excellent value.

RECOMMENDED WITH RESERVATIONS

Brigham's Chocolate Ice Cream

$3.59 for 1 quart

Tasters liked this "refreshing but potent" ice cream, but it was deemed "too sweet" and "airy."

RECOMMENDED WITH RESERVATIONS

365 Every Day Value Chocolate Ice Cream

$4.49 for a half gallon

This store brand from Whole Foods markets was downgraded for its "robust cocoa powder" flavor and "gummy, powdery" texture.

RECOMMENDED WITH RESERVATIONS

Turkey Hill Dutch Chocolate Ice Cream

$2.50 for a half gallon

Tasters thought this inexpensive brand was "too sweet" and "artificial."

RECOMMENDED WITH RESERVATIONS

Breyers Chocolate Ice Cream

$3.99 for a half gallon

This popular brand received low scores for its "mild chocolate flavor" that reminded one taster of "cake batter." Tasters also panned the "icy" and "quick-to-melt" texture.

RECOMMENDED WITH RESERVATIONS

Edy's Grand Chocolate Ice Cream

$3.99 for a half gallon

Tasters compared the flavor to "chocolate milk" or "soft-serve" ice cream. Several complained about "malty," "artificial" flavor.

ANGEL FOOD CAKE

WHAT WE WANTED: A tall, perfectly shaped angel food cake with a snowy-white, tender crumb, encased in a thin, delicate, golden crust.

Although most angel food cakes contain no more than six ingredients, there are literally hundreds of variations on this basic theme. The type of flour used, the baking temperature, the type of sugar, and even the use of baking powder—a serious transgression, according to most experts—are all in dispute. What is not in dispute is that angel food cake requires a delicate balance of ingredients and proper cooking techniques. If leavened with just beaten egg whites (as is the custom), this cake can be fickle.

An angel food cake is distinguished by its lack of egg yolks, chemical leaveners, and fat. Other cakes also use beaten egg whites for leaveners, but there are differences. Chiffon cake contains egg yolks, which makes for a slightly heavier, moister cake. Sponge cake also includes whole or separated eggs; it, too, is denser and more yellow than angel food cake.

The six ingredients found in every angel food cake are egg whites, sugar, flour, cream of tartar, salt, and flavorings. Most recipes start by beating the egg whites. Mixer speed is critical for well-beaten whites. We found that starting at high speed will produce quick but inconsistent results. To create the most stable foam, beat the whites at low speed to break them up into a froth. Add the cream of tartar and salt, increase the speed to medium, and beat until the whites form very soft, billowy mounds. When large bubbles stop appearing around the edges, and with the mixer still on medium, add the sugar, a tablespoon at a time, until all the sugar has been incorporated and the whites are shiny and form soft peaks when the beater is lifted. The mass should still flow slightly when the bowl is tilted. Do not beat until the peaks are stiff; we found that this makes it difficult to fold in the flour, deflating the whites and therefore reducing volume.

Because there is no fat in angel food cake, sugar is critical to its taste and texture. We tested confectioners' sugar and found that the cornstarch in it makes the cake too dense. Superfine sugar is simply too fine, making a soft cake with little substance. We found that granulated sugar is best in this recipe.

Flour sets the cake batter, but because it also adds weight, the flour should be as light and airy as possible. We found that cake flour, which is finer than all-purpose flour, is easier to incorporate into the beaten whites without deflating them. The lower protein content of cake flour results in a more delicate, tender crumb, which we preferred. No matter what kind of flour is used, we found sifting to be essential; it makes the flour lighter in texture and easier to incorporate into the whites. Sift the flour twice—once before measuring and once before adding it to the beaten whites—for maximum lightness.

Egg whites, sugar, flour, and cream of tartar will produce a good-looking angel food cake that is sweet but bland. Salt is added for flavor and also helps stabilize the beaten whites. Other common additions are vanilla and almond extract (we like to use both), which add flavor without changing the basic chemistry of the batter. You can add grated citrus zest or a little citrus juice; we prefer the latter because zest can mar the perfectly soft texture and white color of the cake. We found that high-fat flavorings, such as grated chocolate and nuts, greatly affect the cake's texture, and we prefer to stick with simpler flavorings.

We tried using some baking powder for added leavening and stability but found that the resulting cake was not as white and had a coarser crumb. Adding baking powder also felt like cheating. If you separate and beat the egg whites properly, there should be no need to add baking powder.

Our most intriguing experiment involved oven temperatures. We baked the same recipe in the same pan at 300, 325, 350, and 375 degrees, baking each cake until it

tested done with a skewer and the top bounced back when pressed lightly. Surprisingly, all the cakes cooked evenly, but those baked at 350 and 375 degrees had a thicker, darker crust, while the cakes baked at 300 and 325 degrees had a more desirable, delicate, evenly pale golden crust. After many taste tests, we decided that 325 degrees was the ideal temperature.

The best tool we found to remove an angel food cake from the pan is a thin, flexible, nonserrated knife that is at least five inches long. Tilt the pan at a right angle to the counter to make it easy to work the knife around the sides. Insert the knife between the crust and the pan, pressing hard against the side of the pan, and work your way all around the cake. To cut around the central core of the pan, use a long, thin skewer. Invert the pan so that the cake slides out, then peel off the parchment or waxed paper. If using a pan with a removable bottom, slide the knife blade between the cake and the sides of the pan to release it. Present the cake sitting on its wide, crustier top, with the delicate and more easily sliced bottom crust facing up.

To cut the cake, use a long, serrated knife and pull it back and forth with a gentle sawing motion. When we tried using the specially made tool for cutting angel food cake—a row of prongs attached to a bar—it mashed and squashed this tender cake.

WHAT WE LEARNED: Beat the egg whites to soft peaks (not stiff peaks) so it's easier to incorporate the flour. Add cream of tartar and sugar to the egg whites to help stabilize them. For an ethereal texture, use cake flour (rather than all-purpose) and sift it twice.

ANGEL FOOD CAKE

Serves 10 to 12

Sift both the cake flour and the granulated sugar before measuring to eliminate any lumps and ensure the lightest possible texture.

1	cup (3 ounces) sifted plain cake flour
1½	cups (10½ ounces) sifted sugar
12	large egg whites (1¾ cups plus 2 tablespoons), at room temperature
1	teaspoon cream of tartar
¼	teaspoon salt
1½	teaspoons vanilla extract
1½	teaspoons juice from 1 lemon
½	teaspoon almond extract

1. Adjust an oven rack to the lower-middle position and heat the oven to 325 degrees. Have ready an ungreased large tube pan (9-inch diameter, 16-cup capacity), preferably with a removable bottom. If the pan bottom is not removable, line it with parchment paper or waxed paper.

Q&A

What's the best way to separate yolks from whites?

Many recipes, especially for cakes, call for room-temperature eggs. For example, angel food cake should be made with room temperature egg whites. But separating room-temperature eggs can be tricky, as the warm yolks can easily break and fall into the whites. Yolks are much more taut and less apt to break into the whites when cold. Always separate eggs straight from the refrigerator and then bring the eggs to room temperature if necessary. Also, it's always a good idea to separate each egg over a smaller bowl before adding the yolk and white to another bowl. That way, if a yolk breaks into a white, it won't ruin a big bowl of whites.

---

2. Whisk the flour and ¾ cup of the sugar in a small bowl. Place the remaining ¾ cup sugar in another small bowl next to the mixer.

3. In the bowl of a standing mixer, or with a handheld mixer, beat the egg whites at low speed until just broken up and beginning to froth. Add the cream of tartar and salt and beat at medium speed until the whites form very soft, billowy mounds. With the mixer still at medium speed, beat in the ¾ cup sugar, 1 tablespoon at a time, until all the sugar is added and the whites are shiny and form soft peaks. Add the vanilla, lemon juice, and almond extract and beat until just blended.

4. Place the flour-sugar mixture in a sifter set over waxed paper. Sift the flour-sugar mixture over the whites, about 3 tablespoons at a time, and gently fold in, using a large rubber spatula. Sift any flour-sugar mixture that falls onto the paper back into the bowl with the whites.

5. Gently scrape the batter into the pan, smooth the top with a spatula, and give the pan a couple of raps on the counter to release any large air bubbles.

6. Bake until the cake is golden brown and the top springs back when pressed firmly, 50 to 60 minutes.

7. If the cake pan has prongs around the rim for elevating the cake, invert the pan onto them. If the pan does not have prongs, invert the pan onto the neck of a bottle or funnel. Let the cake cool completely, 2 to 3 hours.

8. To unmold, run a knife around the edges of the pan, being careful not to separate the golden crust from the cake. Slide the cake out of the pan and cut the same way around the removable bottom to release, or peel off the parchment or waxed paper, if using. Place the cake, bottom-side up, on a platter. Cut slices by sawing gently with a large serrated knife. Serve the cake the day it is made.

Q&A

Is it necessary to sift presifted flour?

Flour companies sift their product to remove lumps and any foreign material. At home, bakers sift to aerate flour so that it will blend more easily into a batter. (Unsifted flour takes longer to incorporate into delicate batters and can lead to overmixing.) Presifted flour will become compact during shipping and should be sifted again if a recipe calls for sifted flour. This is especially important when making cakes.

Some recipes call for sifting dry ingredients in order to mix them evenly. This is especially true of older cookie recipes. We find this is unnecessary and instead use a wire whisk to combine dry ingredients for cookies. In this case, unsifted flour won't cause the dough to deflate or lose volume.

EQUIPMENT CORNER: Bundt Pans

UTTERLY SIMPLE TO MAKE, YET POSSESSING A DELICATE elegance, the Bundt cake is a staple of any bake sale or neighborhood get-together. Unlike other cakes, Bundt cakes need no adornment; their distinct shape and texture speak volumes about their content. So what makes this cake so special? Bundt pans, which were introduced by NordicWare (which is still in possession of the registered trademark) in the 1950s, are based on the traditional cast-iron kugelhopf molds of Eastern Europe. What defined kugelhopf cakes was the distinctive, decorative shape that the molds imparted on the dough. This tradition has continued, and to this day, more so than in any other savory or sweet preparation, the pan is the defining characteristic of a Bundt cake. Of course, quality ingredients and a great technique will dictate the cake's flavor, but only the perfect pan can create this distinctively ridged loaf with its perfectly bronzed, symmetrical curves. Having baked quite a few cakes in our time, we understand that not all pans are created equal, so we set out to find a Bundt pan capable of generating a beautiful and delicious cake worthy of its esteemed history.

In our search for pan perfection, we tested eight so-called nonstick pans that ranged in price from $9.99 to $27.99. Each pan had a simple ridged design and a minimum capacity of 12 cups. In order to assess their performance, we baked both our chocolate Bundt cake and a vanilla pound cake in each pan. Aside from evenness and depth of browning, the ease of release was our top concern. All of the chocolate cakes released easily, but some of the pound cakes did stick, most notably in the Kaiser ($17.99), Calphalon ($24.99), and NordicWare Bubble ($9.99). All of the pound cakes baked properly, but cooking times deviated by as much as 10 minutes and some of the cakes were not evenly browned—the Silicone Zone Pan ($19.99) baked a cake with no color at all. The KitchenAid ($24.99), Exeter ($14.99), Silicone Zone, and Kaiser lost points for design flaws—specifically, an unsightly crease where the center tube and the ring were joined. The NordicWare Platinum ($27.99) took top honors for best shape, deepest and most evenly browned exterior, and easiest release. The runner-up was the Baker's Secret, picked up at our local supermarket for a mere $11.99. Although it was made of lightweight material, it passed all of our tests with above-average results.

Rating Bundt Pans

WE TESTED EIGHT BUNDT PANS WITH A MINIMUM CAPACITY OF 12 CUPS. IN ADDITION TO PREPARING OUR chocolate Bundt cake in each pan, we baked vanilla pound cakes to test for evenness and depth of browning as well as ease of release. The pans are listed in order of preference. See www.americastestkitchen.com for up-to-date prices and mail-order sources for top-rated products.

HIGHLY RECOMMENDED
NordicWare Platinum Series, 12-Cup Bundt Pan
$27.99

Thick, durable, cast aluminum produced even browning and a clean, well-defined shape. The most expensive pan tested, but a winner across the board.

RECOMMENDED
Baker's Secret Non-Stick Fluted Tube Pan
$11.99

The best buy of the group, this inexpensive pan outperformed most others, including more expensive pans.

RECOMMENDED WITH RESERVATIONS
NordicWare "Colors," Bubble Non-Stick
$9.99

This flimsy pan had a nice shape but lost points in release tests.

RECOMMENDED WITH RESERVATIONS
Exeter Fluted 10-Inch Pan
$14.99

This poorly designed pan had decent browning but some sticking problems.

RECOMMENDED WITH RESERVATIONS
KitchenAid Fluted Cake Pan
$24.99

A wide rim made for easy handling, but the exterior was very slippery.

RECOMMENDED WITH RESERVATIONS
Kaiser Noblesse Bundform, 12-Cup Non-Stick
$17.99

Cakes clung to this lightweight pan with barely detectable ridges.

NOT RECOMMENDED
Calphalon Crown Bund Pan, Commercial Non-Stick
$24.99

Non-stick? Not in our tests. Cakes stuck seriously to this weighty pan, and they also failed to brown evenly.

NOT RECOMMENDED
Silicone Zone Bundform Pan
$19.99

This pliable pan was hard to handle and produced cakes with flattened tops. Because this pan is silicone and heat resistant, it does not brown the cake.

Jack explains the results of our cream cheese tasting as Chris tries several samples.

PUMPKIN cheesecake

Pumpkin cheesecake stands second to the traditional pumpkin pie as a holiday dessert. Those who suffer from pumpkin pie ennui embrace pumpkin cheesecake as "a nice change," but the expectations are low.

Undoubtedly, pumpkin cheesecake can be good in its own right, though it rarely is. The tendency is for extremes in texture—dry, dense, chalky cakes or wet, soft, mousse-like ones. Flavors veer from far too cheesy and tangy or pungently overspiced to noxiously sweet or totally bland. Merely mixing a can of pumpkin into a standard cheesecake batter doesn't work; the texture is amiss (leaden and sloppy), and the pumpkin flavor is thwarted. And then there are soggy, grease-leaching crumb crusts—a common problem in most every recipe we tried.

The promise of this recipe is so high, so we were willing to get to work. But we never figured it would take 30 cheesecakes—that's more than 11,000 grams of fat and 150,000 calories—to develop a great recipe worthy of the finest holiday dinner.

IN THIS CHAPTER

THE RECIPES

Spiced Pumpkin Cheesecake
Pumpkin-Bourbon Cheesecake
    with Graham-Pecan Crust
Brown Sugar and Bourbon Cream

SCIENCE DESK

Is a Water Bath Worth the
    Trouble?

TASTING LAB

Cream Cheese

PUMPKIN CHEESECAKE

WHAT WE WANTED: A creamy cheesecake with a velvety smooth texture that tasted of sweet, earthy pumpkin as well as tangy cream cheese. And, of course, it had to have a crisp, buttery, cookie-crumb crust.

Pumpkin cheesecake has two distinct components—a crumb crust and a lush cream cheese filling. To make a crumb crust for pumpkin cheesecake, our options were ground-up vanilla wafers, animal crackers, gingersnaps, and graham crackers. The first two were too mild-flavored for the spicy filling. Gingersnaps were well liked for their spicy bittersweet molasses notes, which balanced well against the pumpkin flavor of the cake, but no matter the brand or the amount of butter and sugar we added—and despite prebaking—they refused to form a crust that retained its crispness.

With graham crackers we had success. Five ounces of crackers (nine whole ones), crushed to crumbs, formed a substantial crust. Too little butter and the crust was not cohesive; 6 tablespoons was just the right amount. Too little sugar and the crust was not adequately sweet; 3 tablespoons was a good amount. Pressed into the bottom of the springform pan and baked until browned around the edges, the graham crackers formed a sturdy, crisp, buttery crust. (Without prebaking, the crust became a pasty, soggy layer beneath the filling.) We then replaced the granulated sugar with dark brown sugar to replicate the molasses flavor of the gingersnaps, but the sugar's moisture caused sogginess, so we went back to granulated. To increase spiciness, we added doses of ground cinnamon, cloves, and ginger.

Anyone who has prepared fresh pumpkin for pumpkin pie can attest to the fact that cutting, seeding, peeling, and cooking fresh pumpkin is not time and effort well spent. Opening a can takes only a few seconds; preparing fresh pumpkin takes a few hours. Moreover, all pumpkin cheesecake recipes call for canned pumpkin.

With a working recipe pieced together, we found that one can of pumpkin and 1½ pounds of cream cheese made a tall, handsome cake with a balance of tang and earthy pumpkin flavor. We were using granulated sugar to sweeten the cheesecake, but we surmised that brown sugar, with its molasses flavor, would add depth and richness. We were wrong. Substituted for the entire amount of granulated sugar, brown sugar only mucked up and masked the flavor of the pumpkin while giving the cheesecake a dirty brown hue (this was especially true of dark brown sugar). We tried lesser and lesser amounts until eventually there was none.

According to recipes, most pumpkin cheesecakes, unlike plain ones, require neither sour cream nor heavy cream. No matter. We tried them both (after all, none of the recipes we had tried hit the mark). Sour cream, even in small amounts, was too assertive; its tang eclipsed the delicate flavor of the pumpkin. On the other hand, heavy cream—a cup of it—made the cheesecake feel and taste smooth and lush. It seemed to mitigate the slightly mealy fibrousness of the pumpkin and enrich the cheesecake without obscuring the pumpkin flavor. It did, however, affect the texture, making it loose and soft. Not wanting to compromise the richness, we attempted to remedy the problem by adjusting the eggs, but to no avail. We then tried flour and cornstarch in hopes that one would absorb excess moisture, but both resulted in a starchy, pasty, unappealing texture.

As we were reevaluating heavy cream as an essential ingredient, a colleague suggested cooking the pumpkin before adding it to the cheesecake. It then occurred to us that if we could remove some moisture from the pumpkin, perhaps we could improve the texture. We emptied a can of pumpkin into a nonstick skillet and cooked it until it had lost a surprising amount of moisture—nearly five ounces, or more than half a cup. The cheesecake made with this "dried" pumpkin had a thick, plush, velvety texture to match its rich flavor.

The downside to cooking the pumpkin, which involved frequent stirring and then a cooling period, was that it meant paying the pumpkin more attention than we wanted. Simply draining it did not work. In our numerous dealings with canned pumpkin, we noticed that it had cohesion and a nonstick quality. We spread the pumpkin onto a baking sheet lined with paper towels—like spreading frosting on a cake—and then pressed additional paper towels down on its surface to wick away more moisture. In seconds, the pumpkin shed enough liquid (about four ounces) to yield a cheesecake with a lovely texture, and the paper towels were peeled away almost effortlessly.

With the essential ingredients determined, we turned to eggs. After making some 10 cheesecakes with different amounts of egg in various configurations (whole eggs, egg whites, and egg yolks), we had discovered a surprising range of textures, from stiff and dry to waxy. Five whole eggs produced our favorite cheesecake, one that was satiny, creamy, and unctuous.

Finally, we worked on refining the flavorings. Vanilla and salt were good additions, as was a tablespoon of lemon juice for brightness. Sweet, warm cinnamon was favored at the fore; sharp, spicy ground ginger and small amounts of cloves, nutmeg, and allspice produced, in unison, a deep,

resounding flavor but not an overspiced burn.

In its springform pan, a cheesecake can be baked either directly on the oven rack like a regular cake or in a water bath like a delicate custard. The cake baked in a water bath was undeniably better than the version baked without a water bath. (For more information, see page 323.) We tried a few different oven temperatures, and 325 degrees worked best. At higher temperatures, the water in the bath reached a simmer; at lower temperatures the cheesecake took an inordinate amount of time to bake.

We sliced the cheesecake into neat wedges and served it with bourbon-and-brown-sugar-laced whipped cream (many at first decried this as over-the-top, but they were silenced after a single taste). At last, here was a pumpkin cheesecake that pleased the pumpkin pie traditionalists and that for the others was a nice change from "a nice change."

WHAT WE LEARNED: Start with a basic graham cracker crust that is flavored with ground ginger, cinnamon, and cloves. For the filling, dry canned pumpkin on paper towels to remove excess moisture and rely on heavy cream—not sour cream—for added richness. Add pumpkin-friendly spices to the filling and bake the cheesecake in a water bath for a smooth, creamy texture.

SPICED PUMPKIN CHEESECAKE

Serves 12 to 16

Depending on the oven and the temperature of the ingredients, this cheesecake may bake about 15 minutes faster or slower than the instructions indicate; it is therefore best to check the cake 1¼ hours into baking. Although the cheesecake can be made up to 3 days in advance, the crust will begin to lose its crispness after only 1 day. To make slicing the cheesecake easy and neat, use a knife with a narrow blade, such as a carving knife; between cuts, dip the blade into a pitcher of hot water and wipe it clean with paper towels. The cheesecake is good on its own, but the Brown Sugar and Bourbon Cream (recipe follows) is a grand addition.

crust

9	graham crackers (5 ounces), broken into large pieces
3	tablespoons sugar
½	teaspoon ground ginger
½	teaspoon ground cinnamon
¼	teaspoon ground cloves
6	tablespoons (¾ stick) unsalted butter, melted

filling

1⅓	cups (10⅓ ounces) sugar
1	teaspoon ground cinnamon
½	teaspoon ground ginger
¼	teaspoon ground nutmeg
¼	teaspoon ground cloves
¼	teaspoon ground allspice
½	teaspoon salt
1	(15-ounce) can pumpkin
1½	pounds cream cheese, cut into 1-inch chunks, at room temperature
1	tablespoon vanilla extract
1	tablespoon juice from 1 lemon
5	large eggs, at room temperature
1	cup heavy cream

1. FOR THE CRUST: Adjust an oven rack to the lower-middle position and heat the oven to 325 degrees. Spray the bottom and sides of a 9-inch springform pan evenly with nonstick cooking spray. Place the graham crackers, sugar, and spices in a food processor and process until evenly and finely ground, about fifteen 2-second pulses. Transfer the crumbs to a medium bowl, drizzle the melted butter over them, and mix with a rubber spatula until evenly moistened. Turn the crumbs into the prepared springform pan and spread the crumbs in an even layer, following the illustrations on page 321. Bake until fragrant and browned around the edges, about 15 minutes. Cool on a wire rack to room temperature, about 30 minutes. When cool, wrap the outside of the pan with two 18-inch-square pieces of heavy-duty foil; set the springform pan in a roasting pan.

2. FOR THE FILLING: Bring about 4 quarts water to a simmer in a stockpot. While the crust is cooling, whisk the sugar, spices, and salt in a small bowl; set aside. Line a baking sheet with a triple layer of paper towels. Spread the pumpkin on the towels and cover with a second triple layer of towels. Press firmly until the towels are saturated. Peel back the top layer of towels and discard. Grasp the bottom towels and fold the pumpkin in half; peel back the towels. Repeat and flip the pumpkin onto the baking sheet; discard the towels.

3. In the bowl of a standing mixer, or with a handheld mixer, beat the cream cheese at medium speed to break up and soften slightly, about 1 minute. Scrape the beater and the bottom and sides of the bowl well with a rubber spatula. Add about a third of the sugar mixture and beat at medium-low speed until combined, about 1 minute; scrape the bowl and add the remaining sugar in two additions, scraping the bowl after each addition. Add the pumpkin, vanilla, and lemon juice and beat at medium speed until combined, about 45 seconds; scrape the bowl. Add 3 of the eggs and beat at medium-low speed until incorporated, about 1 minute; scrape the bowl. Add the remaining 2 eggs and beat at medium-low speed until incorporated, about 45 seconds; scrape the bowl. Add the heavy cream and beat at low speed until combined, about 45 seconds. Using a rubber spatula, scrape the bottom and sides of the bowl and give a final stir by hand.

4. Pour the filling into the springform pan and smooth the surface; set the roasting pan in the oven and pour enough boiling water to come about halfway up the sides of the springform pan. Bake until the center of the cake is slightly wobbly when the pan is shaken and the center of the cake reads 150 degrees on an instant-read thermometer, about 1½ hours (see note). Set the roasting pan on a wire rack and cool until the water is just warm, about 45 minutes. Remove the springform pan from the water bath, discard the foil, and set on a wire rack; run a paring knife around the inside edge of the pan to loosen the sides of the cake and cool until barely warm, about 3 hours. Wrap with plastic wrap and refrigerate until chilled, at least 4 hours or up to 3 days.

5. TO SERVE: Remove the sides of the pan. Slide a thin metal spatula between the crust and pan bottom to loosen, then slide the cake onto a serving platter. Let the cheesecake stand at room temperature about 30 minutes, then cut into wedges (see note) and serve with Brown Sugar and Bourbon Cream, if desired.

PUMPKIN-BOURBON CHEESECAKE WITH GRAHAM-PECAN CRUST

Follow the recipe for Spiced Pumpkin Cheesecake, reducing the graham crackers to 3 ounces (5 whole crackers), processing 2 ounces chopped pecans (about ½ cup) with the crackers, and reducing the butter to 4 tablespoons. Omit the lemon juice from the filling, reduce the vanilla extract to 1 teaspoon, and add ¼ cup bourbon along with the heavy cream.

TECHNIQUE:
Pressing the Crumbs into the Pan

1. Use the bottom of a ramekin or drinking glass to press the crumbs into the bottom of a buttered springform pan. Press the crumbs as far as possible into the edges of the pan.

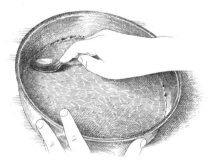

2. Use a teaspoon to neatly press the crumbs into the corners of the pan to create a clean edge.

BROWN SUGAR AND BOURBON CREAM

Makes about 3 cups

1	cup heavy cream
½	cup sour cream
⅓	cup (2⅓ ounces) packed light brown sugar
⅛	teaspoon salt
2	teaspoons bourbon

1. In the bowl of a standing mixer or with a handheld mixer, whisk the heavy cream, sour cream, brown sugar, and salt until combined. Cover with plastic wrap and refrigerate until ready to serve the cheesecake, at least 4 hours or up to 24, stirring once or twice during chilling to ensure that the sugar dissolves.

2. When ready to serve the cheesecake, add the bourbon and beat the mixture at medium speed until small bubbles form around the edges, about 40 seconds; increase the speed to high and continue to beat until fluffy and doubled in volume, about 1 minute longer. Spoon the cream onto individual slices of cheesecake.

TECHNIQUE: Chilling the Bowl to Make Whipped Cream

For the best results, you should chill a bowl before whipping cream in it. For many cooks, the freezer is either too small or too full to accommodate a large bowl. Here's how to accomplish this task outside of the freezer.

1. At least 15 minutes before whipping the cream, fill the bowl with ice cubes and cold water and place the whisk (or beaters from an electric mixer) in the ice water.

2. When ready to whip the cream, dump out the ice water, dry the bowl and whisk, and add the cream. The bowl will stay cold as you work, and the cream will whip up beautifully.

SCIENCE DESK:
Is a Water Bath Worth the Trouble?

A WATER BATH IS COMMONLY CALLED FOR IN THE BAKING of cheesecakes and custards. The theory is that a water bath moderates the temperature around the perimeter of the pan, preventing overcooking at the edges. To figure out exactly what's happening, we prepared two identical cheesecakes and baked one directly on the oven rack and the other in a water bath. Both were removed from the oven when their centers reached 147 degrees. The cake that had been baked in a water bath was even-colored and smooth; the other cake was browned and cracked. A quick comparison of the temperature at the edges of the cakes confirmed what we suspected. Upon removal from the oven, the cake that had had the benefit of a water bath was 184 degrees at the edges, whereas the edges of the cake baked without the water bath had climbed to 213 degrees.

Why was the cheesecake baked in a water bath 30 degrees cooler at the edges than the cake baked without a water bath? Although in both cases the oven had been set to 325 degrees, a water bath cannot exceed 212 degrees, as this is the temperature at which water converts to steam.

Why did the cheesecake baked in the water bath have an even and uncracked top? By moderating the temperature of the cheesecake, the water bath prevented the cheesecake top from inflating like a soufflé. In addition, the water bath added considerable moisture to the oven (more than four cups of water evaporated from the bath during cooking). The added moisture helped to keep the top of the cake supple, which discourages cracking.

TASTING LAB: Cream Cheese

SUPERMARKET SHELVES AREN'T EXACTLY OVERFLOWING with cream cheese options. Whenever we need cream cheese in the test kitchen, we instinctively reach for Philadelphia brand. But is Philadelphia the best or just the most familiar and widely available?

To find out, we gathered all the types of cream cheese we could find: a paltry five, three of which were Philadelphia products (Philadelphia ⅓ Less Fat, Philadelphia Whipped, and original Philadelphia); the other two were organic brands. We tasted them plain and in our New York Cheesecake—we figured the flavors in our Spiced Pumpkin Cheesecake would be distracting.

Tasters judged the cream cheeses on richness, tanginess, creaminess, and overall quality, and one product swept both the plain and cheesecake tastings in all categories: Philadelphia. Though some liked the easy spreadability of Philadelphia Whipped (we let the tasters try the cream cheese on bagels after they tasted each sample plain) and most were enthusiastic about buttery Organic Valley (our second-place finisher), overall the familiar Philadelphia held its place as the cream cheese of choice in the test kitchen.

GETTING IT RIGHT:
Most Cheesecakes Need a Water Bath

A water bath guarantees a cheesecake with a smooth, creamy texture. We baked two cheesecakes until the center reached 147 degrees. One was baked with a water bath; the other without. Note the differences in temperature at the edges of these two pieces. See Science Desk above for an explanation.

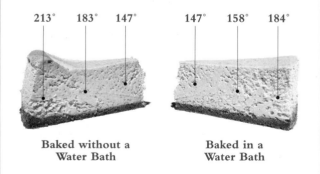

213°   183°   147°   147°   158°   184°

Baked without a
Water Bath

Baked in a
Water Bath

Although Philadelphia was the clear winner, all but one of the products tasted are recommended. Despite our hopes to the contrary, Philadelphia ⅓ Less Fat tanked, coming in last. While we would have been thrilled to offer low-fat cream cheese as a suitable substitution in our cheesecakes, the artificial flavor and stiff texture forced it out of consideration.

Q&A

How do you prevent cheesecakes from cracking?

Cracks are usually caused by overbaking and can be avoided by removing the cheesecake from the oven when the internal temperature taken on an instant-read thermometer reads 150 degrees. Running a paring knife around the inside of the springform pan as soon as the cheesecake comes out of the oven is also a good idea; if the edges stick to the pan, a crack can form as the cheesecake cools and shrinks.

Note that if you take the temperature of the cheesecake multiple times you can do more harm than good. Puncturing the surface again and again will weaken the structure of the cheesecake and can cause cracks. Consequently, we recommend that you take the temperature of the cheesecake only once or, if necessary, take the temperature again through the initial thermometer hole at the center of the cake. You can eliminate this risk altogether by taking the temperature of the cheesecake from the side, approaching the center through the part of the cheesecake that rises above the pan.

Rating Cream Cheeses

FIFTEEN MEMBERS OF THE *COOK'S ILLUSTRATED* STAFF TASTED ALL OF THE CREAM CHEESES BOTH PLAIN AND baked in our New York Cheesecake. The cream cheeses are listed in order of preference based on their combined scores in the two tastings. All brands are available in supermarkets.

RECOMMENDED

Philadelphia Original Cream Cheese

$1.99 for 8 ounces

"Milky" and "very flavorful" was the overall assessment of this supermarket staple. This classic choice won both the plain and the cheesecake tastings, earning high marks for its creamy texture.

RECOMMENDED

Organic Valley Organic Cream Cheese

$2.45 for 8 ounces

Tasters called this sample "mild," "buttery," and "slightly waxy." It finished a strong second in the cheesecake tasting and was tied for second in the plain tasting. In both cases, panelists praised its creamy texture.

RECOMMENDED

Horizon Organic Spreadable Cream Cheese

$1.99 for 8 ounces

"Bland" and "not bad" was the general consensus about this brand, which performed better in the cheesecake tasting than when sampled plain.

RECOMMENDED

Philadelphia Whipped Cream Cheese

$2.99 for 12 ounces

Tasters liked the tangy flavor of this product but complained about its airy consistency. One taster wrote, "light texture—not what I want in a cream cheese." This sample fared better in the plain tasting than when baked in the cheesecake.

NOT RECOMMENDED

Philadelphia ⅓ Less Fat Than Cream Cheese

$1.99 for 8 ounces

"Chalky" and "pasty" were the two most common complaints about this reduced-calorie, reduced-fat Neufchâtel cheese. It fared OK in the plain tasting (although tasters wanted more creaminess), but tasters felt it compromised the quality of the cheesecake.

Our individual chocolate volcano cakes can be portioned into baking dishes a day in advance and then baked as needed.

FOUR-STAR desserts

When our test cooks eat in restaurants, they always come back to the kitchen and talk about the dessert. Dramatic and artful presentations rightfully garner a lot of attention. But we're most interested in how these desserts taste. Many modern pastry chefs include several components in their desserts, offering a mix of flavors, textures, and temperatures on one plate. These creations seem light-years ahead of the usual pies, cakes, and cookies we usually serve at home. But are they?

Over the years, we've discovered several spectacular four-star desserts that are actually pretty simple, at least in theory. Our goal was to identify two such modern classics and figure out ways to make them even more approachable for the home cook.

The first dessert, a molten chocolate cake paired with an espresso ice cream bombe, is a fresh interpretation of a well-worn (and sometimes tired) restaurant classic. The second dessert is more exotic. It starts with the common pairing of blue cheese and pears but then cooks the pears and uses a caramel sauce flavored with black pepper to unite the two main elements. Novel flavors with dramatic presentation. Could we really make these desserts suitable for a weekend dinner party?

CHOCOLATE VOLCANO CAKES WITH ESPRESSO ICE CREAM

WHAT WE WANTED: A warm chocolate cake with an intense chocolate flavor, served with a cooling scoop of equally potent espresso ice cream.

Restaurant menus often offer a molten chocolate cake, but we have had our share of bad molten cakes—usually raw-tasting and soggy or reheated and stale. That said, we were impressed with a version from Ixora restaurant in Whitehouse Station, New Jersey. Served straight out of the oven with a hot, rich, liquidy center, Ixora tempers its intensely flavored cake by serving a tiny, chocolate-coated, ice cream bombe alongside. The dramatic range in temperatures, powerful chocolate punch, and visual appeal make this dessert appear far more difficult and time-consuming than it really is. Using a durable cake batter and a minimal number of ingredients, this dessert can largely be prepared up to 24 hours in advance.

Combining the features of both a brownie and a fallen chocolate cake, the exterior walls of the individual cakes are toothsome and sturdy while the centers are smooth and creamy, and the tops become shiny and appealingly cracked as they bake. The batter has a high proportion of sugar and chocolate, like a fudgy brownie, yet the cake gets its basic structure from eggs and egg yolks, much like a fallen chocolate cake. The original recipe called for extra-bittersweet chocolate, which is somewhat difficult to find. We approximated the intense flavor by using both a supermarket bittersweet chocolate and a few ounces of unsweetened chocolate. With a little cornstarch to stabilize the chocolate and a complete absence of both chemical leavening (such as baking powder or soda) and whipped eggs (which could deflate over time), this batter has been engineered to be unfailingly successful regardless of how hot, hectic, or harried the restaurant's kitchen might get.

We found it easiest to portion the batter into individual ramekins as soon as it was mixed. The cakes can then be either baked right away or wrapped tightly with plastic wrap, refrigerated, and baked straight from the refrigerator at a moment's notice. Although the cakes could be served right in their ramekins, we preferred to unmold them onto individual plates so they could nuzzle up to the ice cream. To help the cakes fall right out of the hot ramekins without a struggle, we found it helpful to butter and sugar the ramekins before pouring in the batter.

Offering bites of relief from the intense, lava-hot cakes, the ice cream bombes are small domes of espresso ice cream coated with a thin shell of hardened chocolate, like a bonbon. After attempting to replicate these morsels on several occasions, we realized that this is one task best left to professionals. In order to thinly coat the ice cream, we found it took multiple dips into chocolate that was melted to a very specific temperature. If done any other way, the chocolate coating either became too thick or slid right off the ice cream. Instead, we liked a scoop of the espresso ice cream placed on the plate next to the hot cake.

The restaurant makes its own espresso ice cream, but in the spirit of home cooking, we found it just as satisfying to mix finely ground espresso beans into coffee-flavored ice cream. After the ice cream is softened on the counter for a few minutes, the ground espresso can be folded in using a rubber spatula. Lastly, we noted that a sprinkling of confectioners' sugar over the cake and plate not only helped prevent the scoop of ice cream from sliding around but also made the dessert look truly impressive.

WHAT WE LEARNED: Duplicate the flavor of hard-to-find extra-bittersweet chocolate by combining regular bittersweet chocolate with a little unsweetened chocolate. Cornstarch makes the batter remarkably stable and ensures that the cakes rise in the oven. To approximate the intense flavor of the restaurant's espresso ice cream, simply fold some finely ground espresso beans into store-bought coffee ice cream.

CHOCOLATE VOLCANO CAKES WITH ESPRESSO ICE CREAM

Serves 8

Use a bittersweet bar chocolate in this recipe, not chips—the chips include emulsifiers that will alter the cakes' texture. The cake batter can be mixed and portioned into the ramekins, wrapped tightly with plastic wrap, and refrigerated up to 24 hours in advance. The cold cake batter should be baked straight from the refrigerator.

espresso ice cream

2	pints coffee ice cream, softened
1½	tablespoons finely ground espresso beans

cakes

10	tablespoons unsalted butter, cut into ½-inch pieces, plus more for buttering the ramekins
1½	cups (10½ ounces) granulated sugar, plus more for dusting the ramekins
8	ounces bittersweet chocolate, finely chopped
2	ounces unsweetened chocolate, finely chopped
2	tablespoons cornstarch
3	large eggs, at room temperature
4	large egg yolks, at room temperature
2	teaspoons Grand Marnier (or other orange-flavored liqueur)
	Confectioners' sugar, for dusting the cakes

1. FOR THE ICE CREAM: Transfer the ice cream to a medium bowl and, using a rubber spatula, fold in the ground espresso until incorporated. Press a sheet of plastic wrap flush against the ice cream (see the illustration on this page) to prevent freezer burn and return it to the freezer. (The ice cream can be prepared up to 24 hours ahead.)

2. FOR THE CAKES: Lightly coat eight 4-ounce ramekins with butter. Dust with sugar, tapping out any excess, and set aside.

3. Melt the bittersweet and unsweetened chocolates and 10 tablespoons butter in a medium bowl over a medium saucepan of simmering water, stirring occasionally, until the chocolate mixture is smooth. In a large bowl, whisk the 1½ cups sugar and cornstarch together. Add the chocolate mixture and stir to combine. Add the eggs, egg yolks, and Grand Marnier and whisk until fully combined. Scoop ½ cup of the batter into each of the prepared ramekins. (The ramekins can be covered tightly with plastic wrap and refrigerated for up to 24 hours.)

4. Adjust an oven rack to the upper-middle position and heat the oven to 375 degrees. Place the filled ramekins on a rimmed baking sheet and bake until the tops of the cakes are set, have formed shiny crusts, and are beginning to crack, 16 to 20 minutes.

5. Transfer the ramekins to a wire rack and cool slightly, about 2 minutes. Run a paring knife around the edge of each cake. Using a towel to protect your hand from the hot ramekins, invert each cake onto a small plate, then immediately invert again right-side up onto 8 individual plates. Sift confectioners' sugar over each cake and the area of the plate where the ice cream will be placed. Remove the ice cream from the freezer and scoop a portion on top of the confectioners' sugar, next to the cake. Serve immediately.

> **TECHNIQUE:**
> **Keeping Ice Cream Fresh**
>
> To prevent ice crystals from forming on the ice cream, press plastic wrap flush against the surface of the ice cream before covering it with a lid.
>
>

EQUIPMENT CORNER:
Handheld Mixers

IN HEAD-TO-HEAD COMPETITIONS IN OUR TEST KITCHEN, standing mixers always outperform handheld mixers (see page 302 for details). Simply put, a standing mixer offers greater flexibility and versatility. The most obvious difference is brute force. Any decent standing mixer can knead bread dough, but even the best handheld mixer fails miserably at this task. A standing mixer also frees up the cook to take on other tasks. While these two advantages are dramatic, for many day-to-day uses, handheld and standing mixers are actually quite similar. When making cake batters and cookie doughs, whipping cream, and beating egg whites, we have found that a handheld mixer can yield the same results as a standing mixer, albeit a little more slowly.

In addition, a handheld mixer costs a fraction of a standing mixer, and it's also compact and easily transported. If your workspace or budget is restricted, a handheld mixer can prove most valuable, especially if you don't want a mixer for bread making and you don't mind standing by the bowl as the mixer does its work. But this calculation only makes sense if you invest in a good handheld mixer—and that's easier said than done.

Over the years, we've been disappointed by many handheld mixers; they can be little more than glorified whisks. And who hasn't encountered the disconcerting smoky odor of a handheld mixer's motor as the beaters slog their way through a particularly stiff dough? These experiences notwithstanding, the promise of a good handheld mixer—reliable performance easily had, and at a low cost—beckoned. And so we assembled eight leading models to see if we could separate the wimps from the workhorses.

Lack of power isn't the only complaint we've had with handheld mixers. With a standing mixer, splattering isn't much of an issue because the whisk sits deep into the bowl. A handheld mixer, however, can spray both the counter and the cook as the beaters whirl away. When whipping cream, we found that most mixers splattered on some level, but the best mixers kept the mess in the bowl; the worst managed to propel flecks of cream up to eye level, which was not appreciated.

All of the mixers were able to beat egg whites to stiff peaks. The main discrepancy resided in the "feel" of the mixer as it beat the whites; some felt unwieldy (and thus received a rating of "fair" on this task), while others felt controlled (and were rated "good"). We also found that certain beater styles were more efficient at beating egg whites. Actually, in recent years, many mixers have abandoned the old-style beaters with flat tines and a center post for a more streamlined wire beater without the hard-to-clean center post. Some manufacturers still offer both styles, while others are also throwing in a bonus whisk attachment. One model in our testing offered all three.

In our tests, we found that the wire beaters were the best choice as they were the most versatile of the three beater styles. They proved good for thin batters, thick doughs, and liquids and were the easiest to clean—by far. And not too far behind were the flat beaters with center posts (the classic attachment), which we found to be a decent choice. They creamed butter and sugar nicely, tending not to spread ingredients to the outskirts of the bowl. They also did a nice job beating egg whites quickly; however, the center post caused thick doughs to become clogged in the beaters. We did not like any of the whisk attachments tested. They were downright flimsy and inefficient and caused a significant amount of splattering.

On the whole, making pound cake seemed the perfect test for a mixer's effectiveness at creaming. Traditional pound cake contains no chemical leaveners; its rise comes from creaming the butter and sugar until they are light and fluffy. Proper aeration is key to avoiding an overly dense cake. The eight mixers tested made cakes that rose to heights within ¼ inch of one another—a range so negligible that this test counted for little in the overall ratings.

The test that really separated the winners from the losers was mixing peanut butter cookie dough. Unlike chocolate chip cookie dough, which is easy enough to mix by hand if necessary, thick, stiff peanut butter cookie dough requires a determined motor. Of the eight mixers tested, only the KitchenAid and the Braun did not hesitate once the dry ingredients were added to the sticky mix of peanut butter, eggs, and butter. Four of the mixers struggled but ultimately managed to tough it out as the dough began to come together or the mixing speed was increased. Two models could not complete this task and landed at the bottom of our ratings.

Somewhat to our surprise, wattage was not a good indicator of power. Of the mixers that fell into the run-of-the-mill category, one had the highest wattage of all eight mixers tested, another the lowest. KitchenAid, the maker of our winning mixer, did not even post the machine's wattage on its box or in its literature.

Because so many consumers judge the power of an appliance by its wattage, we asked KitchenAid about this. A representative explained that unlike most manufacturers, which use AC (alternating current) motors, KitchenAid uses a DC (direct current) motor, which it finds to be less heavy, less noisy, and more powerful than AC motors. The company also claims that this motor is more energy-efficient and requires less wattage to operate. (KitchenAid would not disclose the exact wattage required.) In sum, the KitchenAid representative said, wattage is not always the best measurement of power when buying small electrical appliances. Our science editor explained that wattage is a measure of input—the amount of power a motor is taking in to operate. If a motor is not designed to work efficiently, it can require more input, or wattage, without necessarily delivering more output—that is, a stronger performance.

Secondary to power, although still significant, was design. Most of the mixers weighed in at around 2 pounds, 2 ounces, but some felt much heavier than others and were more fatiguing to use. For example, mixers with angled handles let you relax your elbow at your side. Those with horizontal handles (parallel to the machine's body) make it necessary to lift your elbow in order to hold the machine

upright. This posture quickly proved tiring. Balance of weight and the shape of the handle grip also affected fatigue. The number of speeds didn't seem nearly as important as the range of power within those speeds. The Braun, for instance, with just three speeds, outperformed many models with seven speeds.

Both the KitchenAid and the Cuisinart came with an on/off switch, which we considered a welcome safety mechanism—just in case the machine gets plugged in before the beaters are inserted. We were also big fans of Oster's retractable cord (press a button and the cord automatically winds into the mixer's housing). A round cord design was also preferred to a flat cord with a crease up the center, because the former is much easier to wipe clean.

Overall—and as expected—most of the mixers we tested had their shortcomings. But the KitchenAid was the total package: powerful, quiet, controlled, and compact. It was a pleasure to use. Of course, this machine came with the highest price tag: $70. Braun, the runner-up, was cheaper by $20 but lacked the KitchenAid's finesse. Considering the proven versatility of this mixer and the fact that our favorite standing mixer sells for about $250, maybe $70 doesn't seem so unreasonable after all.

Rating Handheld Mixers

WE TESTED EIGHT HANDHELD MIXERS, EVALUATING EACH ACCORDING TO PRICE, ATTACHMENTS, DESIGN, AND performance in the following tests: whipping cream, beating egg whites, mixing pound cake batter, and mixing peanut butter cookie dough. The mixers are listed in order of preference. See www.americastestkitchen.com for up-to-date prices and mail-order sources for top-rated products.

HIGHLY RECOMMENDED

KitchenAid 7 Speed Artisan Mixer, Model KHM7T $69.99

This mixer never slowed or hesitated when mixing stiff peanut butter cookie dough. The mixing action was notably "neat," "smooth," and "controlled" compared with that of others. It took the longest of all mixers to whip cream and beat egg whites—admittedly, with barely any splattering.

HIGHLY RECOMMENDED

Braun MultiMix 4-in-1, Model M880 $49.99

This mixer worked through thick cookie dough without slowing. A total of three speeds could have felt limited if the rates didn't feel just right. A more angled handle with a narrower grip would have been more comfortable.

RECOMMENDED

Bosch TurboBeat Hand Mixer, Model MFQ2100UC $59.99

The beater design of this model is similar to Braun's and thus is extremely efficient at whipping. Its motor was quiet—"like a modern-day sewing machine"—and the overall operation felt smooth. The beaters slowed some when making cookie dough, but increasing the speed took care of this.

RECOMMENDED

Cuisinart SmartPower Electronic Hand Mixer, Model HTM-7L $49.95

An on/off switch, digital touchpad display, and good overall balance were clear design strengths of this mixer. It didn't "bite into the cookie dough," however, requiring the mixer to be pushed through the dough, at which point the beaters turned but didn't appear to be blending anything.

RECOMMENDED

Black & Decker PowerPro, Model #MX85 $19.99

This mixer began to smell when mixing peanut butter cookie dough. Increased speed helped, but the mixer still had to be pushed through the dough, as the beaters didn't grab it. It did just fine when it came to lighter jobs, such as whipping.

RECOMMENDED

Oster Easystore Hand Mixer, Model 2491 $24.99

The performance of this mixer was top-notch, but it couldn't handle the cookie dough, which became clogged inside the flat beaters. We loved the retractable cord for neat storage but found the handle hard to hold.

NOT RECOMMENDED

Hamilton Beach Power Deluxe Mixer, Model 62695 $29.99

The square edges on this mixer's wire beaters clanged and rattled against the sides of the bowl. Splatters from whipping cream reached eye level, and the beaters repeatedly bogged down in cookie dough as the motor emitted a burning odor. The mixer vibrated noticeably during use.

NOT RECOMMENDED

Farberware Hand Mixer, Model FPHM600 $24.99

While there was some bogging down of beaters during the cookie dough test, our biggest complaint was this mixer's tendency to fling ingredients around and out of the bowl. The handle was so thick that even a tester with large hands struggled to maintain his grip.

CARAMELIZED PEARS WITH BLUE CHEESE AND BLACK PEPPER–CARAMEL SAUCE

WHAT WE WANTED: A new spin on pears and cheese with caramelized, tender pears and a spicy caramel sauce.

When we first tasted this dessert from Tea Tray in the Sky in Cambridge, Massachusetts, we knew it was special. An updated version of the classic combination of pears and blue cheese, this dessert starts with pears that are caramelized, rendering them soft and golden. Although the pears are tasty on their own, it is the rich caramel sauce, surprisingly flavored with crushed black pepper, that really sets this dessert apart. Served on an early menu from the café, this incredible dessert sounded so delicious that we tracked down the chef and coerced the recipe from his memory.

At the café, the caramel sauce was made in advance, while the pears were cut, dipped in sugar, then seared in a hot nonstick pan to caramelize per order. This multipot method makes sense in a restaurant because it limits the amount of last-minute work during dinner service, but it

doesn't make sense for the home cook. To streamline the recipe, we found it easy to cook the pears right in the caramel sauce, saving time and eliminating some dirty dishes. We brought water and sugar (the basis for caramel sauce) to a boil in a skillet and slid the pears into the hot mixture and let them cook in the slowly browning caramel. Because this method actually cooks the pears in the sauce, we found it best to use firm pears that could take the extensive amount of heat. Also, we noted it was easiest to trim the bottom of the pears so that they stand upright on the plate before cooking them, as opposed to after.

With our first batch, we tried removing the pears from the pan before we stirred the heavy cream into the caramel to finish it. This didn't work so well: The pears turned unappetizingly sticky as they cooled, having been essentially cooked in sugar candy. For our next batch, we tried adding the cream to the pan around the pears as they finished caramelizing, which transformed the sticky sugar syrup into a smooth sauce that slid right off the pears. We let the pears drain for a few minutes on a wire rack set over a rimmed baking sheet before serving. After removing the pears, we were able to season the sauce left in the skillet with just the right amount of black pepper and salt.

The presentation of this elegant and sophisticated dessert can be as dramatic or casual as the mood dictates. Whether served individually with an attractive wedge of blue cheese and a fancy swirl of sauce or presented to the table family-style on a platter, passing the sauce and cheese separately, it is the surprising combination of flavors that makes this dessert so good.

WHAT WE LEARNED: Rather than making the caramel sauce in advance and cooking the pears to order in a separate pan (as a restaurant would do), cook the pears and caramel sauce together. It's essential to use firm pears that can withstand a fair amount of heat.

CARAMELIZED PEARS WITH BLUE CHEESE AND BLACK PEPPER–CARAMEL SAUCE

Serves 6

Any type of pear can be used in this recipe, as long as it is firm. See the illustrations on this page for tips on preparing the pears.

⅓ cup water

⅔ cup (4¾ ounces) sugar

3 firm pears, halved, seeds removed with a large melon baller, and ¼ inch trimmed off the bottom of each pear half so it will stand upright

⅔ cup heavy cream
Salt

¼ teaspoon whole black peppercorns, roughly crushed (see the illustrations on page 335)

3 ounces strong blue cheese (such as Stilton), cut into 6 attractive wedges

1. Place the water in a 12-inch nonstick skillet and pour the sugar into the center of the pan, taking care not to let the crystals adhere to the sides of the pan. Bring to a boil over high heat, stirring occasionally, until the sugar is fully dissolved and the mixture is bubbling wildly. Add the pears to the skillet, cut-side down, cover, reduce the heat to medium-high, and cook until the pears are nearly tender (a paring knife inserted into the center of the pears feels slight resistance), 13 to 15 minutes.

2. Uncover, reduce the heat to medium, and cook until the sauce is golden brown and the cut sides of the pears are partly caramelized, 3 to 5 minutes. Pour the heavy cream around the pears and cook, shaking the pan back and forth, until the sauce is a smooth, deep caramel color and the cut sides of the pears are beautifully golden, 3 to 5 minutes.

3. Remove the pan from the heat. Using tongs, carefully remove the pears from the pan and place cut-side up on a wire rack set over a rimmed baking sheet. Cool slightly.

Season the sauce left in the pan with salt to taste and the crushed black pepper, then pour it into a liquid measuring cup.

4. Carefully (the pears will still be hot) stand each pear half upright on an individual plate and arrange a wedge of the blue cheese beside it. Drizzle the plate and some of the pear with the caramel sauce. Serve immediately. (Alternatively, the pears can be stood upright on a large serving platter, and the warm caramel sauce and the blue cheese can be passed separately.)

TECHNIQUE: Coring a Pear

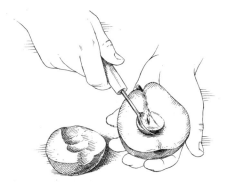

1. Cut the fruit in half from stem to blossom end. Use a melon baller to cut around the central core with a circular motion.

2. Draw the melon baller from the central core to the top of the pear, removing the interior portion of the stem as you go.

TECHNIQUE: Crushing Peppercorns

A. Chefs frequently use the back of a heavy pan and a rocking motion to grind peppercorns.

B. Or, you can spread the peppercorns in an even layer in a zipper-lock plastic bag and whack them with a rolling pin or meat pounder.

A NOTE ON CONVERSIONS

SOME SAY COOKING IS BOTH A SCIENCE AND AN ART. We would say that geography has a hand in it, too. Flour milled in the United Kingdom and elsewhere will feel and taste different from flour milled in the United States. So we cannot promise that the loaf of bread you bake in Canada or England will taste the same as a loaf baked in the States, but we can offer guidelines for converting weights and measures. We also recommend that you rely on instincts when making our recipes. Refer to the visual cues provided. If the bread dough hasn't "come together in a ball," as described, you may need to add more flour—even if the recipe doesn't tell you so. You be the judge. For more information on conversions and ingredient equivalents, visit our Web site at www.cooksillustrated.com and type "conversion chart" in the search box.

The recipes in this book were developed using standard U.S. measures following U.S. government guidelines. The charts below offer equivalents for U.S., metric, and Imperial (U.K.) measures. All conversions are approximate and have been rounded up or down to the nearest whole number. For example:

1 teaspoon = 4.9292 milliliters, rounded up to 5 milliliters

1 ounce = 28.3495 grams, rounded down to 28 grams

Volume Conversions

U.S.	METRIC
1 teaspoon	5 milliliters
2 teaspoons	10 milliliters
1 tablespoon	15 milliliters
2 tablespoons	30 milliliters
¼ cup	59 milliliters
½ cup	118 milliliters
¾ cup	177 milliliters
1 cup	237 milliliters
1¼ cups	296 milliliters
1½ cups	355 milliliters
2 cups	473 milliliters
2½ cups	592 milliliters
3 cups	710 milliliters
4 cups (1 quart)	0.946 liter
1.06 quarts	1 liter
4 quarts (1 gallon)	3.8 liters

Weight Conversions

OUNCES	GRAMS
½	14
¾	21
1	28
1½	43
2	57
2½	71
3	85
3½	99
4	113
4½	128
5	142
6	170
7	198
8	227
9	255
10	283
12	340
16 (1 pound)	454

Conversions for Ingredients Commonly Used in Baking

Baking is an exacting science. Because measuring by weight is far more accurate than measuring by volume, and thus more likely to achieve reliable results, in our recipes we provide ounce measures in addition to cup measures for many ingredients. Refer to the chart below to convert these measures into grams.

INGREDIENT	OUNCES	GRAMS
1 cup all-purpose flour*	5	142
1 cup whole-wheat flour	5½	156
1 cup granulated (white) sugar	7	198
1 cup packed brown sugar (light or dark)	7	198
1 cup confectioners' sugar	4	113
1 cup cocoa powder	3	85
Butter†		
4 tablespoons (½ stick, or ¼ cup)	2	57
8 tablespoons (1 stick, or ½ cup)	4	113
16 tablespoons (2 sticks, or 1 cup)	8	227

*U.S. all-purpose flour, the most frequently used flour in this book, does not contain leaveners, as some European flours do. These leavened flours are called self-rising or self-raising. If you are using self-rising flour, take this into consideration before adding leavening to a recipe.

†In the United States, butter is sold both salted and unsalted. We generally recommend unsalted butter. If you are using salted butter, take this into consideration before adding salt to a recipe.

Oven Temperatures

FAHRENHEIT	CELSIUS	GAS MARK (IMPERIAL)
225	105	¼
250	120	½
275	130	1
300	150	2
325	165	3
350	180	4
375	190	5
400	200	6
425	220	7
450	230	8
475	245	9

Converting Temperatures from an Instant-Read Thermometer

We include doneness temperatures in many of our recipes, such as those for poultry, meat, and bread. We recommend an instant-read thermometer for the job. Refer to the table at left to convert Fahrenheit degrees to Celsius. Or, for temperatures not represented in the chart, use this simple formula:

Subtract 32 degrees from the Fahrenheit reading, then divide the result by 1.8 to find the Celsius reading.

EXAMPLE:
"Roast until the juices run clear when the chicken is cut with a paring knife or the thickest part of the breast registers 160 degrees on an instant-read thermometer." To convert:

160°F − 32 = 128°
128° ÷ 1.8 = 71°C (rounded down from 71.11)

INDEX

INDEX

Tongs, recommended, 49
Tortillas:
    Chicken Enchiladas, *91,* 160–64
    rolling, 164
Trichinosis, 55
Tube pans, filling, 308
Tubetini, 26

V

Veal shanks, in Osso Buco, 246–49
Vegetable peelers, rating of, 33–34

W

Walnut Crescent Cookies, 301–2

Water, bottled:
    tap water vs., 251
    tasting of, 249–52
Water baths (science desk), 323
Waxed paper, parchment paper vs., 299
Whipped cream:
    Brown Sugar and Bourbon, 322
    chilling bowl for, 322
    Tangy, 308
White beans:
    canned, tasting of, 27
    Pasta e Fagioli (Italian Pasta and
        Bean Soup), 24–26, *199*
White chocolate, in Blondies, 287–88
White wine, non-alcoholic substitute
    for, in pan sauces, 77

Whole-wheat flour, in yeasted breads,
    218
Wood chunks, soak-ahead, 125

Y

Yeast:
    designer (science desk), 275
    see also Breads, yeasted
Yogurt Sauce, 191, 192

Z

Zucchini, Chicken Soup with Shells,
    Tomatoes and, 22